D0919522

Sexuality in the Arab World

Sexuality in the Arab World

Edited by

Samir Khalaf and John Gagnon

SAQI

London San Francisco Beirut

ISBN (10): 0-86356-948-X
ISBN (13): 978-0-86356-948-7

Published in 2006 by Saqi Books

A full CIP record for this book is available from the British Library.
A full CIP record for this book is available from the Library of Congress.

Manufactured in Lebanon

SAQI

26 Westbourne Grove, London W2 5RH
825 Page Street, Suite 203, Berkeley, California 94710
Tabet Building, Mneimneh Street, Hamra, Beirut
www.saqibooks.com

Contents

Living with Dissonant Sexual Codes

Samir Khalaf

> *To an unexpected and unusual degree, sexuality has become a battleground for contemporary political forces ... It seems that for many, the struggle for the future of society must be fought on the terrain of contemporary sexuality. As sexuality goes so does society. But equally, as society goes, so goes sexuality.*
>
> Jeffrey Weeks, *Sexuality*

The Arab world, perhaps more so than other socio-cultural settings, has been undergoing some profound and unsettling transformations in sexual and gender relations. The sexual realm, particularly in recent years, has been subjected to conflicting and dissonant expectations and hence has become a source of considerable uncertainty, ambivalence and collective anxiety. Such pervasive confusion has been rendered more acute by personal feelings of impotence and the inability of individuals to adapt or negotiate a coherent identity which allows one to live with such contested and shifting sexual codes.

This confusion and uncertainly, almost a textbook instance of anomie since the culture is extolling inconsistent and irreconcilable normative expectations, is compounded by at least three overriding realities. First, and like elsewhere, the very nature of sexuality and human intimacy and the perspectives employed to account for the transformations they are beset with continue to be contested. Second, some of the inveterate and deep-seated traditional values, particularly those which are undermining the centrality and coherence of the family, primordial and religious loyalties, are also being challenged. Until recently such conflict was largely manageable. The advent of global, transnational and postmodern venues of communication, consumerism, popular culture and mass 'infotainment' – with all their digital and virtual technologies, websites and chat-rooms – have however exacerbated the magnitude and intensity of conflict. The risks and anxieties generated by such compelling incursions have compounded further the process of forging coherent and meaningful self identities. Hence efforts and processes for safeguarding and enhancing one's social worth, autonomy and sense of wellbeing are being rendered more problematic. This is taking place, incidentally, at a time when the power and importance of sexuality in defining self and morality are becoming more central and overpowering.

It is these and related manifestations which inform the chapters in this volume. Despite their range and scope – the different topics and issues they address and varying historical contexts and local settings – they all converge on how individuals and groups are living with such dissonant sexual codes and cultural scripts. What are some of the striking manifestations of such lived realities; both at the macro and micro levels? What concrete forms are such behavioural strategies assuming and what are some of their projected future prospects?

In his packed but cogent and wide-ranging chapter, an elaboration of his keynote address for the conference, John Gagnon highlights the shifting paradigms in the character of sex research as it struggled to explore the changing nature of sexuality, gender and reproductive life. Incidentally Gagnon himself during much of his prolific scholarly career has been deeply engrossed in exploring the changing character of sexuality and sexual research. As early as the mid-1960s, beginning with his collaborative work with William Simon on *Sexual Deviance*, he established himself as one of the most prominent scholars, both by way of his empirical research and conceptual and theoretical analysis, of the changing story of sexual research within the changing contexts of states, cultures, colonies and globalization. Throughout his work he was particularly interested in the history of comparative social research and the cross-national and cross-cultural approaches to sexuality. Doubtlessly, the most striking was his participation with E. O. Laumann and S. Michael (1992) in the controversial National Health and Social Life Survey, the first such national survey of sexual conduct since Kinsey's in 1948. In this regard we could not have possibly recruited a more appropriate colleague to situate and frame the diverse contributions within a meaningful context.

Interestingly, he prefaces his essay by indicating how the early interest in sexuality was in part associated with the Enlightenment in Europe and the larger colonial narrative regarding the enhanced estimate of the sexual attractions of the 'other'. It was not until the nineteenth century in the West that a new 'scientific' attention began to shift from a concern with the sexual, gender and reproductive life of the 'other' to sexuality among the Europeans themselves.

With colonization, particularly since it involved the transplantation of nineteenth-century Christian scripts, these cultural encounters assumed, by and large, four distinct strategies or options. First, there was the destruction of all pre-existing state structures and local cultures and their replacement with European state and even religious institutions. This was largely the experience of Spain in Latin America. Second, the 'reservationization' of indigenous groups to create the image of a desolate 'empty land' to be appropriated by Christian settlers, as was the case of the colonization of North America, Australia and Argentina. A third option meant the creation of 'faux' or artificial state-like institutions with efforts to evangelize local groups. Finally, a fourth encounter was the creation of 'third cultures' in regions such as the Middle East, China and India in which semblance of state agencies predated contact.

As will be seen, virtually all the episodes and case studies explored here – the dissonant forces underlying sexuality in fin-de-siècle Beirut; the tensions nineteenth-century Lebanese emigrants faced in sustaining a 'modern' sense of self while preserving the indigenous virtues of modesty and family honour; symptoms of sexual dysfunction in the diaspora; the sexual victimization of Asian domestic servants; the strategies of upper-class Syrian women and their ploys in safeguarding sexual purity and chastity as 'social capital'; the conflict and personal anguish Tunisian young women face in reconciling the fashionable and liberal lifestyles demanded by their contemporary peers in the city with the reserved and modest expectations of their family and traditional village community; the predicaments young students face as they forge coherent sexual identities in the permissive setting of an American university; an emergent gay subculture, as the gay community in postwar Beirut begin to realize substantial footholds in establishing a formal voluntary association, a periodical and a website to safeguard their rights and interests; and finally the role of contemporary Arabic poetry and literature in the articulation of desire and sexual fantasies – involve sustained efforts to evolve such manifestations of 'third' cultures with their associated hybrid spaces and zones of autonomy.

Gagnon correctly observes that all four colonial strategies involved different levels and directions of change in sexual conduct, gender and reproductive practices. In most early encounters, vectors of change were either though religious or proto-medical agencies. Subsequently, processes of change were brought about through the presence of permanent commercial, governmental and military personnel. After the Second World War, in most post-colonial settings, these transformations were sparked by the advent of globalization, mass media and the itinerant tourist traffic and the like.

In the main part of his erudite and well-informed chapter, Gagnon explores factors associated with the rise of 'scientific', i.e. secular and empirical, research on sexuality; particularly in Germany, Austria, England, France and then its ultimate transfer to the US after the Second World War. First in medicine and then through the spread of the contentious views of Freudian psychoanalysis, something akin to a revolution in thinking about the origins and justifications of sexuality became quite widespread. This initial surge, however, was short-lived. The rise of collectivist and ideological mass movements after the First World War (both right and left), had a repressive impact on ideas and the intellectual climate favouring research on sensitive topics associated with sexual conduct and reproductive behaviour. The transfer, however, of sexual research to the US, stimulated by variants of psychoanalytic perspectives and cross-national surveys, revitalized interest in the study of sexuality. It also opened up venues for research on sensitive topics (i.e. homosexuality, masturbation, oral sex, eroticism, pornography and women's sexual desires) thus far considered inaccessible.

Of course the landmark national survey of Alfred Kinsey and his colleagues (1948, 1953) had a far-reaching impact not only in encouraging cross-national research but also in changing the prevailing deviant perspectives on sexuality. Stigmatized sexual conduct, conventionally treated as 'sick', 'perverse', 'aberrant', 'immoral' started to be normalized and largely perceived as nonconforming or unconventional. It was also then, particularly with the growth of academic studies, that many forms of sexual conduct became to be treated as victimless crimes. It was within such an intellectual setting that social constructionism, labelling and symbolic interactionism started to displace the earlier essentialist views and evolved into a dominant sociological perspective for the exploration of various forms of sexuality.

Gagnon explores four additional factors which, in his view, were instrumental in reshaping the direction of research, particularly the advocacy of policy studies associated with the changing modes of sexual conduct. First, the extension of state interests brought added and legitimate concerns about the moral and ultimately public health implications of changes in the sexual conduct of the young. Research output added to the contested and acrimonious debate over the nature of sexual education and provision of contraception to the sexually active. Second, the epistemological crisis in anthropology, generated by the exploration of cross-cultural differences in sexuality, was also vital. As Gagnon puts it:

> the colonial district officer was replaced by the elected or appointed officials of the new nation states. The political realities that the colonial situation allowed the anthropologist to ignore now became critical (e.g. most anthropologists came from the colonizing states and their citizenship was not a matter of contention, after independence most anthropologists became foreigners, in some sense guest workers). As the process of colonization was usually geographically and culturally specific, so was the process of decolonization.

Equally critical, this epistemological crisis had also direct implications for how and what kind of knowledge becomes legitimate. Hence the forms of inquiry and methodological strategies became highly contested. Again, Gagnon is forthright:

> The question of the anthropologist's relation to these peoples and his or her role in their continued subjugation and the role that the relationship played in the production of what was believed to be knowledge became a foreground theoretical issue in the field for some years. This issue of the cultural relation between the knower and the known, between the researcher and the data, was less intense in those areas in anthropology which seemed to serve a practical purpose. Thus medical anthropology retained its sense of humane purpose under the umbrella of health and development. Unlike those whose interests in the 'others' were scientific enlightenment the medical anthropologist seemed less vulnerable to issues of epistemological doubt.

Third, issues of feminism, particularly as women were negotiating zones of autonomy and 'third spaces' in their efforts to safeguard their rights and interests, were also critical in the cultures which sent anthropologists to live among the 'others'. It was also then, and not necessarily associated with feminist studies, that research on 'homosexuality' and 'queer' studies in the West, particularly in the US, transmuted itself into gay and lesbian lifestyles and subcultures.

Finally, and perhaps most compelling, is the impact of HIV/AIDS epidemics. Incidentally, Gagnon himself and his colleagues were actively involved, shortly after the epidemic (now pandemic) entered the public sphere in 1981, in designing field studies and survey research to fill the glaring gap in knowledge at the time. All the critical and vital data on numbers of sexual partners, types and frequency of sexual contacts, let alone the epidemiology of the virus, were absent. His analysis here, because of his direct personal involvement, is both probing and enlightening. He has much to say about the 'moral' and 'political' crisis and the acrimonious divisions associated with the public debate raging at the time over issues of sexuality, gender, reproduction and the role of civil rights movements mobilized by new waves of women's and gay liberation. The inferences one can draw regarding appropriate theoretical paradigms, research strategies and agendas for redemptive social action and public policy; particularly with regard to the 'calculus of worry' and the balance of national interests are instructive and challenging.

Sexuality, Gender and Class in Beirut as a Colonial City

To illuminate his historical portrait of sexuality, gender and class relations in Beirut at the turn of the nineteenth century, Jens Hanssen prefaces his chapter with a depiction of the graphic touristic impression the city left on an Austrian traveller in 1911. The scene which captivated and befuddled the tourist was not just the display of elegance, glamour and savoir-faire among the patrician elite of Beirut's high bourgeoisie, but rather how familiar and ordinary the dazzling scene seemed to him. The tourist, with a consular official, were attending an Italian puppet show in a theatre next to Place des Canons (*Sahat al Burj*). As they were about to enter the theatre their attention was drawn to the following:

> An elegant carriage drawn by two magnificent horses stopped in front of the staircase. A young gentleman in an immaculate blazer and a red Tarbush stepped out and helped a lady descend dressed in

> a flowing Frou Frou of silk pleats, in flashing diamonds, a layering of Brussels laces and a scent of some provocative perfume. She had the appearance of a typical European lady of fashion. He belonged to one of the immensely rich local Syrian patrician families in this trading city. These young people go to Europe, especially Paris, for a few years and return with a firm command of several European languages, good etiquette and particularly with many new business connections. Their vast fortunes never leave the country, and the merchant dynasties marry amongst themselves.

As the show ended and the lights went on, he could from his box seat on the balcony observe the scene more clearly: 'ladies of the Syrian notability ... with glittering and glamorous European dresses ... knew how to wear the volume of laces, the incredible wealth of jewellery with grace and matter-of-factness and with a truly aristocratic calm and self-confidence'. The Austrian tourist ends his tale with a sinister jibe at the nonchalant predispositions and abandon with which the Francophiles of Beirut indulged their sexual escapades with no trace of shame or guilt. The indulgent Parisian girls seem equally blasé and do not appear to mind being taken for a ride, as it were.

A nuanced and intuitive reading of this vignette allows Hanssen to frame and extrapolate the basic themes and concerns of his chapter. First, while sexuality and gender constructions were crucial in forging a middle-class identity, they also embody the conflict over patriarchy and masculinity which were still prevalent in society at the time. Second, that it was those and other symptoms of promiscuity and sexual license which must have induced the colonialists to address issues of public health and hygiene in their urban policies and planning. As Hanssen puts it,

> The Orientalist discourses on Beirut shifted from sexual conquest to behavioural containment as French hygienists struggled to come to terms with the city's fast-paced growth and transformation that threatened the health of the foreign community and integrity of the established, local male elite.

Finally, and perhaps most relevant to the major thrust of his chapter, the conduct of sexuality reveals some of the inherent dissonant forces associated with the inability of local groups to cope with the exigencies of Western modernity.

The central and most poignant piece of his chapter is the public drama surrounding the tragic life and death of Najla Arslan, a scion of a princely family of Shuwayfat. She harboured a passionate love for her paternal cousin. Both lovers, who were educated at a Jesuit College, managed to keep their liaison secret until they announced their intention to get married in 1893. Her outraged father felt betrayed by his daughter for he had promised, without her consent, her betrothal to the son of the clan's most powerful political *Za'im*. The unfolding public drama which involved of the imperial Sultan in Istanbul, the feudal elite, the Ottoman Pasha and the public in Beirut, ultimately ended in her confinement in a mental hospital in Istanbul.

This tragic episode was an expression of the abiding tension, just nascent at the time, inherent in the failure of Beirut's middle class despite its emancipatory norms and expectations to liberate itself or challenge the resilient patriarchal and feudal authority. It is also a reflection of a deeper structural tension: a desire to seek Western education, yet to hold it accountable for undermining traditional virtues of family honour and engendering the demoralization and vulnerability of youth.

Sexuality and Honour among Lebanese Emigrants

While Jens Hanssen was concerned with the disjunction between the aroused sexual expectations of the new middle class and the resilience of the traditional culture, Akram Khater shifts his analysis to the travails and anxieties of Lebanese emigrants as they struggled to adapt to the requirements of the new middle class in the *mahjar*, particularly regarding practices of love, sexuality and gender, and the traditional norms of family honour and modesty the emigrants carried over with them to the 'New World'. While Hanssen notes the impressions of an Austrian tourist, Khater draws on the views of two leading journalists that appeared in *al-Huda*, the mouthpiece of the Syrian-Lebanese community. One decries women's work as 'a disease whose microbes have infested healthy and sick bodies alike ... which leads women to lewd, filthy and wanton behavior'. The other bemoaned its effects on their honour and that of the Syrian community. During the thirty–year historical interlude of concern to Khater (1890–1920), the Arabic press in the *mahjar* was relentless in expressing its anxiety about the threats to women's honour as they ventured into the public sphere, particularly if they were to seek employment in factories. Indeed, the 'factory girl' became an epithet and the equivalent of a sexually fallen women. As Khater puts it:

> Women's bodies and sexuality thus became contested sites of cultural and social politics which found expression in private conversations and letters as well as across newspaper columns. Sexuality among Lebanese emigrants became self-consciously part of a public identity that was in state of constant flux brought about by contradictory norms of behaviour. While this tension was never fully resolved, it did bring about a set of discordant changes in notions and practices of love, sexuality and gender roles that were an essential aspect of the creation of a new Lebanese emigrant middle class in the *mahjar* and, later, in Lebanon.

Khater's informed and intuitive analysis of the tensions migrants faced as they were compelled to adapt to prevailing middle-class normative expectations is enlightening in more than one respect. He is persuasive in demonstrating how the migrants' experience in the New World was transformative in an existential and fundamental sense in that it entailed socio-cultural contacts which necessitated a profound examination of their individual and collective identities and the cultural baggage they carried over with them from Lebanon. It was the prospects or apprehensions of women's venture into the public sphere which sparked this crisis.

The emigrant community was far from uniform in its views. Traditionalists who had defined women's work as pathology or disease that was defiling the communal body were, to a large extent, in conformity with Anglo-Saxon bourgeois moralists who saw the commitment to middle-class sensibilities and lifestyles as prerequisites for entry into mainstream America. To them the sanitized and orderly nuclear family would be a shelter against uncouth and boorish behaviour. Within such a compliant and felicitous setting, women's sexuality and desires would remain under the control of the husband, while he would naturally indulge his wild escapades in the city.

The more liberal elements within the emigrant community were not as offended or threatened by women's work. They were of the view that women's honour, like pure gold, will not be tainted or despoiled if she ventures into the public domain outside the surveillance of her family. Opinion columns in *al-Huda*, as noted by Khater, reminded readers that women after all worked in silk-reeling factories back home without any risk of immorality and dishonour. Such a claim, incidentally, needs to be qualified since *karkhane* (i.e. silk-reeling factories where women were assembled outside the purview of their families) became morally suspect.

Little wonder that houses of prostitution at the turn of the century acquired such a stigmatized public image and nefarious identity.

Khater goes further, to advance the argument that anxiety over women's identity was not grounded in the wish to protect her honour or the traditional construct of patriarchy. He maintains that many of those objecting to woman's work saw it as a departure not only from village norms, but more importantly from the standards of the middle class in America. More interesting perhaps, he also argues that, although the concern with woman's work was not completely freed from the fears about immorality and dishonour, anxiety over licentious sexuality shifted away from its class context to focus more on individual character and morality.

Despite the apprehensions the Lebanese immigrants continued to harbour towards sexuality and women's modesty, there were elements within the community who were receptive to acquiring some of the liberal lifestyle features and mannerisms of the New World: fashionable clothes, new individualized and romantic perceptions of marriage and the popularity of the romance novel as a new Arabic literary genre espousing love as the highest ideal a woman should aspire to and debunking arranged marriages. Most visible perhaps was the abandon with which women flaunted modern styles of clothing:

> Their clothes appear consistently (except for the few posed 'traditional' attire photos) to be in the latest American style and their faces are always made up. In other words, throughout these moments of self-representation, these women chose (and/or were allowed) to uncover their hair, highlight their bodies in tight-fitting dresses, and attract the eye of the beholder with make-up applied generously. It would seem, then, that they were attracting the viewer to their bodies, faces and in essence to their sexuality as women.

Khater concludes his chapter by drawing a few conceptual inferences which reinforce the underlying premisses and themes of other chapter and the overall perspective of this edited volume; namely that the normative and behavioural dimensions of sexuality should not be treated as merely predetermined. Nor should the primordial desires be dismissed or relegated to the private sphere and, hence, outside the purview of scholars. Khater, likewise, gives added credence to Foucault and other constructionist perspectives on sexuality. In other words, sexuality is not merely a physical urge that calls for gratification. Rather it is a construct of power relations which involves constant negotiation between individuals and their socio-cultural settings.

Sexual Dysfunction and the Disaffection of Diaspora

Ghassan Hage dips into his vivid ethnographic data to probe a few of the manifestations of the interplay between migration and sexuality, a problem rarely explored before. His protagonist, Adel, is a Lebanese village migrant living in Boston who has persuaded himself to recognize and agonize over his 'erectile dysfunction' (termed 'Dephallicization' by Hage) as an inevitable affliction of his marginalized life in diaspora and his unremitting nostalgia to reconnect with Lebanon by way of reclaiming his damaged identity.

Adel's disempowerment and the 'symbolic castration' he was progressively suffering is not, as Hage reminds us, a unique or rare predicament. Such perceptions of colonially subjugated 'Third World' males were apparent in the works of Frantz Fanon (1986), Edward Said (1979), Mrinalini Sinha (1995), among others. In this sense Adel's phallic inadequacies become largely a by-product of his progressive feelings that he does not 'have what it takes' – be it money, lack of prestige, lack of 'modernity' or patriarchal authority to validate himself as an American citizen.

Interesting as this is, Hage does not stop here. He goes on to argue how the physical loss of phallic power is itself made to stand for the loss of social power. In such instances it acquires all the trappings of a 'culturally acquired disposition to think of one's masculinity and social power in a penis-centred way'.

One of the overriding themes of Hage's ethnographic portrait is the amplified dissonance between the phallocentrism of Adel's childhood socialization in his Lebanese village – embodied in graphic episodes, festivals and traditional *dabkeh* dance which accentuate the eroticism of male–female posturing and the anguishing dephallicization he suffered in diaspora.

Though phallic-centred, the cultural scripts a young man receives are nuanced and situational. Since women in the village are normally categorized as those 'for marriage' or those you flirt with and 'show off' to, exhibiting one's sexual powers for the latter is condoned but for the former it is condemned and considered vulgar. Hage, more explicitly, points out that it is

> rude to act in a too stud-like way towards village girls in the sense that it is rude to be too sexual about women you may potentially marry. To such women you exhibit the social traits of your masculinity (gender without sex, so to speak): toughness, rationality, dependability, etc ... You only emphasize your sexual/physical masculinity to those who are outside the 'official' marriageable realm. This is partly an extension of the logic of the arranged marriage whereby marriage decisions are not supposed to succumb to the irrational flows of desire but have to be rational, business-like decisions. This also extends into a division between women who embody reproductive sexuality and the others who embody sexuality for fun.

Though based on a rather unusual case study, Hage deftly extracts from his engaging protagonist meaningful empirical and conceptual realities. Two, in particular, stand out. First, the village cultural scripts internalized by Adel which sanctioned the categorization of women into two distinct entities – those who embody reproductive sexuality and others who embody sexuality for fun – are expressive of an abiding preference for endogamous and arranged marriage still pervasive in village culture. Indeed, it reinforces the logic of arranged marriages whereby such vital and weighty decisions are not entirely left to the whims and irrational longings of spurious desire and hunger for lust. Rather, marriage, particularly since it reinforces family solidarity and kinship loyalties, is prone to be motivated by rational, instrumental and business-like concerns.

Second, on a more conceptual level, Adel's grappling with his sexual identity runs counter to the views of Anthony Giddens (1992) and Zigmund Bauman (2003) in their analysis of the changing characters of intimacy, sexuality and eroticism in today's world. For example, what Giddens terms 'plastic sexuality' (i.e. sexuality for fun) emerges when it became technologically possible to free it from reproductive sexuality. In other words, since reproduction can now occur without sexuality, intimacy is thus liberated from all the constraints and imperatives of replenishing the species. Sex becomes predominantly a matter of personal interest. Likewise, Bauman's 'liquid love' conjures up images of transient, ephemeral encounters; a joint product of liquid modern life settings and consumerism as the chosen and sole available strategy of 'seeking biographical solutions to socially produced problems'.[1]

The Sexual Victimization of Asian Domestic Servants

While Ghassan Hage elucidates the sexual travails and anguish Adel suffered because of the cultural baggage he carried over with him to Boston, Ray Jureidini is, in some respects, concerned with the converse process: the sexual victimization of Asian domestic servants and the threats they generate within the middle-class Lebanese family. Because of the presence of a massive and growing supply of displaced migrants with visibly different attitudes and modes of sexual conduct, the domestic sphere of the family becomes a highly charged emotional and sexual arena.

Jureidini begins his chapter by exposing the images and perceptions of maids in Arab households with special focus on Lebanon. The bulk of the material is extracted from an extensive empirical survey which explored two distinct dimensions of the phenomena. It offers first a stereotypical profile of the domestic servant as portrayed and represented in Arabic literature, popular films and the mass media. Second, the views of employers, household heads and other family members on matters such as the fear and control of sexuality, public image and conduct of the domestic servant are analyzed and accounted for.

Altogether, it is possible to discern three distinct perceptions of the maid's sexuality. First, she is treated as an asexual being; one whose sexuality is denied. Second, and at the other extreme, she is seen as a highly erotic and sexual being. This, Jureidini maintains, carries two dissonant implications: that the maid's sexuality is legitimate and, hence, available for the taking. Indeed, in some reported incidences, she provides sexual release to both adults and adolescents in the household. Parents, in fact, not only turn a blind eye, but are known to encourage their young sons to initiate, as it were, their rites of passage into manhood and validate their heterosexual masculinity and sexual prowess with the accessible and willing house maid. In this regard she becomes, clearly, a more affordable and convenient outlet than commercial prostitution and street walkers. It is also less of a health hazard since the wife/mother dutifully takes her for regular medical inspections. She also allays, by doing so, her anxiety over the embarrassing prospects of her pregnancy. Finally, and more compelling, she is perceived as a source of seduction and family disputes. Much like the classic anti-wife *Jariah* she is the threat to the well-being of the family.

Though pervasive, the varying forms, manifestations and disheartening consequences of domestic labour remain perhaps as the quintessential invisible, overlooked and marginal entities. Despite their ubiquitous presence and consequential roles they play in reinforcing the well-being of middle-class families, the lives, working conditions and abuse domestic servants are subjected to remain largely muffled and unrecognized.

The synopses he provides illuminate the nature of illicit sexuality (i.e. underhanded, morally abhorrent, dirty) and the contested relations between middle-class women and men in relation to domestic servants. Jureidini borrows the apt dual metaphor of 'marginal insiders' and 'intimate outsiders' employed by Michel Gamburd (2000) in her study of Sri Lanka's migrant housemaids as part of the growing mass of transnational labour. Also, some of his interviews reveal that the disreputable and stigmatized public image of Asian housemaids, as lusty and oversexualized women indifferent to the normative standards of honour and shame of their host countries, is overstated. Though lumped together, they do not constitute a homogeneous and undifferentiated category. Filipinos, Sri Lankans and Ethiopians differ markedly in their behaviour, reputation and licentious predispositions. Some are highly virtuous, regular churchgoers and seem attentive to observing their religious duties. There is, however, persuasive evidence to support the claim that they do suffer more than their share of sexual harassment and abuse. Like other forms of domestic violence, such forms of abuse are masked from public view. Nor do they receive the corrective or remedial attention they deserve.

Jureidini extracts another instructive inference from his ethnographic data which bear a few compelling implications for the role of the family as a redemptive refuge, or haven, for domesticity, intimacy and privacy. The growing presence of such 'intimate outsiders', in the midst of this most private of all sanctuaries, has been a source of tension and uncertainty.

Female Chastity as 'Social Capital'

Another more substantive issue which has direct bearing on the control of women's sexuality also remains shrouded from public recognition or concern. At least it has not, perhaps because of its inaccessibility to direct research, attracted the attention it deserves. The chapter by Christa Salamandra breaks new, and much needed, ground. Making judicious and creative use of Pierre Bourdieu's analysis of distinction, taste, image-consciousness, Salamandra draws on her probing ethnographic fieldwork to explore how upper-class Syrian women manipulate the appearance of sexual purity and chastity as forms of social capital.

In a shame-oriented culture where sexual modesty is a highly cherished and jealously guarded expectation, any threat to it can have ominous implications for a woman's marriage prospects, let alone the honour and social standing of her family. Salamandra is fully aware that this longing of the Syrian woman to cultivate an attractive outward appearance and sex appeal – how they comport themselves, the spaces and encounters they seek to display and enhance their bodily endowments – are clearly not unique to the upper-class Damascene women she was studying. By treating, however, the phenomena as a 'chastity capital', a few of its unusual Syrian manifestations become more pronounced. First, there are symptoms of growing conflict generated by the dissonance between the burgeoning access to novel trends and venues of consumerism and the surviving traditional values of sexual modesty, family honour and patriarchy, the seeming preponderance of fashionable clothing, cosmetic stores, beauty parlours and the like should not be taken to mean that these venues and what they request are now widely accepted. Indeed, Syrian women seem more taxed than their cohorts elsewhere in the Arab world by the process of negotiating a coherent and workable identity that reconciles the virtues inherent in both sets of expectations and cultural scripts.

Salamandra's grounded ethnographic data allows her to suggest that at least in contrast to Cairo, where a thriving industry in ornate *hijab* clothing offers an alternative to the bland styles worn in Syria, Damascene women are left with the more cumbersome task of forging reconciliatory strategies incorporating both stylistic features. Such efforts have not been very comforting. Indeed, as Salamandra argues, 'woman find it difficult to maintain a stylistic middle ground between the invisibility of *hijab*, and the flamboyance of the coquette'. As one Damascene woman put it (in English), 'we have cockteasers and muhajjbat, and nothing in between!'

Second, the obsession with safeguarding and enhancing one's 'chastity capital' also accounts for the competition, often assuming intense rivalry, between women in pursuit of this scarce and cherished resource. This competitive display is so pernicious that it does not only appear in public gatherings. It also intrudes into the sanctuary of close communal networks and circles. Since prospects for any intimate encounters or liaisons are still tabooed, the gaze assumes special prominence. Hence the stakes and public regard for the 'representational self', to invoke Goffman (1959), become very high indeed. Incidentally, it is not only the gaze of men they are after. They are as eager to draw the attention of other women, given the pivotal role mothers, sisters and aunts play in finding an eligible young man a suitable bride. It is precisely such women who are more likely to be familiar with the physical and bodily endowments and the intimate personal history of the prospective wife.

So engrossed are women in the competitive struggle to acquire all the outward trappings of the coveted 'chastity capital', little else seems to matter. Certainly not the seemingly expendable common decencies of courtesy to friends. Salamandra dwells on this point to cast doubt on the alleged inferences feminist anthropologists often make regarding the large residue of social harmony and genial comradeship which still prevails among Middle Eastern women. Behind the appearance of intimacy, harmony lurks bitterness and jealousy. In the midst of such sinister and menacing settings, where outward sociability is often laced with inner and masked hostility, Syrian women admitted that it was difficult for them to sustain any genuine and trusting friendships with other women.

Finally, and perhaps most central to Salamandra's overriding concern with 'chastity capital', particularly within the context of an acute marriage market, is her central premiss that sexual appeal, how to procure it and gain access to spaces in which to display it, is surpassing other conventional measures of social worth and esteem. Such consuming negotiating strategies come naturally with a cost. Women, much more than men, continue to bear a disproportionate part of the burden. They remain 'victims' of the inconsistent demands inherent in the two salient cultural scripts: they are expected first to be sexually attractive. This abiding norm is internalized by early childhood socialization where young girls are encouraged and admired for being coquettish, coy, even flirtatious. Peer pressure during puberty and tantalizing media images of global consumerism, which place a high premium on sensuality and eroticized images, accentuate such expectations. But this is in stark opposition to another more impermeable cultural script; a taboo-like condemnation of any form of sexual conduct or intimacy. This, if anything, is a textbook instance of anomie. Syrian women, in other words, like elsewhere in the Arab world, continue to bear the brunt of negotiating an identity which allows them to manage or reconcile those two dissonant demands. They are admired and revered for being sexually attractive but doomed and admonished if they dare to translate this into a form of sexual activity.

Beauty, Body Image and Sexuality

The story of El-Hem, the young and dynamic Tunisian girl, poignantly told by Angel Foster, bespeak of a similar irredeemable tension. The life of the bright and determined girl who left her village (Gafsa) in pursuit of university education in Tunis has much to share with her counterparts in Damascus. The ambivalence, distress and personal anguish women like her suffer are also reflective of the dilemmas they face as they attempt to negotiate the dissonance inherent in the two disparate sets of expectations: the fashionable, thin, svelte figure with stylish clothes and demeanour demanded by her contemporary peers in the city to accentuate the glamour and the body image of a liberated women were pitted against the reserved and modest expectations of her family and traditional village community. Poor El-Hem had to shuttle back and forth, at a rather exacting toll; emotional, scholastic and health-wise.

Her expectations were so irreconcilable that she remained a misfit in both settings. In Tunis, she felt tired, distracted and unable to devote her undivided attention and resources to her studies. She became anorexic. She dyed her hair blonde and wore fashionable clothes. Upon her return to Gafsa after her first year in the city, her parents were shocked and dismayed. Their concern, of course, was that with such an overhaul of her outside appearance, her prospects for marrying a man from the village were grim. She conceded to parental pressure to stay within the conventional and tested standards of beauty; namely to cultivate bodily features of being round and plump. But she did so with the inner resolve that when she returned to Tunis she would remodel herself to the fashionable ideals of her peers and the trendy urbane culture of the city.

This back-and-forth shuttling left her bewildered and confused. In Tunis, as Foster put it,

> she felt good about the way she looked and the way men responded to her. For the first time in her life she had boyfriends, and she knew she wouldn't have been able to date if she had continued to look like a rural woman from the centre of the country. But when she returned to her rural village, she no longer felt like she fit in and she feared no one would want to marry her.

Nowhere is this dissonance as visible as in the competing pressures young women are facing regarding conceptions of beauty and bodily image. Both expectations are compelling and difficult to resist. Her family and village community, to safeguard her marriageability, expect her (indeed demand) to subscribe to the cherished and inordinate virtues of voluptuousness; a body type normally associated with maternity, fertility and a high premium placed on sexual modesty. On the other hand, and largely due to the infusion of Western media images, many women are now desiring the more fashionable elements such as lighter hair, fairer skin and trimmer and leaner bodies.

The tensions inherent in such dichotomies are not as benign as they appear. They have implications for women's perceptions of self-worth, their relationships with others and sexual expressions. Clearly El-Hem was a 'victim' of such discordant cultural scripts. If anything, her emotional vulnerability and inability to measure up to the scholastic expectations are symptomatic of such tensions. She twice failed her final examinations and at the age of twenty-six she remained in her final year at the university.

Forging Coherent Sexual Identities in an Ambivalent Cultural Setting

Such symptoms of tension and anomie are not only salient among women in the fairly conservative and traditional communities of Damascus and Tunisia. They also prevail in the comparatively more liberal and permissive settings of college students at the American University of Beirut (AUB), an institution known for its tolerant and cosmopolitan lifestyles. By extracting written and oral narrations from students in her creative writing courses, Roseanne Khalaf was able to identity and account for their views and perceptions on the nature and place of love, romance and sexuality in their lives. In intimate, often graphic and explicit personal narrations, students in the relatively free and uncensored classroom setting seem similarly plagued by disjunctive cultural expectations.

Roseanne Khalaf frames her study by depicting the unusual predicament two of her students faced since both – for strikingly different reasons – were unable to participate in the spirited class discussions. Both requested instead that they do so in the privacy of her office. One, a veiled, reserved student in her late teens or early twenties a by-product of a traditional Druze family, was adamant about not adjusting her white veil to uncover her mouth while speaking. Her muffled speech was inaudible to her colleagues in class. The other is a fashionable 'postmodern' student keen on displaying all the faddish artifice in vogue among her trendy peers. The rings which pierced her lips and tongue virtually disabled her speech.

Both, in other words, are 'damaged' and 'deformed' by the very values they were subscribing to. Though polarized, both represent extreme but salient reactions to the unsettling transformations affecting the nature of sexuality, intimacy and gender relations. In the words of Roseanne Khalaf, 'the outwardly timid and reserved veiled student, along with her dauntless and liberated cohort, who flaunts the rings on her tongue and other parts of her sparsely dressed body as "emblems of honour" and daring, represent extreme modes of adaptation which are, no doubt, manifest elsewhere in the Arab World'.

Though contrived, the classroom setting, as a contact zone and safety net, was transformed into something akin to a 'third space' where students fell free to articulate their most intimate views and anxieties away from the repressive public gaze. Despite the seeming homogeneity of the class, students drawn together in a presumably humanistic setting of an American liberal education, their views were multiple and wide-ranging. They converge, in fact, on a set of six themes which epitomize the contested and negotiated character of sexuality in everyday life.

What stands out first is the generational (parent/child) differences as an expression of the discrepant sexual ideologies of parents and children. Students are inclined to perceive sexuality in fairly positive terms as forms of self-fulfilment. They also act on their libidinal desires regardless of romantic attachments or marital prospects. Parents, on the other hand, as perceived by their children, are seen as being alarmed by the permissive atmosphere of free sexuality unrestrained by love and marriage. They condone physical intimacy only as a prelude to lasting and secure relationships. Indeed, a girl's virginity, as one student put it sinisterly, is treated by her parents as the most effective ploy to 'trap a worthy spouse'!

Roseanne Khalaf treats the parent/child dualism as symptomatic of the moral divide which differentiates their views with regard to love, sex and intimacy. In this sense parents are more apt to be regarded as *romantics*, is that they are more prone to view sex as a mode of expressing intimate feelings which cannot and should not be divorced from love and affection. Young students, on the other hand, by challenging such archaic orthodoxies, are more *libertarians* in that they are bent on freeing sex from the excessive strictures of custom and tradition.

With noted cynicism, some students are fully aware of the insincerity and duplicity of their parents in that they do not live up to the high moral grounds they preach. Though a few are outraged by their parents' social hypocrisy they treat this 'jarring dissonance between their overt righteousness and covert misconduct as a microcosm of the deepening malaise they see elsewhere in society'.

The insincerity of their parents, Khalaf cautions, should not be dismissed lightly. It compounds the moral outrage of the younger generation. It is particularly poignant because they are, as a consequence, 'trapped in a socio-cultural setting where they are still expected to pay deference to parents whose values and conduct are no longer meaningful to their own situations'. They, and other mainstream groups and communal arbiters, are no longer their appropriate role models. Instead, they are compelled to look elsewhere for the more painful task of forging a more coherent sexual identity.

Another theme emerges from Khalaf's analysis of her student's narrative voices; namely, that the younger generations, perhaps more than other groups, are compelled to grapple more intensely with efforts at negotiating and constructing an identity to accommodate the shifting and inconsistent sexual codes they are facing today. 'It is not surprising', she tells us, 'that within such a fluid and negotiable setting, virtually everything becomes charged with sensual, erotic undertones and, hence, highly contested. Seemingly mundane and prosaic matters – i.e. dress codes, speech styles and the freedom to imagine alternate sexual attributes and practices – begin to assume primacy.'

Not unlike the Damascene elite women of Salamandra, AUB students are also keen to make effective use of all the ploys for eroticizing their bodies as part of the competitive game to seduce and attract the male gaze. They are also sending a confounding message: that 'men can only look, not touch'. Much like the 'cockteasers' in Damascus, in other words, their ploys are designed to arouse the men but also to keep them at a safe distance. More, however, than their Syrian counterparts, students in Lebanon seem more permissive, uninhibited and explicit in their language, rhetorical expressions and actual conduct. Indeed, indulging in sexual escapades becomes an unalloyed libidinal drive to be heeded with abandon and for all to see.

Khalaf leaves us with one final compelling inference. Though her data represent the cloistered views of students sheltered in the comfort zone of a classroom, we need not belittle or dismiss such voices. As several observers have noted, sketchy and marginal as these voices may seem, they have a way of eventually intruding upon the mainstream scripts and conventional codes. At the least, they serve to sustain the fluidity of sexual identities and public discourse.

The Prospects for Gay Space in Beirut

One of the most resourceful, often unintended, by-products of hosting a conference on the sensitive and largely overlooked dimensions of sexuality is the impetus such occasions provide in spurring further efforts into exploring other such 'tabooed' topics. Virtually all the contributions in this volume are groundbreaking in this regard. Sofian Merabet and Jared McCormick must be particularly complimented for their ability to get into and provide such an intimate and reflexive analysis of the fluid and fluctuating features of emergent gay space – the harbingers of a community or subculture – in the postwar setting of Beirut.

Merabet focuses on different spaces within Beirut which come close to the creation of what he terms 'queer space' or 'homosexual sphere'. These are often spaces in which the socially assumed dichotomy between public and private become obsolete and gives way to what he perceives as *zones of encounters*; namely, mostly urban sites that attempt to transcend spatio-temporal fixities. Although abstract at times, Merabet does nonetheless provide an insightful analysis of the prospects for the gay, particularly when they no longer feel 'protected by the imperial garments of social conformity'. They are consequently compelled to seek 'authentic zones of encounters that may become, in the long run, socially transforming sites that unquestionably sanction the assertion of a lasting *visibility* and difference'.

Since the gay men do not as yet constitute a 'gay community' which socially identifies itself with its homosexual orientation, they employ diverse, often conflicting, strategies for approaching and coping with their particular lived realities. More explicitly, how can they celebrate or at least act on their differences without sacrificing their visibility?

Merabet asks a meaningful conceptual and methodological question which has clear implications for how one is to undertake research on sensitive topics in a fluid and ambiguous spatio-temporal setting. How is it possible, he asks, for an anthropologist to 'represent theoretically the appropriation of a space deemed queer in Beirut'? His answer, prosaic and mundane as it might seem, is persuasive and relevant to the exercise he has in mind. Much like the quintessential Parisian 'flaneur' of Walter Benjamin, the idle stroller continuously adrift in the city, he chose to capture Beirut's countless congregations of sites and cultural references, by literally walking through the city.

Merabet's concern here extends beyond state suppression or official persecution, itself legitimized by Article 534 of the Lebanese Penal Code which outlaws all 'sexual activity that is contrary to nature'. Instead he is more interested in the complex dynamics of what he calls an internal as well as perpetually internalized homophobia that is operative and very much present within (and not merely without) the homosexual sphere in Lebanon. By walking through such urban sites – 'Café Sheikh Manoush', the Corniche, local bathhouses, Ramlet al-Bayda, Hamra etc – he is able to highlight some of the socio-historical attributes they share. He is unequivocal in his constructionist perspective:

> Queer space, like all spaces in and outside Lebanon, is socially constructed. It comes and goes, and usually calls forth certain social relations within the homosexual sphere as well as between that sphere and the larger normative worlds that perpetually affect it. For many of those who appropriate it on a daily basis, queer space is both freeing and trapping. It offers an opportunity for persons separated in other respects to come together in a particular place at a particular moment. Yet, by being a potential motivator, it also functions as a frustrator in the shape of a catalyst that every so often reinforces the very social normativities it wants to defy.

He makes judicious and creative use of Lacan's 'Mirror Stage', Merleau-Ponty's 'phenomenology of the essences' to account for how appearances, in the so-called social mirror of Lebanese serendipities, invite the 'invisible to become visible'. 'By giving way to an opening, this perceived space can potentially develop into a sort of 'third' or 'alternative' space which is neither real nor fictive, but an authentic zone of encounter that may become, in the long run, a socially transforming site that unquestionably sanctions the assertion of a lasting visibility and difference.' Likewise, he dips into the views of André Breton's 'espace intérieur', Benjamin's 'profane illumination' and Bataille's 'transgressions' in tackling the sensitive subject of socially marginalized identities in a place like Beirut.

Writing in 2003, at a time gay encounters were still amorphous and unanchored in any grounded realities, subcultural attributes or legitimate associations, Merabet has no other choice but to be discursive in his treatment of what were at the time no more than symptomatic precursors of hopeful prospects for consolidating the 'zones of encounters' into more concrete entities. Two years later, by the time McCormick was conducting his field research, much more tangible material was at his disposal. The prospects Merabet was anticipating had already started to appear by 2005.

The initial manifestations of burgeoning gay social scene or community have begun to surface. Discussions of homosexuality are now part of the public discourse. More compelling, Lebanon can now boast of being the first country in the Arab world to establish a gay rights voluntary association (Helem, the Arabic world for dream and acronym for *Himaya Lubnaniyya lil Mithliyeen*). While states in the region are still prosecuting gays (in Iran and Iraq they are still executed), Helem has a regular periodical (*Barra*), its own website and a guide which offers inventories of gay-friendly clubs, bars and safe cruising areas. As a result, the number of gays who have recently 'come out' and who are actively engaged in defending their lifestyle and associated freedoms are becoming more audible. Its recently installed website is already being inundated by over 50,000 hits per month.

Despite the overt liberalization and less inhibitive socio-cultural setting, the evidence McCormick extracts from his recorded interviews reveals that most Lebanese are still averse to considering a gay way of life as acceptable. This is why many of his twenty informants lead portions of their lives covertly, particularly in relation to their family. Usually, the father is kept in the dark. At least he is the last to know. Hence, the delicate balancing act – being 'in/out' of the closet – is still riddled with tension, ambivalence and personal anguish. It is interesting to point out in this regard that the six men who returned from at least eight years of experience abroad clearly show less dissonance between their lived and gay identity. In fact, quite a few who have come out recently appear to display many of the Western gay archetypes as a guide and role model in validating their own gay identity. They also are the groups who assume leadership roles in the affairs of Helem.

McCormick devotes the bulk of his essay to demonstrate how three circumstances have had a transforming effect on the process or redefining global transplants to accommodate local realities: the establishment of Helem; the role of the internet, chat-rooms and other electronic and digital networks and information technologies; and, finally, the advent of globalization, particularly the changing character of consumerism and marketing.

McCormick ends with a fairly positive conjecture; i.e. that this quest to forge a local gay identity is groundbreaking. It is bound, despite the travails it is currently embroiled in, to play a transforming role in the advancement of sexuality and gay rights in Lebanon and perhaps elsewhere in the Arab world.

Eroticism in Contemporary Arabic Poetry and Literature

In some obvious and significant respects, Arabic poetry and literature have always served as vectors not only for the articulation of desire and erotic fantasies, but where sexuality is manipulated as a powerful and subversive weapon. The liberties poets and novelists are prone to take – both in the raw, graphic, often blasphemous language they employ and in their pointed attacks against repressive authoritarian cultures where religious and social taboos prevail – are coveted venues for erotic longings. In this context eroticization of the human body and, of course, the carnal sexual act itself must be viewed, as As'ad Khairallah reminds us in the opening passage of his chapter, in two contexts: first and, naturally, as an outlet for satisfying one's libidinal desires; second, and perhaps more relevant to some of the concerns of this volume, as an act of defiance or snubbing one's nose, as it were, against the dominant discourse lodged into the social, political, religious and moral fabric of society.

Indeed, the oppositional tone of sexual expressions, Khairallah correctly maintains, has become more salient since the early 1970s, particularly among transnational intellectuals and poets, whose rejection of sexual taboos and related inhibitious have become more vilifying because of its perceived links with the revival of assertive fundamentalism. Khairallah, in fact, goes further to argue that, given this confrontational character of contemporary Arabic poetry, the evocation of love and romance as an existential experience often becomes secondary to the underlying intention of the poet to dramatize the evils inherent in all restrictive ideologies and taboos. Even in such instances, however, the celebration of the sheer ecstasy and sensuality of the sexual act, without the inhibitions of moral turpitudes of outworn perceptions of innocence and sin, have become more pronounced in recent years.

To highlight the erotic imagination in modern Arab poetry, Khairallah dwells on two poets: Amjad Nasir, a Jordanian, and Abdu Wazin, a Lebanese. Both are in their early 50s and both, in his view, depart markedly from the 'love poetry' prevalent during the 1950s and 1960s. The two texts he analyses – Nasir's *Surra man Ra'aki* (Joy to your Beholder, 1994) and Wazin's *Hadiqat al-Hawass* (The Garden of Senses, 1993) – are treated as instances of 'erotic poetry' in that the individual and his body are seen as the 'final source of redemption. In this respect, instead of dying for a remote abstract cause, the only thing which seems worth living and dying for is love. Physical love for a specific body, in other words, and not love for humanity, nature, or God is the source of well-being.'

Khairallah tells us that the metaphor of hunter and prey informs much of Nasir's concept of sex and longing for desire. It is though a ritual hunt which often takes on patriarchal values and imagery without apologizing for them. As such, the prey

> is generally linked to a treasure, a prize, a trophy, but mostly to a symbol of fertility in the shape of a fruit or a plant ... the female organ appears as a flower, a truffle, or a pear. But the male, the primitive male, is far from being a gatherer. He is a hunter who is mostly likened to a ferocious animal, a lion, a tiger, a panther, a male viper.

The most striking feature of Nasir's poetry, in Khairallah's view, is the mixture between a docile and nearly worshipping attitude in front of the female sex, on the one hand, and the burst of violent emotions and intentions, on the other. So we often read incantations full of submissive admiration. The equally striking attribute is the interplay between the sacred and profane. The metaphoric lyricism, imagery and graphic language he uses is often an interplay between dissonant forces of the sacred and profane.

Khairallah concludes his analysis of Nasir's poetry by asking a pertinent question: Is it love or sex? Is the body in his poetry sacred or profane? His answer veers, unequivocally, in the direction of the sacred. This is seen in the lyrical, nuanced, evocative rendering of a women's body as a 'sacred fruit' as though it were a 'hymn inspired by the mythology of Mesopotamia, Cannanite or biblical injunctions'. Here Khairallah does not refrain from casting a few legitimate aspersions at the comparatively more blasé, lovesick and romanticized treatment of amatory encounters one finds in the works of Nizar Qabbani, Hashim Shafiq among other bourgeois perceptions. In contrast to such banal, prosaic and passionless renderings, Nasir's poetry

> embodies the overwhelming desire of a male hypnotized by his own craving to possess the female ... the love act is seen as a wild and

> brute force resembling an aggressive fight with a sacred bull, having the final kill as its climax. The urge is so strong the lovers cannot help but yield to their devouring desire. Thus the act is not a simple sexual exercise nor does it resemble an encounter at a whorehouse. The ritual hymns and litanies which inform and sustain its basic tone bestow a sacred atmosphere on the whole scene.

In contrast to Nasir's perception of sexuality as a sacred prey, Abduh Wazin's *Hadiqat al-Hawass* (The Garden of the Senses) is much less concerned with lovemaking in itself, or the longing to act on one's wildest desires than in the body-in-love as a venue to a hidden world which happen to fascinate the poet. This is why Wazin's text is more meditative, narcissistic and contemplative. Though the book was censored in Lebanon, it is really not pornographic despite its occasional lapse into the minute graphic depiction of various bodily parts and love making. As a meditation on life and death, sexual encounters lose their violent libidinal urgency. They also have little to do with the recurrent sullen moments of brooding and narcissistic self-contemplation.

In exploring the nature of sexuality, fantasy and violence in Lebanon's postwar novel, Maher Jarrar adopts a constructionist perspective extracted from the premises of Jeffrey Weeks (1986) and Anthony Giddens (1992); namely that sexuality is not pregiven or prearranged, rather it is a product of negotiation, struggle and human agency. He prefaces his discussion by pointing out an interesting reality, that virtually all the studies exploring the interplay between sexuality and the Lebanese civil war, as portrayed in the novel, have been almost exclusively the monopoly of women authors. He is not though an uncritical admirer of this profusion of writing, though it has sparked a literary imagination of immense proportions among a new generation of women writers.

Foremost, he asserts that most of this output, albeit impressive and engaging in parts, fails to provide a persuasive and grounded view of the impact of protracted civil unrest on gender relations or in the alternative strategies they propose for ameliorating the traditional sources of women's oppression and marginalization.

To explore how the Lebanese postwar novel is employing sexuality and endowing it with a more explicit and graphic language to articulate its interplay with the socio-cultural setting it is embedded into, Jarrar uses the protagonists in three recent novels published between 2001 and 2002: Rashid al-Da'if's *Tustufil Myrel Streep*, Ilyas Khuri's *Yalo* and 'Alawiyya

Subh's *Maryam al-Hakaya*. The novels display little restraint in depicting graphic sexual encounters, bordering at times on lurid erotic fantasies and hard pornography. This is particularly visible in 'Rashshud', the main protagonist of al-Da'if's novella. Rooted in his traditional and patriarchal middle-class community, he is symptomatic of many of the double standards and social hypocrisy so typical of such conservative settings. For example, he condemns pre-marital sex and condones honour crimes. Of course, he himself is absolved of such moral restrictions. He harbours no misgivings whatsoever when he tries to rape the neighbourhood's veiled seamstress when she comes to fix their curtains at home. He also indulges all his sexual fantasies with abandon and no feelings of guilt.

Jarrar, however, does not confine himself to an exposure of the sexually explicit, linguistic liberties and aberrant conduct of his main characters. To his credit he makes efforts to extrapolate a few meaningful inferences about the forms and outcomes of sexuality as a literary genre in a postwar setting like Beirut.

It is hoped by now that the chapters to follow, despite their varied scope and historical settings, constitute more than just a collection of disparate contributions selected arbitrarily from the larger pool of conference proceedings. They are all informed by a coherent set of premises which elucidate the interplay between sexuality and society. Indeed, by providing further vivid and grounded evidence of the social construction of sexuality, we are in effect highliting the adaptive strategies individuals and groups are resorting to in forging meaningful sexual identities. Such efforts, as will be apparent, are not as benign and unproblematic. They are particularly poignant because they demand a keen predisposition to live with dissonant sexual codes and cultural scripts. To paraphrase Jeffrey Weeks's epigram which prefaced this chapter, much of the struggle for the future of Arab society could well be fought on the terrain of contemporary sexuality. 'As sexuality goes', he asserts, 'so does society. But equally, as society goes, so goes sexuality'.

Bibliography

Bauman, Z. *Liquid Love*, Cambridge: Polity Press, 2003.

Fanon, Frantz, *The Wretched of the Earth*, New York: Grove Press, 1961; orig. in French.

Gagnon, John H., and Simon, William, eds, *Sexual Deviance*, New York: Harper &

Row, 1967.

Gamburd, Michel, *The Kitchen Spoon's Handle: Transnationalism and Sri Lanka's Migrant Housemaids*, Ithaca, NY: Cornell University Press, 2000.

Giddens, A., *The Transformation of Intimacy: Sexuality, Love and Eroticism in Modern Societies*, Cambridge: Polity Press, 1992.

Goffman, E., *The Presentation of Self in Everyday Life*, New York: Doubleday, 1971.

Kinsey, Alfred C., Pomeroy, Wardell B., and Martin, Clyde E., *Sexual Behavior in the Human Male,* Philadelphia: Saunders, 1948.

Kinsey, Alfred C., Pomeroy, Wardell B., Martin, Clyde E., and Gebhard, Paul, H., *Sexual Behavior in the Human Female,* Philadelphia: Saunders,1953.

Laumann, E. O., Gagnon, J. H., Micheal, R. T., and Micheal, S., 'A Political History of the Adult Sex Survey', in *Family Planning Perspectives*, vol. 26, no. 1, 1994.

Said, Edward W., *Orientalism,* New York: Pantheon Books, 1978.

Sinha, M., *Colonial Masculinity: The 'Manly Englishman' and the 'Effeminate Bengali' in the Late Nineteenth Century*, Manchester: Manchester University Press, 1995.

Weeks, Jeffrey, *Sexuality*, London: Routledge, 2004.

Note

1. Z. Bauman, *Liquid Love*, Cambridge, 2003, p. 44.

States, Cultures, Colonies and Globalization: A Story of Sex Research

John H. Gagnon

An interest in the sexual lives and practices of 'others' can be documented from the very beginning of the written record in the West. Between the Greeks of the fourth century BCE and the anthropologists of the nineteenth century there is a long, though fragmentary, record of travellers' tales and diaries, ships captains' logs and churchmen's records about the sexual lives and practices of the 'others'. It is with the Enlightenment in Europe that we find the recovery of the classical Greek intuition that there might be some attractions to living like (or at least among) the barbarians, an intuition that would grow into an intellectual movement in the nineteenth century.[1] Part of this movement, which was an important subtext in the larger colonial narrative, was an improved estimate of the sexual attractions of the 'other' (both men and women) and their life ways in contrast to the sexual limitations of European cultures.[2] It is perhaps only with this early decline in the dominance of evangelical Christian modes of thought in relation to the 'other' (all non-Christian 'others' were to be converted or exterminated) that such alternative 'multicultural' or 'relativistic' visions of the 'other' could be entertained.

It was in the nineteenth century in the West that a new 'scientific' attention began to move from a concern with the sexual, gender and reproductive life of the 'others' to sexual, gender and reproductive life among the Europeans themselves. These new studies of 'what are we like' or, more often, what are 'some of us like', focus first on the demographic bases of state power (how many of us are there?) and then somewhat later, are we (meaning the populace of the nation) sufficiently well fed, housed, and healthy so that an army can be raised, a navy manned, or factories and fields made productive. This, of course, led to the question of 'are there too many of us' or more commonly 'are there too many of the "others" among us?' The intellectual and moral problem of how to justify the European domination of the other 'others' in the new claimed colonies was solved by placing them lower on the ladder erected on evolutionary models and thinking of these 'others' as a burden rather than a benefit.

These two foci of interest, the interest in *the ways of life* of the 'other' elsewhere and an interest in *the quality of the population of the state* began as relatively separate enterprises in their earliest days. At the same time both had comparativist tendencies even as they developed independently. In the 'health of state' tradition (that which would become *cross-national* research) there was always an interest in the health of competitive states. At one time or another, one or another European state worried about the powers of a changing menu of other states and as the balance of national interests shifted so did the balance of worry. Part of this calculus of appropriate worry were the numbers, health and morale of the populace of the nation states which were on the scales. The beginning of 'cross-national research' was a concern with the balance of military and commercial power between European states (and in later periods, the United States and Japan).

In what would become the study of *ways of life* (in this case, what would become anthropology), the early ships logs of Wallis, Bougainville and Cook (and in this latter case, those of Joseph Banks) to the South Pacific became the basis for debates about the comparative quality of the cultural practices of the Polynesians and the Europeans.[3] Whether there was something to be learned about how to live from the 'others' was a fraught question in late Enlightenment Europe.[4] The more thoughtful of these commentators understood that the 'others' were in far greater danger from the Europeans than the Europeans were from the 'other'.

The territorial division of labour between these two approaches to the study of social life began in their earliest moments. Those interested in the health of the state tended to focus on the 'us' in contrast to other states, while those interested in 'ways of life' tended to focus on the 'them' outside the confines of Europe. Given the interest of early anthropologists in the evolution of cultures it is not surprising that individual anthropologists migrated to those locales in which recognizable state institutions were either unknown or could be classified as 'primitive'. It was in these regions that the colonizing states began to install simulacra of their own religions, administrative practices, legal systems (and courts and prisons), commercial institutions and among the more enlightened, schools and medical institutions.[5] That these institutional forms were imposed on geographical entities which contained culturally diverse populations did not trouble the colonizers (and indeed probably made social management easier). Thus the anthropologists began to produce 'objective knowledge' within the institutional and ideological structures created by other more powerful agents of the colonizing states, often treating the colonial realities (e.g. forced labour for infrastructure building) as if they did not exist. The history of colonial practices (and anthropological knowledge) varies in different geographical and cultural settings depending on the level of development of both the colonized and the colonizers at the moment of contact and the subsequent historical relations between them (and between the colonizing states).

What is important in terms of sexuality, gender and reproduction is the routine installation of institutions or institutional arrangements which would to a greater or lesser degree allow the export of nineteenth-century Christian scripts for appropriate (and inappropriate) sexual, gender and reproductive practices. The colonizing process largely occurred in four ways, with quite different consequences for the peoples being colonized.[6] One strategy was the destruction of pre-existing state structures, local cultures and populations (by conquest or disease) and their replacement with European state structures (including religions), for example, Spain in Latin America.[7] A second was the extermination or reservationization of indigenous peoples (again by conquest or disease) to create the image of an 'empty land' to be freely appropriated by Christian settlers, for example, the colonists in North America, Australia and Argentina.[8] A third was the creation of 'faux' state-like institutions in those places in which they did not yet exist along with the religious evangelizing of the local populations, for example, most of sub-Saharan Africa. And a fourth was to create 'third cultures' in those places in which state-like structures predated contact, for example, the Middle East, Japan, China and India.[9] In some regions with populations that were composed of social formations with varying prior political, social and cultural histories, for example, the components of the Ottoman Empire, India and the islands of what is presently Indonesia, all of these techniques were employed.

All of these colonial strategies involved different levels of change in sexual, gender and reproductive practices. In most locales the earliest agents of change were through the agencies of religion and proto-medicine, though in some cases a major force was the sexual mixing of colonial and native populations, for example, Latin America. In later periods the processes of change were effectuated through the presence of various permanent (the military, governmental and commercial) personnel. Since the end of the Second World War (the 'post-colonial' period) these changes have been facilitated by the globalization of the mass media and an increase in foreign transient population flows in the form of the growing numbers of tourists and retired persons from the first world. In the interconnected domains of sexuality, gender and reproduction, the narrative of colonization is dismayingly local, involving issues of the historical moment when colonization took place, the level of economic, political and technological development of both the colonizing state and those colonized, the pre-existing patterns of sexual, gender and reproductive life in each culture (or cultures) and the degree to which colonizing states were able to coerce change in the areas of sexuality, the relations of the genders, and the production and training of children.

The Rise of Sexual Science

The history of what might be considered 'scientific' (meaning secular and empirical) research on sexuality (and it is possible to overestimate how much research actually took place) over the period 1880–1980 has to be understood in terms of its place in the larger process of 'secularization of the world through science' which has been taking place since Newton and Leibnitz.[10] Sex research emerges in its 'modern' form in the late nineteenth century in Europe and took its first independent secular construction in medicine as the result of new discoveries in biology – the cumulative influence of Pasteur, Koch among many others.[11] Prior to the late nineteenth century sexual conduct was understood and managed through everyday sex beliefs that were distantly scripted by religion and/or the law. Sexual practices were understood as either virtuous or vicious, or law abiding or criminal, among elites, but at the local level they were more informally governed (i.e., informality does not imply liberatory). In a world of limited centralized surveillance local cultural rules were probably often diverse though framed by intermittent religious or state interventions.

The great and uneven transformation of the West from rural to urban and from agricultural to industrial in the nineteenth century was accompanied by the partial movement of sexuality, gender and reproduction into the world of the secularity. In its earliest phase this did not mean that specific sexual practices or arrangements condemned by religion ceased to be stigmatized, only the 'explanations' or the 'whys' of sexual conduct began to change. However, the recasting of these practices into a secular framework opened opportunities for empirical study and debate. In this process new distinctions between the approved and disapproved in sexual life were introduced as various and changing secular disciplines brought their methods and explanations to bear on sexual life. This secular study of sexual conduct began as an intra-European intellectual project centred in Germany, Austria, England and France (and then more widely).[12] First in medicine, particularly among students of mental illness, and then in that branch of medicine which became psychoanalysis, a revolution in thinking about origins and justifications for various forms of sexuality began.

While it is Freud who is most commonly thought of as the centre of this revolution, there was a large supporting cast who contributed to these changes.[13] However unsupported (and ultimately unsupportable) the contentions of psychoanalysis might have been, it was the most important and influential system of ideas about sexuality in the early twentieth century. Indeed, the interesting question about psychoanalysis may not be whether it was so, but why so many have believed that it was a correct version of the world of sexuality, gender and reproduction. Self-consciously usurping sacred versions of the proper sexual life, psychoanalysis replaced the critical distinction between *virtue and vice* with that of *the normal and the perverse*. At the same time psychoanalysis often allocated specific sexual, gender and reproductive practices and actors to the same side of the dichotomy as did the criminal law and religious doctrine. What was virtuous became the normal, what was vicious became the perverse.

This rapid change of thinking about sexuality in particular (traditional thinking about gender and reproduction changed more slowly) began in earnest in the more pacific moments of the closing decades of the nineteenth century. However, its pace and direction was blunted in the context of the violent military, economic, and political events of what the historian Eric Hobsbawn has labelled the 'short' twentieth century. Even as sexual reform in general and psychoanalysis and its variants became important ideas in the European landscape, the great European civil war (1914–45), which eventually came to involve the whole world, shattered the social and cultural situation of new thinking about sexuality. The post-

First World War rise of collectivist movements of the right and the left repressed ideas about sexual reform and often exterminated or dispersed the holders of these new ideas about sexual life. By the end of the Second World War the movement toward sexual research and sexual reform had been largely transferred to physically safer confines of the United States.

It was in the United States that many of the important figures committed to changed thinking about sexuality, particularly in psychoanalysis, found refuge and new audiences. As they settled in and successfully promoted variants of psychoanalysis among cultural elites, the American sex researcher Alfred Kinsey and his colleagues were carrying out their landmark survey studies of sexuality which served to introduce the people of the United States to a changing sexual world.[14] National in scope, these surveys (whatever their technical defects and they were numerous) represented an important step toward a *cross national* perspective on studying sexuality.[15] The Kinsey studies were, of course, confined to one country (they were also restricted to the young, the better educated, the white, the northeast region of the United States), but the *idea* of the sex survey as the appropriate method to study sexual life of a nation and its comparative implications as a method was confirmed in the national mind. Kinsey treated all forms of sexual expression as normal within the range of mammalian sexual behaviour, a view that widely expanded the domain of legitimate sexuality. Behaviours still treated as perverse in the psychoanalytic tradition became biologically (and culturally) normal. Homosexuality, oral sex, masturbation, women's sexual pleasure were moved from one side of the sexual ledger to the other, from sinful and perverse to evolutionarily normal. At the same time the very criteria of normality were shifted from the behaviour of the individual to the possibilities of the species.

The focus on sexual life at the intra-national level by Kinsey did not replace the earlier considerations of a comparative 'cross-cultural' interest in the sexual lives of 'the others'. During the 1930s Margaret Mead compared the quality of the lives, including the sexual, of the young people that she studied in Polynesia with those of young people in the United States. In a reversal of the conventional colonial impulse (but following the subversive Enlightenment perspective) Mead and other anthropologists began to praise the practices of the peoples they studied.[16] At the same time the actual amount of research on sexuality in anthropology that was reported remained modest until the 1960s and after. While 'cross-cultural' research on sexuality was undertaken in this period, data collection on sexuality during fieldwork was often self-censored and data that were collected in fieldnotes did not appear in published works.[17] 'The sexual life of savages' was more often a topic of gossip at anthropologists' meetings than the topic of professional reports. It was possible for an acute observer of research trends in anthropology to point out the dearth of field reports on the sexual life of the 'others' in anthropology in the United States.[18]

The Second World War saw in the United States a major expansion of the use of survey methods to study both the state of the nation at large and the military in particular. The purpose in these cases was not comparative and did not focus on sexuality, but resulted in the institutionalization of the survey method as a way of measuring multiple aspects of a nation at war that would be deeply consequential in terms of governmental practice in the postwar period. This vast information-gathering campaign was extended to the military and the postwar analysis of that effort in the volumes of *The American Soldier* represents an important continuation of the nineteenth-century efforts at state formation and societal management.[19] At the same time the 'cross-cultural' tradition was recruited to the war effort as attempts were made to understand our enemy (the 'others') through comparative studies of 'national character'. Particularly focusing of the Japanese (who were perceived as more 'other' than the Germans until the postwar confrontation with the Holocaust) such studies of 'enemy others' had a considerable purchase in the intellectual life of the United States during the cold war.[20] Even as serious doubts emerged about the concept of 'national character' and whether nation states (or even small societies) were sufficiently homogeneous in personality terms to have a common 'cultural character' this tradition of viewing a nation state as composed similar 'others' (as in the Germans or the French) has significant vitality even at the present moment.[21] As the 'other' becomes the enemy, the danger of the 'otherness' to our cultural uniqueness and virtue becomes more accentuated.

Internal to the United States the national survey tradition in *sexuality* did not immediately take hold in the academy. It was not that *no* scientific studies of sexuality were undertaken – both fieldwork studies (of the anthropological sort undertaken by sociologists and anthropologists) and careful surveys of some populations, particularly of young people's attitudes and their behaviours, started in the 1950s and early 1960s. The fieldwork studies treated previously highly stigmatized sexual conduct as 'non-conforming' or 'unconventional' rather than 'sick' or 'perverse'. The *deviant* was contrasted with the *conforming* and both were treated as local social conventions rather than as universal laws. It was out of these academic studies that many forms of sexual conduct that differed from the norm became treated as victimless practices which should no longer be treated as criminal.[22] These studies were important in establishing a basis for a social constructionist view of sexuality during the early 1970s.[23]

Academic survey studies on sexuality conducted during the 1960s and 1970s usually focused on young people, given the long-standing national concern with what was viewed as the changing role of sexuality during adolescence. During the early 1970s these concerns of the sexuality of young people became narrowly focused on questions of teen pregnancy, particularly among minority groups.[24] A number of demographic and birth control surveys of young women with a limited number of questions about coitus were undertaken and data reported.[25] This was also the era in which other federally supported studies were begun which aimed at measuring demographic patterns among women of child-bearing age (beginning in 1973 and continuing at six-year intervals, these studies were conducted by the National Center for Health Statistics and called the National Surveys of Family Growth). These studies were beginning a new tradition of demographic and health oriented surveys within the Federal health establishment aimed at the creation of measures of the sexual and reproductive health of the nation. In their beginnings they were carefully restricted to a narrow range of sexual concerns.

Other than a small national survey of college students conducted in 1967, there were no studies of sexuality that replicated the range or purposes of the Kinsey study, that is, a general report on the sexual life of the nation. The Kinsey studies of sexuality in the mid-century (conducted between 1938 and 1953) remained a singularity in the scientific community until nearly a decade into the HIV/AIDS epidemic in the 1990s. This absence of academic survey research on sexuality did not restrain the conduct of mass media mail-in surveys (usually called 'Reports' to echo 'the Kinsey Report') on their readership.[26] These questionnaire studies were conducted widely in the post-Kinsey era. Nearly all these surveys were defective methodologically and intellectually. Most recently (in 1994) a national sex survey meeting the rules of telephone random sampling was conducted by a major media outlet, suggesting both the increasing sophistication of the media and the willingness of Americans to talk about their sexual lives on the phone with a stranger.[27]

The survey as an intra-national method of choice attained an internal normalcy as a method of 'national' fact finding and societal bookkeeping in the immediate post-Second World War period for governmental agencies, media institutions, political parties, private corporations and for research communities in economics, sociology and political science. The community of surveyors soon became a disciplinary entity comprising a separate set of technical professionals with their own organizations, journals and practices. Survey specialists worked in the academy, in the government, in commercial polling and in private corporations that maintained polling arms. The survey of public opinion (and the conduct of the public) became part of the normative practices of society in the United States, the populace became used to reading about polls and many were responsive to the pollsters at their door or on their telephones. The national poll reaffirmed the national solidarity of the American people because it assumed the cultural homogeneity of the populace. The random survey assumed the notion that only a 'representative American' in the statistical sense would answer the door or pick up the phone. The success of the intra-national survey movement in the United States has been replicated in the rest of the world. Within nearly all economically advanced major nation states, surveying the populace has become a normal practice. These survey practices have resulted in a comparative international academic survey movement (institutionalized as the International Social Survey Programme) that has steadily expanded since the end of the Second World War, in part modelled on the General Social Survey in the United States. The specifically comparative research programme includes thirty-nines states at the time of writing.

Until the emergence of the HIV/AIDS epidemic the interest in sexual practices had remained modest not only in the intra-national arena, but in international comparative surveys as well. The issues of sexuality, gender and reproduction first moved into the domain of normal survey practices of the nation state through studies of population and contraception. Driven by concerns about world overpopulation after the Second World War and the feared increase in less desired social groupings, investments were made in the academic study of population and the creation of the specialty interdisciplinary field of demography. A series of surveys was undertaken in the United States and then in other nations, primarily in those that were thought to be less developed, to measure population growth and the success of techniques of population control (the World Fertility Surveys were undertaken 1972–84, followed by the Contraceptive Prevalence Surveys

1977–85 – both surveys were funded by the United States government. These two surveys became the Demographic and Health Surveys which have had a continuous existence since the mid-1980s and have been part of the portfolio of research conducted by the USAID. With the onset of the HIV/AIDS epidemic these surveys increased the numbers of questions on sexual conduct. It is important to note that these were not 'sex surveys', they were studies of fertility, family planning and, latterly, health that included a limited number of questions about sexual conduct.

The extension of state interests to sexuality was politically cautious in all arenas, with only a few sexuality questions which were used to identify the coitally active. Little information was gathered about sexual practices other than coitus between women and men and coitus was often measured using only such items as 'when was the last time ...' or 'how often in the last month ...' At the same these questions were the opening move in the inclusion of sexuality and sexuality related issues into the agenda of social bookkeeping of the nation state. These surveys which indicated that more young people were becoming coitally active earlier in life had the unintended consequence of creating increased levels of social concern and conflict about the 'moral' implications for the nation of changes in the sexual life of the young. The increasingly acrimonious debate over the amount and kind of sexual education and the provision of contraception for the coitally active young was in part fuelled by the results of this survey and antedated similar debates in the HIV/AIDS era.[28]

As the survey tradition blossomed within nation states and in cross-national research programmes, the anthropological exploration of cross-cultural differences in sexuality was facing a quite different set of issues. The peoples of pre-colonial anthropology were rapidly replaced by the nation states often created by the departed colonial nation state. The colonial district officer was replaced by the elected or appointed officials of the new nation states. The political realities that the colonial situation allowed the anthropologist to ignore now became critical (e.g. most anthropologists came from the colonizing states and their citizenship was not a matter of contention; after independence most anthropologists became foreigners, in some sense guest workers). As the process of colonization was usually geographically and culturally specific, so was the process of decolonization. In sub-Saharan Africa the new nation states developed their own political and economic agendas with peoples who were loyal to traditional groupings as well as to the new nation itself. In many parts of the world insurgent groups from the left and the right emerged, only sometimes as part of the cold war rivalry between the US and the USSR. These confrontations resulted in hot and cold wars in which anthropologists and their 'peoples' were often involved.[29]

The epistemological crisis in anthropology can in part be assigned to its changing relation to what were its subject peoples – in both senses of being subjected peoples and peoples as subjects.[30] The question of the anthropologist's relation to these peoples and his or her role in their continued subjugation and the role that the relationship played in the production of what was believed to be knowledge became a foreground theoretical issue in the field for some years. This issue of the cultural relation between the knower and the known, between the researcher and the data, was less intense in those areas in anthropology which seemed to serve a practical purpose. Thus medical anthropology retained its sense of humane purpose under the umbrella of health and development. Unlike those whose interest in the 'others' was scientific enlightenment, the medical anthropologist seemed less vulnerable to issues of epistemological doubt. Yet it is important to remember that significant cross-cultural research on *sexuality-related issues* was in fact being conducted in the 1960s and 1970s. This work was often driven by concerns with the role of women in various cultures and this took the anthropologist into the issues of relations between women and men, reproduction, household labour and women's rights. Here the medical anthropologist and non-medical anthropologists could meet about issues of substance and theory. Sexuality began to be studied in the context of gender, rather than in the context of reproduction.[31]

Issues of feminism and women's roles and rights were now critical in the cultures that sent anthropologists to live among the 'others'. As a consequence these issues became central for many anthropologists, both women and men. In addition, as study of 'homosexuality' in the West, particularly in the United States, transmuted itself into the study of 'gay life' or 'gay men and lesbians', similar sexual practices became noticeable, understandable and reportable to usual audiences of the anthropological literature as well as to international policy-makers.[32] The sexuality of the 'other' became more and more a topic that could be addressed in the sending cultures and as a consequence more and more normalized as a topic of conversation and potential social transformation.

The HIV/AIDS Epidemics

The HIV/AIDS epidemics have had fundamental consequences for research on sexuality, if not always for sexual practices. Within a relatively short time after the epidemic entered its public phase in 1981 in the United States the role of particular sexual practices in the transmission of the virus became well known (as did the role of contaminated injection equipment among drug users and contaminated blood and blood products)[33]. At the same time it was clear that there were quite different epidemics in various regions of the world that were being driven by different sexual and non-sexual practices and differing co-factors that facilitated infection. What was universal in these differing epidemic situations was the lack of research knowledge about sexuality either within specific cultural groups or within different nation states. The filing cabinet which was meant to contain scientific knowledge about sexuality was largely bare, like the fabled cupboard of Mother Hubbard.[34]

The lack of quantitative survey data was particularly problematic for epidemiologists who wished to estimate the future course of the epidemic, but found that the critical data on numbers of sexual partners, types of sexual practices and frequencies of sexual conduct were largely missing for nearly all social groups in all regions of the world. A similar lack of fieldwork studies focusing on the cultural aspects of sexuality resulted in a different set of problems for disease prevention. Such studies of the ways in which sexual scripts (which specified sexual practices) were embedded in the life ways of a cultural community could be especially valuable in understanding how to design appropriate prescriptions for what would be labelled 'behaviour change'. Thus if one knew exactly how sexual life was managed by everyday people in the normal course of life, one could know how to introduce messages that might reduce risky conduct or might increase the use of preventive measures such as condoms. In addition such field studies might also be useful in the design of survey studies by informing the survey research of how to design and word questions that would yield accurate and reliable knowledge for differing cultural groups within multicultural states.[35]

Not only was the scientific cupboard relatively bare of knowledge, the researchers who were first confronting HIV/AIDS in the United States found themselves in a deeply politically divided situation when dealing with issues of sex, gender and reproduction. HIV/AIDS was viewed by a significant minority of people in the United States as primarily a 'moral issue' rather than as a purely secular health issue.[36] This conflict antedated the first public recognition of the existence of the virus and was the result of a conservative reaction to a number of human rights movements, some with strong programmes dealing with sexual, gender and reproductive rights, that emerged in the 1950s and 1960s. The civil rights movement for racial equality was rapidly followed by the second wave women's movement and the movement for gay liberation.[37] These movements produced a powerful response among religious and social conservatives, particularly in the Southern states of the US that had attempted to secede over the slavery issue during the nineteenth century. The political support of the Democratic Party for civil rights during the 1960s produced a defection of the Southern states to the Republican Party, an opportunity which they quickly seized.[38] This fundamentalist religious movement organized to resist women's choice about abortion, sex education in the schools, the homosexual 'agenda', pornography, and easily accessible contraception as well as other issues that seemed to them to contravene biblical Christian dogma about sexuality, the proper roles assigned to men and women, and the rights of the unborn.[39] All of these issues and others were clumped together in an 'issues basket' labelled 'family values'. Beginning with the Reagan administration this movement has become part of the 'base' (reliable voters, political workers and fundraisers) for the Republican Party.

When the HIV/AIDS epidemic appeared in the United States it was quickly clear that the religious right and its supporters in the Republican Party would resist a purely secular and health oriented policy toward both those afflicted and those at risk as well as the prevention programs that would be considered effective by health officials. The epidemic was then centered on gay men, already anathema to the religious right; drug users, on whom the US polity had been making war for half a century; and racial and ethnic minorities and immigrants. Only haemophiliacs, persons infected through transfusions, and those infected through mother–child transmission were 'innocent' victims.[40] The attempt to define the infected as victims of their own misconduct was widespread, as was the general torpor of the Reagan-Bush administrations in response to the epidemic. The fundamental message from the right was that it was already known what the appropriate sexual script was (i.e. sexual abstinence outside of a marriage between man and a woman) and the problem of HIV/AIDS was simply the failure of people to adhere to this script.

This conception was vigorously contested by supporters of gay liberation (both women and men), members of the women's movement and other groups with strong commitments to secular, reformist or liberatory approaches to issues of sexuality, gender and reproduction. The epidemic in the United States has evolved in the context of this struggle between the 'moralist' and the 'secular health' perspective. This has had two consequences for the research on the sexual aspects of the epidemic and prevention strategies within the United States and because of the singular importance of the United States in international affairs has had important influences on both HIV/AIDS research and prevention in the international arena. In the United States the presence of individuals from the religious right as officials in both the executive and congressional branches of government has regularly delayed, modified or prevented various sex research initiatives. In addition the membership of the fundamentalist movement has been regularly mobilized to influence decision-making about policies, research studies and prevention programmes with which they disagree. At the same time it must be understood that often these efforts only serve to slow down or temporarily sidetrack the policies, studies or programmes of which they disapprove, since such policies, studies or programmes have the support of their secular, more health and human rights oriented opponents.

The consequences for the Federal health establishment have been complex. The health establishment is largely committed to positivist and empirical science (as in 'evidence based medicine') and health researchers and policy-makers have found the existence of a new class of political 'commissars' onerous. At the same they are employees of the government and their conduct is strongly influenced by the political composition and ideologies of those currently in political power. The people in political power set policies which the civil servants are expected to implement – the former are the political masters of the latter. Even though many government scientists may have disagreed with the Reagan 'go slow' response to the epidemic, very few resigned their government posts and most worked within the policy restrictions which were imposed on them. At the same time various sex research programmes, which the right opposed, did finally go forward, often delayed by a number of years, and when completed usually failed to influence policy (e.g. the vast body of evidence is that clean needle exchange programmes not only work to reduce infection, but do not lead to greater drug use.[41] Such programmes are not supported by the Federal government and attempts to promote them are often defeated. Former President Clinton has reported that, when he was in office, he did not support such programmes even though it was apparent to him that they worked.

The history of the first national survey of sexual conduct since Kinsey (the National Health and Social Life Survey conducted in 1992) is a good example of this conflicted process.[42] Such a survey was proposed by the National Academy of Sciences early in the epidemic when it became clear that the Kinsey studies were half a century old, were methodologically limited and could not be safely used to estimate the size and direction of the epidemic or to estimate the effects of programmes of behaviour change. Preparatory work was undertaken using government funds, but when the proposal to do the study was submitted Federal funds were withdrawn not only for this study of adults, but from a comparable study of youth and a linked but approved study of sexual networks as well. This study in a much reduced size was undertaken with private funds and published in 1994. Other survey studies on sexuality were funded in this period by different agencies (the national surveys conducted at the Center for AIDS Prevention studies funded by National Institute for Mental Health are an excellent example); however, most surveys were narrowly focused on AIDS related sexual issues. They were studies about sexuality in the context of AIDS, rather than the study of AIDS in the context of sexuality.

Perhaps the most interesting outcome of this social conflict over sexuality has been, first, that the traditional religious groups have been fighting a delaying action against empirically based research projects on sexuality, largely slowing rather than preventing them, and, second, that changes in sexual conduct of the populace of the United States, as measured by these surveys, have been largely moving in directions antithetical to those proposed by religious conservatives.[43] Under the guise of studies of 'risk behaviour' and with the goal of 'healthy youth', high school students are now being routinely asked questions by state and Federal questioners that would have been forbidden 15 years ago (see the Youth Risk Behavior Surveillance System which has been in place since 1992) and questions about specific sexual practices such as oral and anal sex are asked in face-to-face computer assisted surveys funded by the Federal government under the guise of regular studies of family growth (see the most recent reports from last cycle of the National Survey of Family Growth conducted by the National Center for Health Statistics). These studies produce evidence of increasing levels of sexual liberalization among the population of the United States even in the context of governmental conservatism. Other studies suggest that both sexual conduct and attitudes to sexuality, particularly toward same gender sexuality (homosexuality), are changing among the young in similar directions.

Beginning in the early 1990s a number of international surveys of sexual conduct were undertaken in response to the HIV/AIDS epidemic. While there was little methodological overlap and little consultation between the national research teams, these studies were the opening moment in producing reasonably high quality survey data on sexual life in various nation states. While nearly all of the studies had certain constraints because they were driven primarily by concerns with HIV/AIDS they were sufficiently alike to able to produce cross-national comparative studies of sexual practices that suggested interesting commonalties in the sexual practices of the populations in a number of European nation states, the United States and Australia. Similar studies have been undertaken in Latin America and mainland China which have received limited attention in the press. It is clear that, given enough emphasis on the health aspects of sexuality, many nation states are willing to add sexuality to their research portfolios.

In addition to these general population level surveys a large number of local surveys have been undertaken among groups who were thought to be 'at risk' for infection. In many cases these were multi-centre interview studies of specific classes of respondents (e.g. injection drug users, young urban gay men, men who were prostitutes, college youth, women sex workers) which were intended to measure infection prevalence or to assess various intervention techniques. The number of such studies over the last twenty-five years within the United States has been very large, large enough indeed, for judgments to be made of 'best intervention practices'. All of this research has been governed by interests in AIDS, not interests in sexuality. Thus the studies of young gay men in urban settings yields little knowledge about the relation of changes in gay life and the reasons for differential levels of infection among young men of different ethnic backgrounds in different cities. Sex is not treated as a social practice embedded in larger lives of young men, but as a simple vector for virus transmission. It may well be that after twenty-five years of sex related research on AIDS we will end up knowing as little about sex as we did before the epidemic began.

At the international level the AIDS epidemic has produced a number of nation level studies, some at the national and regional level with sampled populations, but are more often multi-site ones that single out specific populations for estimating the size of the epidemic (e.g. pregnant women attending pre-natal clinics) or groups thought to be at risk (e.g. sex workers in specific sites). Nearly all of these studies are interview surveys rather than full ethnographic field studies and many of the research populations suffer from undocumented and unconsidered selection effects. The move towards the rapid 'interview survey' in AIDS research is partially a response to the perceived need for rapid data and to meet the scientific illusion of similarity of questions produced by the use of similar interview schedules for all respondents. Protocol driven studies which are based on fixed instruments were used in the first WHO sponsored knowledge, attitude and sexual partners studies, but this project largely failed to produce comparable research results because of sampling and other difficulties. The failure of these studies led to a turn to small-scale 'qualitative' studies largely based on interviewing of respondents who were similar in some attributes but whose representativeness was unknown.

The AIDS epidemic has not been productive of knowledge about sexuality or gender largely because the research projects occasioned by the epidemic have been limited to variables that seem obviously related to the issue of transmission or to variables whose change would indicate that levels of risk of transmission has gone up or down (e.g. condom use or numbers of partners in a given time period). The role of sexuality in the wider social life of the respondents is largely unexamined, the studies are not of ways of living in which sexuality is embedded, but are of the variables that are related to measuring transmission or responses to interventions. In these studies sexuality is a problem, but it is not problematized. Not all studies suffer from this defect, but nearly all of those designed and funded by various centralized national or international health care institutions do.[44]

The decline of fieldwork or ethnographic studies of sexuality in the AIDS arena represents a serious methodological lack. The emphasis on the small-scale survey as the only representative of 'qualitative research' has increased the speed of output of data collection and publication, but no longer supplies the thick description that is needed to place a practice in the larger context of cultural life. What sex means to men and women in various cultural situations and its importance (or unimportance) to non-sexual aspects of living is rarely addressed in issues of how often, how many, and did you use a condom the last time and on to the next respondent. In the absence of a deeper understanding of multiple ways in which sex plays a role in everyday life in specific cultures, the insertion of a new cultural element (a condom) into the ongoing condom-less scripts for coitus is unknowable.

At the same time the international AIDS arena has become subject to the political struggles over sexuality, gender and reproduction that complicate research and everyday sexual life in the United States. Faith-based (meaning Christian) evangelical missionary institutions from the United States (and other centres of Christian belief) have had a long and continuing international history in both the colonial and post-colonial periods. The Christian presence in many countries has now had a sufficient duration that only the historically minded remember that it is not an indigenous religion in many parts of the world prior to colonial expansions. At the same time Christianity or some syncretic forms of Christianity are now widespread in many countries that are dealing with AIDS. It is therefore not a surprise that programmes that support strict Christian versions of how to deal with HIV transmission receive funding from various arms of the United States government.

Nations, Cultures and Globalization

In the history of comparative social research, the cross-national and the cross-cultural approaches have often been seen as competitors, with the practitioners of the one eager to point out the scientific limitations of the other. In some cases the criticisms are technical – pointing out that in this or that survey the sample was defective in one or another ways or that the field worker did not ask all respondents the same questions. In other arguments there are disputes at a higher level, that surveys cannot spend enough time with the respondents to get the truth or that the field worker is only one person reporting on a complex reality. In some circumstances it is a debate between the quantitative and the qualitative, between a thin description, but representative sample, and a thick description, but only a few respondents or informants. This debate is now largely formulaic and the points and counterpoints are largely routine and the critical strictures on each method are probably correct.

In practice those doing research recognize the limitations of all research strategies in producing an 'objective' or veridical view of a complex social or cultural situation. The sample survey and the ethnographic study are designed to do different things and conflicts in findings are problems to be parsed and understood as either unique to the specific inquiry or as consequences of the general limitations of a given strategy of inquiry. The complementary nature of research methods has begun to be recognized in such strategies as 'triangulation' studies which use a multi-method approach to understand local situations. At the moment such studies often only include 'qualitative' and 'quantitative' methods in the here and now. It would be an advance if such studies adopted a more historical approach and included data on the economic and political context in which the problem resided (invoking the intellectual tradition of political-economy). There are actually only a few studies of sexuality which have tried to move away from the individual and interactional levels to issues of the political economy of the sexual. Such approaches are found more often (though not routinely) in the study of gender and reproduction.

This is another reason to adopt a less conflictual strategy in dealing with cross-national and cross-cultural approaches to research on sex, gender and reproduction: there are actually no nation states which have a singular culture. Survey researchers recognize this at the moment of analysis when they divide up the sample by various important variables, for instance, gender, class, occupation, religion, age and the like. The aggregation of individuals on the basis of any one of these variables offers a useful, but incomplete picture of cultural variations within any 'master status' such as class or gender. Men and women are often different, but within the category 'woman' or 'man' there is internal variation which is not accounted for by adding additional variables in one or another ways. Adding variables such as older, richer, working, church attending to the variable 'woman' may extract more variance, but there is always something left over that should not be assigned to error rather to than lack of measurement of unrecognized sources of variation.

Multiculturalism makes the state a fuzzy unit of analysis. One does not have to leave Europe or the United States to find examples of the truism that all states are multicultural. In the United States the extraordinary importance of 'being a real American' rests on the fact that it is a nation state composed of former and current immigrants who have extraordinarily diverse cultural origins (including sexual, gender and reproductive practices). It is obvious that nation states change their borders in war and peace (what is France with and without the Alsace or Austria without the South Tyrol?). The extermination of the Jews, the expulsion of the German populations from Eastern Europe after the Second World War, the collapse of the Soviet hegemony over the Baltic states in the west and the Islamic states in the south involve deep cultural change. States in Europe often have two or more important language groups, which are waxing or waning in cultural and political significance (this waxing and waning includes the selection of sexual and reproductive partners) depending on the historical moment.

We usually think of cultures as long-lasting, and there are differences that we easily recognize as having cultural consequences or having the capacity for a 'way of life' to be formed around them. Thus religion, region, ethnicity, even living in the countryside or the city have an easily recognized potential for culture building. These are taken for granted sources of 'cultural' differences. But if culture means 'a way of life to which its members are committed' then there are many foci of social practices or individual identities that can become the basis for cultural difference. In recent times 'cultures' have been formed around sexual preferences or practices (gay and lesbian cultures, transgendered cultures, the cultures of prostitution). What were once 'deviant' subcultures or ancillary cultures have become new cultural formations with boundaries, memberships, ideologies and politics.

In the words of Idries Shah:

> Different sections of the community are, to all realities, nations ... The clerics, doctors, literary men, nobles, and peasants really could be called nations; for each has its own customs and castes of thought. To imagine that they are the same as you simply because they live in the same country or speak the same language is a feeling to examined.[45]

The implications of this recognition that all states are multicultural, that the current cultures within a state are always in the process of change and that new cultural formations are always being produced in agreement or resistance to what appear to be the central cultural formations in the nation state. Such dynamic changes are profound for all aspects of social research. In this introduction we have only considered issues of sexuality and sex research, but all aspects of research which examine social units from a comparative perspective face the same problematic. There are no fixed and permanent units of analysis: nations, cultures and individuals are in states of change, some rapidly, others more slowly, but changing they are.

A Coda: Resistance

The history of comparative research has been largely the history of research done on the 'other'. Even intra-national research has usually been conducted for the purposes of the 'few' rather than the 'many'. One of the features of the contemporary world has been the increasing resistance of the 'other' to research driven by the interests of the powerful either in other states or those in positions of power within a state. This resistance to the practices and interpretations of the dominant expert has been critical in the rise of the civil rights movement, the women's movement, and the gay and lesbian movements in the United States since the Second World War. They have each rejected an aspect of the research programmes of white heterosexual men in the human sciences and have created a set of 'critical' theories of race-ethnicity, gender and sexuality.[46]

Similar forms of resistance to research conducted by those newly construed as the 'colonizing other' are now prominent in the international arena as members of various states, religions, and ethnic groups are engaged in struggles against the way they have been characterized in the sciences of the former colonial states.[47] In some cases this resistance has been extended to secular explanations of religious belief in general and to Western psychological explanations of everyday conduct among those being studied (the resistance to Freudian explanations of Hindu beliefs is a recent example). The current anti-sex research programme of the religious right in the United States is one important example of the ways in which secular science is now engaged in a struggle to maintain its authority to explain the world. While a great deal of attention is now being paid to conflict between 'evolution' and 'intelligent design' in the United States, this is only a symptom of a much deeper crisis of authority which has significant ramifications for studies in the social conflicted domains of sex, gender and reproduction.

Notes

1. The belief that Europeans had nothing to learn from the 'Indians' of Tahiti has been echoed by contemporary religious conservatives who have reacted to findings of Gilbert Herdt about the practice of insemination of boys by young men among the Sambia (not their real name), a tribal group living in Papua New Guinea (Herdt, 1987). To the Sambia the practice ensures the maturation of boys into men, to

the religious conservative it seems a form of homosexual child abuse. The citation of Herdt's work in report of the National Academy of Sciences on HIV/AIDS provoked a strong negative reaction from the right (Turner et al., 1989).

2. There is an extraordinary contrast between anthropological reports of 'primitive' peoples and the writings of native African novelists (usually writing in French or English) about conditions in the same regions. Anthropological reports are stripped of the colonial context, while the novelists highlight the issues of coerced labour, forced religious conversion and the seizure of land and resources. See Beti (1971), Ngugi (1977), Jumban (1980, Armah (1968), Munoye (1971) among many examples.
3. The role of the nascent medical profession in creating the great fear of masturbation in the early seventeenth century in the West should be viewed as part of the history of 'ethno-medicine' or 'magical' thought rather than as a empirical precursor of modern medicine. Tissot was called a physician, but he was only historically earlier, rather than a scientific ancestor of Pasteur or Koch. The fact that contemporary medical practice also involves magical or non-empirical thinking does not justify the notion that the history of medicine is somehow intellectually continuous (Laqueur, 2003).
4. Embedded in these studies is preliminary research on sexuality and sexually transmitted diseases of white and black American soldiers. These findings are unobtrusively but brilliantly reported by sociologist Shirley Star. Still other unanalysed reports on the US military in the Second World War remain in the national archives.
5. It is important to keep in mind that Kinsey had much greater ambitions than the sociological study of sexual life in the United States at a given historical moment. He was interested in establishing an evolutionary template for the normal expression of sexuality in 'males' and 'females', a template that was discernible even after the distortions and inhibitions that resulted from cultural repressions. However even Kinsey could appeal to the overarching values of the state when, after a litany of state initiated intrusions into the sexual life of the individual, he asks, 'in an age which calls itself scientific and Christian, we should be able to discover more intelligent ways of protecting social interests without doing such irreparable damage to so many individuals and to the total social organization to which

they belong' (Kinsey et. al., 1953: 21).

6. In the interests of full disclosure I was a co-investigator and co-author of works from this study. I was also personally attacked on the floor of the United States Senate by Senator Jesse Helms for my participation in the research and there were some discussions over whether the funding of the research would be facilitated by my leaving the project
7. Globalization for these critics is colonization by with another name and with new practices, leaving intact the older system of power relations and exploitation of the weak by the strong.

Bibliography

Aistrup, Joseph A., *The Southern Strategy Revisited: Republican Top-Down Advancement in the South*, Lexington, KY: University Press of Kentucky, 1996.

Altman, Dennis, *The Homosexualization of America: The Americanization of the Homosexual*, New York: St Martin's Press, 1982.

Armah, Ayi Kwei, *The Beautiful Ones are Not Yet Born,* London: Heinemann, 1969.

Benedict, Ruth, *The Chrysanthemum and the Sword: Patterns of Japanese Culture*, Boston: Houghton Mifflin Co, 1946.

Bennet, Amanda, and Sharpe, Anita, 'AIDS Fight is Skewed by Federal Campaign', *The Wall Street Journal*, 1 May 1996.

Beti, Mongo, *The Poor Christ of Bomba*, London: Heinemann, 1971.

Bland, Lucy and Doan, Laura, eds, *Sexology in Culture: Labeling Bodies and Desires*, Chicago: University of Chicago Press, 1998.

——*Sexology Uncensored: The Documents of Sexual Science*, Chicago: University of Chicago Press, 1998.

Boot, Max, *The Savage Wars of Peace: Small Wars and the Rise of American Power*, New York: Basic Books, 2002.

Brooks, Peter, 'Gauguin's Thatian Body', *Yale Journal of Criticism*, vol. 3, no. 2, 1990.

Bullard, Alice, *Exile to Paradise: Savagery and Civilization in Paris and the South Pacific, 1790–1900*, Stanford, CA: Stanford University Press, 2000.

Chirot, Daniel, *Social Change in the Modern Era*, San Diego: Harcourt Brace Jovanovich, 1986.

Clifford, James and Marcus, George E., eds, *Writing Culture: The Poetics and Politics of Ethnography,* Berkeley, CA: University of California Press, 1986.

Cohen, Bernard S., 'Representing Authority in Victorian India', in Eric Hobsbawn and Terence Ranger, eds, *The Invention of Tradition*, Cambridge: Cambridge University Press, 1983.

De Certeau, Michel, *The Practice of Everyday Life*, Berkeley: University of California Press, 1984.

D'Emilio, John, *Sexual Politics, Sexual Communities: The Making of a Homosexual Minority in the United States, 1940–1970*, Chicago: University of Chicago Press, 1983.

——*Making Trouble: Essays on Gay History, Politics, and the University*, New York: Routledge, 1992.

Duberman, Martin B., ed. , *Queer Representations: Reading Lives, Reading Cultures*, Center for Lesbian and Gay Studies Book, New York: New York University Press, 1997.

Escoffier, Jeffrey, *American Homo: Community and Perversity*, Berkeley: University of California Press, 1998.

Fanon, Frantz, *The Wretched of the Earth*, New York: Grove Press, 1961.

Fausto-Sterling, Anne, *Myths of Gender: Biological Theories about Women and Men*, 2nd edn, New York: Basic Books, 1992.

Ferguson, Niall, *Empire: The Rise and Demise of the British World Order and the Lessons for Global Power*, New York: Basic Books, 2003.

Fogel, Robert William, *The Fourth Great Awakening and the Future of Egalitarianism*, Chicago: University of Chicago Press, 2000.

Gagnon, John H., 'Reconsiderations', *Human Nature*, vol. 1, no. 10, 1978.

—— 'Disease and Desire', *Daedelus, Journal of the American Academy of Arts and Sciences*, vol. 118, no. 3, *Living with Aids: Part II*, 1989.

——'Epidemics and Researchers: AIDS and the Practice of Social Studies', in Gilbert Herdt and Shirley Lindenbaum, eds, *Social Analysis in the Time of AIDS*, Newbury Park, CA: SAGE, 1992.

——'Others Having Sex with Others: Captain Cook and the Penetration of the Pacific', in Gilbert Herdt (ed.), *Sexual Cultures, Migration and AIDS: Anthropological and Demographic Perspectives*, Oxford: Oxford University Press, 1997.

——*An Interpretation of Desire*, Chicago: University of Chicago Press, 2004.

——'Sex Research and Sexual Conduct in the Age of AIDS', *Journal of the Acquired Immune Deficiency Syndromes*. vol. 1, 2004.

Gagnon, John H., and Simon, William, eds, *Sexual Deviance,* New York: Harper & Row, 1967.

——*Sexual Conduct,* 2nd edn, Piscatawory, NJ: Transaction Books, 2005.

Gaylin, Willard, Glasser, Ira, Marcus, Steven, and Rothman, David, *Doing Good: The Limits of Benevolence*, New York: Pantheon Books, 1981.

Herdt, Gilbert, *Guardians of the Flutes: Idioms of Masculinity*, New York: Columbia University Press, 1987.

Hobsbawn, Eric, *The Age of Extremes: The Short Twentieth Century 1914–1991*, London: Penguin, 1994.

Hobsbawn, Eric, and Terence Ranger, eds, *The Invention of Tradition*, Cambridge: Cambridge University Press, 1983.

Inkeles, Alex, *The Soviet Citizen: Daily Life in a Totalitarian Society*, Cambridge, MA: Harvard University Press, 1959.

Institute of Medicine and National Academy of Sciences, *Confronting AIDS: Update 1988*, Washington, DC: National Academy Press, 1988.

——*Confronting AIDS*, Washington, DC: National Academy Press, 1986.

Jumban, Kenjo, *The White Man of God*, London: Heinemann, 1980.
Kern, Stephen, *The Culture of Space and Time: 1980–1918*, Cambridge, MA: Harvard University Press, 1983.
Kinsey, Alfred C, Pomeroy, Wardell B., and Martin, Clyde E., *Sexual Behavior in the Human Male*, Philadelphia: Saunders, 1948.
——*Sexual Behavior in the Human Female*, Philadelphia: Saunders, 1953.
Laqueur, Thomas W., *Solitary Sex*, New York: Zone Books, 2003.
Laumann, E. O., Gagnon, John H., Michael, R. T. and Micheals, S., *The Sexual Organization of Sexuality*, Chicago: Chicago University Press, 1994.
——'A Political History of the Adult Sex Survey', in *Family Planning Perspectives*, vol. 26, no. 1, 1994.
Leveton, Lauren B., Sox, Harold C. Jr, and Sotto, Michael A., eds, *HIV and the Blood Supply*, Washington, DC: National Academy Press, 1995.
Levine, Martin P., Nardi, Peter M., and Gagnon, John H., eds, *In Changing Times: Gay Men and Lesbians Encounter HIV/AIDS*, Chicago: University of Chicago, 1997.
Lewis, Bernard, *Islam and the West*, New York: Oxford University Press, 1993.
Luker, Kristin, *Abortion and the Politics of Motherhood*, Berkeley: University of California Press, 1984.
McNeill, William H., *Plagues and Peoples*, New York: Anchor Books, 1989.
Marshall, Donald S., and Suggs, Robert C., eds, *Human Sexual Behavior: Variations in the Ethnographic Spectrum*, New York: Basic Books, 1971.
Mead, Margaret, *From the South Seas: Studies of Adolescence and Sex in Primitive Societies*, New York: William Morrow & Co, 1939.
——*And Keep your Powder Dry: An Anthropologist Looks at America*, New York: Wiliiam Morrow & Co, 1942.
——*Soviet Attitudes toward Authority: An Interdisciplinary Approach to Problems of Soviet Character*, New York: Rand Corporation and McGraw-Hill, 1951.
Moore, H. L., *Feminism and Anthropology*, Minneapolis: University of Minnesota Press, 1988.
Moorehead, Alan, *The Fatal Impact: An Account of the Invasion of the South Pacific, 1767–1840*, New York: Harper & Brothers, 1966.
Munoye, John, *Oil Man of Obange*, London: Heinemann, 1971.
Nagel, Janet, *Race, Ethnicity, and Sexuality: Intimate Intersections, Forbidden Frontiers*, New York: Oxford University Press, 2003.
Nathanson, Constance, *Dangerous Passage: The Social Control of Women's Adolescence*, Philadelphia: Tample University Press, 1991.
Ngugi, wa Thiongo, *Petals of Blood*, New York: E. P. Dutton, 1977.
Normand, Jacques, Vlahov, David, and Moses, Lincoln E., eds, *Preventing HIV Transmission: The Role of Sterile Needles and Bleach*, Washington, DC: National Academiy Press, 1995.
Plummer, Ken, *Intimate Citizenship: Private Decisions and Public Dialogues*, Seattle: University of Washington Press, 2003.
Polanyi, Karl, *The Great Transformation*, Boston: Beacon Press, 1957; original 1944.
Ranger, Terence, 'The Invention of Tradition in Colonial Africa', in Eric Hobsbawn

and Terence Ranger, eds, *The Invention of Tradition,* Cambridge: Cambridge University Press, 1983.

Robinson, Paul, *Opera, Sex and Other Vital Matters*, Chicago: University of Chicago Press, 2002.

Rubin, Eva R., ed., *The Abortion Controversy: A Documentary History*, Westport, CT: Greenwood, 1994.

Rubin, G., 'Thinking Sex: Notes for a Radical Theory in the Politics of Sexuality', in C.S. Vance, ed., *Pleasure and Danger: Exploring Female Sexuality*, New York: Routledge & Kegan Paul, 1984.

Said, Edward W., *Orientalism*, New York: Pantheon Books, 1978.

Schur, Edwin M., and Bedau, Hugo Adam, *Victimless Crimes: Two Sides of a Controversy*, Englewood Cliffs, NJ: Prentice-Hall, 1974.

Scott, James C., *Seeing like a State: How Certain Schemes to Improve the Human Condition have Failed*, New Haven: Yale University Press, 1998.

Shah, Idries, *Caravan of Dreams*, London: Quartet Books, 1973.

Stouffer, Samuel A., Suchman, E. A., DeVinney, L. C., Star, S. A., and Williams, Jr, R. M., *The American Soldier: Adjustment during Army Life. Studies in Social Psychology in World War II*, vol. 1, Princeton NJ: Princeton University Press, 1949.

——*The American Soldier: Combat and its Aftermath*, vol. 2, Princeton: Princeton University Press, 1949.

Tavris, Carol, and Wade, Carole, *The Longest War: Sex Differences in Perspective*, 2nd edn, San Diego: Harcourt Brace Jovanovich, 1984.

Turner, Charles, Miller, Heather, and Moses, Lincoln, eds, *AIDS, Sexual Behavior and Intravenous Drug Use*, Washington, DC: National Academy Press, 1989.

Useem, John, and Useem, Ruth Hill, *The Western-Educated Man in India: A Study of his Social Roles and Influence*, New York: Dryden Press, 1955.

Useem, John, Useem, Ruth, and Donoghue, John, 'Men in the Middle of the Third Culture: The Roles of American and Non-Western People in Cross-Cultural Administration', in *Human Organization*, vol. 22 Fall, 1963.

Vance, Carole, 'Anthropology Rediscovers Sexuality: A Theoretical Comment', in *Social Science and Medicine*, vol. 33, no. 8, 1991.

Wallace, Anthony F. C., *Culture and Personality*, New York: Random House, 1971.

Wallerstein, Immanuel, *The Capitalist World Economy*, New York: Cambridge University Press, 1974.

Young, Robert, *Postcolonialism: An Historical Introduction*, Malden, MA: Blackwell, 2001.

Zelnik, Melvin, Kantner, John F., and Ford, Kathleen, *Sex and Pregnancy in Adolescence*, Beverly Hills: SAGE, 1981.

Notes

1. Peter Brooks, 'Gauguin's Tahitian Body', Yale Journal of Criticism, vol. 3, no. 2, 1990, pp. 51–90; Alice Bullard, *Exile to Paradise: Savagery and Civilization in Paris and the*

South Pacific, 1790–1900, Stanford, CA, 2000.

2. Alan Moorehead, *The Fatal Impact: An Account of the Invasion of the South Pacific, 1767–1840*, New York, 1966; John H. Gagnon (1997), 'Others Having Sex with Others: Captain Cook and the Penetration of the Pacific', in Gilbert Herdt, ed., *Sexual Cultures, Migration and AIDS: Anthropological and Demographic Perspectives*, Oxford, pp. 23–38.
3. Gagnon, 2004.
4. Moorehead, 1966.
5. Terence Ranger, 'The Invention of Tradition in Colonial Africa', in Eric Hobsbawn and Terence Ranger, eds, *The Invention of Tradition*, Cambridge, 1983, pp. 211–63.
6. Daniel Chirot, *Social Change in the Modern Era*, San Diego, 1986.
7. William H. McNeill, *Plagues and Peoples*, New York, 1989.
8. Frantz Fanon, *The Wretched of the Earth*, New York, 1961; de Certeau, Michel, *The Practice of Everyday Life*, Berkeley, 1984.
9. John Useem and Ruth Hill Useem, *The Western-Educated Man in India: A Study of his Social Roles and Influence*, New York, 1955; John Useem, Ruth Useem and John Donoghue, 'Men in the Middle of the Third Culture: The Roles of American and Non-Western People in Cross-Cultural Administration', Human Organization, vol. 22 Fall, 1963, pp.169–79.
10. Stephen Kern, *The Culture of Space and Time: 1880–1918*, Cambridge, MA, 1983.
11. Lucy Bland and Laura Doan, eds, *Sexology in Culture: Labeling Bodies and Desires*, Chicago, 1998; Lucy Bland and Laura Doan, eds, *Sexology Uncensored: The Documents of Sexual Science*, Chicago, 1998.
12. See the bibliography in Kinsey et al., *Sexual Behavior in the Human Male*, Philadelphia 1948.
13. Bland and Doan, 1998, 1998, Gagnon, 1973.
14. Kinsey et al., 1948, and *Sexual Behavior in the Human Female*, Philadelphia 1953.
15. Gagnon, 1978.
16. Margaret Mead, *From the South Seas: Studies of Adolescence and Sex in Primitive Societies*, New York 1939.
17. Donald S. Marshall and Robert C. Suggs, eds, *Human Sexual Behavior: Variations in the Ethnographic Spectrum*, New York, 1971.
18. Carole Vance, 'Anthropology Rediscovers Sexuality: A Theoretical Comment', in *Social Science and Medicine*, vol. 33, no. 8, 1991.
19. Stouffer et al., *The American Soldier: Adjustment during Army Life. Studies in Social Psychology in World War II*, vol. 1, Princeton NJ, 1949.
20. Mead, 1942; Benedict, 1946; Inkeles 1959.
21. Anthony F. C. Wallace, *Culture and Personality*, New York, 1971.
22. Edwin M. Schur and Hugo A. Bedau, Edwin M., *Victimless Crimes: Two Sides of a Controversy*, Englewood Cliffs, NJ, 1974.
23. For a collection of such field studies, see John H. Gagnon and William Simon, eds, *Sexual Deviance*, New York 1967.
24. Constance Nathanson, *Dangerous Passage: The Social Control of Women's Adolescence*, Philadelphia, 1991.
25. Melvin Zelnik et al., *Sex and Pregnancy in Adolescence*, Beverly Hills, 1981.
26. Paul Robinson, *Opera, Sex and Other Vital Matters*, Chicago, 2002, pp. 185–205.
27. http://abcnews.go.com/images/Politics/959a1AmericanSexSurvey.pdf.
28. Nathanson, 1991.
29. Max Boot, *The Savage Wars of Peace: Small Wars and the Rise of American Power*, New York, 2002; Eric Hobsbawn, *The Age of Extremes: The Short Twentieth Century 1914–*

1991, London, 1994.

30. James Clifford and George E. Marcus, eds, *Writing Culture: The Poetics and Politics of Ethnography,* Berkeley, CA 1986; John H. Gagnon, 'Epidemics and Researchers: AIDS and the Practice of Social Studies', in Gilbert Herdt and Shirley Lindenbaum, eds, *Social Analysis in the Time of AIDS*, Newbury Park, CA, 1992.
31. See H. L. Moore, *Feminism and Anthropology*, Minneapolis, 1988; G. Rubin, 'Thinking Sex: Notes for a Radical Theory in the Politics of Sexuality', in C.S. Vance, ed., *Pleasure and Danger: Exploring Female Sexuality*, New York, 1984.
32. Dennis Altman, *The Homosexualization of America: The Americanization of the Homosexual*, New York 1982; John D'Emilio, *Sexual Politics, Sexual Communities: The Making of a Homosexual Minority in the United States, 1940–1970*, Chicago 1983, and *Making Trouble: Essays on Gay History, Politics, and the University*, New York, 1992; Martin B. Duberman, ed., *Queer Representations: Reading Lives, Reading Cultures*, Center for Lesbian and Gay Studies Book, New York, 1997.
33. Institute of Medicine and National Academy of Sciences, *Confronting AIDS: Update 1988*, Washington DC, 1988.
34. John H. Gagnon, 'Disease and Desire', *Daedelus, Journal of the American Academy of Arts and Sciences*, vol. 118, no. 3, *Living with Aids: Part II*, 1989.
35. Gagnon, *An Interpretation of Desire*, Chicago, 2004.
36. Martin P. Levine et al., *In Changing Times: Gay Men and Lesbians Encounter HIV/AIDS*, Chicago, 1997.
37. Gagnon and Simon, *Sexual Conduct,* 2nd edn, Piscatawory, NJ, 2005, pp. 235–77.
38. Joseph A. Aistrup, *The Southern Strategy Revisited: Republican Top-Down Advancement in the South*, Lexington, KY, 1996.
39. Levine, 2002; Kristin Luker, *Abortion and the Politics of Motherhood*, Berkeley, 1984; Eva R. Rubin, ed., *The Abortion Controversy: A Documentary History*, Westport, CT, 1994.
40. Lauren B. Leveton et al., *HIV and the Blood Supply*, Washington, DC, 1995.
41. Jacques Normand et al., eds, *Preventing HIV Transmission: The Role of Sterile Needles and Bleach*, Washington, DC, 1995.
42. E. O. Laumann et al., *The Sexual Organization of Sexuality*, Chicago, 1994 and 'A Political History of the Adult Sex Survey', in *Family Planning Perspectives*, vol. 26, no. 1, 1994.
43. Laumann et al., 1994.
44. Gaylin et al., *Doing Good: The Limits of Benevolence*, New York, 1981, for the downside of doing good.
45. Idries Shah, *Caravan of Dreams*, London, 1973.
46. For gender see Carol Tavris and Carole Wade, *The Longest War: Sex Differences in Perspective*, 2nd edn, San Diego, 1984; Anne Fausto-Sterling, *Myths of Gender: Biological Theories about Women and Men*, 2nd edn, New York, 1992; for sexuality see Rubin, 1984.
47. The debate about Orientalism is relevant, see Edward Said, *Orientalism*, New York, 1978, and Bernard Lewis, *Islam and the West*, New York, 1993.

Sexuality, Health and Colonialism in Postwar 1860 Beirut

Jens Hanssen

Not far from the Place des Canons (Sahat al-Burj) we found ourselves in front of a house with large, lit-up windows. We descended the rickety wooden stairs that were covered by an inviting red carpet. Downstairs a man got up from his wooden table to greet us with a bow. An Italian show. While we were still deliberating, an elegant carriage drawn by two magnificent horses stopped in front of the staircase. A young gentleman in an immaculate blazer and a red Tarbush stepped out and helped a lady descend dressed in a flowing frou-frou of silk pleats, in flashing diamonds, a layering of Brussels laces and a scent of some provocative perfume. She had the appearance of a typical European lady of fashion. He belonged to one of the immensely rich local Syrian patrician families in this trading city. These young people go to Europe, especially Paris, for a few years and return with a firm command of several European languages, good etiquette and particularly with many new business connections. Their vast fortunes never leave the country, and the merchant dynasties marry amongst themselves. However pleasant and polite these distinguished patricians are towards the Europeans, they do not allow them to gain a durable foothold in their society.

Of such a dynasty was this man. And the lady? Looking over his shoulder secretively, the consular official whispers: 'His girlfriend. From Paris ... absolutely authentic! Direct import. He has brought her himself.'

We decided to enter the theatre and followed the young man and his girlfriend. The box where we were placed was one of many on an encircling balcony. It was not exactly comfortable, but the arrangement permitted one to bend over the low railings and chat

> animatedly with the neighbours to the right and left.
>
> [When the show was over, it] was greeted with frenetic applause by the audience. The lights went on and I could have a look around the theatre. In the boxes on the balcony, the ladies of the Syrian notability sat in their European dresses. It was glittering and glamorous as if these women were not sitting on the pathetic balcony of a puppet theatre, but within the mirrored walls of any one of the largest opera houses in Europe. And the ladies knew how to wear the volume of laces, the incredible wealth of jewelry with grace and matter-of-factness and with a truly aristocratic calm and self-confidence ... A tad too much in some aspects which was surely added here and not in Paris or Vienna. And these ladies were free, they went about unveiled. Opposite us sat the young man with his girlfriend from Paris. They sat next to each other, engaged in a casual conversation, a bit bored, like people for whom leisure is a social duty.
>
> Two boxes to our right sat two elderly women with three young girls. The young man greeted them and they reciprocated with a friendly nodding of their heads. 'It is his mother,' said the consular official, 'and the young girls are his sisters.'
>
> I found it strange indeed, that one should present one's girlfriends with such aplomb. 'My god, what do you want? Nobody finds anything wrong with it. One keeps these ladies like racing horses. It is part of good form.' 'And these girlfriends never complain?' 'Most of them know exactly the habits of this country. Many have already come several times. Should, for whatever reason, the relationship come to an end, one sunny morning the young lady will receive magnificent jewelry and a small letter which will inform her in elegant French that the next Messagerie Maritime steamer sets sail on such and such a day. A ticket for the journey and a transfer to a Paris banker for a handsome sum will be included. So far, nobody has had to complain.'[1]

This account of an episode that occurred in Beirut sometime in the first decade of the twentieth century is excerpted from an Austrian book published in 1911, *Romantische Reise im Orient*. It presents Beirut as an unexpected place in which gender and class relations unsettled the passing foreigner. What was so unexpected to the author, however, was not the city's quaint exoticism or sexual mystique – conventional tropes of Orientalism – but rather the opposite: how unsettlingly familiar it was. It appears that to tourists like K. H. Strobel, Beirut was 'a subject of a difference that [wa]s almost the same but not quite.'[2] This chapter sets out to explore the historical anthropology of Beirut's social structure, class consciousness and the concomitant colonial discourses of intervention it generated. On the one hand, I argue that sexuality and gender constructions were central to the forging of middle-class modes of identification and to the conflicts over patriarchy and masculinity that ensued in Beirut and Mount Lebanon. On the other hand, discourses of promiscuity and sexual excess brought colonial hygienists onto the stage of urban politics and planning. Over the course of the nineteenth century, Orientalist discourses on Beirut shifted from sexual conquest to behavioural containment as French hygienists struggled to come to terms with the city's fast-paced growth and transformation that threatened the health of the foreign community and integrity of the established, local male elite. Finally, I argue that this colonial anxiety provided French colonialism with a psychological aetiology that culminated in a racialized pathology of Syrians.

As far as conventional Orientalist travel narratives of Beirut go, K. H. Strobel's *Romantische Reise* is a remarkably self-conscious account of an Austrian traveller on the increasingly busy tourist trail from Istanbul to Damascus, Jerusalem and on to Egypt. In his theatre scene, the participant observer is not quite in control of the goings-on he describes as he mocks himself for the ways in which the nonchalant behaviour of Beirut's Francophile elites spoils the romantic expectations he had held. It is as if Strobel and other less sensitive visitors were finding it difficult to place late Ottoman Beirut on a cultural map.

Strobel's account stands out because the author neither cites previous travel accounts nor constructs an antiquity-referential discourse of the Orient's present urban decay. Both were common narrative features of Edward Said's critique of Orientalism: representing 'the Orient' as Europe's past and inferior other, and reducing it to the physical place where exotic desires are fulfilled. Strobel, clearly, had a keen eye for the contradictions of everyday life and the way ordinary occurrences he witnessed in Middle Eastern cities were surprisingly familiar in unfamiliar settings. He documents with great alacrity the growing macadamization of downtown Beirut and speculates on the passing of the camel as the main mode of transportation. Elsewhere, he is impressed how Beirut's police provided safe cordons for night-time walkers by communicating through an ingenious whistle system between the dark patches of the newly installed gas lamps.[3]

Checked against historical sources, such representations of social spaces can provide meaningful insights. In the second half of the nineteenth century, regular steamships industrialized the Mediterranean transport system, Beirut's merchants established outlets in most European ports, Lebanese emigration reached the Americas and a steady stream of Eurotourism from Ottoman lands trickled into European capitals, tying together leisure and pleasure activities of an emerging Mediterranean cruise society.[4] Venues like the *Masrah al-Jadid* (The New Theatre) on Beirut's ostentatious Sahat al-Burj were popular as well as contested sites of modern entertainment. It was listed as a new nocturnal 'hotspot' in the 1910/11 edition of the Beirut Directory.[5] The same place was the ugly scene of European vandalism in 1911. A circle of local freemasons had invited a travelling troupe of French actors to perform Eugène Sue's *Le Juif errant*. This enraged Jesuit students who ransacked the theatre.[6]

The Parisian literary scene had discovered Beirut back in the 1840s and 1850s. The correspondence between Gustave Flaubert, Maxime du Camp, Gérard de Nerval and Théophile Gautier are replete with lewd references to promiscuity in Cairo, Beirut and other cities in the Ottoman Empire.[7] This metropolitan circle's trusted local anchor in Beirut was the director of the French post office in Beirut and a recognized Orientalist painter. Flaubert, who visited Camille Rogier (1810–96) in 1850, wrote home that 'we have discovered that him and us are of the same band of artists'.[8] But Flaubert and de Nerval found it hard 'to penetrate these fortresses of maternal and paternal power' in Beirut and complained that sexual 'adventures here are rarer than in Cairo'.[9] Only ten years later, however, prostitution was recognized as a social and cultural problem after civil war in Mount Lebanon brought in a French 'peace-keeping' force of thousands of soldiers. The postwar condition changed this idyllic, if straight-laced image in ways that deeply affected relations with – and the perception of – foreigners in Beirut.

Even though such travel accounts as Strobel's are, of course, also fictional in the sense of being a crafted narrative, if cross-referenced with multi-archive research and embedded in a local historical context, they do shed light on the interplay between the city and the West, observer and the observed, expectations and adjustments. The unplaceability of cities like Beirut for Europeans contributed to their sense of insecurity and 'precarious vulnerabilities'.[10] Worse for our befuddled visitor, not only is the distant Orient much closer culturally than expected but its merchant elites straddle the apparent East–West divide so easily that a regular sexual network seems to have been operating at the time of Strobel's visit. Passing visitors could shrug off their unease with innocuous humour and self-mockery. As I will argue below, however, resident professionals like Boyer launched a wholesale, intrusive assault on the ways in which Beirutis lived their lives.

Gendered Class Definitions

The above traveller's tale is shot through with bourgeois male envy and a pervading foreign sense of exclusion from the scot-free frivolities of local elites that 'do not allow them to gain a durable foothold in their society'. Its allusion to the link between 'Westernization', sexuality and the double standards of a morally corrupt local elite anticipates twentieth-century Marxist critiques of economic alienation, nationalists' romantic notions of aboriginal history, and Islamicist discourses of contaminated cultural authenticity.

In Beirut, class consciousness was interlaced with discourses on gender, masculinity and missionary colonialism since the mid-nineteenth century. In fact, I argue it was a constitutive element of Beirut's remarkable development into a major Mediterranean port-city, a regional immigration hub and a launching pad for competing European and Ottoman civilizing missions over the Arab provinces of the Ottoman Empire.[11] European missionaries and Ottoman state schools vied with each other in moulding faithful and literate subjects; legions of international health officials cooperated to reconfigure urban space in noble struggles to stem epidemics and prevent diseases; European investors, Ottoman governors and private merchants battled over concessions, infrastructural development projects and public construction permits.

Beirut's commercial ascent dates back to the late Napoleonic period when Beiruti businessmen bypassed the regional monopoly system controlled by the powerful governors of Acre and sold goods directly to British merchant ships.[12] Under Egyptian occupation (1831–40), Beirut's harbourfront – deliberately neglected by the rulers in Acre – was developed to service the growing trade volume passing to and from Mount Lebanon and the Damascene hinterland. Each year the port-city attracted thousands of immigrants seeking to partake in the economic windfall. Local traders and notables from other towns and cities in the Arab provinces expanded their businesses in the import-export of luxury goods. Most important, Beirut became the entrepot of an enormously profitable silk trade with Europe.[13] Beirut's remarkable development was striking because, in spite of considerable European participation, Beirut merchant houses accumulated the lion's share of wealth. Beirut was set for a bright future.

Economic growth was only temporarily halted when in the summer of 1860 a large-scale civil war erupted in the mountains above Beirut, killing an estimated 20,000 people and displacing many more.[14] Refugees flooded into the port-city in search for shelter and humanitarian relief provided by international agencies.[15] Not everyone had access to these alms, however. The struggle for survival drove dozens of destitute widows and orphans into the arms of idle soldiers willing to pay a franc (or five piastres) for sexual gratification. The long presence of stationary troops which were prevented from occupying the Levant by the diplomatic manœuvres of the British and Ottoman envoys, put a severe strain on the moral fabric of Beirut. Local and foreign residents alike were appalled at the soldiers' rampant behaviour, blatant indiscretions and daily molestations on the streets.

From 1860 onwards, anxiety and insecurity permanently hampered the optimism of Beirut's merchant middle class. Local intellectuals who outgrew the parochial missionary schools they had attended as teenagers began to raise concerns over the future of their country, urging their compatriots to overcome poverty, exploitation, sectarian prejudice and superficial imitation of 'Western habits'.[16] The memoirs of the Beirut-born Cairo-based intellectual Jirji Zaydan (1861–14) offer a succinct description of an emerging class consciousness. He divides Beirut society into 'three distinct classes'. *Al-khassa* – the distinguished elite – consisted of 'the people of the government and the rich'. This class possessed social and economic capital which the *al-'amma* – the undistinguished general public – lacked. Zaydan considered this low class 'the riff raff, the artisans, all the other people with menial occupations, and the small merchant'. They were 'immoral crooks' and 'idle vagrants' who got drunk and 'were uneducated because of the few schools available'.[17]

But Zaydan insisted he and other members of Beirut's literary circles were distinct from both classes. An independent 'third class after the unrest [of 1860]' emerged which he identified as a kind of local *Bildungsbürgertum* – or educated bourgeoisie. Educated at Christian missionary schools, 'especially the American, English, and German ones ... they founded schools in order to spread the knowledge and culture of modern civilized Europe [and] were determined to change the social norms'.[18] The particular position of this emerging intellectual middle class was far from stable or uncontested. As a young street boy, Zaydan himself held this group in contempt 'because they did not quarrel or beat each other and did not drink'.[19] From Zaydan's memoirs it becomes apparent that this *Bildungsbürgertum* was alienated from both the ordinary people – the *ahali* – and the local elites. Both considered their thoughts and appearance 'in sinful breach with tradition manifesting effeminateness and licentiousness'.

Beirut society at mid-century silenced critiques of existing norms and habits by 'emasculating' their articulators – a common strategy in bourgeois societies. The status of the emerging intellectual middle class was further delegitimized by the apparently alien way they dressed, talked, sat down at tables and mingled freely with women. Young men wearing trousers in particular were branded as foppish. Conversely, the disciples of this new generation of writers and educators were 'convinced that people who wore *bantalunat* [tight trousers] were of higher intelligence, wider knowledge and better judgment than those wearing the *sirwal*'.[20] Stigmatized as Westernizers and 'cross-dressers', Beirut's early intellectual class was struggling to find a public. It did not help that they themselves were intolerant *vis-à-vis* the behaviour of the established feudal and nouveau riche elites on the one hand and the lower classes on the other. Journalists, teachers and city councillors frequently expressed angst and anxiety about the city's future and about the lower classes and drifters that the growing city attracted. Butrus al-Bustani feared in 1860 that this 'dreadful volcano' might erupt once again. Khalil Khuri, the editor of Beirut's first newspaper, warned that Beirut 'was infested with growing numbers of base scum (*al-asafil wa al-ajlaf*)' from foreign ships and he hoped that tightened passport controls would 'cleanse Beirut from the human rabble (*lil-tanzif min al-awbash*)'.[21]

After 1860, fear and demonization lay at the heart of Beirut's bourgeois project of modernity. From the 1870s onwards, new newspapers were overflowing with admonitions of idleness, gambling and late-night bouts as detrimental to social productivity, and therefore irresponsible and immoral activities, and always a possible root cause of renewed sectarian conflict. By the end of the nineteenth century public intellectuals had come to constitute an influential social class in their own right because they dominated Beirut's local education system and the Arabic print media. Schools and newspapers had a tremendous effect on post-1860 urban culture. As new institutions of cultural production, notions of public good and self-improvement, they destabilized elite conventions of patriarchy and challenged those among the *ahali* who pursued social emancipation through sectarian politics.[22]

Love and Family Honour

As a consequence of these turbulent social dynamics and rebellious discourses, Beirut at the turn of the century was full of unexpected encounters and associations. It was a subversive place to live in, where existing values could be threatened at every street corner and in every newspaper column. Students, families, visitors and government officials were constantly forced to readjust conventional wisdoms.

The tension between the aspirations of the *Bildungsbürgertum* on the one hand and the general uncertainty and unstable social categories on the other was hardest for those who attempted to change their class affiliation or move beyond their station, and on dependants, especially women and teenagers. The fate of one Najla Arslan is a case in point.[23] She was born in Shuwayfat around 1870, the ancestral hometown of the Arslan clan in the Shuf Mountains above Beirut. The only child of a lesser family branch, her parents 'wanted to make every effort to provide her with a good education and to bring her up well'.[24] But as events around their beloved daughter unfolded, the promising young woman found herself exposed to a web of patriarchy, patronage and honour as well as the widening tensions between city and Mountain.

While at Lazarist School she met and fell in love with Amin Majid, a paternal cousin who studied at the Jesuit College in Beirut. They somehow managed to keep their passion secret until they decided to get married in 1893. Even though they had not consulted their parents, they had reason to hope that their parents would agree as they met the endogamous convention as first cousins. Instead, things went sour for Amin and especially for Najla. Her father, Khalil, felt betrayed by his daughter for he had promised her to the son of the clan's powerful political boss, Mustafa Arslan. Her father decided to break her resolve by placing her under house arrest and when she was recaptured after a dramatic escape, her uncle tortured her by staging a mock execution of his son's rival, Amin Majid.[25]

Her father was deeply offended by his daughter's ingratitude and regretted that he had sent her to a missionary school whose 'seductive influence' made her fall for 'an imitator of European ways'.[26] Her behaviour defied his paternal authority, jeopardized the family's reputation and – by failing to honour his 'gentleman's agreement' – challenged his masculinity. Najla for her part somehow managed to petition the Sultan in Istanbul, pleading for imperial support against her unlawful confinement:

> I am twenty-five years old and a mature adult. Yet, my family insists that I marry a person whom I do not want to marry. I cannot find any refuge or helper but Your Compassionate Imperial Majesty. Please rescue me from the torment and oppression to which I am subjected and which endangers my life just for having a wish in perfect accord with the *Shari'a*![27]

The problem for Najla was that her uncle, Mustafa Arslan, was not only a chauvinist brute but also an important pillar in the delicate balance of power that was the postwar government of Mount Lebanon – in other words, not even the Ottoman governor would risk alienating him over a young rebellious woman.[28] After a year of confinement high up in the Shuf Mountains, news spread to Beirut that Najla was suffering physical and mental abuse. Pressured into reluctant action and alarmed by the sorry turn of events, Governor Na'um Pasha finally chose to act. He ordered her release and forced the marriage consent of Najla's distraught father. By this time, however, Najla bore 'signs of psychological disturbance' that certified her of unsound mind.

Her story had become a medical case and, in the wider picture, a bone of contention between family authority and state welfare. Although Na'um Pasha refused to interfere in the 'local customs' of the Druze community at the beginning of this case, he now ordered that the woman be taken out of the family's custody and submitted as a patient to the care of the medical profession of the state. She was shipped to Istanbul where the Sultan personally attended to the well-being of the provincial princess, and where she was diagnosed with 'mania' and delivered to the leading mental hospital in Istanbul. The case disappeared into the anonymity of the Ottoman archives and with it the voicelessness of Najla Arslan. Her father had believed that education held the key to Najla's fulfillment but did not bargain for the possibility that she might use this education against the kind of authority and dependency his feudal lineage bestowed on him. From the perspective of the daughter, the 'age-old' reign of endogamy proved a false pretension for patriarchal marriage-control because in her case the beloved was a paternal cousin and therefore perfectly suitable in the formal sense. The patriarchal honour system that had emerged when Ottoman rule introduced the *iqta'* system of hereditary landholding was adapted to the seemingly unstable and fleeting capitalist conditions of *fin de siècle* Beirut. Najla may have been of the first female generation who were victims of the failure of Beirut's middle class to emancipate itself from the dictates of the *al-khassa* establishment, as the latter, as reinvented 'aristocrats of office', successfully absorbed bourgeois aspirations into their power base. It is also a reflection of the appearance of a distinct state-sanctioned 'aristocracy of office' vying for positions in the Administrative Council in postwar Mount Lebanon.[29]

For the father, this tragic episode was indicative of a deep personal crisis that *fin de siècle* Beirut generated for many parents. On the one hand, professionals like Khalil recognized that in a changing world their children's future lay in trade and education. On the other hand, European commerce and culture proved volatile and led to uncontrollable side-effects. Fathers like Khalil Arslan were trapped by the 'fantasies of the possible'.[30] More generally perhaps, Najla's case anticipated a more systematic victimization inherent in the unresolved relationship between the Lebanese nation state and the new guises of local customary patriarchy.

French Colonial Anxieties

Khalil Arslan argued in a letter to the Sublime Porte that one of the main reasons why he rejected his daughter's marriage to Amin Majid so vehemently was the latter's exposure to Jesuit missionary education. This charge raises suspicions of cultural schizophrenia and mental instability. The Ottoman government officials who dealt with Najla Arslan's case may or may not have accepted this explanation. To blame European desires on deeper structural injustices and personal problems was certainly a common means to get the imperial government in Istanbul on one's side, as missionary influence was regarded as a serious threat to the sovereignty of the Ottoman state.[31]

In a place and time like *fin de siècle* Beirut, this ever-looming trope of European background machinations requires critical reflection. I argue that if we consider the European presence not as external or coincidental to social conflict but as central and causally linked to it, the assumed stable nature and omnipotence of the colonial enterprise in the Levant quickly dissolves. Ussama Makdisi has argued this eloquently in the case of the Protestant missionaries.[32] It is equally pertinent in the comparatively understudied case of Catholic colonialism, in particular since the Jesuits' position in France was often less secure and less aligned with metropolitan power centres than the various Protestant missions in Britain and the US.[33] Before Lebanon was officially mandated to France by the League of

Nations in 1920, the French colonial presence manifested itself in various ways and went through a number of metamorphoses. The main thrust of French intervention in Beirut and Mount Lebanon had been the Jesuit mission which returned to the Levant in 1831 after sixty years' absence.[34] Their imprint was cultural in general and religious in particular. Their educational work, which addressed particularly the Maronite community, had long constituted a most reliable avenue of French colonial designs and culminated in 1881 when the Vatican granted the papal seal to the Université St. Joseph.[35] If this missionary conduit was never entirely abandoned and continued to be strong in the French share of the Lebanese silk production, the thwarted policy of occupying the Levant after the civil war of 1860 was driven by military circles. Towards the end of the century, the dominant role of the Jesuits on the ground was superseded by concerns about economic competition with Britain over investments in the entire region of Bilad al-Sham.[36] Port constructions, railways, tramways, road networks and gas-lighting projects multiplied the economic stakes and scales to such an extent that they somewhat dwarfed the traditional Catholic commitment to the 'Maronite Mountain'.

In the last fifteen years of the nineteenth century, medicine and public health provided another important and hitherto underestimated avenue of French colonial intervention in the Levant. The particular features of this new kind of intervention were of an entirely different nature from the missionary philanthropy and emergency relief put in place in 1860. The founding of the French Medical Faculty at the Université St. Joseph in 1883, marks the entry French officials into the realm of governance. They began to take part in public health surveys and special commissions dispatched to the Arab provinces of the Ottoman Empire. But most significantly for our analysis of French colonial anxiety in *fin de siècle* Beirut, they penned reports such as Benoît Boyer's *Les conditions hygiéniques actuelles de Beyrouth*, which was published in Lyon in 1897.

Boyer's survey of Beirut deserves special attention because it marked a new turn in French colonialism in the Levant.[37] With Boyer, cultural and economic concerns were incorporated or developed into a biological and scientific intervention in the city as a whole – one in which sexuality and race emerged as pathogens of some inherent inability to cope with Western modernity. Dr Benoît Boyer came to Beirut with strong recommendations from the Hospice Civil de Lyon where he graduated in 1881. This city was long linked to the Lebanese silk trade and the Jesuit mission in the

Ottoman period, and 'would play a major role in convincing the French parliament to take on Syria and Lebanon as mandates after World War I'.[38] Significantly, neither he nor his successors at the French Medical Faculty were practitioners of tropical medicine – a prerequisite for French doctors preparing to serve in more distant colonies. He was hired as Professor of Therapeutics and Hygiene and served in Beirut from 1889 to 1897. A number of his local medical students, who helped him conduct research on climate and morbidity statistics, later went on to become medical authorities in their own right.[39] Boyer served on the 1895 commission to establish the cause of that year's deadly typhoid outbreak; a year later, at the request of the Ottoman governor, he penned *Les conditions hygiéniques*.

This brief outline of Boyer's career gives us a sense of the position Beirut occupied in France's imperial circuit. It reflects the perceptions that many Europeans had of this late Ottoman city as a surprisingly familiar yet – in unexpected ways – different place. It was precisely this ambivalence, I suggest, that led to the kinds of charges and claims the author of *Les conditions hygiéniques actuelles de Beyrouth* made about 'Syrian/Oriental' sexuality, psychology and morbidity.

Before I delve into the text itself, it is important to note that the Ottoman governor commissioned the report and granted Boyer the necessary *passepartout* to enter all private homes and public installations necessary. In other words, *Les conditions hygiéniques* must also be understood in the context of urban reforms under Sultan Abdülhamid II. The Ottoman government had long institutionalized the empire's health system. In the 1830 and 1840s it set up and enforced quarantines from Mosul to Mecca, effectively turning the Ottoman Empire into Europe's eastern bulwark against those epidemics that emerged further east.[40] With the support of European consultants the Ottomans defeated the plague and by 1881 the municipality banished cholera from Beirut.[41]

Les conditions hygiéniques is a 174-page survey of the health risks and pathologies in and of Beirut. It contains a few images but unlike many other European representations of Bilad al-Sham and the Middle East more generally, Boyer's book contains no portraits of half-naked women, 'degenerated natives' or 'exotic nobles'. Instead, we find illustrations of 'state-of-the-art' waste disposal machines, a sewage system, 'healthy' house typologies and a map of Beirut. Boyer is neither driven by libidinal desires nor sexual conquests *à la* Flaubert, Gautier and de Nerval. Containment was his overarching mission: sealed containers for human excrement, temperance of human pleasures and segregating prostitutes in a tightly policed red-light district. A deep fear of excess and immoderation creeps in on every page of Boyer's health report.

The author insisted that Beirut's new quarters required cosmetic surgery if it was to live up to its potential to become a truly great city. Generally, the municipality had done a good job, Boyer commented, but failed to take the necessary drastic actions in the 'depraved old town'. Only a total 'disembowelling (*éventration*) would set Beirut free from the urban chains' and emulate 'the great European cities'.[42] Just seven years after the publication of the *Mémoires* of the infamous Prefect of Paris, this very Haussmannian term was applied to Beirut.[43] That a public hygienist, not a modernist planner or militiaman, should first advocate gutting downtown Beirut suggests that there has existed since the nineteenth century a close ideological and institutional link between public health and urban planning. Indeed, Haussmann himself used the term *éventrement* when he referred to piercing wide boulevards through the densely populated and subaltern quarters of medieval Paris.

The study of the role of public hygienists in urban development might appear unattractive, quaint and trivial. But let us recall Dominique Laporte's polemic account against the figure of the public hygienist as the 'prince consort of bourgeois civilization':

> The hygienist is a hero. He overcomes the most visceral repugnance, rolls up his shirt sleeves, and takes on the *cloaca*. He faces the foul unnamable and speaks of that thing of which no one else will speak ... he alone makes it speak ... What drove them to speak so earnestly of a 'revolution of cesspool drainage', to press for evacuation systems, particular modes of transport, formulas for purification? They expected nothing short of the eradication of all ills and, in the most sublime cases, the assurance of everlasting universal harmony. Essays and reports were drafted with prophetic faith. Not one of these revolutionary heroes doubted for an instant that his invention of a separator, a ventilation system, a new form of toilet bowl, or a mobile urinal would transform the future of humanity.[44]

The biting sarcasm aside, Laporte raises a fundamental point about Boyer's new kind of quasi-missionary zeal and an unprecedented comprehensive urban approach to colonial intervention. Boyer's tract, notes Michel Foucault (1978), contains the first systematic biopolitical representation of Beirut. With a penchant for apocalyptic drama, Boyer argues for a political technology that catapults every aspect of human life – from dietary to sleeping habits; from urban to family planning – onto the domain of state knowledge/power, to be monitored, acted upon and transformed for the health benefit of the social body. Legions of 'doctors, engineers, inspectors, architects [and] administrators' needed to be mobilized in order to survey statistically a sexually active population.[45] And since Boyer worked closely with the Ottoman authorities, the state was poised to become the protector of social purifications to prevent nineteenth-century spectres of biological and/or cultural degeneration.

Boyer's narrative embodied the *fin de siècle* tensions between scientific knowledge, secular authority and imperial power on the one hand and physical vulnerability, colonial anxiety and bourgeois insecurity on the other. Whereas early nineteenth-century missionaries perceived illness in Syria as the physical incarnation of a metaphysical flaw, as a surface reflection of a deeper spiritual malaise, by the late Ottoman period, illness had been relocated to a biomedical framework. Illness was still a morality tale in which physical disease followed from an inherent flaw, but the source of that flaw had migrated from the metaphysical to the scientific. Like his counterparts at the Syrian Protestant College, Boyer offered explanations that were rooted in secular knowledge that nevertheless invoked ineffable causation. In Boyer's case this cause was rooted in psychology.

Chapter five of Boyer's tract, 'On Morbidity in Beirut', provides a ten-page classification of the frequency of illnesses and diseases Boyer and his colleagues registered. Boyer incorporated European class- and gender-based notions into his racialized portrayal of 'Orientals'. This emerges most clearly in his depiction of tuberculosis, the centrepiece of his description of morbidity in Beirut.[46] Its exceptional virulence in Syria seemed odd to Boyer and his colleagues. Back in 1847 the long-serving French director of the quarantine, Dr Sucuet, declared that tuberculosis was 'virtually unknown' in the country. Moreover, Boyer mused that the rampant malaria in Syria should have held the number of tuberculosis cases to a minimum. He recorded almost 3,000 cases of malaria for 1896. Boyer had to look elsewhere for an answer.

He found his answer in the 'current social conditions'.[47] Primary among these social conditions was the 'psychology of the Syrian'. By appealing to psychology, he reconciled the mid-nineteenth-century discourses of emotionality and passion with the notion of contagion, which had taken centre stage by the end of the century. Boyer writes:

> Consider the alcoholic and venereal excess, long night-outs, the emotions of gambling, the manœuvres of masturbation – repeated up to fifteen times per day [evidence of an existing discourse] – and one will not be surprised that the psychological misery of these overworked youths, debilitated by constant heat and chronically fainting of hunger, one fine day manifests itself in a fast-spreading tuberculosis affliction.[48]

Personal excess was mirrored in material concerns:

> In his quality as an Oriental, the Syrian loves luxury, splendour and ceremonial. External appearance and ostentation of wealth is the object of particular attention. Above all, the Syrian lives for the gallery; nothing is too dear to him to attract the admiration of his neighbour.[49]

Young family members of the social elites were diagnosed as particularly prone to conspicuous consumption and Europeanization. Of their salary of 50 francs, they spent up to 15 francs on luxury cigarettes, 'and every Sunday they parade in their carriages or on their horses in a suit to match their aristocratic aspirations. In order to maintain their station, they blackmail and suck their parents dry while economizing on a healthy diet'.[50] The Beiruti youth lived above its station, both in terms of expenditures and social character. Boyer's consumptives had partaken of too many of Beirut's urban pleasures, or in other words, they were simply *too* Westernized for their own good. The Beiruti 'Oriental' existed in the liminal and unviable space between a Levantine premodernity and the city's all-too-real contemporary social transformations.

Boyer viewed tuberculosis, like hysteria and neurasthenia, as physical symptoms of social diseases with distinctly feminine underpinnings. This explained why 'Orientals' were victims of the disease – and also why women were at even greater risk of disorders afflicting the nervous system. Their conditions owed much to the effects of 'new more or less relaxed morals, material preoccupations and depravation to which women are subjected in order to satisfy the caprice of their outfit'. These new conditions, he continued, 'lead us to *anticipate* an increase of these manifestations of hysteria'.[51] Boyer represented neither the repression of the female body behind a veil or into a corset, nor the incarceration of women in the confines of a harem, as a root cause for hysteria, but rather the opposite: astonishingly, too much liberty and leisure caused Beiruti women's susceptibility to disease.

In Boyer's scientific narrative the 'Syrian/Oriental' body is treated as a metonymy for Beirut's body politic writ large, and 'irregularities' of sexual behaviour and individual habits reflected larger deficiencies of the social organism. Here, the public hygienist's mania for cleanliness is merely a manifestation of a deeper anxiety about the close contact between the local population and the European communities who were no longer composed of the 'pioneers' – consuls, missionaries and merchants. According to consular statistics, the population of the French 'colony' alone rose from 600 to 1,400 between 1891 and 1897.[52]

Unlike colonial cities in North Africa, foreigners in Beirut did not reside in a designated parallel city set apart from the local population. Diplomats, pastors, doctors and businessmen rented floors or entire buildings from landowners in residential areas adjacent to the old city. Although these residences tended to be near educational facilities in respectable neighbourhoods like Zokak el-Blat or Ashrafieh, often foreigners lived on the geographical fringes in Ras Beirut and on the margins of respectable locations. Behind the coastal entertainment and hotel district of Zaytuneh, for example, which towards the end of the century gained a reputation for nocturnal revelry, lay the highest concentration of foreign consulates in the city.[53] The creation of the province of Beirut in 1888 generated a veritable investment rush into Beirut: the port was enlarged, a huge department store was raised on the harbour front, a railway line to Damascus was built and tracks for five tramway lines were laid.[54] As a tangible consequence male European labour arrived in Beirut, especially French contractors in one of the growing numbers of construction and insurance companies. Hundreds of engineers, accountants, not to mention uncountable unaccountables, moved to Beirut to work.

Boyer's chapter 5, which closes with a section on 'Mortality and Morbidity of the French', expressed the growing sense of vulnerability in the foreign establishment in Beirut: the rise of non-elite foreigners mingling with local lower classes and partaking in sex and alcohol bouts. Foreign semi-skilled and menial labour is more exposed to the extreme climate's health risks. Although 'Beirut poses no difficulty to adapt' and 'the acclimatization of the [French?] race is perfect', among construction workers – 'even foremen and engineers charged with surveying and directing the works' – contagious diseases like typhoid fever and malaria multiplied. It was clearly worrying to public hygienists and the general project of imperial expansion into the Levant that in the 'French colony' – as among the 'natives' – tuberculosis was the most frequent cause of death. Boyer therefore admonishes his readers that if the French 'want to last in Syria, they need to lead a life void of excess and overwork'.[55] This brings us back to the issue of prostitution which Boyer identified as a serious urban problem because the existing officially licensed brothels, *maisons de tolérance*, were insufficiently isolated and demarcated from the rest of the city. Moreover, many prostitutes lived elsewhere among 'respectable' people and only came to work in the evening.[56]

After the enlargement of the port of Beirut in 1895, some of the *maisons de tolérance* moved to the vicinity of the city's growing administrative and commercial centre. According to a onetime head of the guild of porterage, 'the *Suq*, as it was called since then, established itself in *Suq al-khammamir* [the wine sellers' market], between the Petit Serail and the port east of the Muslim cemetery'.[57] At around the same time, the cemetery was destroyed to make way for the development of the expanding port facilities.[58] With the return of the French army in 1920 the *maisons de tolérance* moved to an area then popularly known as *wara' al-bank* ('behind the bank') or *al-Manshiyya* behind the former Ottoman Bank building just east of Sahat al-Burj. According to the accounts of an old Beiruti, 'the number of prostitutes (*al-mumsat*) rose to around 850 Arab women from Syria, Palestine and Lebanon and no less than 400 foreign girls – Greek, Turkish and French'.

The developments troubled health professionals who saw themselves as the first line of defence against the transmission of diseases from Asia to Europe. The overlapping geographies of high and low life, foreign and local quarters and moral and immoral pursuits in Beirut compounded their dilemma precisely because they defied the clinical separations upon which scientific intervention – as well as, incidentally, identity politics – depended. Dr Boyer died before his colonial successors and Lebanese nationalists set out to disentangle the 'mess' that was *fin de siècle* Beirut during the Mandate period. Ironically, he succumbed to a disease he had admonished the Beirut municipality to take preventive measures against two years earlier – typhoid fever.

Boyer's narrative may have been no more than a reflection of commonly held perceptions of degeneration, social evils and bodily abuses in France. Or Beirut may have functioned as a laboratory to test medical assumptions in France. I believe its significance is greater than that. Boyer's survey was probably the earliest and most comprehensive example of biopolitics in the Arab provinces of the Ottoman Empire. The very emergence of a joint Franco-Ottoman biopolitics attests to a realization that the empire was 'an arena of momentous change and dynamism'.[59] Boyer's putting-health-into-discourse suggests that, in *fin de siècle* Beirut, Orientalist knowledge acquired another of its many skins. Evidence everywhere showed that 'the East' was unchanging no more. Rather change needed to be managed and incrementalized, lest unknown or unwanted social and psychological consequences occurred. Beirut's middle-class intellectuals and Ottoman bureaucrats shared some of Boyer's fears and anxieties about the city. The similarity belies a fundamental difference. Boyer's discourse would form part of a larger claim to political control and comprehensive urban reconfiguration at the earliest convenient time. For Beirut's intellectuals cultural critique was an aspect of consolidation of their own vision and of Beirut's autonomy, whereas for the French political establishment criticism would be the basis for undermining that autonomy. Recent research on the history of European empires has brought out the intimate connections between sexuality, health and colonialism and the racial categorizations that underlie this relationship. In particular the work of Ann Laura Stoler suggests that human intimacy and social instability, as much as clear-cut abstractions of power, military conquest and economic and sexual exploitation, have been at the centre of colonial experiences around the world.[60] In late Ottoman Beirut as in other radically changing cities with large European communities, fear of licentiousness and containment occupied the minds of colonial health professionals as much as local male elites. In this light, the tragic fate of Najla Arslan is neither a remnant of unchanging patriarchal practices nor some easily isolatable 'indigenous' phenomenon but rather a 'symptom' of the fundamental changes in a city which was both invitingly familiar and menacingly unfamiliar to both foreign and native inhabitants.

Bibliography

Akarli, E., *The Long Peace, Ottoman Lebanon, 1860–1920*, London: Centre for Lebanese Studies and I. B. Tauris, 1993.

Akarli, E. (2005), 'Daughters and Fathers: A Druze Damsel's Experience (1894–1897)', in Karl Barbir and Baki Tezcan, eds, *Identity and Identity Formation in the*

Middle East: Essays in Honour of Norman Itzkowitz (forthcoming).
Arslan, K. (1897), 'Letter to the Sublime Porte', as quoted in Akarli, 'Daughters and Fathers', in Karl Barbir and Baki Tezcan, eds, *Identity and Identity Formation in the Middle East: Essays in Honour of Norman Itzkowitz* (forthcoming).
Barud, Antoine, *Shari' al-Mutanabbi, hikayyat al-bagha' fi Lubnan*, Beirut: Haqa'iq Wa Arqam, 1971.
Bayly, S., 'Racial Readings of Empire: Britain, France and Colonial Modernity in the Mediterranean and Asia', in C. A. Bayly and L. Fawaz, eds, *Modernity and Culture: From the Mediterranean to the Indian Ocean*, New York: Columbia University Press, 2002.
Bhabha, H., 'Of Mimicry and Man', in F. Cooper and L. A. Stoler, eds, *Tensions of Empire: Colonial Cultures in a Bourgeois World*, Berkeley and Los Angeles: California University Press, 1997.
Boyer, B., *Conditions hygiéniques actuelles de Beyrouth et de ses environs immédiats*, Lyon: Imprimerie Rey, 1897.
al-Bustani, B., *Nafir Suriyya*, issue 6, 8 November 1860.
Chevallier, D., *La société du Mont Liban à l'époque de la révolution industrielle en Europe*, Paris: Librairie Orientaliste Paul Geuthner, 1971.
—— 'Lyon et la Syrie en 1919: les bases d'une intervention', in his *Villes et travail en Syrie du XIX au XX siècle*, Beirut: Maisonneuve & Larose, 1982.
Debbas, F., *Des Photographes à Beyrouth 1840–1918*, Paris: Marval, 2001.
De Nerval, G., *Voyage en Orient*, Paris:Maison Michel Levy Freres, 1884.
Deringil, S., *The Well-Protected Domains: Ideology and the Legitimation of Power in the Ottoman Empire, 1876–1909*, London: I. B. Tauris, 1998.
Fawaz, L., *Merchants and Migrants in Nineteenth Century Beirut*, Cambridge, MA: Harvard University Press, 1983.
Foucault, M., *The History of Sexuality: An Introduction*, vol. 1, New York: Vintage, 1978.
Hadikat al-Akhbar, 17 January 1861.
Hanssen, J., 'Public Morality and Marginality in fin de Siècle Beirut', in E. Rogan, ed., *Outside In: Shifting Boundaries of Marginality in the Modern Middle East*, London: I. B Tauris, 2002.
—— *Fin de siècle Beirut*, Oxford: Oxford University Press, 2005.
Haussmann, G. E., *Mémoires du Baron Haussmann*, vol. 3, Paris: Harvard, 1890.
Heyberger, B., *Les Chrétiens du Proche-Orient au temps de la Réforme Catholique (XVIe–XVIIIe Siécles)*, Rome, 1994.
Heyberger, B. and Walbiner, C., eds, *Les Européens vus par les Libanais à l'époque Ottomane*, Beirut: Orient Institute, 2002.
Ismail, A., and Chehab, M., *Documents diplomatiques et consulaires relatifs à l'histoire du Liban*, vol. 16, Beirut: Éditions des Œuvres Politiques et Historiques, 1976.
——*Documents diplomatiques et consulaires relatifs à l'histoire du Liban,* vol. 18, Beirut: Éditions des Œuvres Politiques et Historiques, 1979.
Jabir, Bahjat, '1913 bidayat al-'asr al-dhahabi fi Lubnan li-aqdam mihna', *an-Nahar*, 28 March, 2000.
Khalaf, S., 'Primordial Ties and Politics in Lebanon', *Middle East Studies*, vol. 4, 1968.

Khater, A. F., *Inventing Home, Emigration, Gender and the Middle Class in Lebanon, 1870–1920*, Berkeley: California University Press, 2001.
Laporte, D., *History of Shit*, tr. N. Benabid and R. el-Khoury, with an introduction by R. el-Khoury, Cambridge, MA: MIT Press, 2000.
Makdisi, U., 'Reclaiming the Land of the Bible: Missionaries, Secularism, and Evangelical Modernity', *American Historical Review*, vol. 120, 1997.
——*The Culture of Sectarianism: Community, History and Violence in Nineteenth Century Ottoman Lebanon*, Berkeley: California University Press, 2000.
Ministère des Affaires Etrangères, Paris, *Correspondance Consulaire Commercial, Turquie–Beyrouth*, vol. 12, Beirut, 1897.
Panzac, D., *Quarantaines et Lazarets: L'Europe et la Peste d'Orient*, Aix-en-Provence: Edisud, 1986.
Philipp, T., *Acre: The Rise and Fall of a Palestinian City. World Economy and Local Politics,* New York: Columbia University Press, 2002.
Pouillon, F., 'Un ami de Theophile Gautier en Orient, Camille Rogier: réflexions sur la condition de dragoman', *Bulletin de la Société Theophile Gautier*, vol. 12, 1990.
Shorrock, W., *French Imperialism in the Middle East: The Failure of Policy in Syria and Lebanon, 1900–1914*, Madison: University of Wisconsin Press, 1975.
Spagnolo, J., 'The Definition of a Style of Imperialism: The Internal Politics of the French Educational Investment in Ottoman Beirut', *French Historical Studies*, vol. 9, 1973.
Strobel, K. H., *Romantische Reise in Orient,* Berlin: Vita, 1911.
Stoler, A. L., *Race and the Education of Desire: Foucault's History of Sexuality and the Colonial Order of Things*, Durham: Duke University Press, 1995.
——*Carnal Knowledge and Imperial Power: Race and the Intimate in Colonial Rule*, New York: Columbia University Press, 2002.
Thompson, E., 'Neither Conspiracy Nor Hypocrisy: The Jesuits and the French Mandate in Syria and Lebanon', working paper at the Belagio Conference on Alturism and Imperialism: The Western Religious and Cultural Missionary Enterprise in the Middle East, 2002.
Université Saint Joseph, *Bulletin de l'association des anciens élèves de la faculté*, Beirut, 1908.
al-Unsi, A., *Dalil Bayrut wa Taquim al-Iqbal li-sanat* 1327h *(1909–1910)*, Beirut: al-Iqbal, 1910/1911.
Wielandt, R., *Das Bild der Europäer in der Modernen Arabischen Erzähl- und Theaterliteratur,* Beirut: Orient Institut, 1980.
Zaydan, J., *Mudhakkirat*, ed. and tr. Thomas Philipp as *–ur—i Zaidab: His Life and Thought.*, Beirut: Orient Institut, 1979.

Notes

1. K. H. Strobel, *Romantische Reise in Orient*, Vienna, 1911, pp. 34–40.
2. H. Bhabha, *Of Mimicry and Man*, Los Angeles, 1997, p. 153.
3. K. H. Strobel, p. 42.

4. For further details see A. F. Khater, *Inventing Home, Emigration, Gender and the Middle Class in Lebanon, 1870–1920*, Berkeley, 2001; B. Heyberger and C. Walbiner, eds, *Les Européens vus par les Libanais à l'époque Ottomane*, Beirut, 2002.
5. al-Unsi, *Dalil Bayrut wa Taquim al-Iqbal li-sanat* 1327h *(1909–1910)*, Beirut, 1910/11, p. 160.
6. A. Ismail and M. Chehab, *Documents diplomatique et consulaires relatifs à l'histoire du Liban* (Beirut, 1979), pp. 362–5; *Lisan al-Hal*, 1911.
7. F. Pouillon, 'Un ami de Theophile Gautier en Orient, Camille Rogier: reflexions sur la condition de dragoman', *Bulletin de la Société Theophile Gautier*, vol. 12, 1990.
8. As quoted in F. Debbas, *Des Photograpes a Beyrouth 1840–1918*, Paris, 2001, p. 34.
9. G. de Nerval, *Voyage en Orient*, Paris, 1884, p. 82.
10. A. L. Stoler, *Race and the Education of Desire: Foucault's History of Sexuality and the Colonial Order of Things*, London, 1995, p. 97.
11. J. Hanssen, *Fin de siècle Beirut*, Oxford, 2005.
12. T. Philipp, *Acre: The Rise and Fall of a Palestinian City. World Economy and Local Politics*, New York, 2002.
13. D. Chevallier, *La société du Mont Liban à l'époque de la révolution industrielle en Europe*, Paris, 1971, pp. 196–7.
14. B. al-Bustani, *Nafir Suriyya*, issue 6, 1860.
15. L. Fawaz, *Merchants and Migrants in Nineteenth Century Beirut*, Cambridge, MA, 1983.
16. R. Wielandt, *Das Bild der Europäer in der Modernen Arabischen Erzähl- und Theaterliterature*, Beirut, 1980; al-Bustani.
17. J. Zaydan, *Mudhakkirat*, Beirut, 1979, p. 147.
18. Ibid., p. 148.
19. Ibid., p. 149.
20. Ibid., pp. 156–7.
21. *Hadikat al-Akhbar*, 1861.
22. U. Makdisi, *The Culture of Sectarianism: Community, History and Violence in Nineteenth Century Ottoman Lebanon*, Los Angeles, 2000.
23. E. Akarli, 'Daughters and Fathers: A Druze Damsel's Experience (1894–1897)', 2005.
24. I am indebted to the author's kindness in making available his Ottoman archival research and discussing his work prior to publication.
25. E. Akarli, 2005.
26. Ibid.
27. Ibid.
28. E. Akarli, *The Long Peace, Ottoman Lebanon, 1860–1920*, London, 1993, pp. 53–7.
29. S. Khalaf, 'Primordial Ties and Politics in Lebanon', *Middle East Studies*, vol. 4, 1968.
30. This is the apt title of Ussama Makdisi's 1997 PhD thesis.
31. S. Deringil, *The Well-Protected Domains; Ideology and the Legitimation of Power in the Ottoman Empire, 1876–1909*, London, 1998.
32. U. Makdisi, 'Reclaiming the Land of the Bible: Missionaries, Secularism, and Evangelical Modernity', *American Historical Review*, vol. 120, 1997.
33. Jesuit institutions were outlawed in the Hexagon in 1773, 1828 and 1880. This state persecution at home, however, linked them that much closer to French colonial enterprises abroad.
34. B. Heyberger, *Les Chrétiens du Proche-Orient au temps de la Réforme Catholique (XVIe–XVIIIe Siécles)*, (Rome, 1994).
35. J. Spagnolo, 'The Definition of a Style of Imperialism: The Internal Politics of the French Educational Investment in Ottoman Beirut', *French Historical Studies*, vol. 9, 1973.

36. W. Shorrock, *French Imperialism in the Middle East: The Failure of Policy in Syria and Lebanon, 1900–1914*, Madison, Wisconsin, 1975.
37. A. Ismail and M. Chehab, *Documents diplomatiques et consulaires relatifs à l'histoire du Liban*, vol. 16, Beirut, 1976, p. 430; Ministère des Affaires Étrangères, *Correspondance Consulaire Commercial, Turquie–Beyrouth*, vol. 12, Beirut, 1897.
38. E. Thompson, 'Neither Conspiracy Nor Hypocrisy: The Jesuits and the French Mandate in Syria and Lebanon', Working paper, 2002, p. 2; D. Chevallier, 'Lyon et la Syrie en 1919: les bases d'une intervention', Beirut, 1982, p. 198.
39. Université St. Joseph, *Bulletin de l'association des ancient eleves de la faculte*, Beirut, 1908.
40. D. Panzac, *Quarantaines et Lazarets: L'Europe et la Peste d'Orient*, Aix-En-Provence, 1986.
41. J. Hanssen, *Fin de siècle Beirut*, Oxford, 2005.
42. B. Boyer, *Conditions hygiéniques actuelles de Beyrouth et de ses environs immédiats*, Lyon, 1897, p. 5.
43. G. E. Haussmann, *Mémoires du Baron Haussmann,* vol. 3, Paris, 1890, p. 54.
44. D. Laporte, *History of Shit* (Ca,bridge, MA, 2000), pp. 118, 123.
45. B. Boyer, p. III.
46. The fact that, at the end of this section, Boyer informs the reader that this section was made publicly available in Arabic in the local Francophile newspaper *al-Bashir* is significant for the question of the study's audience and local impact.
47. B. Boyer, p. 119.
48. Ibid., pp. 120, 127.
49. Ibid., p. 119.
50. Ibid., p. 119.
51. Ibid., p. 130.
52. A. Ismail and M. Chehab, 1976, p. 430.
53. J. Hanssen, 'Public Morality and Marginality in *fin de Siècle* Beirut', London, 2002.
54. J. Hanssen, 2005.
55. B. Boyer, 1897, pp. 144–5.
56. B. Boyer, 1897, pp. 134–5.
57. Antoine Barud, *Shari' al-Mutanabbi, hikayyat al-bagha' fi Lubnan*, Beirut, 1971, p. 5.
58. See Bahjat Jabir, '1913 bidayat al-'asr al-dhahabi fi Lubnan li-aqdam mihna', *an-Nahar*, 28 March 2000.
59. S. Bayly, 'Racial Readings of Empire: Britain, France and Colonial Modernity in the Mediterranean and Asia', New York, 2002, p. 286.
60. A. L. Stoler, *Race and the Education of Desire: Foucault's History of Sexuality and the Colonial Order of Things*, London, 2002.

Like Pure Gold: Sexuality and Honour amongst Lebanese Emigrants, 1890–1920

Akram F. Khater

In 1903, Yusuf al-Za'ini, a Lebanese immigrant in New York, wrote an article in *al-Huda* newspaper proclaiming women's work as 'a disease whose microbes have infested healthy and sick bodies alike', and that leads women to 'lewd, filthy and wanton behavior'.[1] Five years later another emigrant, Yusuf Wakim, wrote with concern about this same matter of women's work and its effects on their 'honour', and that of the 'Syrian' community. He recounted that he knew 'of one man who left his wife in Mexico with three children and came to Pennsylvania, [where] he met an emigrant woman who was still young ... [the two] went together to New York ... living in a house whose owner is also living with his female partner'.[2]

These were not isolated concerns, but rather fairly widespread tensions precipitated by the emigration of over 120,000 villagers (men and women) from the mountains of Lebanon to the United States, between 1890 and 1921. A slightly larger number of Lebanese emigrants made their way to Central and South America during this same period. In that thirty-year period the Arabic press published a stream of articles expressing individual and collective anxieties about women's 'honour' in the *mahjar*.[3] It appeared to many of these observers that women's departure from the private 'home' into the public arena for work threatened to erase the moral boundaries which defined the social and cultural contours of that community.

For such observers, these boundaries were all the more critical at a time when emigrants were forced to articulate and uphold a 'modern' sense of self against a hegemonic American middle class that – for the most part – shunned them as part of a suspicious 'East', as much as it was bent on transforming them from 'Old World' peasants to a 'New World' working class.

For other members of the community of Lebanese emigrants, concern over women's work appeared misplaced and misguided. They regarded women's work as a necessary 'evil' that in no way tarnished their honour. Rather, for these more liberal writers, any moral confusion which had befallen the community derived from men acting fast and loose with women's reputations, and from women who reduced themselves – through enslavement to fashion trends – to beautified commodities.

Women's bodies and sexuality thus became contested sites of cultural and social politics which found expression in private conversations and letters as well as across newspaper columns. Sexuality among Lebanese emigrants became self-consciously part of a public identity that was in state of constant flux brought about by contradictory norms of behaviour. While this tension was never fully resolved, it did bring about a set of discordant changes in notions and practices of love, sexuality and gender roles that were an essential aspect of the creation of a new Lebanese emigrant middle class in the *mahjar* and, later, in Lebanon. It the story of these historical changes which will occupy the rest of the chapter.

Going to Amirka

Peasants emigrated from Mount Lebanon to the Americas because they thought they needed to and because they could. As with other parts of the nineteenth-century world, this small Eastern Mediterranean Arab area attracted European capitalists seeking markets for their manufactured goods and sources of raw material for their factories. In this instance it was silk that brought merchants from Marseilles and Lyons – through local intermediaries – to the villages that dotted the Mount Lebanon range. Higher prices offered for silk cocoons enticed local producers to sell to the newcomers as well as to increase their production. Typically – as the story usually goes at some point during the incorporation into the world capitalist market – after a decade or so the prices started fluctuating. By the 1870s they had stagnated because of the entry of China and Japan into the market, especially as the latter was bent on industrializing through a massive production of higher quality silk. The opening of the Suez Canal in 1869 and steamboat navigation contributed to the saturation of the silk market and to the fall in prices. Finally, the death blow came from European-manufactured synthetic fibres which – starting in the 1880s – steadily undermined the silk market. For many villagers in Mount Lebanon this historical process had an intimate impact on their daily lives. After two decades of prosperity – in which some experienced a better standard of living that translated into, among other things, a doubling of the population – they saw themselves sliding back into poverty and dispossession of their land. This was effectively making them landless labourers rather than peasants. In an effort to counter this undesirable end, about one-tenth of the peasant population opted to send their daughters to work in silk factories. This family strategy for financial survival strained the gender 'contract' to its breaking point,[4] because it placed unwed women (for the most part) in morally compromising situations. The reputation of young women who worked in these establishments became the subject of gossip and innuendoes to the point where the term 'factory girl'[5] became an epithet and the equivalent of a sexually fallen woman. Thus, even before waves of immigrants made their way across the Atlantic to the Americas, women's work outside the boundaries of family labour was a source of sexual anxieties and crises. This threat was serious enough for the Maronite church to try to prohibit women from working in the silk factories by circulating an ecclesiastical letter which described factory work as immoral for women.[6] When that proved ineffective, the church resorted to pleading with the French ambassador in 1867 to pressure the French owners of these factories to abstain from hiring women.[7] Nor was the outcry only ecclesiastical in nature, for some peasants and many more *shuyukh* petitioned the Maronite patriarch and government to put an end to women's employment in those factories. The whole matter finally receded from the limelight when factory owners began overwhelmingly to hire women, and – more importantly perhaps – when it became obvious that peasants were still intent on sending their daughters to the factories despite the threats of the church.

This strategy did not completely solve the problem, particularly as the factories were underfunded and could not compete with the technological superiority of French factories. Thus, by the early 1890s the decision to emigrate appeared as the most financially viable alternative. At the same time it was possible for large numbers of families – and individuals – to implement this decision because of Lebanon's unusual political status within the Ottoman Empire. After the 1860 civil war European powers

– bent on increasing their influence in the region – worked with some local elites to force the Ottoman government to provide Lebanon with a semi-independent status and greater personal freedom of movement for its inhabitants. The peasants in turn used these two elements to their advantage by circumventing intermittent Ottoman regulations against emigration. Combined, the hard socio-economic realities and political-administrative loopholes translated into the emigration of over 120,000 individuals and families (in all combinations) from Mount Lebanon to the United States, between 1880 and 1920. Another 120,000–180,000 emigrated to South America during this same period. Statistics on this matter are rather difficult to assess accurately.[8]

Very few of the men and women who left Mount Lebanon for 'Amirka' thought they would stay long. They expected to land somewhere, work for a while to gather money, and return home to live as financially comfortable landowning peasants. Focused as they were on these straightforward goals, it was only the most clairvoyant amongst the emigrants who could have anticipated the complex reality ahead. Even fewer could have foretold that the days spent peddling lace and buttons, shopping for food and clothes, and strolling in the streets of their temporary communities would be transformative. Almost none would have expected their experiences in the *mahjar* to entail social and cultural contacts that necessitated a self-conscious examination of their individual and collective identities. Yet, all of this did happen, and women's work was one of the main catalysts for these events.

Gender, Sexuality and Identity

It was quickly evident to many emigrants that everyone who could had to work outside the house in order to make ends meet, and to gather enough money to fulfill their dreams of return to a comfortable life in Lebanon. Practically every adult, and many children, had to walk long miles, stand for many hours or sew late into the night just to make a living. Women were no exception. In droves they left the 'house' and went into the 'public' spaces to make money. Although we really do not know the exact numbers of women who worked at peddling or some other jobs, we can estimate that it was a majority. In New York, for example, we know that *officially* 38.1 percent of immigrant Lebanese women worked in either peddling or at a factory. Further south the numbers were smaller but not by much.

Ignacio Klich estimated that in Argentina somewhere around one-fifth of the women worked alongside their husbands, and Charles Knowlton dismissed immigrant women's work as minimal in Brazil by noting that only a quarter worked.[9] In fact, it is quite certain that immigrant women *worked at earning money* in far larger numbers, albeit in ways oblique to the eyes of male observers. Based on interviews with immigrants in the US, Alixa Naff[10] contends that anywhere between '75 and 80 percent of the women peddled during the pioneer years [1880s–1910]'. Even women who never peddled, or who left that task, worked in other venues. Many helped in family stores, sewed items at home that were later sold by a male relative, and some even worked as servants in houses of rich immigrants. Informally, women took in boarders, cleaned and cooked and made certain of a modicum of order in a chaotic world and time. That alone was of immense – albeit non-monetary – value to the whole family.

Going back to the 'tangible', we find many testimonials to the long days and hard work women put into making certain their families (in the *mahjar* or back home) survived. In the words of one descendant of immigrants: 'Women weren't afraid and were strong and even women up to seventy years of age peddled'.[11] Even while allowing for a good deal of romanticizing of the past, such comments were repeated by enough different sources to make them apt in their description of at least some of the women immigrants. Budelia Malooley, for instance, recounted how:

> Mother arrived and started to peddle in Spring Valley ... must have been in her mid-teens at the time. She resumed peddling on her return to Spring Valley from Lebanon after my father died and I was born [about the first part of 1904]. She'd make $5 to $10/week. She'd have to send money back to Rachaya to support my sister and brother.[12]

Women were drawn to peddling for several reasons. Primarily, and as noted above, most families would not have attained their financial goals without the work of women. At other times women had no other option but to work as they were the sole or main 'breadwinners'. For Sultana al-Khazin work was a necessity of survival for her and her children. Sultana travelled to Philadelphia in 1901 to join her husband. However, upon arrival she discovered, much to her dismay, that he was living with another woman named Nazira. His plan was for all of them to live together in the same house as one family. Sultana was not quite so cavalier – to say the least – in her approach to marriage, so she packed up the three children and moved out on her own. Soon she was selling linens door to door.[13] Some women lost their husbands not to infidelity but to death. They, equally, had to contend with raising a family on their own. Alice Assaley was widowed when she was only in her twenties. In order to raise her son and daughter without her husband or any other male relatives, Alice worked first as a janitor and later as a peddler in Springfield, Illinois.[14]

Louise Houghton remarked on another reason for women's work while discussing the misguided attempts of American social workers to induce 'Syrian' women to abandon peddling for more 'honorable and lady-like' pursuits. Rhetorically she asked: 'Why should she [emigrant] give up the open air, the broad sky, the song of the birds, the smile of flowers, the right to work and rest at her own pleasure to immure herself within four noisy walls and be subject to the strict regime of the clock?'[15] Of course, one must take the pastoral bit about 'song of birds' and 'smile of flowers' with an immense grain of salt; life on the road was hardly this romantic. However, hidden amidst the flowery language is a good deal of common sense and truth. Peddling for some women was not only a necessity, but an escape. Mayme Faris, for example, vividly remembers arguments between her father and mother about the latter's peddling activities.

> My mother peddled when my father had the [supplier's] store. It was a controversy between them; he didn't like her to; he didn't like her independence. She wanted more for them. She worked hard; two or three days after my sisters were born, she would be up washing and not long after that she'd take her stuff and peddle. Once my father got mad and destroyed her satchel – in front of the other peddlers and the women who lived around there too. No, she wasn't disgraced ... She stopped it for a while and when she felt they needed more money, she would go. But independence was a big thing in [women's] lives.[16]

Sophia Mussallem was equally persistent and restless in seeking financial independence. Starting in 1885, when she first emigrated to the United States at the age of fourteen, she worked. From Milwaukee, Wisconsin to Green Bay and Watertown, then across to the Oklahoma Territory she peddled all the way to Muskogie. Throughout her expeditions she stashed away money for the dream of owning a store, which she finally accomplished in Muskogie.[17] And Oscar Alwan's mother made more money as a peddler than did his father. 'She was a strong woman ... She was never afraid, people [in upstate New York] loved her and waited for her to arrive. She knew how to deal with people, she was a good saleswoman'.[18]

Their desire for work as well as their need and reasons for employment were hardly uniform, but the fact that most worked, at one time or another, outside the 'house' is the common thread running through their varying experiences. Leaving the 'private' space of the house and sallying forth on a daily basis into the 'public' world of city streets was a new experience for most of these women – even when work was not. On a daily basis their work brought them into encounters with men who were not related to them. This took place on the street or at homes where these women peddled. For those women who worked in factories their day was spent on an assembly line interacting with Irish, Italian, or native-born American men. In other instances, women peddlers worked right alongside male peddlers who were acquaintances or whom they met through the network of peddlers. For example, on one of his peddling trips Faris Naoum was accompanied by a fellow villager's wife. One night, he wrote:

> [W]hen I asked for sleep and said she was my wife, they would not believe me ... We had left the town about one mile when I saw ... a small building. I jumped the fence ... it had windows and a round door which was closed. I opened my kashshi (*qashé*) and I used a scissors, No. 9, [to open the window] and we entered.[19]

These circumstances of intermingling between the sexes – regardless of how innocent they all were – produced situations rife with rumours of 'misconduct'.

The overcrowded living circumstances of the emigrants did little to assuage anxieties about 'unbridled' sexuality. Counting emigrant families and apartments in New York, one observer found that over 70 percent of the 'families' lived in apartments that rented for less than $14 per month, and that were made up of two rooms or one.[20] On average, the same observer calculated methodically, four to five people lived in these apartments. The 'scientific' tone of these characterizations becomes slightly more impassioned when the report states 'the number of baths in the Syrian homes ... can be counted on the fingers of one hand, and there are very few private closets ... many [of which] are constructed in the illegal sink fashion'.[21] Taking baths 'on Saturdays' meant a galvanized steel tub sitting in the middle of the kitchen with a stream of relatives and neighbours swirling around the lone bather. In outlying areas crowding was even more intense. In an article titled (in a straightforward racist fashion) 'Don't Like Arabs', which appeared in the 16 July 1901 edition of the *Cedar Rapids Evening Gazette*, neighbours complained of 'the deportment of fifty Arabians who represent the colony [of Lebanese emigrants] living in a building ... at 1220 South Third Street'. The building included only two apartments and a store below them, which made for very dense living conditions. Squeezing together for warmth and frugality was also common amongst immigrants in Fort Wayne, Indiana. By sleeping ten, twelve, or even twenty 'souls' to a room in the 'hotel' of Salem Beshara, emigrants limited their rent to 5 or 10 dollars a month.[22]

Cramming into an apartment meant that there were 'strangers' in the midst of 'families'. Boarders were a necessary part of the formula of cutting costs. Many families took in boarders because the dollar or two they paid reduced rent costs by 10 to 20 percent. For those desperate to save money this was nothing to scoff at. Out of a total population of 1891 emigrants in Brooklyn, some 464 were boarders; men and women who were not directly related to the family with whom they were staying. Living cheek-to-cheek put much added pressure on the social privacy of families. Coming from a society that was suspicious of admitting 'strangers' into the physical spaces of the 'family' for fear of a *fadiha* (scandal with sexual overtones), boarders added significantly to the social stresses surrounding these folks. How were parents to keep the 'honour' of their daughters from being sullied with rumours and innuendoes? How was a husband to guarantee that nothing unseemly would transpire between his wife and a boarder? These were difficult questions, not easily answered given the financial realities.

Thus, women's work in 'public' spaces as well as the living conditions of most (but certainly not all) immigrants threatened middle-class notions of social order by casting doubts on morality and honour. In an article that appeared in *al-Huda* in 1903, Elias Nassif Elias, a regular and early contributor, contended that women's work tarnished the honour of the 'Syrians'. To make his point, Elias wrote of an experience he had while sitting in the lobby of the Central House hotel, in Bridgewater, Maine. 'While talking with some men about various matters,' he wrote, '[we heard] a light knock on the door, so one of us got up to open only to find a Syrian woman weighed down by her heavy load ... and she sighed saying: "I will sell to those men for the amount of 4 or 5 dollars and I do not care if they laughed at, or made fun of, me."'[23] With the stage set,

Elias proceeded to describe a scene in which the 'American' men ask the 'Syrian' woman to do various 'humiliating things' (such as letting one of the men tie her shoes) that carried dishonourable overtones. Elias could not stand the situation any more, so ... he left without identifying himself as a compatriot of the woman. Without reflecting on the irony inherent in his lack of intervention in the 'degrading' affair, Elias proceeded – in his composition – to reproach the 'Syrians' for letting 'their' women work. He scathingly asked, 'Oh, you dear Syrians who claim honour ... is it honorable to send your women to meander and encounter such insults?'[24] As more of the immigrants made the move from itinerant peddling to a 'respectable' settled life, such questions only became more persistent and the tone and intensity of opposition to women's work grew more strident.

But the 'concern' was not just about protecting an 'honour' grounded in the 'traditional' construct of patriarchy. Many of those objecting to women's work saw it as a departure not only from village 'norms', but more importantly from the standards of the middle class in America, into whose ranks they were trying to gain entry. Using clinical terms, women's work was identified as the 'disease' that was 'infecting' the communal body, and simultaneously destroying 'traditional honour' and 'modern morality'. In a singular turn of phrase, then, these authors collapsed women's economic independence with sexual freedom, and termed both as detrimental. Part of the 'cure' for these problems was to subjugate women to male authority and confine them to the 'home'. This recommendation echoed the fears of the larger American middle class of sexuality and the restrictions which its members applied to confine female sexuality within the house. In the 1860s American writers on sexuality such as Dr R. T. Trall placed the 'passional expression of love' in the house and attributed its control to the woman. And while admitting the possibility that women can experience sexual pleasure, he and other writers either subordinated female sexual desire, or lust, 'to the passive, loving faculties of feminine character or denied [it] entirely'.[25] And like the Anglo-Saxon bourgeois moralists who surrounded them, these authors sought then to universalize the 'true' gender identity that derived from middle-class history and sensibilities. In fact, other authors argued that the only way to avoid the 'fall' of women into 'ruin' is to mix with 'middle classes of America' and not the lower classes 'with whom we the Syrians mingle'.[26]

In the imagination of such emigrants, a woman's place was clearly within a middle-class house which included only the immediate family of husband, wife and children. This was to be a sanitized space where foul language and rough play would be banished and where order in every aspect of life (theoretically in any case) presided over chaos. One American reformer depicted this life in the following manner:

> The social and moral life of a smaller family where the father earns enough to support wife and children, and where the mother can devote her time to the care of them, and where neither she nor the children go out and help in the support of the family, is superior to that of a family with a large number of children where the wife and often the older children must slave.[27]

Within such an isolated environment, sexuality would once again be contained within the marital contract and bond. More specifically, women's sexuality would be (again, at least, theoretically) controlled by the husband, who nonetheless would continue to have access to sex through his commutes into the 'city' and public life from the privatized suburbs.

Immigrants who sought to become 'American' adopted more and more the dominant middle-class discourse on gender roles, sexuality and the family as a means of entry into mainstream America. For those, and there were many, who felt alienated from America and its middle-class lifestyle, the search for a confirmation of identity and communal boundary took them – first verbally, and later physically – across the Atlantic. Amongst immigrants *zajal*, or popular poetry, experienced a renaissance after the 1890s.

The criticism levelled against women's work was met with objections from more liberal elements within the immigrant community. These contrarian views did not advocate women's work as inherently good, but rather as a necessary evil. Articles and editorials appearing in Arab-American newspapers sought to dispel concern over women's labour by making statements to the extent that a woman's honour, 'like pure gold', will not be tarnished by work. To emphasize that last point, *al-Huda* reminded its readers that women had worked in the silk factories of Mount Lebanon without any visible side-effects; and that was long before they had arrived in 'Amrika'.[28] Speaking from an equally 'modernist' and middle-class perspective, these latter writers tended to emphasize that the fault lay not with the women but with their 'lazy' or 'incapacitated' husbands or fathers. Read, for example, the following rejoinder by Nasrallah Faris. Reacting to Nassif Elias's story of the woman peddler in

Bridgewater, Maine, Nasrallah wrote:

> [W]e agree with the writer that women should not travel to sell if her husband is capable of properly taking care of her needs and the needs of her house, but if that woman had emigrated and left in the country a sick man ... or one heavily indebted then is it not permissible for her to sell? Or if her husband is with her and he was sick, then who will take care of him, or if he was a gambling drunkard then how can she depend on him?[29]

Afifa Karam, one of the earliest and most prolific women writers in the *mahjar*, took up the same theme in a later article. Addressing those writers who were maligning the 'honour' of women peddlers, she wrote: 'you ascribe licentiousness, depravity and immorality only to the [female] *qashé* sellers, but you are wrong because an immoral woman is not constrained from committing ugliness simply because she is living in palaces, or because she is imprisoned there'.[30]

Although women's work is not completely dissociated from the risk of immorality and dishonour, the anxiety over unbridled sexuality is shifted away from class and more onto individual character and personality. Afifa Karam, for example categorized and evaluated 'womanhood' by creating four mutually exclusive and idealized types of 'woman'. In this construction, a woman – as an individual – is either 'good', 'deceitful', 'working' or 'ignorant'. The 'good' woman is the one who attends to her duties and helps her mother, and who later as a bride makes her husband happy and makes her house a paradise. 'Working' women on the other hand are not – 'God Forbid' – necessarily without morals, but they do exist in an environment that is filled 'with dangers' which could compromise their honour. However, for Karam, the worst two kinds of women are the 'ignorant', one who is 'the disease of civilization and the curse of modernization', and the 'deceitful' woman who pretends to be 'good' but is in reality a 'snake that poisons the honey of life'.[31] Superficial beauty, powdering the face and wearing corsets to make thin waists were all considered frivolous affairs by Karam, with the purpose simply to physically attract men and appeal to their 'animal' instincts. In still another article, Ms Karam chided men who, she argued, seduced innocent women and brought 'dishonour' upon them by promising marriage only to take advantage of their bodies. Carnality, in her view, was the common and negative denominator in both of these instances ('deceitful' women and rapacious men), and it was directly responsible for the 'sorry' state of the immigrant community.

Thus, Afifa Karam still regarded sexuality outside marriage as a threat to family and community even if she saw its causes as men's rapacious appetites and 'ghoulishness'.[32] To civilize these monsters and eradicate the implied sexual predatory behaviour of men – let loose by the absence or even collapse of communal boundaries – Karam also advocated the construction of an ideal middle-class family. However, in this family, where the woman is respected, educated and house-bound, the man has to contain his sexuality within the household by refraining from visiting coffeehouses, cinemas and houses of ill-repute.[33] The house itself remains desexualized in the writings of these liberal emigrant thinkers, where every depiction of such abodes is full of marital bliss deriving from proper table manners, wholesome evenings of reading and needlework, and where the children are always in the presence of their parents. Any notion of physical tenderness let alone unbridled sexual pleasure is absent from these prosaic portraits.

'A Shiver of Pleasure ...'[34]

Yet, while most liberal and conservative elements within the Lebanese immigrant community saw sexuality as a danger to the cohesion of community (for differing reasons), there were others who regarded it as a trope of liberation from the stifling strictures of the old or new mores of the community. These views were expressed in a variety of manners stretching from new styles of clothing that celebrated (and flaunted according to some observers) a person's individual sexuality, to new definitions of marriage as (at least in part) a romantic union of two individuals and not so much their families, to new Arabic literary genres that was manifested in large part as the romance novel. Throughout, love and sexuality were articulated into new subjective, individualized forms that were, explicitly and implicitly, criticisms of the very attempts to subdue emotions and contain sexuality within the bourgeois household.

From the multitude of photographs that were taken of immigrants (and shared with those remaining in Lebanon) the changes in the presentation and representation of oneself become quite evident. At the most basic level, what is striking is that individuals, couples, families and groups posed for photographs taken in studios or in public. This visual recording and dissemination of self represents a degree of individuation and self-consciousness that was uncommon and unavailable (technologically or socially) before. But more to the point, the staged poses, struck in these photographs, and the clothes displayed a very different approach to self and sexuality at least among those in the photographs.[35] For example, around 1905 a young couple stood for a photographer. Both looked straight self-assuredly at the lens in an almost challenging manner. The woman wore a tight dress that cinched her waist and highlighted her bodice, while her hair was lifted off her neck and he eyes and lips were heavily made up in what can be seen as a 'provocative' manner.[36] Moreover, with her hand over the man's shoulder she appears to be crossing a physical boundary, particularly since it is not clear that the two are married. This image is even more striking when contrasted with pictures taken during the 1890s where the woman generally has a less 'confrontational' relationship with the camera, and where she appeared as a support for the man, with a child or space between them. Creating even more sexual ambiguity and tension are a series of photographs depicting working women.[37] Many of these were of emigrant factory workers wearing overalls and holding wrenches or other implements of their work.[38] Both in clothes and equipment it is quite evident that these particular women were neither contained at home nor abiding by middle-class gender roles. Wearing 'men's' clothes and wielding 'men's' equipment they would most certainly have been a jolt to the sensibilities of observers like Yusuf Wakim and Yusuf al-Za'ini who, along with other Lebanese immigrants, were strenuously advocating a clear separation of male and female roles in life and appearances. Working-class women – continuing the tradition of silk 'factory girls' – made a mockery of the proposed norms of femininity. They appeared, at least in the photographs, strong, without a man, and in pants. They worked in shoe, glass, automobile and steel factories alongside Italian, Polish and other immigrant men. They worked graveyard shifts as well as regular shifts. In this manner, every part of their day appeared to middle-class observers to transgress community boundaries (class, ethnicity and gender), thus heightening anxieties about sexuality.

At another level, practically every other photograph available in the Smithsonian archives show that women donned shorted haircuts, or styled their hair in a manner that highlighted their necks. Their clothes appear consistently (except for the few posed 'traditional'-attire photos) to be in the latest American style and their faces are always made up. In other words, throughout these moments of self-representation, these women chose (and/or were allowed) to uncover their hair, highlight their bodies in tight-fitting dresses, and attract the eye of the beholder with make-up applied generously. It would seem, then, that they were attracting the viewer to their bodies, faces and in essence to their sexuality as women.

Incessant comments in the Arab-American press of those times about women's increasing and excessive concern with appearances confirm these observations. Writing in *al-Sa'ih*, Sarah Abi al-'Ala' noted caustically that

> a woman does not adorn herself with jewelry except that the man want her to, and she does not put on creams and powders except that he is searching (desperately) for the white [skin] and red [lipped] young woman, and she does not wear a corset except for the fact that he requires the narrow waist, and she does not wear low-cut dresses but for the fact that he desires to take pleasure in staring at her chest ... They call us ladies when we are anything but that for them, in reality we are nothing but commodities for them and they are the merchants and customers.[39]

Other commentators directed their criticism against the women who participated in public displays of feminine sexuality which Abi al-'Ala' criticized. One female author sarcastically described the 'apparition' of a young middle-class woman in these words:

> [She had] a skin covered with powders and a waist that squeezed by a corset until it practically equaled her neck in thinness. And she was wearing an expensive silk dress ... and on her head a white hat from which dangled ostrich feathers ... and on her hands two gloves of smooth leather that she was busy putting them on ...[40]

In addition to photography, newspapers, and fashion, the novel was another medium where new concepts of sexuality and the emotional self were explored and proposed as the new social norms. As a literary genre exciting the imagination of young men and women of the emigrant middle classes, the novel was revolutionary by definition.[41] Richard Gray noted for German bourgeois literature that novels were 'a muffled protest by middle-class writers against the alienating and reifying tendencies of the bourgeois episteme within whose (signifying) parameters they and their texts necessarily operate'.[42] Between 1890 and 1914 romance novels became readily available to literate audiences in the *mahjar*. They were either serialized in the immigrant press or sold as books through the growing number of bookstores which catered to the emigrant community, and they were either written by émigrés, were authored by writers in Egypt or Lebanon, or translated into Arabic from French.[43] This expanding repertoire of literature provided texts which described the category of 'woman' and explored her social relations to friends, family, and most powerfully to lovers. A common thread ran through most of these early Arabic romance novels: a young woman struggles to sort out the complexities of her feelings towards a young man. A competing woman, disapproving and unyielding parents, or another man intrude into her relationship and force her to evaluate her love. In one such story – *Countess Sarah* – we read the following impassioned plea on the part of young man:

> I swear to you that I would die for you; I beseech you to listen to what I have to say because you must know the truth so that you will not continue to blame me. I never loved Sarah after I fell in love with you ...[44]

Within this story and many others, the young female protagonist was portrayed as an individual whose emotions and decisions were ultimately hers to make; even if they were encumbered by family considerations. This notion was made possible by the power of love, even as it stood in testament for that power. This was made explicit in a novel emblazoned with the dramatic title *Martyr of Love*. On one of its pages we find Emily riding in a carriage alongside a Mr Falkland:

> While he was looking for something in the pocket of the carriage, his hand touched Emily's so he squeezed it without paying attention, because he felt a power that made him do so. When Emily felt the strength of the touch she pulled her hand away quickly, and Falkland noticed that it was visibly shaking so he did not dare raise his eyes to her face. But his touch of his beloved's hand at that moment was enough to cause great changes in his life ...[45]

Other romance novels presented love as the highest ideal to which a woman – and a man – should aspire. In one such tale – *Love Not Money* – a young woman's marriage was being arranged by her mother to an older but wealthy man. Painting a fairly unattractive image of the mother, the author of the novel wrote:

> Truth is that marriage did not occupy the thoughts of Canair much. But her mother, who cared more for material than essential things,

> had painted marriage as something that is the duty of every young woman ... But she [the mother] said nothing of familial love ... but Canair ... had very different opinion to those of her mother's, and she saw in marriage more than inheriting money and wealth.[46]

These sentiments were equally found in romance novels that were located in an 'Eastern' context. Jirji Zaydan (1861–1914) was amongst the most prolific authors of such stories that were predominantly written as historical fiction. With titles such *The Bride of Furgana*, *The Beauty of Karbala*, and *The Young Woman of Ghassan*, Zaidan evoked romantic nostalgia for the Arab past, and its 'traditions' of courtship and *hubb*, or love. In each tale a woman and a man struggle – amidst political turmoil – to overcome all the obstacles placed in the way of their love. In each story love is seen as a virtue that should – even if it did not in reality – erase class boundaries and dispense with social customs.

On one side we find, then, romantic images which idolized love as individual freedom from parents, even when it led a woman – through marriage – into the middle-class 'female' sphere. On the other side was the reality which most young women and men experienced: parents who were indeed quite instrumental, to say the least, in the selection of a husband. Caught between these conflicting aspects of life, some young men and women tugged and pulled against the ties that bound them. Even if few ever succeeded in breaking free (and that possibility must have been quite unsettling for many young people), some struggled to be free in their choice. Here again we need not exaggerate the scale of this change to appreciate its impact. Love had existed before, and few men and women had eloped when their parents refused to allow them to marry. Marriage was more often than not a family affair that was meant to solidify social and economic relations within the clan. In that context, love was an option that would *possibly* develop after betrothal. If it did not then that was not tragic since marriage was meant for the purpose of procreation and not individual happiness. Such considerations contrasted sharply with the expectations that some middle-class young women and men harboured about romantic love. These expectations made for many disappointments in marriage, as attested to by the numerous articles that complained that many husbands treat their wives like 'servants', and which counselled men to treat with their wives with love and kindness 'even after the honeymoon is over'.[47]

The hypocrisy of this contradiction was also noted by not too few fiction writers, whether in the *mahjar* or in Lebanon. Gibran Khalil Gibran was one who incorporated a critique of the social reality into his short stories. In 'Warda al-Hani', published in 1908 in *al-Arwah al-Mutamarrida* (Spirits Rebellious) we read a very blunt indictment of the hypocrisy of middle-class society. A middle-class man complains to his friend, the narrator, that his wife – Warda al-Hani – had deserted him for a pauper. A few days later the narrator meets Warda and hears her singing. In the ensuing encounter Warda tells her story of betrothal to Rashid Na'man the middle-class man who was her senior by twenty-two years. Despite his kindness and generosity, Warda was not happy in her marriage because 'I knew that a woman's happiness is not dependent on a man's fame, his domination or his generosity ... but in love binding her spirit and his together.' Thus she left Rashid for the man she loved, because she saw herself as 'whoring and deceitful in the house of Rashid Na'man because he made me his bed companion through the rules of custom and tradition before heaven made me his wife by the ruling of the spirit and affection'. Middle-class morality was thus turned on its head. What was sanctioned as a lawful and moral marriage becomes prostitution, and what would have been considered immoral became sanctioned by God and heaven. Hence, middle-class social custom and 'tradition' appear as the underlying cause for unhappiness.

These narratives were complex and conflicting in their depiction of gender. Most proclaimed the right of a woman to choose her beloved without interference from her family, and without succumbing to the consideration of wealth. However, none could imagine a woman who did not crave the love of a man, or who would not desire to be ultimately married. None could conceive of sexuality other than physical intimacy between a man and a woman. In other words, marriage was still considered the 'natural' state of existence for a young woman outside her parental household, even as these tales spoke of different ways to get to that state. Women who appeared in these tales of romance aspired to be nothing more than lovers. Thus, love that was meant to liberate a woman from her patriarchal prison only appears to land her in another; this one of her own choice. These limitations in the critique of middle-class society arise from the fact that most authors were themselves of that class. Hence, their verbal barbs were directed from within an edifice, and had the effect of pushing at its boundaries and displacing them without destroying them. This political-critical equivocation stems from 'an ideologically motivated retraction of their own spontaneous critical insights into the guiding sociopolitical, economic, and discursive practices of the bourgeois episteme'.[48]

Despite this inherent contradiction, romance novels, along with new fashion, photography and the press, created a critical space from which to question the boundaries inscribed in middle-class gender roles. For fleeting moments, these novels allowed their female protagonists a subjective individuality that extracted them from the larger objectified category of 'woman'. In the context of the turn of the century these novels appear as radical rejection of the 'rational' and stultifying domesticity and hypocritical middle-class morality that were the hallmarks of an indigenous 'modernity' in the making. Moreover, clothes and novels gave some women the social and cultural tools with which to explore and express desire. Sexuality, then, became an explicit part of defining a 'modern' identity for Lebanese immigrants in the first two decades of the twentieth century. On one hand, controlling and disciplining sexuality was central, in the eyes of some observers, to creating a 'respectable' and modern middle class in the *mahjar*. For others, the real essence of modernity was shunning the societal strictures and allowing individuals to express themselves freely. Perhaps the most well-known writing on this subject is Khalil Gibran's *The Prophet.* His romantic philosophy pertaining to the idea of individuality can be seen in chapter 4, 'Children', where he says:

> Your children are not your children. They are the sons and daughters of Life's longing for itself. They come through you but not from you, and though they are with you, yet they belong not to you. You may give them your love but not your thoughts. For they have their own thoughts.

This became a mantra of sorts for the generation of immigrant children.

Still others worked assiduously to ignore the subject altogether by retreating into a nostalgia which depicted the life left behind in Mount Lebanon in hyper-romanticized imagery. *Zajal*, or folk poetry, which blossomed in the *mahjar*, became the most popular vessel for these soft-hued images. These poems evoked a simpler life amidst figtrees, grapevines, terraced fields full of flowers, and the certainty of peasant family.[49] Yet even these who chose to ignore the subject did so self-consciously in a manner that still reacted to sexuality by desexualizing every image of life in Lebanon.

These tensions imbued sexuality among immigrants with a history of changes, accommodations, and continuities. While this may appear rather obvious, the fact is that far too often the ideas and practices of sexuality have been presented in Middle Eastern studies as primordial desires that change little if at all. Moreover, sexual relations are regarded as private matters which have remained until recently – by design or neglect – outside the purview of scholarly analysis. Yet, and as Foucault has argued in his *History of Sexuality*, sexuality is not simply a physical urge that needs to be satisfied, but rather it is a construct of power relations that involves individuals and society. What was considered acceptable sexual behaviour among Lebanese immigrants, for example, was hardly an agreed upon subject. Extra-marital affairs, display of women's bodies, control over female sexuality and expression of desire were all issues that the immigrant community had to confront in ways that were not necessary or 'normal' back in their villages. Regardless of how they approached these and other issues – and there were myriad reactions – what is clear is that sexuality became a central element in how the immigrant community defined itself *vis-à-vis* the larger American society and that of their villages left behind. In other words, sexuality was very instrumental in shaping the power struggles and relations along the lines of gender, class and ethnicity. Equally, these other elements of individual and communal identity were critical in the definition of sexuality, love and desire. The tensions, confusions and contradictions that were part and parcel of this history were carried back with returned emigrants – along with their grandfather clocks, fedora hats, and other material objects – to their villages and towns in Lebanon and thus in turn became part of that history.

In fact, one can argue that these uncertainties and debates have historically played a role in shaping modern Lebanese society and its contradictory approach to sexuality. As with the immigrants of the 1890 and early 1900s, today's Lebanese are torn between displaying their bodies in a hyper-sexualized fashion while maintaining 'traditional' conservative views about sexual relations. Equally, the hypocrisy which characterized the immigrant middle-class sanctification of sex as permissible only within the bounds of marriage even as husbands engaged in extra-marital sex remains common in today's Lebanon. Finally, the struggle to control women's bodies, either through desexualizing or sexualizing their appearance, is a common thread that links the two historical periods. Therefore, to understand the history of the immigrant community is not to capture the stories of those peasants who left Lebanon for the Americas, but it is indeed to understand the history of Lebanon itself.

Bibliography

Allen, Roger, *The Arabic Novel: An Historical and Critical Introduction*, Manchester: University of Manchester Press, 1982.

Allen, Roger, Kilpatrick, Hilary, and Moor, E. de, eds, *Love and Sexuality in Modern Arabic Literature*, London: Saqi Books, 1995.

Chehab, Maurice, *Dawr lubnan fi tarikh al-harir*, Beirut: Publications de l'Université Libanaise, 1967.

Faris, Nasrallah, *al-Huda*, 1903, vol. 6, 88:3, 1903.

Gray, Richard T., *Stations of the Divided Subject: Contestation and Ideological Legitimation in German Bourgeois Literature, 1770–1914*, Stanford: Stanford University Press, 1995.

Houghton, Louise, 'Syrians in the United States,' 3 parts, *The Survey*, vol. 26, nos. 1–3, 1911.

Jabbour, Abdel Nour, *Étude sur la poésie dialectale au Liban*, Beirut: Publications de l'Université Libanaise, 1957.

Karam, Afifa, *al-Huda*, vol. 6, 115:2, 1903.

Khater, A., 'From 'House' to 'Mistress of the House': Gender and Class in 19th Century Lebanon', in *International Journal of Middle East Studies*, no. 28, 1996.

Knoph, S. Adolphus, 'The Smaller Family,' *Survey*, no. 37, 1916.

Miller, Lucius Hopkins, *Our Syrian Population: A Study of the Syrian Communities of Greater New York*, San Francisco: R. D. Reed, 1969.

Naoum, Faris, Hand-written Memoirs, Smithsonian Institute, Naff Arab-American Collection, 1957.

Ryan, Mary, *Cradle of the Middle Class: The Family in Oneida County, New York, 1790–1865*, New York: Cambridge University Press, 1981.

Tannous, Afif, *Trends of Social and Cultural Change in a Lebanese Village: Bishmizeen*, PhD dissertation, Yale University, 1939.

Wakim, Yusuf, 'Necessity for Putting a Limit of Law that Prohibits the Emigration of the Syrian Woman to American,' *al-Huda*, 13 January 1908.

al-Zai'ini, Yusuf, 'Female Qashé Sellers,' *al-Huda*, 12 July 1903.

Notes

1. Yusuf Al-Za'ini, 'Female Qashé Sellers,' *al-Huda*, 12 July 1903, p. 2.
2. Yusuf Wakim, 'Necessity for Putting a Limit of Law that Prohibits the Emigration of the Syrian Woman to American,' *al-Huda*, 13 January 1908, p. 4.
3. Among the various newspapers that were published between 1890 and 1914 (and thereafter), are *al-Naser*, *al-Ayam*, *al-Bayan*, *al-Sayeh*, *Kawkeb American*, *al-Kawn*,

and *al-Huda*. What makes these newspapers relevant in understanding the history of the immigrant community is the fact that they quickly became public community forums and attained a widespread circulation. For example, *al-Huda* (arguably one of the two most popular newspapers), had a circulation of over 12,000 copies by 1904, or about 10 percent of the immigrant population. When taking into consideration that the newspaper was often (but certainly not always), mailed to a household then the percentage figure doubles if not triples. Finally, newspapers were read communally in coffeehouses and shared by various people. Altogether, then, articles which appeared in these various publications were seen by a good many of the immigrants, and reflect some of the discussions within their community.

4. Akram Khater, 'From 'House' to 'Mistress of the House': Gender and Class in 19th Century Lebanon', in *International Journal of Middle East Studies*, no. 28, 1996, pp. 325–48.
5. Afif Tannous, *Trends of Social and Cultural Change in a Lebanese Village: Bishmizeen*, PhD dissertation, 1939, p. 656.
6. Maurice Chehab, *Dawr lubnan fi tarikh al-harir*, Beirut, 1967, pp. 48–9.
7. *Correspondence Commerciale, Beyrouth 1864–1867*, vol. 7.
8. For further details, see Albert Hourani and Nadim Shehadi, *Lebanese Migration in the World: A Century of Migration*, London, 1992.
9. Ignacio Klich, 1992 and Charles Knowlton, 1992.
10. Naff, 1980, p. 178.
11. Ibid.
12. Ibid.
13. Naff, 1991.
14. Naff, 1980.
15. Louise Houghton, 'Syrians in the United States,' 3 parts, *The Survey*, vol. 26, nos. 1–3, 1911, p. 648.
16. Naff, 1980.
17. Ibid.
18. Ibid.
19. Faris Naoum, Hand-written Memoirs, Smithsonian Institute, Naff Arab-American Collection, 1957.
20. Lucius Hopkins Miller, *Our Syrian Population: A Study of the Syrian Communities of Greater New York*, San Francisco, 1969, p. 16.
21. Ibid., p. 9.
22. Ibid., p. 46.
23. Elias, 1903, p. 2.
24. Ibid.
25. Mary Ryan, *Cradle of the Middle Class: The Family in Oneida County, New York, 1790–1865*, New York, 1981, p. 105.
26. *al-Huda*, 1905, p. 3.
27. S. Adolphus Knoph, 'The Smaller Family,' *Survey*, no. 37, 1916, p. 161.
28. *al-Huda*, 1899, pp. 15–17; 1906, p. 3.
29. Faris, 1903, *al-Huda*, 1903, vol. 6, 88:3, p. 3.
30. At the beginning of this article, Afifa Karam (1903/6; 115: 2) wrote, without the slightest hint of sarcasm, 'I read above the article of [Yusuf al-Za'ini titled 'Women Qash Sellers' words from *al-Huda* asking "educated men to respond and criticize" without including educated women. But I ask *al-Huda* to excuse this action of mine [writing in response].' At the end of the article, the editor of *al-Huda* wrote: 'We wish more educated women were like the writer of this article, not afraid to appear in a literary

setting nor of the objections against them by foolish people ...' Both comments were indications that the entry of women writers into this field was a fairly novel event.

31. *al-Huda*, 1900, p. 2.
32. *al-Huda*, 1900, p. 3.
33. Afifa Karam, *al-Huda*, vol. 6, 115:2, 1903, p. 2.
34. This is a quote taken from a scene described in *Jihad al-muhibbin*, of one of Jirji Zaidan's sixteen historical romance novels. The two protagonists (a Coptic upper-class young woman and a rising Coptic engineer) encounter each other in the dusk of a November evening, and through a series of oblique references arrive at the climactic conclusion where they both discover their love for each other. At that moment, 'a shiver of pleasure went through Nassima's body and words were no longer necessary ...' (Zaidan, 1950, p. 34).
35. Obviously, there are many who rejected either photography or its public display of the private. Yet, the few or many (since we do not know the numbers) who accepted the medium of photography remain very relevant because they present an alternative or a challenge to the accepted status quo. In that sense, the number of individuals and photos is irrelevant.
36. Museum of American History, 1908.
37. Ibid.
38. In a survey conducted around 1902, Lucius Hopkins Miller found that a little over a quarter of the Lebanese emigrant population living in New York City was engaged in industrial factory work (Miller, 1969, p. 11).
39. Abi al-'Ala', 1912, p. 6.
40. al-Muhazab, 1907, p. 2.
41. Roger Allen, *The Arabic Novel: An Historical and Critical Introduction*, Manchester, 1982; Allen et al., *Love and Sexuality in Modern Arabic Literature*, London, 1995.
42. Gray, 1995, p. 2.
43. Advertisements in newspapers like *al-Huda*, *al-Sa'ih*, *Syrian World* for such bookstores became quite common by the end of the 1890s and thereafter. For example, between 1900 and 1912 *al-Huda* newspaper ran over 100 advertisements for various bookstores, as well as specific novels.
44. *Lubnan*, 1907, p. 4.
45. *Lubnan*, 1895, p. 4.
46. Ibid.
47. Articles of this nature were published in *Lubnan*, *al-Bashir*, *al-Hasna'*, *Fatat Lubnan*, *al Muqtataf* (Egyptian magazine published by Lebanese immigrants) and *al-Huda* in New York.
48. Richard T. Gray, *Stations of the Divided Subject: Contestation and Ideological Legitimation in German Bourgeois Literature, 1770–1914*, Stanford, 1995, p. 5.
49. Abdel Nour Jabbour, *Étude sur la poésie dialectale au Liban*, Beirut, 1957, pp. 140–2, 152.

Migration, Marginalized Masculinity and Dephallicization: A Lebanese Villager's Experience

Ghassan Hage

Adel was born in a Northern Lebanese village in 1956. When I met him, he had been living in a town not far from Boston (which I will simply call Boston) for eighteen years. He is a close friend of my key informant there.[1] He is often present either at the family events that my informant organizes, or in certain 'boys only' outings to bars and strip-joints that the latter particularly enjoyed. Adel himself became for a while a major source of information about his relation to, and perception of, the family I was researching. After two years of knowing him, we've gradually become close as he gave himself an 'I'll be your spy while you're away' role on my behalf. The incident I am about to describe happened during my mid-2002 ethnographic visit to the US.

After a night of heavy drinking at a suburban strip-joint, it was decided that Adel was not in a position to drive home. Having maintained myself in a state of relative sobriety to continue indulging in my anthropological voyeurism, I ended up driving Adel home in his own car and staying at his place. I had done so on a number of occasions before and came to know his wife and children well. During the drive I noted that he was unusually silent. As I stopped the car in front of the house, he didn't make any move to leave. I looked at him somewhat puzzled by both his silence and his immobility, thinking that maybe he was even drunker than I thought. But he turned to me and said hesitantly: 'Docteur ... I want to ask you about something'. Somewhat dramatically, he made me promise 'not to tell anyone'. He then told me that for some time now he had been getting very anxious about his capacity to perform when about to have sex. This was leading him to have erection and ejaculation problems. He explained that it began to happen, first, when he was having sex with his wife, but now, he has the same problem 'even with prostitutes'. He did disappear with one of the women during our long stay at the strip-joint. So I gathered that he had a fresh experience of his problem that evening. Finally, he asked me if my knowledge of 'this "analysis of feelings and soul" (*tehleel'l el ehsehs wil nafs*) you talk about' can help cure him. He meant psychoanalysis.

In the course of my fieldwork, I am repeatedly asked the question 'But what is it exactly that you do?' I usually interact with this type of questions strategically. I reply by providing information which I hope will make those listening more comfortable in understanding why I ask them the sort of questions I ask.[2] It was in that spirit that on an occasion during a previous visit, I tried to explain the significance of the psychoanalytic orientation of my work and the kind of issues and approaches that psychoanalytic anthropology entailed. Since then, Adel had asked me about psychoanalysis on a number of occasions. But it took the raising of his sexual performance problems that night to make me aware that his interest, which in retrospect was somewhat odd, was not born out of pure curiosity.

Something else began to make sense that night. Although, as I said, Adel and I had become close, he has always insisted on referring to me with the classical French-Lebanese hybrid: 'el-docteur.' Some of my informants use 'docteur' or 'doctor' occasionally, often to gain a form of symbolic capital by association when introducing me to others. Adel, however, uses it all the time. That night I began to strongly suspect that Adel's 'docteuring' me had nothing to do with my PhD.

I told Adel that I was not qualified to deal with his problem and I casually asked him if he has tried to use Viagra. He obviously had been contemplating it for he had accumulated a considerable amount of folk knowledge about it. He said that he was too scared to take it, mentioning 'three day long erections that you cannot hide', heart attacks and a host of other things that the drug was supposed to cause. I said that he could go to a psychotherapist to counsel him but that he should probably see a doctor first. He said he would be ashamed to go and see anyone in Boston and that if anyone around him knew he would be dishonoured: 'I cannot tell anyone here ... neither a Lebanese nor a foreigner.[3] I can only tell you.' He then started telling me how he has always confided in me because he has always noticed that I was 'not like the others'. He said that he was struck by the fact that I don't gossip about people 'like the other Lebanese', or judge and 'say bad things' about anyone when we're talking about them. He informed me that he noticed this especially during my last visit when we were discussing Nabil's (my informant) sister. She lives alone and has had three consecutive boyfriends in the last two years. This has generated some classical 'moralistic' arguments about her lifestyle between enthusiastically assimilated 'modernists' defending her 'individual freedom' and traditionalist defenders of the Lebanese moral order condemning her 'moral depravity', as well as other in-between positions. He said that he thought about telling me about his problem then, but he didn't muster enough courage. He reiterated that he trusted me and that he was certain that what he tells me will remain between him and me.[4]

I experienced the fact that he noted that 'I do not judge' as a small anthropological victory, as I often work hard on projecting that Spinozist 'do not condemn, do not laugh, do not hate, just understand' aura. And although I could not understand why he wouldn't tell a 'foreigner', I felt the same about his confiding in me, given his stated inability to tell either 'a Lebanese or a foreigner'. I think that, to him, I was in a category in-between 'both a Lebanese and a foreigner' and 'neither a Lebanese nor a foreigner'. To me this was the ideal position to be in as a researcher working with Lebanese people.[5] I asked Adel how his wife felt about this. His face changed and he said as if struck with fear: 'I hope you're not going to talk to her about this.' I said that he knew very well that I wouldn't but that I just wondered if she hadn't suggested he does something about it. He said that he simply doesn't talk to her about it.

I continued stressing to Adel that, notwithstanding his position – 'honour or no honour' as I somewhat flippantly said – he must just go and get some medical advice about his problem. He insisted that he couldn't. But he then told me that, when he was in Lebanon (three years earlier), he made a special visit to Mar Charbel, seeking a miraculous recovery. St Charbel is Lebanon's quintessentially indigenous Maronite Catholic saint recognized by Rome. He is so because he embodies a fusion of religious and nationalist symbolism. Adel even maintained that it 'helped a bit' at first, but when he was back in Boston his problems resumed.

'It's all got to do with me being here', he suddenly said. I asked him what he meant. He said that he is 'one hundred percent sure' it is all related to him living in Boston. I asked him how come he is so sure. He told me that 'five, six years ago' he went through a stage where he started feeling very nostalgic about Lebanon and where he began reflecting about his life in the US. This is when he 'realized' that he had made a big mistake migrating. Then 'it all happened at once' he said. He became depressed, dissatisfied with everything and along with that started experiencing sexual problems.

He concluded by saying to me in English, 'I know I have wasted my life.'

I replied in a consoling manner that this surely cannot be the case, emphasizing that he has a nice family and a good job. But Adel broke into a full-on depressive rave about his social and family life in Boston. He told me that his job stinks, that 'after twenty years of hard work' he cannot stop working for a single day without having to plan it way in advance and that he cannot even afford to go to Lebanon when he wants to. Not like Nabil, he pointed out, who goes whenever he likes. He also began comparing his wife's work (his wife is an accountant) where she deals with 'high-status people' (*'aalam zaweht*) while he constantly deals with *'aalam 'aayfeen rabbun*. This is somewhat hard to translate. It literally means: 'people who have given up their God'. But this is not to indicate immoral or 'bad' people. Rather it is used to signify people who are low on social and cultural capital: uninteresting, unsophisticated, low social status, etc. Adel said that this is why no one really respects him, not even his kids ... 'Kids don't have respect for their parents in this country even if they are Einstein, let alone someone uneducated with a lousy job like me.' 'And anyway you can't control kids here', he continued. While the Einstein bit was a specific Adel addition, the 'no respect ... no control' was a classical first generation migrant theme when speaking of their children. Although it was 4 in the morning when I was alone in the spare room in Adel's house, I spent the rest of the night writing both the content of the conversation and notes around it.

When I woke up the next day it was almost midday. Adel and his wife had already gone to work, and his kids had gone to school, but he left me his car keys and a note saying that I could use the car if I wanted to. I could not wait to see him again. I rang him and said I would drive his car to his workplace and join him for his lunch break. I informed him straightforwardly that I had been thinking about how he has come to see his perceived failure to succeed as a migrant as the cause of his problem. I said I would like him to talk to me about how he felt, not only now, but also about his sexual life before he left Lebanon, and in the early stages of his migration ('as much as you are willing to reveal, but you can leave out the pornographic bits', I joked). I reiterated that this had nothing to do with curing him. I told him straight out that I didn't think that he was right about the connection he made between migration and his sexual performance, but that I was nevertheless interested in the fact that he made that connection. This particular point should be made clear. Although I have to admit that the possibility of a causal relation between Adel's sense of loss of social power and his 'erectile dysfunction' did, naively, come to my mind as he was telling me about his problems in the evening, by the morning I had realized that the idea was rather farfetched, and that in any case I was not equipped to investigate it. Adel leads what is by any standard a very unhealthy lifestyle. He is overweight; he never exercises, chain-smokes, consumes a lot of alcohol, and has high blood pressure. As I learnt later, reading some of the medical literature around the subject, many of these are suspected to be correlated with erectile dysfunction. Furthermore, erectile dysfunction can itself be the cause of low self-esteem rather than vice versa.

Nevertheless, I strongly suggested to Adel that even though what I was asking him to participate in had nothing to do with curing him, things might become clearer and he might feel better by talking to me about it and reflecting on the issue. I was expecting that now that he was no longer in a 'drunken state' he might refuse or would take his time before agreeing. To my astonishment, he agreed on the spot. He clearly felt a strong desire to talk about his situation. This is how I began a series of informal interviews with him that took place during three visits to Boston over two years (2002–3). During that time, I also visited his village while on fieldwork nearby and had various conversations with his friends, his elders and other people who remembered him.[6]

I have used the information I managed to collect, backed with my other ethnographic notes on migration and sexuality, to construct a kind of social history of the way Adel has lived his sexuality. In so doing, my primary aim has been to establish the relationship between Adel's mode of sexual identification (his conception and projection of his sexual viability), and its relationship to his mode of social identification (his conception and projection of his social viability). Most importantly, I have tried to explore the way this relationship between sexual viability and social viability was transformed by the social locations and the various cultural milieus he has occupied along his migratory trajectory. I cannot, of course, within the space of this chapter, go through this whole history. I will be concentrating on Adel's formative years in the village which were, analytically, a very important part of my investigation. To put things in perspective, I begin by presenting a very quick history of Adel's trajectory so far, to make the reason behind my choice clearer.

A Short History of a Migratory Process of Dephallicization

Adel was born in a Maronite village in North Lebanon, near Zgharta, the main Maronite town in the north. He attended primary school in the village.

For his secondary schooling he was first sent to a private Christian Brothers school, the well-known 'Frères' of Tripoli (the capital of north Lebanon and about an hour's drive from the village at the time). But he only stayed there for two years as his father, who owned the only grocery store in the village, could no longer afford the fees. He tried to continue his education in a public school but, according to him, 'it was disastrous', and he left school after he did his 'Brevet' – a certificate marking the end of 'middle school' (year 9). He then joined a technical school where he studied 'mechanique'. In 1971, he began work in the mechanical repairs section of the Shekka cement company (a large employer of industrial labour in the north of Lebanon, and about an hour's drive from the village) but continued to live at home. In mid-1975 he lost his job. The Lebanese civil war had already started and in 1976 he became a full-time Phalangist militiaman. Like most Northern Phalangists he was implicated with the forces that assassinated Tony Frangieh in 1978 and had to leave his village.[7] Also like many of them he moved to the Christian coastal town of Jbeil where he lived between a Phalangist barrack and his paternal aunt who resided in the town. In 1980, he had a disagreement with members of some kind of militia subgroup close to Samir Geagea, the leader of the northern Phalangist forces at the time. He was relocated to the Christian suburb of Beirut Ashrafieh. But he remained with what became the Lebanese Forces, serving with a group led by Elie Hobeika, one of the key leaders of the militia. He was lightly injured in the bomb that assassinated the leader of the Lebanese Forces and Lebanese president-elect, Bashir Gemayel. Soon after, in late 1983, his maternal uncle managed to bring him to Boston. He worked as a truck driver delivering home construction timber (doors, windows, etc) in his uncle's company for about a year. Then he ran the truck repair workshop of the company for another two years. Finally, he separated the truck repair shop from the company and moved it to new premises (still servicing his uncle's business, though servicing many other companies in the area, as well). This was partly an assertion of independence and partly the result of growing personal tensions between him and his uncle's son George (born in the US in 1973) who had begun to take over his father's business. Part of the tension was that George, who was married to a German-American woman, and is considered by his own family as 'too American', held Adel in contempt. This led to a particularly tense relationship, especially as George's sister Juliette (born in the US in 1963) 'fell deeply in love' (her own words) with Adel, who also emphasizes love as a primary force in the relationship. 'I loved her from the day I arrived in America', he said. George, however, feels that Adel is 'all looks and nothing else' and apparently has said so to Adel to his face. For

Adel, 'George was a wimp' who is jealous because 'no woman would bother looking at him when he is walking down the street'.

Today George and Adel are barely on speaking terms, even though, or perhaps because, in mid-1986 Adel did marry Juliette. By Lebanese standards Adel has 'married well', in that his maternal uncle's family was considerably wealthier than his own. However, George's disapproving gaze which, as I was to discover, has been internalized and constantly hovers around Adel, works to constantly inferiorize him. In a kind of aristocratic logic which emphasizes those who are superior 'by essence' rather than 'by achievement', the gaze reminds him that the very conditions of the possibility of 'doing well' out of a marriage is precisely to be 'not doing so well' originally. It declares to Adel: 'you are of lowly origins'. That Adel has internalized that gaze is itself function of his own class sensitivities: his missed but aspired-for elite education, his joining of the Phalangist Party which accentuated among its members at the time, particularly the militia, on one hand, a modernist individualism opposed to rampant forms of political patronage in Lebanon (often referred to as political feudalism), and on the other hand, a form of petty bourgeois class resentment, heavily laced with envy, towards richer people. Adel has openly admitted his resentment of the Lebanese upper classes who, as he put it, 'made us fight a war to protect their interests'. He also quite candidly detailed his involvement in stealing jewelry from rich people's chalets and bungalows after a major military action aimed at disarming a rival Christian militia (Dany Chamoun's 'Tigers' of the National Liberal Party). The operation involved a raid on two middle-class beach resorts where Dany Chamoun and other leaders of his militia were located. 'I bought myself a BMW and was partying with lots of beautiful Ashrafieh women for a while', he said.

Adel also felt forms of class resentment towards his own wife who was much better educated than he was. When the children grew up, Juliette returned to university, and resumed a career as a reasonably successful accountant (she has worked continuously as the accountant for her family's company). This, as we have already seen, has accentuated the anisogamic resentment Adel felt towards his wife's family. Furthermore, he also experienced resentment over what he sees as 'losing' (his word) his children to his wife's family, even though he recognizes that this was inevitable given that his own family were in Lebanon. All this was bound to generate a sense of domestic disempowerment for someone who is as traditionally patriarchal as Adel. (He says without blinking things like *ana mafrood koon rabb el'ayli* ('I am supposed to be the god of the family') which is a highly traditionalist conception of the male patriarchal role for someone his age.) This domestic disempowerment not only increased when his business stalled in the mid-1990s, but it was also superimposed on a wider social disempowerment resulting from the way he lived his Lebanese-ness in Boston.

First, because of his already damaged and brittle sense of patriarchal power, Adel perceives the US state as a competitor for the domination of his familial realm, that is, as a competing patriarch. He is genuinely haunted by the thought that 'you can't even slap your kid here', which he repeatedly mentioned when describing his life in the US, although his wife and kids say that he has never been violent or ever had the disposition to slap the kids in the first place. All state laws designed to empower women or children within the domestic space are experienced as an 'intrusion' into what he sees as 'his' domain.

Second, Adel is (paradoxically) an assimilationist. While he complains that life in America is inferior to life in Lebanon because of drugs and homosexuality among the youth, and says that one can be 'too American' (which is 'bad'), he also states unequivocally that 'the West' and 'America' are 'modern' and 'superior' in everything else. He is highly committed to the idea of 'American democracy' where you don't follow someone 'just because they are from family so and so'. To him, to be more *moderne* (always used in French) means above all to have more money, more education, live in nice (meaning new and big) houses, and more goods. In this he is no different from many Christian Lebanese migrants from his class background. And like many of them, his excessive enthusiasm for their specific version of Western modernism translates into racism towards Muslim Lebanese who are perceived as bringing the collective Lebanese down in the struggle to achieve modernity. He proudly displays Jewish American newspapers in his shop to make sure that 'no Palestinian or Muslim does business with me'.

His overemphasis on 'marrying for love' is also an indication of this modernistic aspiration, as he uses it to demarcate himself from, and express a sense of superiority over, the Lebanese who engage in 'arranged marriages'. But because of his low stock of 'modernistic cultural capital', his 'trying to be western/modern' always generates the sense of inferiority common among those who are 'furiously trying to be' while the gaze of the other is always telling you that you are 'nowhere near'. With a paradoxically Fanon-like situation, this actually leads Adel to dread any contact with middle-class Americans who seem to put him face to face with his 'trying to be' self.[8] Adel's sensitivity towards telling an American doctor about his condition, which I initially thought was rather strange, is better explained by this positioning of the middle-class 'American' as the ultimate example of modernity, a severe judge always out to evaluate how modern 'others' can be, and someone always ready to condemn them for their failure to be 'modern' enough.

This short account of Adel's migratory trajectory should be enough to give an understanding of the sense of disempowerment that he has experienced in the process of migrating to the US. That this experience can be expressed as a form of symbolic castration is not hard to see. In many masculine forms of domination, 'having what it takes' to be the legitimate holder of patriarchal power within the family and society is captured with a metaphorically phallic language. The literature on migration is full of allusions to phallic loss in describing the ways in which migrant males lose their culturally specific patriarchal power in the process of migration. Words that suggest symbolic castration, like effeminization and emasculation, are often used to describe this.[9] Castration itself is also used, of course. These are often borrowed from an earlier usage of the concepts in describing colonially subjugated 'Third World' males. Needless to say, such perceptions are strongly present in the works of Frantz Fanon, Edward Said, Mrinalini Sinha, among others.[10] From this perspective Adel's phallic experience is a process of increasingly feeling a lack of 'having what it takes', whether it is a lack of money, a lack of prestige, a lack of 'modernity' or a lack of patriarchal authority.

However, notwithstanding the truth of the above, such a dwelling on 'metaphoric' or 'symbolic' castration is not entirely satisfactory in dealing with Adel's situation. For here we have a further step in the process of signification where the physical loss of phallic power, a form of biological castration, is itself made to stand for the sense of loss of social power, symbolic castration. This is not entailed by the metaphoric usage of castration which does not presuppose a penis-centred experience as such.

It could be said that it is simply pure chance that has allowed for such a process of signification. That is, it so happened that Adel suffered from a sense of social disempowerment at the same time as he experienced some form of 'erectile dysfunction'. In an extension of the common folk association of social power with phallic symbols, Adel comes to associate 'not being able to do something social' with 'not having what it takes to do something sexual'. I am not rejecting this explanation. What I want to emphasize, however, is that not all males will make such an association with the same strength. My already existing ethnographic notes on the sexuality of the Lebanese male villagers in Lebanon and in the diaspora, Adel's own language which is full of metaphoric usage of the penis[11] and his initial insistence on a social/psychological explanation of his medical condition lead me to think that there is also something culturally specific concerning the strength with which the association between social power and the power of the penis is made: a culturally acquired disposition to think one's masculinity and social power in a penis-centred way. This is a slightly edited version of a couple of paragraphs I wrote in my notebook after talking to Adel in mid-2003. It can still serve as a good introduction to the questions preoccupying me here:

1) In the West the penis's social/public value as a symbol of masculinity in everyday life has markedly decreased. Those who valorize their masculinity through a valorizing of their penis are perceived as immature (teenagers) or vulgar (working-class). Perhaps it is because of this that it has become common today, especially under the influence of Lacanian literary studies, to speak of any patriarchy as 'phallocentric' and 'phallocratic' but implying that this is always *metaphorically* or *symbolically* so to the point of vacating the actual imaginary of the penis from the metaphor.[12] 2) However, this actually stops us from differentiating between 'actually phallocentric' and 'metaphorically phallocentric' masculine cultures. 3) There are certain cultural milieus where there is nothing metaphoric about phallocentrism and phallocracy. It seems increasingly so to me that, for Adel, like for a number of Lebanese males from his age group in the villages, phallic power is above all just that: the power of the penis. And phallocentrism also means above all just that: all power is centred around the penis. (I say above all because even then there clearly remains a lot of room for metaphoric phallicity.) 4) In this kind of phallocentrism, the penis itself becomes the site of a condensation of all that signifies patriarchal masculine social power, whether in the realm of the sexual (men's domination over women), the familial (men's domination within the family) or the social (men's domination within a society). Thus, the penis comes to *embody* social power, not just *signify* it. This raises some important anthropological and theoretical questions:

- Am I right in thinking that this masculinity is at the intersection of cultural forms that are, in turn, specifically Mediterranean, rural and class-based – upper working class/lower middle class types?
- Does the process of 'civilizing' masculinity (as in Norbert Elias's conception of the civilizing process) involve its increased detachment from the biological phallus? And, therefore, is this penis-centred masculinity a sign of a primarily 'Third World' and 'underdeveloped' masculinity?
- Maybe just as racist discourse in the West today (which we may want to call advanced or civilized racism) has discarded biological

> difference in the name of cultural difference between 'races', patriarchal discourse likewise increasingly discards the biological as the site of sexual difference?

It is from this perspective that Adel's formative years in his village, where he lived until he was twenty-two years old, acquire their centrality. Analysing the male sexual culture of the village, particularly among people of Adel's age and class background, makes it clear that it is there that Adel acquired the disposition to see in his penis this 'condensation of sexual, familial and social viability' I refer to above as the mark of 'real' phallocentrism.

Penis-centred Masculinity in a Lebanese Village

One does not have to stay long in the village to note that 'the social order functions as an immense symbolic machine tending to ratify the masculine domination on which it is founded', as Bourdieu argues on the strength of his Kabyle ethnography.[13] But one can also quickly note with Bourdieu that, likewise,

> manliness, virility, in its ethical aspect, i.e. as the essence of the *vir*, *virtus*, the point of honour (*nif*), the principle of the conservation and increase of honour, remains indissociable, tacitly at least, from the physical virility, in particular through the attestations of sexual potency ... which are expected of a 'real' man. Hence the phallus, always metaphorically present but very rarely named, concentrates all the collective fantasies of fecundating potency.[14]

Bourdieu here still sees the male's lived 'phallicity' as metaphorical. For example, in analysing the male physical posture, the men in the village are perceived to be walking with bodies that are erect like the phallus. I suppose what I am aiming to describe are men whose masculine posture is not primarily manifested by being erect *like* the phallus, but rather in standing in such a way that they make sure that their phallic region *is* perceived as a, if not the, key part of them: for example, arching their body in such a way that the crotch is obviously protruding and confronting. What we have is a male sexual culture where the penis, even if always 'clothed', is an important part of what Goffman calls the 'front' in the masculine 'presentation of the self in everyday life'. We can speak of a discursive and practical construction of a penis-centred worldview that internalizes its priorities into the male body, curving it accordingly.

Appreciative penis talk directed at boys begins very early in life. Both men and women while pampering and playing with male babies employ, very often publicly, words like *Te'berni zabertak* and *tislamli hal anburah*, both roughly signifying a kind of submissive love of the boy's little penis and aimed at anthropomorphizing it. This can include actually catching the penis between the fingers and wiggling it playfully while uttering the words. Later, adult males, often engage in a public check-up of the state of the boy's penis saying *farjeeneh wayn sernah* (let us see where we're at), but also importantly, associating its state with other forms of social power: *Shawfeeneh hal anburah. Saar feenah neflah?* (Let me see this penis. Are we ready to plough the field?). I recorded these forms of interactions only recently and it is likely that they were more pervasive in Adel's time.

But perhaps no ethnographic detail can capture this early centring of the penis as well as a (rather exotic) ritual that Adel himself told me about. From his late teenage years and until he left his job, Adel was, according to himself and to others in the village who were his friends at the time, 'very popular' with women. One older woman said to me that he was *mitl el-amar* ('like the moon' – commonly used to define people considered physically beautiful). A close friend of his still in the village said that: 'We used to spend our time after work and on the weekends *am 'n nammer*' (literally: 'playing a number', which means making a number of oneself (showing off) in front of women), and that 'Adel was *malak el tenmeer*' (the king of the show-offs).

As I was discussing this with him, I said to Adel jokingly 'So you clearly weren't shy with women'. Adel enigmatically replied: 'How can you be once they've made you do *a'sit el-dabboor* (the sting of the wasp)?' Here is the rest of the taped conversation:

> G: What is that?
> A (smiling): You've never heard of *a'sit el-dabboor*?!
> G: No. Sorry!
> A: When you are very young ...
> G: How young?
> A: I don't know, five or six years old. Anyway, someone among the elders (*el kbaar*) takes your pants off.
> G: Wait ... who do you mean by 'the elders'? [My mind, unrealistically, had started ticking in the direction of Herdt's *Guardians of the Flutes*.][15]
> A: Well, your father, an uncle or one of their close friends ... but your father has to be there or no one would do it otherwise.

G: OK ... and then?

A: Well they take your pants off and they put you behind a girl your age and they keep pressing you and rubbing you on her until you get a little erection.

G [with a genuine sense of having missed out on an important Lebanese cultural tradition]: Are you serious?!

A: Yes.

G: I can't believe it. I've never heard of anything like this before ... certainly hasn't happened to me ... wait before you go on. I've got too many questions. Let's see ... uh, I'll come back to the questions, so what happens next? After you get an erection?

A: That's it. They all start clapping, often some of them wiggle the boy's penis or pat him on the back while saying things like *bravo 'aleik ... 'emella a'sit al dabour... aah ya Malak*.

G [laughing]: I still find this unbelievable. But what about the girl? What do they tell her?

A [frowning]: Nothing. Everybody is laughing and shouting so most of the time she just thinks it's fun and she laughs too. Though I remember a couple of years before I left the village, we were doing it to the son of George with the daughter of Samira and she [the daughter] started crying hysterically even before the rubbing started and we had to give up!

G: Tell me about when it happened to you, who was present and who was the girl?

A: I only remember vaguely but definitely my father and my paternal uncle were there. I still have an image of them in my mind, laughing their heads off when it was happening. I can't remember who the girl was.

G: But I am intrigued ... I mean, presumably, she is the daughter of a friend of your family or something.

A: I don't remember ... It must have been the daughter of a friend we have stopped seeing since because otherwise people would have continued reminding me of who she was. But yes usually she would be a friend of the family who just happened to be there on the day. And of course her father would be there. You wouldn't do it without the parents knowing. It is never planned, it usually happens after a lunch or dinner party and lots of people are around ...

G: And do you remember anyone your age to whom it was done?

A: Hmm ... actually ... no, I don't remember this. I only remember it with other boys later when I was older.

G: Tell me, did you do it to your son?

A: You've got to be kidding. Can you imagine what 'el Madame' [this is the word, Adel uses sarcastically, in its French-Arabic combination, to refer to his mother-in-law] would say if this happened to her beloved?

G: But you don't have any objections. You'd do it?

A: Yes, of course I would. I think it would be good for him.

G: OK ... your daughter ... if you're around, would you have let this be done to your girl if you are around.

A [smiling]: Yes. Why not? Let her get used to it. This is how it will be in life.

I have asked around the village and in several other villages for accounts of *a'sit el-dabbour*. A number of men in the village have confirmed the practice, though they said that no one does it anymore. But it was clear that the practice was not widespread. It was also looked down upon by the village's 'aristocracy' as 'what the peasants do'. It is also (not surprisingly) disliked by the women. None of them wanted to share their experiences of it as young girls. Many older women told me that they used to leave to another room when 'it' was happening and, as one of them put it, 'leave the men alone to play this disgusting game'. With men and women sitting around her and laughing at what was clearly the telling of a shared memory that is ritually recounted, another woman told me the story of Afifeh who did not allow her daughter be sacrificed and said to her husband 'you let this be done to your daughter and you'll never get to rub your own penis except on the fig tree outside!' The practice does not seem to have been as widespread outside the village. Only a handful of people from other villages, one reasonably far from Adel's village, knew about it. But all have independently detailed it to me in much the same way Adel did.

The event seems to have had a lasting effect on Adel. He said to me that *a'sit el dabbour* often came to his mind when having sex as a young man. Beside being a festival of phallocentrism, what was also interesting were the words uttered to the performing boy once he proves himself capable of having an erection: *bravo 'aleik, 'emella a'sit al dabour. Aah ya Malak!* They roughly mean: 'good on you, he's given her the sting of the wasp. O you king!', bringing a clear association between the possession of a well-functioning penis, the capacity to dominate girls and the capacity to rule within society which is at the core of this 'real' phallocentrism I have been describing.

I think it is this kind of perpetual touching and talking about and around the penis which slowly creates the ultimate male posture of the protruding crotch mentioned above. This posture is particularly emphasized during the traditional *dabkeh* dance where the male arching of the body, accompanied by the display of various forms of physical prowess (the males are said to engage in *'ard adhalat*: literally, muscle exhibition) stands in contrast with the female undulating bodily movements. But the male–female posturing and interaction at such parties actually offer us another important dimension of this phallocentrism: the penis is itself party to the classification of girls by men according to their suitability for marriage and/or sex.

I initially did not pay it much attention when someone, from a village neighbouring Adel's village, told me jokingly that 'men here think with their penis'. I took it to mean what it ordinarily means, i.e. that 'they follow their sexual instincts'. This is because I have heard another person say in the same vein that when it comes to girls, the men of the village don't use their brains, they just 'go where the tip of their penis guide them'. This always gets them in trouble with the men of the villages where the girls they are chasing come from. But I began to notice that the mode of deploying one's crotch was actually an intrinsic part of the way women are categorized.

On one hand, this is very simple: women are classified as 'for marriage' and that's usually the girls of the village,[16] or they are for flirting and 'showing off' with. Exhibiting your crotch to the latter is fine but to the former is vulgar. It is considered rude to act in a too stud-like way towards village girls, in the sense that it is rude to be too sexual about women you may potentially marry. To such women you exhibit the social traits of your masculinity (gender without sex, so to speak): toughness, rationality, dependability, etc. You only emphasize your sexual/physical masculinity to those who are outside the 'official' marriageable realm. This is partly an extension of the logic of the arranged marriage whereby marriage decisions are not supposed to succumb to the irrational flows of desire but have to be rational, business-like decisions. This also extends into a division between women who embody reproductive sexuality and the others who embody sexuality for fun. One should note here that this runs against Giddens's[17] argument that what he calls plastic sexuality (sexuality for fun) emerged when it became technologically possible to free it from reproductive sexuality. He argues that:

> Sexuality came into being as part of a progressive differentiation of sex from exigencies of reproduction. With the further elaboration of reproductive technologies, that differentiation has today become complete. Now that conception can be artificially produced, rather than only artificially inhibited, sexuality is at last fully autonomous.

> Reproduction can occur in the absence of a sexual activity; this is the final 'liberation' for sexuality, which thence can become wholly a quality if individuals and their transactions with one another.[18]

Many cultures have always managed to separate sex for fun and reproductive sex through a simple social technology of domain separation.

Of course, the loves, great and small, that many village boys develop towards other village and non-village girls perturbs the neatness of these domains. Furthermore, witnessing the kind of male–female interactions that go on during various festive gatherings clearly show that this neatness is continuously subverted even when the appropriate behaviour appears to be reasonably maintained. Most males, for example, do not assume that the marriageable women of the village are not interested in their penis exhibitionism. In a kind of displacement of the sexual exhibitionism, you play the stud with the strangers but you are hoping that the women of the village are watching you, for this is where you want to establish your reputation and the reputation of your penis. Indeed, the man who proves himself *fahl* (basically, a stud) does so outside the village. But it is in the village that he is perceived as a holder of a social prestige that can be converted into real social power: for example, he develops a group of other males around him, admirers but people who are also trying to establish their own reputation by rubbing shoulders with him. If he is willing and able to play such a game, this can give him access to the position of middleman for a particular village patron which in turn allows him to have his own clientele.

For all its social power, it is important to realize that such penis-centred masculinity is not a one-way traffic of empowerment. Like all forms of phallic possessions it produces a sense of power laced with a heavy dose of ambivalence and fear of castration. Whether perceived in Freudian terms as the actual penis in the early stages of development or as a general signifier of lack as in the Lacanian tradition where anything can basically play a phallic function, psychoanalytic understandings of the phallus all emphasize its arbitrary value and its dependence on an intersubjective process of valorization. Freud's little Hans remains the best documented example of this fear. The story goes something like this:

> Take two toddlers playing on the floor. Toddler A notices a piece of plastic, maybe a small nondescript section of a broken plastic container. Once she notices it, toddler A goes for it to investigate it. Toddler B notices her going for it. He wonders what it is she is going for. He tries to grab it too, but a bit too late. At the same time

> though, as she is going to pick up the piece of plastic, toddler A sees toddler B also heading towards it a fraction too late. Thus, already in the very first process of going for it as someone from behind is also trying to grab it, she gets her first inkling that maybe this piece of plastic is not just of some interest but also of some importance. So she rushes to grab it and she does. Now she holds it wondering about the importance of this thing 'she has'. Toddler B now is convinced that the piece of plastic must be pretty important given the way toddler A is holding on to it. He plunges on it again to try to snatch it. But now, toddler A can see that toddler B is desperate to have the piece of plastic. She becomes convinced that it must be VERY important indeed and holds on to it even more jealously. And so on ...[19]

This is in a nutshell what phallic logic is all about. It is a social relation which ends up constructing an unimportant element of difference into the most important thing there is. But it also institutes two dramas. The drama of the person who doesn't have 'it': the one who will always think that the other must be better because he 'has it'. But also the drama of the person who has it: here is a person who is being told by 'everything' that he has 'something' important. He expects that 'something' to make him somehow 'feel better' than the one who doesn't have it. But he is not sure whether he actually does 'feel better'. On one hand he is forcing himself to live up to his 'reputation' as the possessor of this important something. On the other, he is worried that maybe his 'something' is not enough, is too small or not working well, and he is about to lose it. It is in this sense that all modes of phallic identification reproduce a paranoid modality of being that is always haunted by the fear of 'castration'. This logic is true, whatever form the phallus take, whether it is a piece of plastic or the penis. In the case we have been examining it is the penis that ends up being invested with this ambivalent power. And its holder is forever fearful of losing what he has.

The disjuncture referred to above between the need to project oneself successfully 'as the possessor of a powerful phallus' and one's inner fears and ambivalence, 'I don't know if my phallus is as good as I am making others believe it to be', helps us understand the weak underbelly of the penis-centred culture of masculinity we have been examining. In a social situation where there are in fact very few women available to have sex with before marriage, the 'stud' has to maintain a public aura among both the men and the women of the village of continuous sexual success in both the number of women and the quality of the sex he is supposed to be having. This necessarily involves the creation of a very complex world of boasting and make-believe that the stud has to work hard to sustain in the face of others. Adel had rather serious trouble trying to tell me how he lived up to his own reputation as a sexual predator when he was living in the village. He was very evasive when I tried to probe where the actual women he managed to score with came from. I said to him: 'you have to embellish reality a bit if you are to maintain your reputation, isn't that so?" He gave me a kind of yes, dressed as a general cultural observation: 'Yes, as you know in Lebanon you have to engage in a lot of *tefsheet* (harmless lying) otherwise people will lose respect for you'!

This phallic disjunction between 'what I want others to believe I am' and 'what I believe I am' in this type of masculinity minimizes considerably the possibility of sexual and social intimacy with women, for to have a sexual relation with a woman is to reveal to her, at least, what kind of lover 'I really am' as opposed to the lover I want others to believe I am. And in a society where one of the standard male stereotypes of women is that they talk too much, this is quite a breach in their carefully constructed public persona! One's fears will be proportional to the gap that exists between the being-for-others and the being-for-oneself. I also suspect that it would be the basis of much subterranean forms of misogynous behaviour for it minimizes the possibility of what Giddens calls 'confluent love', which involves, as he puts it, 'opening oneself out to the other'. The ethos of the phallic conqueror does not allow confluent love as it requires abandoning the defensive mechanism of the sexual warrior: 'I will not be showing my vulnerability' and 'I will continue to project myself as invulnerable'. It seems however, following Giddens, that this is simply an accentuated form of a more general problem.

> Confluent love presumes equality in emotional give and take, the more so the more any particular love tie approximates closely the prototype of the pure relationship. Love here only develops to the degree to which intimacy does, to the degree to which each partner is prepared to reveal concerns and needs to the other and to be vulnerable to the other. The masked emotional dependence of men has inhibited their willingness, and their capacity, to be made thus vulnerable. The ethos of romantic love has in some part sustained this orientation, in the sense in which the desirable man has been represented as cold and unapproachable. Yet since such love dissolves these characteristics, which are revealed as a front, recognition of male emotional vulnerability is evidently present.[20]

This is something the phallic conqueror finds impossible to do.

In the above, I have tried to give an account of the penis-centred nature of the masculinity internalized by Adel during his formative years in the village. By all accounts, including those of his friends and contemporaries, Adel not only was part of this culture but was also a reputed performer in it. This should help us understand the relative strength of his desire to associate his social condition with his erectile dysfunction. As I have pointed out earlier, it is this relative strength that I aimed to demonstrate. But this emphasis should in no sense lead us to think that the cultures of penis-centred phallocentrism and metaphoric phallocentrism are mutually exclusive. Even when a phallic culture is penis-centred, masculinity still depends on a whole series of metaphoric phallic symbols that work to prop up the penis.

Even in penis-centred patriarchies, males still depend on a whole series of phallicized cultural forms which they claim to monopolize. For instance, the rolled up, thick moustache was for a long time such a phallic symbol. Various items of clothing, monopolized by males, have also functioned this way. One example is found in John Gulick's early 1950s ethnography of a northern Christian Lebanese village, not far from Adel's own. Like most ethnographies of the time the text has very little to say about patriarchy and male domination. Yet, in a section dealing with clothing, the anthropologist describes the way younger women, especially those who work in the city, follow modern European styles. However, he continues, the Western practice of women or girls wearing slacks or shorts has been completely rejected. For this there are at least two reasons. One is that the men regard the practice as a usurpation of a symbol of masculine status. The second is that women who wear slacks or shorts are assumed to be of loose morals.[21]

These phallicized cultural forms are not always cultural as opposed to the biological penis. One of the most important phallic signifiers that I have come across in the village and which is strangely unmentioned in the anthropology of kinship is the extent to which males 'have' their fathers' looks. Here we need to recall the important relation between phallic masculinity and patriarchal law. To have the phallus is to be on the side of the patriarchal law and the patriarchal 'order of things'. It is to have the power to act in the name of that law which in the patriarchal family is embodied by the father. The penis of the little boy symbolizes that he, unlike his sister, 'has what it takes' to inherit and occupy the position of the father as the enforcer of the law when this position is vacated. This is an important way in which the penis becomes the signifier of social power. But, in the Lebanese villages, the penis is not the only possession that gives the child such power of inheritance. The physical resemblance to the father also plays a role as a kind of secondary, but nonetheless important, phallic symbol of entitlement.

In a wonderful example of an imaginary power struggle, the Lebanese male villager experiences his child's birth, without the help of a microscope, as a power struggle between his genetic lineage (his blood, his stock, etc) and his wife's genetic lineage. To have a boy rather than a girl is not just to secure the paternal lineage, it is a proof of that his maleness has prevailed over his wife's femaleness in the making of the baby. But to have a boy that resembles you rather than resembling his mother is a further proof of the vitality of the male's stock. Therefore, the son's lack of resemblance to the father becomes a signifier of an imaginary 'genetic defeat' of the paternal lineage which reflects negatively on the phallic power of the father. This makes the father resent the son as an embodiment of his own genetic weakness. In turn, the son being dominated by the genetic lineage of the mother is perceived as effeminized. In Arabic, the maternal uncle is called *khal*. When a man looks like his mother's side of the family he is said to be *m'khawwal*, which means looking like his *khal*. It has been pointed out to me that in Egyptian, the term *khawal*, which clearly has the same roots, is used for 'poofter', and thus also denotes a form of effeminization.

As a holder of the penis/phallus Adel is the legitimate inheritor of his father's position. However, Adel insists that he has had a very problematic relation with his father precisely because he looks 'too much' like his mother's side of the family: 'When he was angry with me, he would always say: *tali' la kahlak Jameel* (you take after your maternal uncle Jameel). Of course, he would not mention my other maternal uncles who are successful. He just mentions Jameel who is known by everyone to be a weak man with many problems.' I also noted that, despite being, as mentioned above, recognized as 'good looking' by many, two people from the father's side of the family have independently commented to me that Adel was 'too good looking', implying a feminine quality.

Interestingly, this, to my mind, has been part of Adel's problem with his mother's family in Boston. He and his cousin (and brother-in-law) mentioned above bear a striking facial resemblance. I think that part of Adel's extreme reaction to him is that he is a reminder of the constant dephallicization he has endured within his father's family because of his looks. This has added a further negative dimension to his migration. For this migration is experienced as form of matrilocalism which has made him now even more separated from the paternal side of the family. It has 'locked him' with his dephallicizing maternal 'look-alikes'.

In the text above, I have increasingly marked a preference for the usage of the notion of dephallcization rather than castration. This is because the above emphasis on the multiple nature of phallicizing and dephallicizing 'possessions' clearly shows that the question of losing or gaining phallic power is not an either you have the phallus/or you don't question, which is often implied by the notion of castration. Rather, the process of phallicization and dephallicization obeys the logic of the more or less. This is important because this means that the experience of dephallicization is not an experience of losing phallic power in an absolute sense, but an experience of decline. This, by the way, fits with the Spinozist logic whereby joy and sadness are respectively experiences of increase or decrease in the body's capacity to reproduce itself. A person A can have 'a lot' of phallic power, so to speak, and experience a decrease which is also experienced as a dephallicization. While a person B with much less phallic power can experience an increase and feel 'on top the world' even if in absolute terms they have 'less' phallic power than person A.

As importantly, the above also invites us not to see Adel's phallic trajectory simplistically as one of phallic power in Lebanon and one of loss of phallic power in the process of migration, and be aware that there are always phallicizing and dephallicizing tendencies operating on the holder of the phallus.

Bibliography

Bourdieu, P., *Masculine Domination*, Cambridge: Polity, 2001.

Fanon, F., *Black Skin, White Masks*, London: Pluto, 1986.

Freud, S., 'Analysis of a Phobia in a Five-Year Old Boy', in *Complete Psychological Works*, vol. 10, London: Hogarth, 1995.

Giddens, A., *The Transformation of Intimacy: Sexuality, Love and Eroticism in Modern Societies*, Cambridge: Polity, 1992.

Gulick, J., 'The Material Base of a Lebanese Village', in Ailon Shiloh, ed., *Peoples and Cultures of the Middle East*, New York: Random House, 1969.

Herdt, G., *Guardians of the Flute: Idioms of Masculinity*, New York: McGraw-Hill, 1981.

Poynting, S., Noble, G., and Tabar, P., 'Protest Masculinity and Lebanese Youth in Western Sydney', *Journal of Interdisciplinary Studies*, vol 3, no. 2, 1998.

Said, E., *Orientalism*, New York: Random House, 1978.

Silverman, K., *Male Subjectivity at the Margin*, New York: Routledge, 1992.

Sinha, M., *Colonial Masculinity: The 'Manly Englishman' and the 'Effeminate Bengali' in the Late Nineteenth Century*, Manchester: Manchester University Press, 1995.

Zizek, S., *Organs without Bodies: On Deleuze and Consequences*, New York: Routledge, 2004.

Notes

1. In my multisited ethnographic research on Lebanese transnational families I move between the different international locations where members the families I am researching have settled. A 'key informant' in a particular location is the person in whose house I stay during my research through whom I access other family members and their activities.
2. Somehow, what I said never seemed to be satisfactory. This is not because I couldn't explain what I was doing but because people found it hard to believe that someone who spends a lot of time travelling and talking to people can actually be doing 'something'. But what is it for? How much money does that make? This was largely because of the Lebanese migrants' unusually strong instrumental sense of work as money-making. My key informant in Venezuela, for example, with whom I have a kind of 'joking relation', continuously 'teases' me about my work. He acts as if he finds it hard to accept that it can be called 'work'. So when I arrive to Caracas, he often sarcastically greets me with: 'So, back here on work, I see, you look exhausted already.' A young family member who was doing a social science postgraduate degree found it extremely liberating to have me around. Most members of the family thought of him as a failure for taking such a path in life.
3. He used *ajnabi*, which means more precisely a Western foreigner.
4. I have of course obtained Adel's permission to write about this. However, needless to say, I have changed his name, his village of origin and the American city where he has settled. Though it is not absolutely crucial for this chapter. I have however tried to maintain a sense of geographical concreteness in that the city where he has settled is very Boston suburb-like.
5. Such a position is probably easier to achieve for a 'post-native' anthropologist like me than it is for a Westerner or a Lebanese. The Lebanese I deal with often tell me that I've become 'too Australian'. So it was not the first time that I was seen as 'Lebanese enough' to understand what another Lebanese was on about but not 'Lebanese enough' to threaten that the knowledge revealed to me will become public knowledge within a specific Lebanese communal milieu. This has led people, on a number of occasions, to confide in me and tell me things I knew very well could not be told to anyone else.
6. I am glad to say that our discussions played an important role in helping convince him to go and see a medical doctor about his problem, which he did in mid-2003. He said to me: 'when you write this tell people that I feel much better!'
7. Tony Frangieh, was the leader of another Christian militia, the Maradah, based in the key northern Lebanese town of Zgharta and with membership from the many surrounding villages. His assassination by Phalangist militias led to the expulsion of all Phalangists from North Lebanon.
8. I gently confronted Adel with this one day after a particularly difficult evening with some of my Anglo-American friends. He first became very upset with me and accused me of acting superior like his brother-in-law. I kept confronting him and said that I could be wrong but that I wanted him to think about it and then tell me if he felt I was right or wrong. He thought to settle it by telling me that it is true that he feels a bit intimated by Americans but it was only because he is living in their country. I said: 'well

think about why you only felt intimated by upper class Americans, then'. He replied: 'well that's because they are the Americans that really count. Who else do you want me to worry about?'

9. see e.g. Poynting et al., 'Protest Masculinity and Lebanese Youth in Western Sydney', *Journal of Interdisciplinary Studies*, vol 3, no. 2, 1998.
10. Frantz Fanon, *Black Skin, White Masks*, London, 1986; Edward Said, *Orientalism*, New York, 1978; Mrinalini Sinha, *Colonial Masculinity: The 'Manly Englishman' and the 'Effeminate Bengali' in the Late Nineteenth Century*, Manchester, 1995.
11. For example, Adel used a very strong penis-based castration metaphor when describing to me the assassination of Bashir Gemayel, the leader of the Lebanese Forces. Gemayel was elected Lebanese president following the Israeli invasion of the Lebanon which tipped the balance of power in favour of the Christians that Gemayel represented. Thus, his election gave these Lebanese Christians a strong sense that finally the time had come where they would be able to really control 'the order of things' in Lebanon. It was a unique and even euphoric sense of social empowerment for the many Christians who always felt until then that the Lebanese order of things could never be their order of things, as it had to be always negotiated with Muslims. Describing how he felt after the assassination, at which, as mentioned, he was lightly injured, Adel said that it was 'like having someone cut it in the middle of your best erection ever'.
12. For further elaboration of this and the centrality of the penis, see K. Silverman, *Male Subjectivity at the Margin*, New York, 1992; S. Zizek, *Organs without Bodies: On Deleuze and Consequences*, New York, 2004.
13. P. Bourdieu, *Masculine Domination*, Cambridge, 2001, p. 9.
14. Ibid., pp. 11–2.
15. In this classic ethnography of a tribe in the eastern highland of Papua New Guinea, Herdt (1981) describes what he called 'ritualised homosexuality' involving adults sucking the penises of young boys and swallowing the semen.
16. There is still a very strong endogamous tendency within the village.
17. A. Giddens, *The Transformation of Intimacy: Sexuality, Love and Eroticism in Modern Societies*, Cambridge, 1992.
18. Ibid., p. 27.
19. S. Freud, 'Analysis of a Phobia in a Five-Year Old Boy', in *Complete Psychological Works*, vol. 10, London 1995, pp. 1–149.
20. Ibid., p. 62.
21. J. Gulick, 'The Material Base of a Lebanese Village', in Ailon Shiloh, ed., *Peoples and Cultures of the Middle East*, New York, 1969, pp. 94–5.

Sexuality and the Servant: An Exploration of Arab Images of the Sexuality of Domestic Maids Living in the Household

Ray Jureidini

A history of domestic service in the Arab world over the past century, or post-slavery period, is a history that has yet to be written. Middle-class and wealthy Arab families have always had access to domestic help and a culture that supports the practice of having a non-family member perform the drudgery of domestic labour. Gender studies on the division of labour between husband and wife have not addressed the role of housemaids in middle-class Arab family life. Since the family is so central to the social fabric of Lebanese society,[1] it is somewhat surprising that the role of the housemaid has not been acknowledged either in Lebanon or elsewhere in the social analyses of Arab families.

This chapter is an exploration, rather than a systematic study, of images and perceptions of sexuality of domestic maids in Arab households, with particular reference to Lebanon. The bulk of the data is extracted from ongoing fieldwork on foreign domestic maids. The exploratory investigation involves two basic dimensions. First, there is a review of the portrayal of domestic maids in Arab literature, film and everyday discourse revealing stereotypical constructions that reach the public sphere through various media. Second, from interviews conducted with employers and other household members in Lebanon, issues of fear and control of sexuality, as well as sexual practices are analysed.

Although the empirical focus begins with two synopses of Egyptian films about maids, they are seen as containing broad representational Arab (and indeed, universal) themes. Supplementing the films is a fictional short story of the transformation of a Lebanese maid into a heroine of the civil war. The discussion of the themes raised employs other material which has some bearing on contemporary Lebanon. For example, interviews were conducted with middle-class employers concerning their perceptions and practices in relation to the sexuality of domestic maids.

Altogether one could infer that there are three conceptions of sexuality of maids from the Lebanese employers' context or perspective. First, the maid is perceived as an asexual being; one whose sexuality is implicitly or explicitly denied. Second, she is seen as a highly erotic and sexual being. This naturally involves two dissonant and conflicting implications: that the maid's sexuality becomes legitimate and available for the taking and, perhaps more compelling, she becomes a source of chaos and seduction, and hence a threat to the integrity and well-being of the family.

Within such a context an effort is made to elucidate three related dimensions. First, and by reviewing salient anthropological and sociological studies of Arab families, I disclose and account for the persistent neglect of studies dealing with domestic servants. Why does such a pervasive problem, with some disheartening consequences, remain under-researched? Second, the nature of illicit sexuality and its implications for the well-being of the middle-class family will be explored. Finally, and within the context of what Gamburd terms as 'marginal insiders and intimate outsiders',[2] I present and analyse some of the variable patterns in the perceptions of sexuality of domestic maids and the persistent abuse they are subjected to.

The Domestic Servant as the Quintessential Marginal and Overlooked Entity

Anthropological and sociological studies of Arab families have typically been concerned with gender and kinship relations.[3] They have overlooked the role, influence and work of domestic maids, even though the notion of 'fictive kin' may have been an appropriate perspective. To give one example, an anthropology masters thesis[4] conducted an ethnography of five families. One family employed a maid, butler, cook and driver; another had a full-time live-in maid; one employed a cleaner for three days a week; another brought in a maid only on Sundays. However, nowhere in the thesis is there any explanation of the division of labour in the household that takes the maid into account. We have no names of the maids and no idea who they were or what they did, who directed them or how. Only the 'kin' of the families seemed to matter. Similarly, in Khater's[5] excellent study of emigration, gender and middle-class families in Lebanon 1870–1920, there is a reference to 1884 when some 4,000 impoverished peasants were working as servants in 'the cities',[6] but no further mention of the issue.

Ignoring the servant class seems to be universal. Elias,[7] for example, notes that, despite the most intimate revelations of European court society, little is known of the lives of servants: 'The court people themselves do not talk much about these serving hands that bear them. The *domestiques* live, as it were, behind the scenes of the great theatre of court life'.[8] In a study of domestic service in seventeenth- and eighteenth-century London, Meldrum[9] has been able to reveal a considerable amount of detail on the sexual relations between maids and masters from cases brought before the London Consistory Court.

The 'invisibility' of the servant class from the perspective of the elite that they serve is given poignancy by a remark in the splendidly authentic murder mystery film set on an English aristocratic estate, *Gosford Park*, directed by Robert Altman. Ignoring the intimate knowledge of the maids and male servants, the police inspector dismisses their involvement: 'We're not interested with the servants, only those connected to the dead man' – or later, as 'Mrs Wilson', head of the female servant staff remarks 'I am the perfect servant – I have no life.' In the film, it is revealed that Mrs Wilson had many years prior been forced to give up her child, fathered by her employer, as many others had. It is interesting that although the 'master' had sired many children from his servants over the years, he is mainly vilified for having placed them in an institutional orphanage, rather than have them adopted into decent homes as he had promised. The silence of the servants is one of the consequences of the civilizing process that relegates sex to the realm of secrecy.[10]

Few contemporary Arabic literary works include maids, though they are more prevalent in films. In novels where they are present Arab maids tend to be treated and respected like daughters of the family as in the maid of Sitti Amina in Nagib Mahfouz's novels, or Zennoub, the maid from Akkar (north Lebanon) in Awwad's 1976 novel *Death in Beirut*. In Huda Barakat's 2001 novel, *The Tiller of Waters* (*Hareth al Miyah* or *Le laboureur des eaux*), the young Kurdish maid, Shamsa, is also an accomplished storyteller who is vivid and full of life, memory and seduction. By contrast, a short story by Haifa Bitar presents a victimized Sri Lankan maid 'Indou', who is abused and beaten by her *madame*. At one point she torments Indou by calling her in while she is making love to her husband, saying, 'You can look if you'd like; it might make masturbation easier for you'.[11]

From a patriarchal perspective, male heads of households having 'affairs' with their servants has not been particularly controversial. Karl Marx, for example, fathered a child with his long-serving housemaid. But of course it goes further back into antiquity. From the second century AD, the text on *The Interpretation of Dreams* by Artemidorus explains that a citizen's dream of copulating with servants and slaves signifies that he will 'derive pleasure from one's possessions, which will grow greater and more valuable'.[12] If the master dreamed himself underneath the servant or slave (whether male or female) in the act of sex, it was interpreted as 'a sign that one will suffer harm from this inferior or incur his contempt'.

More historical literature in English on slavery in the Middle East has been forthcoming of late.[13] For example, Marmon's 1999 study of domestic slavery in the Mamluk Empire explains that, although a pious tradition in Islam exhorted followers to treat slaves with kindness, slavery was specifically 'ownership of the physical person'.[14] Formally this implied that the slave enjoyed unlimited rights, yet was mitigated by a conception that, for male slaves at least, they were humans in a state of suspension until they were freed through various mechanisms of manumission. For female slaves, it meant 'the master's right to unrestricted sexual access as well as his absolute rights over the slave woman's offspring', who could all be freed if the master accepted paternity with the statement *farjuki hurrun* ('your sexual organ is free').[15] The *jawareb* were concubines who were often well educated and trained in the arts as entertainers, as musicians, artists and the like. These women are often depicted in the legendary tales of *The Thousand and One Nights*[16] where concubines were inherently playful, manipulative, sexually insatiable and often sought political and other forms of influence through their masters.

While Elias's lack of knowledge of sexuality between masters and servants in European court society is understandable because of the suppression of sexuality into the realm of secrecy, we do have the benefit of Jonathan Swift's playful sarcasm and misogyny that produced his 'Directions to Servants', where he tells us that the housemaid is likely to become pregnant from the footman; that if the lady's waiting maid is 'handsome', she is likely to have her hand squeezed, her breasts fondled or endure the ultimate sexual requirement by her lord (Swift recommends that the maid should 'make him pay' in accordance with the requirement). The chambermaid's lover will most likely be the coachman or the footman and the butler is likely to 'allure the maids with a glass of sack, or white wine and sugar'.[17] In 'a great family', the waiting maid

> will have the choice of three lovers, the chaplain, the steward, and

> my lord's gentleman. I would first advise you to choose the steward; but if you happen to be with young child by my lord, you must take up with the chaplain ...
>
> I must caution you particularly against my lord's eldest son. If you are dexterous enough, it is odds that you may draw him to marry you, and make you a lady; if he be a common rake ... avoid him like Satan ... and after ten thousand promises, you will get nothing from him but a big belly or a clap, and probably both together.[18]

Here we have a recurrent theme of service and sex. On the one hand there is the relationship between a female serving a male in one form or another as they work in close proximity – sexual liaisons are more likely to develop in confined spaces such as workplaces, farmhouses, kitchens and presidential offices of the White House. The power differentials that may result in sexual relations of exploitation, such as that between employers and employees, teachers and pupils, therapists and patients, priests and parishioners, masters and slaves, presidents and interns – in other words, where a fiduciary relationship exists – are seemingly basic to human affective behaviour.[19]

Pateman argues that there is very little past or contemporary difference in the contractual relations between civil slaves, servants and housewives who 'labour at the behest of their masters'.[20] In an interesting similarity, Marmon explains that in the Mamluk period, *both* marriage and slavery involved:

> a kind of *milk* or ownership. The husband pays a certain sum to his prospective wife through her *wali* or guardian and thus acquires the right to exclusive sexual access, the right to claim her offspring as members of the kinship group, and the right to exercise a fairly broad control over her person and her activities. The jurists described this transaction as resulting in a *milk* or ownership of the woman's sexual organ: '*nikah* (marriage) is a contract, the purpose of which is ownership of sexual access'.[21]

Another view highlights the relationship between dirt and domesticity. Derivative of the work of Mary Douglas, Palmer[22] suggests that, in part, the middle-class unconscious implies an association between 'bad' dirt and 'good' cleanliness. Naturally, this also translates into sexuality: 'dirt and sex live in close association, and women who clean up things associated with bodies find themselves mysteriously deemed sexual and powerful regardless of their actual social status'.[23] To be a 'good woman', the middle-class housewife seeks to maintain her image of 'sexual purity' and 'pristine domesticity' and transfers the 'bad in woman' to the housemaid who is employed to do the dirty work.

Illicit Sexuality and the Middle-Class Family

The association between sexuality and the drudgery of housework has a number of layers in the representation of housemaids, not only in the Western unconscious, but also in the Arab world. The following three synopses illuminate the theme of illicit sexuality (underhanded, morally abhorrent, dirty) and the contested relations between middle-class women and men in relation to domestic maids. The first two synopses are derived from narrative episodes of two popular Egyptian films, the third is extracted from Mai Ghaussoub's *Leaving Beirut* (1998), a collection of vivid portraits of women coping with the travails of civil unrest.

Synopsis 1

In the 1983 Egyptian film, *al-Khadima* (The Maid) – directed by Ishraf Fahmi and starring Nadia al-Jundi – a young woman, Fardous, murders her elderly husband after he catches her with her lover. Widowed, she is offered a job as a well-paid maid at the house of a wealthy middle-aged woman and her only child, Ala', an attractive bachelor. Fardous refuses at first, claiming this kind of work is beneath her. Her lover however encourages her, suggesting she could make a fortune and she accepts. All goes well at first, until, at the suggestion of her lover, she begins to seduce the inexperienced Ala'. Returning from a failed attempt at losing his virginity with an old prostitute, Fardous consoles Ala', suggesting she can 'help' him, but he arrogantly rebuffs her. Fardous responds aggressively: 'Don't think that just because I'm a servant that I'm ignorant and know nothing ... I've tried the world and I know what boys like you want.' Her seduction works and they sleep together. One day, Ala's mother, who is obsessively protective of her son, discovers the affair and dismisses the maid. In a countermove, Fardous convinces Ala' to marry her, thus enabling her to return to the household as a 'mistress' rather than maid, in defiance of the mother. With her new husband's approval, Fardous begins to take charge of the family business, embezzling money with the company accountant, with whom she has an affair. When Ala' catches her in bed with the accountant, he divorces her. She is left with no option but to return to her first lover who subsequently murders her.

Synopsis 2

The film, *Afwah wa Araneb* (Mouths and Rabbits) – directed by Barakat, starring Faten Hamama and Mahmoud Yassin – is similar to *al-Khadima*, but unlike *al-Khadima*'s conniving Fardous, the film's good-natured Neamat earns her class mobility through honesty, industriousness and dedication, in a 'Pygmalion-type' tale.[24] At the beginning of the film, Neamat is a single attractive rural woman, later a hard-working factory worker who supports her sister, who has nine children and an alcoholic husband. She turns down her first suitor because he has not the money to support her and her sister's family. She turns down her second suitor because, while wealthy, he is a corrupt thief. When her first suitor returns with a bundle of money, Neamat's face lights up with the prospect of a comfortable life at last. But when she discovers that he had stolen the money, she turns him down. When her sister and brother-in-law begin plotting to have her marry the wealthy, corrupt suitor, Neamat runs away to the next village where she works harvesting in a large vineyard. She is rapidly promoted to domestic service for the estate's owner, a handsome bachelor, and she becomes increasingly involved in running the estate, taking initiatives, proposing new projects and of course, winning her boss's admiration. One day, accompanying her boss to Cairo, he announces his intention to get engaged to an upper-class woman. Neamat is secretly heartbroken. The new fiancée is instantly suspicious of Neamat and is visibly annoyed that she is given so much importance, credit and praise. Gripped by jealousy, she makes her fiancé decide between her and Neamat. He chooses Neamat and proposes to her. The film ends happily with the two marrying and Neamat's family becoming financially secure forever.

Synopsis 3

In Mai Ghoussoub, 'The Heroism of Umm Ali', in *Leaving Beirut: Women and the Wars Within,* Latifa is a nine-year-old girl from North Lebanon, who was brought to a Beirut household to work as a maid. She quickly becomes the family's scapegoat, particularly for the stepmother, Umm Wasim and her son. Latifa's services to the house are endless, from dawn to the late hours of the night. She is basically enslaved, since she does not get her own salary. Instead, her alcoholic father comes to collect the money every month without even asking to see her or taking her out. One night, Wasim rapes Latifa in her bed, which is made up on the kitchen floor (she

does not have her own room). The family, of course, is quick to conceal the 'accident'. The girl is taken to a clinic to 'restore' her virginity. The story suggests that Wasim continues to sleep with Latifa for a long time. This renders the girl not only a maid, but also a ready source of sexual relief for the household's protected son. Umm Wasim later accuses Latifa of seducing her son in the attempt to win his heart and hand, so as to climb the social strata by having access to the family's resources. Although the family suffers from financial problems, Umm Wasim's apprehension towards Latifa is a classic example of the fear of 'marrying down' as a threat to family status and prestige, even where money is not available to be fretted over. Latifa becomes a teenager while the Lebanese Civil War is in full rage. She comes to admire militia men and decides to join their ranks. One day, while on her way to buy bread for her host family, she leaves, never to return. She subsequently becomes a fearless, militia woman with the nom de guerre, *Umm Ali* ('sister of men'), and proves herself to be the equal of other fighters in battle.

Similar to the two films, Ghoussoub gives the maid Latifa a way out of domestic servitude and transforms her – from the passive subservience of child labour to having agency in early adulthood – through the paradoxical mediation of the civil war. But here, rather than marry, the maid had to adopt the violent ways of men in order to win respect as a woman because of her status. Her victimization at the domestic/familial level is relieved by the armed struggle at the national level.

'Marginal Insiders and Intimate Outsiders'

The three stories, the first tragic, the other two with more romantic endings, raise at least two general issues. First, they depict the threat or 'danger' of maids as strangers – their sexuality and the threat this brings to the middle-class family. Second, maids may be either decent or evil; it is the 'luck-of-the-draw'. And the same may be said of the households they enter into. The family and the domestic sphere is a highly charged emotional and sexual arena.

In the first synopsis, the maid is an evil, self-seeking manipulator. In the second, she is angelic, decent, moral, hard-working and genuinely dedicated to her employer. In the third, she is a victim, abused from childhood, but finds an unusual way out. In all three there are prospects for social mobility – of escaping the world of servitude, particularly in the two films where the maid marries into the employing family. The salience of these stories is that many of the themes resonate in real life. Indeed, considerable evidence

from my fieldwork substantiates these recurrent themes.

Extensive mechanisms are exercised to maintain distinct power and status relations, particularly between the *madame* and maid where the greatest interactional intensity resides. Since the recent displacement of Arab maids from South and West Asia (from Lebanon 1990 and from the Gulf States in the 1980s) the proportion of women whose culture, history and families remain relatively understudied has increased substantively. This is compounded by the element of mystique and dread, particularly since it involves the lives of displaced and marginalized domestic servants.

Asian maids are not only 'strangers' in the house, they are also foreigners and thus ethnically, religiously and visibly different. There is an acculturation process to be undertaken in fulfilling the often idiosyncratic requirements of the Arab family and the *madame*, in particular. However, for Simmel, the formal position of the stranger is at the same time the 'unity of nearness and remoteness'.[25] That is, the presence of the stranger is simultaneously close but distant, familiar but unknown. Much like the stranger, in other words, the domestic servant is largely a byproduct of a permanent and irreconcilable dissonance. The tension of this ambivalence is ever present in relations between the migrant as the stranger in the host community.[26] The maid belongs in the household (in a paid capacity) and is privy to family intimacies but she does not belong to the family and thus cannot participate in those intimacies (although it may be forced upon her). Gamburd suggests something similar in her study of Sri Lankan returnees from the Arab states. Domestic maids, she says, are both 'marginal insiders and intimate outsiders'.[27] Although living in close quarters, privy to the intimate relations between family members – tidying, washing their clothes, cleaning after them, taking care of their children and domestic animals, preparing food, serving and so on – they are nonetheless distinguished, not only in appearance, but in the separation from the family in personal, everyday activities. For example, maids do not usually eat at the same table or at the same time. They do not (or rarely) bring friends 'home', but rather rely upon another maid accompanying a visiting family to make social contact (in the kitchen), or communicate with other maids by so-called 'balcony talk'. Using the insights of Erving Goffman, Rollins points out that the differentiation and inequality of maids is perpetuated by linguistic, physical and spatial 'deference' – calling the employer 'Madame' or 'Sir'; never initiating unnecessary conversation; strict avoidance of touching the body of the employer and maintaining distance throughout the geographical space of the household.[28]

It is interesting to note that, while the kitchen is the main domicile for the maid, in Lebanese families the *madame* of the household is the one who actually cooks the meals. Maids are more usually involved in assisting food preparation, such as cutting vegetables or soaking the rice. However, Western expatriate professionals in Lebanon who consider it a luxury to employ live-in maids, are more likely to allow them to cook meals without supervision. The reluctance of Lebanese to allow a Sri Lankan or Filipina maid to cook for the household – the man of the house in particular – is not entirely explained by fears of pollution, the incompetence of the maids, cleanliness or even the special pride Lebanese have for their traditional cuisine. A suggestion is made in Hansen's 1989 study of servants and employers in Zambia where it is argued that female rural Zambian housemaids have an image of being 'oversexed' and competing for the husbands of their female employers.[29] In order to reduce the possibilities of sexual indulgence, contact with the male head of household is minimized. Hansen explains that bedrooms and the preparation of food are both particularly 'sexually charged' domains. 'Zambian women householders feared that their female servants would mix love potions into the husband's food in order to attract his sexual attentions'.[30] Rather than 'love potions', it may be suggested that boys in Arab families are raised with serious indulgence when it comes to food. In typical Mediterranean fashion, Lebanese mothers (and sisters) serve food to the male members of the household with loving attention to detail. Whoever prepares and serves the food will most likely stir the emotions of the male recipients. The wives are more likely to want to ensure that *they* are the ones who will gain the gratitude and affections that are aroused by food.

By virtue of their outsider status, the presence of live-in domestic workers creates a public space (the maid's work place) located in the private sphere of the home. There is an assumption that, if a maid has her own private room, there is less likelihood of any 'sexual tension' between the maid and male members of the household. Recalling Ghoussoub's story, it is emphasized that the rape of Latifa is on the kitchen floor. In one of my interviews with a female employer I was told:

> Konjeet [the Sri Lankan maid] had been at a previous Lebanese employer for six months when she came to us. We found out (indirectly) that she left the other house because they didn't have a separate room for her. She slept on the balcony and the madam there had two sons ... She was afraid for her.[31]

Proximity and accessibility is naturally of spatial and architectural concern. The maid is assumed to be more 'available' if she sleeps in the kitchen, living room or balcony. If she has her own room, she is considered less accessible. Recent architectural plans indicate that some new apartment buildings in Lebanon are designing the entrance of maids' quarters exclusively from the balcony. The spatial symbolism reflects the desire for a greater separation of the maid from the family. With a stranger in the house, discretion is always required. Such spatial isolation reduces the freedom of intimacy. It also provides greater privacy for the maid and acts as a buffer zone against intrusion.

Deference, distinction and separateness within the household are replicated in attitudes towards activities outside the house, when the maids are beyond the direct surveillance of the family. One thirty-four-year-old employer made it clear that she allows no unaccompanied outings for her Sri Lankan maid. She explained that her attitude developed from a traumatic past experience with an Ethiopian maid who, although single, arrived pregnant:

> We didn't know about it at first because the blood tests they do for maids don't include pregnancy tests. The girl complained of chronic stomach aches. I exempted her from work when this happened. One day, her pains got severe so we called a doctor. He said that she was pregnant and that she was giving birth on the spot, to a premature girl. The pregnancy did not show on her. I was furious. We had to pay the hospital bill for her and had to send her home having paid for the contract with the agency. We had no medical insurance for her. The hospital nuns asked to adopt the child to a black couple who were looking for a baby, so they took her and paid for the incubation. I wanted to fire the maid on the spot because I couldn't trust her anymore.
>
> I took the maid to the police station to break the contract, but there she reported that it was my husband who had made her pregnant and would not give her the baby so they took him in for questioning. We told the police that this was ridiculous. The maid had only been with us for five and a half months while the baby was seven and a half months old. My husband told the police, 'Whose interests are you protecting after all, those of foreigners or Lebanese?' They cancelled the charges and that was that.

The sentiments here are similar to the study of local domestic maids in Ghana by Sanjek who explains that employer objections to 'sexual encounters' are based on the time taken for liaisons and fears that they may become 'lackadaisical about her duties while she is thinking about being with her boyfriend'.[32] More importantly, the employer is also legitimately concerned about fears of pregnancy and the ensuing responsibilities and costs he might have to assume. In Lebanon, opportunities for live-in maids to find partners are few. It is well-known (and normatively accepted) that most migrant domestic maids are not allowed out of the house unaccompanied by a family member. Some are even locked in the apartment during the day or night when the family is absent. It is estimated that there are approximately 120,000 Sri Lankans, 30,000 Filipinas and 30,000 Ethiopians working as housemaids in Lebanon as of January 2004.[33] When asked whether she minded if her Filipina maid went out on a regular basis one Lebanese interviewee clearly did not approve: 'She might find a boyfriend or bring back diseases or get pregnant. It is not convenient for me.' In her study comparing contemporary migrant domestic workers with slavery, Anderson notes:

> Unlike the children of slave women ... the children of domestic workers are not the property of her employers. They serve not to increase the employer's capital but to provide an unwelcome distraction from the domestic worker's main responsibility, which is the employing family rather than her own children. Migrant domestic workers, unlike slave women, are positively discouraged from having children ... Generally, workers are concerned not to get pregnant because they would lose their jobs, yet they are also conscious that in many instances they are forfeiting their own chance to have children by remaining as migrant domestic workers for their crucial reproductive years.[34]

The extent to which domestic maids are willing partners in sexual liaisons with members of the employing family is something that is difficult to ascertain. Seduction may be on either side or it may be coerced. The maid's actions in having sex with the children or with the husband, or just flirting, may be an expression of genuine affection, or a form of assertion of her seductive powers competing with the dominant *madame* of the house.

One Lebanese respondent (fifty years old) admitted that, as a teenager in the late 1960s, he and his close male friends used to regularly compare notes and even enter into competitive discourse about their sexual relations with their respective maids (an Arab maid at that time). When asked how compliant the maid was in all this, he responded that she was a perfectly willing partner – 'she liked it'. He noted that his mother would regularly take the maid to the doctor for a check up to see if she had been having sex with her husband. (How the doctor was able to reassure her is unknown.) Another respondent (Lebanese male in his forties) noted how some mothers and fathers in fact encouraged their sons to have sex with the maid to introduce manhood. So the sexual relations with the domestic maid can be viewed in at least two contradictory ways – one as a threat to the honour and integrity of the family, and the other as providing assistance in the validations of one's heterosexual masculinity. Psychoanalytically, it may be worth pondering over whether the maid here might be an Oedipal 'mother substitute'.

In what must be an exceptional case with very liberal employers, there is the story of the Filipina, Penni, who had been in Lebanon some three years when her friend from the same village in the Philippines arrived. Penni pleaded with another family in the building where a friend (Onti) worked to employ her because she was being abused and her salary was not being paid. On the first night at her new employer's apartment (a retired professional couple with three children still living at home in Ashrafieh), Penni announced that she did not want to sleep in the apartment, but preferred to sleep downstairs with Onti. Neither of the families objected, as it was considered convenient to have both maids content and assisting one another when required. However, Penni began to fret during the following summer when, having moved to the mountains, she was unable to see or be with her partner. The other family subsequently bought an apartment in the same mountain retreat building so they could be together. The happy arrangement has been ongoing for seventeen years. In late 2003, however, both partners (who had been honoured by the priest for their weekly Bible readings at Mass) decided that, in order to be good Christians, they would cease their lesbian sexual relationship and just remain close friends. When asked if this was now a better arrangement, the twenty-five-year-old daughter, who had been brought up by Penni, replied: 'No. We want them to have sexual relations because they are what they are.'

For some people, domestic workers are assumed to be 'sexually available' in addition to their domestic chores. In Europe, advertisements for domestic maids are used as alternatives to advertising for prostitutes.[35] It is for this reason, that single males in Lebanon and elsewhere cannot sponsor a foreign domestic maid. On Saturday and Sunday evenings, Lebanese men of all ages can be seen circling in their cars around a small night club/karaoke bar for Filipinas in Sin El Fil (run by a Lebanese and his Filipina lover). The Filipina in this case was publicly presented as his wife even though everyone knew he was married to a Lebanese. The Filipina was subsequently arrested and deported for operating illegally as a recruitment agent. They cruise around like tomcats in the hope that they can entice one of the women into their car for a good time on their night off.

Incidentally, such instances of prostitution are legion. It is interesting to note the story of MS, a twenty-three-year-old Lebanese AUB graduate with a Lebanese girlfriend. They are close friends but with no sexual relationship between them. He says he loves her a lot. She knows that he has sexual relations with other women, but that, according to MS, 'she knows it is just for the sex'. He says he has 'tried all kinds of women – Lebanese, Ethiopians, Filipinas, Sri Lankans, Russians – but he prefers Ethiopians because they are cheap' (10–15,000LL) and 'they know how to do things'. Although there is an Ethiopian maid in his home, he has never tried to do anything with her. He goes to bars to choose the girls he wants. His friend PT, a twenty-four-year-old AUB student, has also had a Lebanese girlfriend for five years. They too have no sexual relations. He says that once or twice a week he has sex with Ethiopian women, sometimes with more than one at a time. Sometimes more than one guy has sex with the same woman, one after the other. He noted carefully, that 'it is never against her will, because she gets paid from everyone'. He says that Ethiopians are known for their sexual skill and he gets more pleasure from them. It is interesting to note that similar permissive and lusty sexual escapades with Ethiopian women were reported in nineteenth-century Morocco. Ethiopian concubines were considered 'a cool paradise in hot weather and armor against the cold, her touch cures the sufferer, satisfies lust, dispels ills due to cold and damp, and eases back and joint pain'.[36]

It is difficult, of course, to rely confidently on such reports, for young men are typically prone to braggadocio. However it is well-known that, in addition to the Ethiopians, Sri Lankan women who run away from their employers often find the need to prostitute themselves cheaply, servicing mainly Syrian workers as well as Egyptian and Indian labourers, charging just enough for them to survive on a weekly basis. By contrast, other interviews have revealed that Sri Lankans, Ethiopians and Filipinas can be more conservative than the Lebanese families they are in. They are often highly religious, very attentive to observing praying and other religious services whenever possible. For example, in an interview with a thirty-four-year-old employer with two children:

> Q: Are women in your country more sexually free than Lebanese women?
>
> A: I don't know about Sri Lanka in general but the girls who worked at my house were actually more conservative than we are.

> Q: Given the chance, do you think a maid who has a husband back home would seek sexual relations with another man here in Lebanon?
>
> A: She might. They're just like you or me.
>
> Q: Do you prefer a married to a single maid?
>
> A: We've always had married maids. It's a coincidence. I do prefer it though because if she is single she might look for a male friend. If she is married, however, then at least she knows what sex is when she comes to us, and she would probably not look for it. But I don't find maids to be sex-oriented generally.

From a seventy-five-year-old woman with six children:

> In the case of Mala, I never told her anything. One time she told me she was at her cousin, then her uncle, then her sister. Every time she slept out she was at someone new, as if her whole family were here. I never asked her if there was a man in the story because she was married, you see. Anyway, she would have denied it so what would have been the use? If she had said yes, I would have sent her home.

There are occasionally reports of severe sexual abuse and rape of domestic maids. Such reports tend to be more numerous in the Gulf States than in Lebanon, although the frequency of rape can never be known because it often goes unreported. For example, Middle East Watch Women's Rights Project (1992) in Kuwait 'found that one third of the sixty cases they investigated involved rape or sexual assault by employers'. In her study of domestic workers in the Gulf, Sabban states that

> most complaints of sexual abuse reported by foreign female domestic workers were against older men, either in Saudi Arabia, or in the Emirates ... This phenomenon is one of the outcomes of the oil booms ... Elderly males find themselves suddenly rich, but socially frustrated, and with no roles or pleasure. Their first source of pleasure is poor women, whose easier, cheaper and younger sexuality can alleviate their frustrations.[37]

Further, a BBC radio report (4 December 2003) documented the case of Soma, a Sri Lankan, who had returned from domestic service in Lebanon. The following is an extract from the transcript of the report:

> ... forty-one-year-old Soma ... recalls repeated rapes by the eighteen-

> year-old son of her female employer.
>
> 'When I went to his bedroom he closed the door and removed my clothes and his. When I tried to resist he threatened to kill me,' she says.
>
> Soma says she begged him to spare her on the grounds that she had a son his age.
>
> 'Another day, his four friends came to the house. When I took tea to the room they closed the door and kept me on their laps and started to touch my body and abuse me,' she says in tears. All the men then raped her.
>
> There was little comfort from Soma's employer, who seemed to think she had employed a prostitute for her son rather than a cleaner for her house.
>
> 'I complained to his mother and she just said, "I will give you pills to make sure you don't get pregnant" and she beat me.'
>
> Soma eventually escaped from the flat and walked for four hours until she met by chance a Sri Lankan couple who took her home, fed her and took her to the embassy.
>
> Although the rapes were reported to the embassy and police, Soma was just put on a plane home. Nothing happened to her rapists.

It is clear from the report that the maid is treated as an object, rather than as a human being. This objectification is brought into more relief with the case of a twenty-two-year-old Congolese woman (Assina) who, not long after arrival in Lebanon, was found to be pregnant. As she was ill during the pregnancy, she could not work properly. She was returned to the recruitment agency by her employer where she was beaten and had her life threatened. Faced with losing the costs paid to have her brought to Lebanon, the agent allegedly forced her to have an abortion against her will.[38]

It should be noted finally that the reputation of maids in Arab countries can be particularly negative in the countries of origin. In 1996, for example, Colonel Nissanka Wijeratne, then chairman of the Sri Lankan Bureau of Foreign Employment, was quoted as saying: 'The real problem is that 80 percent of the women in Kuwait must sleep with their masters. They are merely regarded as sex slaves'.[39] From interviews with local Sri Lankan men in the village, Gamburd's study of returnee maids from the Gulf shows how suspicion is placed upon Sri Lankan women working abroad. Stories of '[u]nwanted pregnancies, secret abortions and attempted infanticide'[40] are revealed to indicate the health dangers posed, but in reality bring moral questions of promiscuity upon the women more stereotypically. As one male villager explained: 'In the Middle East, Sri Lankan women are like prostitutes ... Muslim people's sons [are] fond of womanizing, and so the family hires a couple of housemaids so that the sons stay home instead of going out'.[41] This was, however, the perception of Sri Lankan men, which bore little resemblance to the stories told by most of the women.

When asked 'Do you think foreign maids have standards of honour and shame for women?' one interviewee said:

> Yes. They are decent people. Once I told her [Sri Lankan maid] to stay away from the window because there are men who might look at her from there and sure enough she never stood by that window again. Also, even though (my husband) is an old man – he's eighty-five – she avoids him, she shies away from him.

There is no way to generalize the sexuality and sexual behaviour of domestic maids and their relations in Lebanese families. In reality, it is most probable that most domestic maids in Lebanon maintain the values of hard work and virtuousness. They are there mainly to earn money for their families back home. It may also be the case that most are treated decently by their employers and with respect and gratitude for their services. The media and social scientists wanting legal and social reform, however, tend to highlight the extreme cases of abuse and exploitation, but these are nevertheless instructive. What is clear is that the existence of maids as strangers in the family can be fraught with sexual fears and sexual tension. A Lebanese television talk-show hostess suggested that the existence of foreign maids in Arab households is 'simply not viable':

> We live in an authoritarian system. The woman is head of the household and runs it in an authoritarian manner. She is responsible for the children and the maid and all aspects of the house. So, she treats the maid the same as she does her children. Her attitude and her moral rules are the same. The same moral principles regarding her daughters' restrictions are applied to the maid. She is not allowed out alone in case she gets involved with a man.

But the fact is that many are 'allowed out' and their public and private visibility in Lebanon continues to increase and community networks invariably develop that give some semblance of at least a temporary 'home'. When contracting or 'importing' migrant domestic labour, it is all too often forgotten by employers that it is more than 'labour' that they are bringing in to the country. Human beings are employed, who have their own hopes and dreams as well as sexual desires and needs. These desires, of at least some women, may be voluntarily suppressed or coercively repressed. Others, however, find ways to fulfill them as best they can. Sexual liaisons between maids and family members of the household sometimes occur and others find partners, whether local Lebanese, from their countries of origin, or from other countries such as India, Egypt or Syria.

Following the civil war in Lebanon, it has been suggested that: 'Given the large-scale devastation of state and other secular agencies and institutions, the family was one of the few remaining social edifices in which people could seek and find refuge in its reassuring domesticity and privacy'.[42] The reassuring domesticity and privacy of many or possibly most households is both enhanced as well as undermined by the employment of migrant domestic workers in Lebanon today. On the one hand, the migrant women are 'admired' for their tenacity and courage to travel to a place such as Lebanon, unaccompanied. On the other hand, they are reviled for that very condition. Those that have left their immediate families behind (often husbands and children) are considered both in terms of pity (*haram*) and scorn (how can they do it?).

The ignorance and cultural 'invisibility' of migrant domestic workers is linked to employers not knowing, or not wanting to be familiar with, the origins of their domestic maids, whether from the Philippines, Sri Lanka or Ethiopia, for long genealogies signify 'power and the exploits of the strong. The "weak" have no genealogies, no roots'.[43] Without their families close by and visible, foreign domestic maids are vulnerable to the fears, fantasies and favours of their employers. While it is preferred that servants remain invisible, they nevertheless pervade topics of conversation in coffeehouses and restaurants that middle-class women frequent during the day. Their sexuality, however, is something that is more associated with the underworld, the dirty side of domesticity.

What seems interesting is that, with the replacement of Arab women with Asian and African migrant domestic maids in Lebanese households, the theme of the maid as a threat, usurping the dominance in the family through her sexual wiles, has disappeared. The cultural and physical difference is more likely to prohibit committed liaisons. It is one thing to marry across class or religion in the Arab world. It is another to break through racial and ethnic barriers. While dalliances seen as exotic by Lebanese men and youth may be increasingly common, the likelihood of such marriages is very slim.

Perceptions of the sexuality of domestic maids do vary as we have seen, but we are still faced with the analytical task of determining why some portray them as victims, while others see them as oversexed and others as normal human beings. Tolerance and abuse both cut across class, religious and gender lines. Following Simmel, the key may be in the peculiar alienated, yet integrated, space of a stranger in the home and the ways that individuals adapt to their foreign environment and the different ways that employers allow or deny them their own sexual agency.

Note

I would like to thank Samar Kanafani for her assistance in the research for this chapter and for her comments on an earlier draft. Thanks to Iman Humaydan for her insightful suggestions on maids in Arab literature. Responsibility for errors and obfuscations of course resides with the author.

Bibliography

Anderson, Bridgit, *Doing the Dirty Work: The Global Politics of Domestic Labour*, London: Zed Books, 2000.

Awwad, Tawfiq, *Death in Beirut*, London: Heinemann, 1976.

Barakat, Huda, *The Tiller of Waters*, Cairo: American University in Cairo Press, 2001.

Bitar, Haifa, 'Indou', in *The Din of the Body* (*Dhajeej al-Jasad*), Beirut: Dar An-Nahar, 2002.

Burton, Sir Richard, tr., *The Arabian Nights' Entertainments*, 12 vols, London: Nichols, 1886.

Diken, Bulent, *Strangers, Ambivalence and Social Theory*, Ashgate: Aldershot. 1998.

Elias, Norbert, *The Court Society,* Oxford: Basil Blackwell, 1983.

Ennaji, Mohammed, *Serving the Master: Slavery and Society in Nineteenth-Century Morocco*, New York: St Martin's Press, 1998.

Erdem, Y Hakan, *Slavery in the Ottoman Empire and its Demise 1800–1909*, Oxford: Macmillan, 1996.

Foucault, Michel, *The Care of the Self*, vol. 3 of *The History of Sexuality*, New York: Vintage Books, 1986.

Gamburd, Michel, *The Kitchen Spoon's Handle: Transnationalism and Sri Lanka's Migrant Housemaids*, Ithaca, NY: Cornell University Press, 2000.

Game, Anne, and Metcalf, Andrew, *Passionate Sociology*, London: SAGE, 1996.

Ghoussoub, Mai, 'The Heroism of Umm Ali', in Mai Ghoussoub, ed., *Leaving Beirut:*

Women and the Wars Within, London: Saqi Books, 1998.
Hansen, K., *Distant Companions: Servant and Employers in Zambia, 1900–1985*, Ithaca, NY: Cornell University Press, 1989.
Joseph, Suad, ed., *Intimate Selving: Self, Gender and Identity in Arab Families*, Syracuse: Syracuse University Press, 1999.
Jureidini, Ray, *Women Migrant Domestic Workers in Lebanon*, International Migration Papers, no. 48, Geneva: International Labour Organization, 2002.
Khalaf, Samir, 'On Roots and Routes: The Reassertion of Primordial Loyalties', in Theodor Hanf and Nawaf Salam, eds, *Lebanon in Limbo: Postwar Society and State in an Uncertain Regional Environment*, Baden Baden: Nomos Verlagsgesellschaft, 2003.
Khater, Akram, *Inventing Home: Emigration, Gender and the Middle Class in Lebanon 1870–1920*, Berkeley: University of California Press, 2001.
Khuri, Fuad, 'The Ascent to Top Office in Arab-Islamic Culture: A Challenge to Democracy', in Paul Salem, ed., *Conflict Resolution in the Arab World: Selected Essays*, Beirut: American University of Beirut, 1997.
Le Gall, Michel, 'Translation of Louis Frank's Memoir on the Traffic in Negroes in Cairo and on the Illnesses to which they are Subject upon arrival there, 1802', in Shaun Marmon, ed., *Slavery in the Islamic Middle East*, Princeton: Markus Wiener, 1999.
Lewis, Bernard, *Race and Slavery in the Middle East: An Historical Inquiry*, New York: Oxford University Press, 1992.
Marmon, Shaun, 'Domestic Slavery in the Mamluk Empire: A Preliminary Sketch', in Shaun Marmon, ed., *Slavery in the Islamic Middle East*, Princeton: Markus Wiener, 1999.
Meldrum, Tim, *Domestic Service and Gender: 1660–1750. Life and Work in the London Household*, London: Longman, 2000.
Middle East Watch, 'Punishing the Victim: Rape and Mistreatment of Asian Maids in Kuwait', Women's Rights Project, 1992.
Myntti, Cynthia, 'Domestic Roles of Arab Women: Case Studies of Beirut Women Concerning Power, Status and Behavior', MA thesis, American University of Beirut, June 1974.
Palmer, Phyllis, *Domesticity and Dirt: Housewives and Domestic Servants in the United States, 1920–1945*, Philadelphia: Temple University Press, 1989.
Pateman, Carole, *The Sexual Contract*, Oxford: Polity Press, 1988.
Rollins, Janet, *Between Women: Domestics and their Employers*, Philadelphia: Temple University Press, 1985.
Rollins, Janet, 'Ideology and Servitude', in R. Sanjek and S. Colen, eds, *At Work in Homes: Household Workers in World Perspective*, Washington DC, American Ethnological Society, Monograph Series, no. 3, 1990.
Sabban, R., 'Foreign Female Domestic Workers in the United Arab Emirates', Paper presented ast the CLARA Workshop on Domestic Service and Mobility. The International Institute od Social History, Amsterdam, 5–7 February 2001.
Sanjek, Roger, 'Maid Servants and Market Women's Apprentices in Adabraka', in R. Sanjek and S. Colen, eds, *At Work in Homes: Household Workers in World*

Perspective, Washington, DC: American Ethnological Society, Monograph Series, no. 3, 1990.

Seng, Yvonne, 'A Liminal State: Slavery in Sixteenth-Century Istanbul', in Shaun Marmon, ed., *Slavery in the Islamic Middle East*, Princeton: Markus Wiener, 1999.

Simmel, Georg, 'The Stranger', in Kurt Wolff, tr. and ed., *The Sociology of Georg Simmel*, New York: Free Press, 1950.

Smith, Monica., 'Beaten, Forced to Abort her Child, a Woman Fights Back', *The Daily Star*, 28 March, 2004.

Swift, Jonathan, 'Directions to the Housemaid', in 'Directions to Servants' in *The Works of Jonathan Swift*, vol. 2, London: Henry Bohn, 1852.

Notes

1. Samir Khalaf, 'On Roots and Routes: The Reassertion of Primordial Loyalties', Baden Baden, 2003.
2. Michel Gamburd, *The Kitchen Spoon's Handle: Transnationalism and Sri Lanka's Migrant Housemaids*, Ithaca, 2000.
3. Suad Joseph, *Intimate Selving: Self, Gender and Identity in Arab Families*, Syracuse, 1999.
4. Cynthia Myntti, 'Domestic Roles of Arab Women: Case Studies of Beirut Women Concerning Power, Status and Behavior', Beirut, 1974.
5. Akram Khater, *Inventing Home: Emigration, Gender and the Middle Class in Lebanon 1870–1920*, Berkeley, 2001.
6. Ibid., p. 61.
7. Norbert Elias, *The Court Society*, Oxford, 1983.
8. Ibid., p. 45.
9. Tim Meldrum, *Domestic Service and Gender: 1660–1750. Life and Work in the London Household*, London, 2000.
10. Norbert Elias, 1983, p. 189.
11. Haifa Bitar, *The Din of the Body* (*Dhajeej al-Jasad*), Beirut, 2002, p. 197.
12. Michel Foucault, *The Care of the Self*, vol. 3 of *The History of Sexuality*, New York, 1988, p. 19.
13. See Bernard Lewis, *Race and Slavery in the Middle East: An Historical Inquiry*, New York, 1992; Y. Hakan Erdem, *Slavery in the Ottoman Empire and its Demise 1800–1909*, Oxford, 1996; Seng, 1999; Michel Le Gall, 'Translation of Louis Frank's Memoir on the Traffic in Negroes in Cairo and on the Illnesses to which they are Subject upon arrival there, 1802', in Shaun Marmon, ed., *Slavery in the Islamic Middle East*, Princeton 1999.
14. Shaun Marmon, 'Domestic Slavery in the Mamluk Empire: A Preliminary Sketch', Princeton, 1999.
15. Ibid., pp. 4–5.
16. Sir Richard Burton, *The Arabian Nights' Entertainments*, 12 vols, London, 1886.
17. Jonathan Swift, 'Directions to the Housemaid', London, 1852, p. 359.
18. Ibid., p. 366.
19. See Anne Game and Andrew Metcalf, *Passionate Sociology*, London, 1996, p. 162, on pupils' sexual desire linked to the desire for knowledge.
20. Carole Pateman, *The Sexual Contract*, Oxford 1988, p. 116.

21. Shaun Marmon, 'Domestic Slavery in the Mamluk Empire: A Preliminary Sketch', in Shaun Marmon, ed., *Slavery in the Islamic Middle East*, Princeton, 1999, p.19.
22. Phyllis Palmer, *Domesticity and Dirt: Housewives and Domestic Servants in the United States, 1920–1945*, Philadelphia, 1989.
23. Ibid., p. 138.
24. This is also the main theme of many British and American films, the most recent being *A Maid in Manhattan*.
25. Georg Simmel, 'The Stranger', New York, 1950, p. 402.
26. Bulent Diken, *Strangers, Ambivalence and Social Theory*, Ashgate, 1998, p. 126.
27. Michel Gamburd, 2000, p. 228.
28. Janet Rollins, *Between Women: Domestics and their Employers*, Philadelphia, 1985.
29. K. Hansen, *Distant Companions: Servant and Employers in Zambia, 1900–1985*, Ithaca, 1989.
30. Ibid., p. 266.
31. It should be noted that, in all interviews with employers, descriptions and explanations of mistreatment of maids tends to be expressed in terms of 'other people', never the interviewee.
32. Roger Sanjek, 'Maid Servants and Market Women's Apprentices in Adabraka', Washington DC, 1990, p. 44.
33. Ray Jureidini, *Women Migrant Domestic Workers in Lebanon*, Geneva, 2002.
34. Bridgit Anderson, *Doing the Dirty Work: The Global Politics of Domestic Labour*, London, 2000, p. 134.
35. Ibid.
36. Mohammed Ennaji, *Serving the Master: Slavery and Society in Nineteenth-Century Morocco*, New York, 1998, p. 34.
37. R. Sabban, 'Foreign Female Domestic Workers in the United Arab Emirates', Amsterdam, 2001, p. 33.
38. Monica Smith, 'Beaten, Forced to Abort her Child, a Woman Fights Back', Beirut, 2004.
39. Michel Gamburd, 2000, p. 212.
40. Ibid., p. 219.
41. Ibid., pp. 219–20.
42. Samir Khalaf, 2003, p. 16.
43. Fuad Khuri, 'The Ascent to Top Office in Arab-Islamic Culture: A Challenge to Democracy', Beirut, 1997, p. 131.

Chastity Capital: Hierarchy and Distinction in Damascus

Christa Salamandra

In Damascus, social identities are increasingly negotiated and contested through competitive consumption and display. This chapter, drawn from ethnographic fieldwork conducted in 1992–4 among the elites of Damascus, explores consumption, display and social distinction among women. Here women emerge as central players in contests over position and prestige; how they comport themselves, what they wear, where they dine and whom they marry may signify, reinforce and even create class affiliation.

The ability to purchase expensive consumer goods, and to be seen in fashionable venues, has long been an important mark of elite status in Damascus. Wealthy women of the 1920s and 1930s, as Elizabeth Thompson has noted,[1] were among the city's first cinema-goers, an activity that required both disposable income and familiarity with French or English. Under the socialist economic policies of the 1960s, 1970s and 1980s, minimal domestic industry combined with import bans to render commodities scarce. Access to consumer goods, such as fashionable clothing, distinguished those with connections to power, and the wealthy who travelled abroad. The Ba'ath Party attempt to rid Syrian society of social hierarchy not only failed, but actually produced new class divisions. During the 1990s, a boom in local production and loosening of import regulations led to an increasing availability of both locally produced and foreign consumables on Syrian store shelves. The commodification of many aspects of social life accelerated, as more commodities and new public leisure sites widened opportunities for social distinction through consumption.

Consumption of the kind engaging people in Damascus both reflects and constructs social differences. My exploration of this phenomenon draws on Pierre Bourdieu's analysis of distinction, which links preferences in cuisine, art, music and home furnishings to income level, educational qualification and social background.[2] Bourdieu's once ground-breaking and now commonplace argument demonstrated that taste is a matter not of individual proclivity but of social position. 'Good taste', the socially acquired preference for high over low cultural forms, serves as cultural capital, an asset not directly material, but one enhancing and reinforcing social position.

The relationship between consumption, display and social identity is explored in a significant body of recent literature. Much of this material shows how the range of commodities now available allows the differentiation and ranking, through consumption, of persons who have no 'natural' relations, such as kin or locality, but instead must state their social position before an audience who otherwise might know little of them. Elite Damascus presents a seeming paradox. Style, leisure activities and displays of wealth have become increasingly significant with economic liberalization. As one informant puts it, elites in Damascus are 'inventing occasions to show off their wealth'. Yet these have not eclipsed the importance of family name. Damascus is still very much like a small town for the middle and upper classes; all appear to know one another. But Damascenes do not actually know each other. They know of and about each other. Damascenes often have at their fingertips detailed information or speculation – family background, income, profession, education – about persons they have never met. Information networks are vast; social networks are much smaller. As people may not know others personally, seeing and perceiving each other became naturally significant. It is here that consumption comes into play. Elite names remain elite, and new names become elite, through public displays of wealth. Older forms of social identification are not disappearing but are being reworked, through consumption, in a new arena, a public culture of hotels, restaurants and cafés. To paraphrase a line from Lampedusa's *The Leopard*, things are changing so that things can remain the same.[3]

In a 'community' where people may not know each other but do see each other, appearances take on great importance. Syrian men are image-conscious – those who can afford it wear expensive clothing, cologne and jewelry and drive flashy cars – but it is women who most often represent familial wealth and status through physical beauty and adornment.

Compounding the importance of image for Syrian women is the

premium placed on the appearance of chastity. An unpopular subject among gender specialists who prefer to emphasize Middle Eastern women's empowerment, the issue of control over female sexuality is profoundly affecting Syrian society in novel ways. The appearance of sexual purity becomes a form of capital for a young woman. Its absence can be disastrous for her future prospects. It can also become ammunition for opposing families to hurl at their enemies. In order to preserve their chastity capital, young women should not be seen interacting with men, particularly one-to-one, before they are engaged. Their moving about the city alone, especially after sundown, is frowned upon. The economic implications of these sanctions are obvious and profound. To paraphrase Bourdieu, women's subjective situation – restricted movement outside the home – is both a precondition and a product of their material dependency.[4]

Although premarital social and even sexual contact between men and women is not unknown, discretion, secrecy and concealment of any such evidence is, of course, crucial. For example, to ensure the appearance of virginity on the wedding night, some women undergo a surgical procedure, 'hymno-plasty', in which the hymen is restitched.[5] Elite districts of Damascus are peppered with small, dark, heavily curtained coffee shops where courting couples can sit together unnoticed. Dates take place either surreptitiously or under the guise of fictional marriage engagement. Ossman points to this problem in urban Morocco where, as in Damascus, young adults have difficulty finding legitimate spaces in which to form opposite-sex relationships.[6] The park and street serve as meeting places, and the gaze is paramount. The same is true in Cairo, where 'there is no socially sanctioned custom for single males and females socializing in an unchaperoned setting'.[7] Young women for whom interaction with men is restricted adopt strategies of attraction through display. Semi-public spaces provide venues for showing oneself to others. The Health Club in Abu Rummaneh, for instance, is an entirely unisex workout place in a neighbourhood largely populated by upper-middle-class, conservative Damascenes. The women who can afford to go there drive or are driven. They tend not to walk on the streets, even in conservative clothing. Yet inside the club they wear heavy make-up, skimpy leotards – often with spaces cut to reveal large sections of bare stomach, back or thigh – and leave flowing their invariably long hair. The club's single, brightly lit, mirror-panelled room seems designed with display in mind, as aerobic classes take place in a cleared area in front of the weights and exercise machines. Those pumping iron – mostly men – can watch the bobbing behinds, delineated clearly in thong-backed leotards, of the women taking step aerobics or body-toning classes. The Health Club is one of the arenas between public and private where young women take advantage of the in-betweenness to show off as much body as possible.

Most semi-public spaces, including professional ones, provide opportunities for attraction. Flirtatiousness, if not the norm, is legion. A Damascene professional told me that a diplomat from the American Cultural Center had suggested starting classes in office conduct for Syrian women. My friend told the diplomat that no one would attend them, as women who work do so to attract husbands, not build careers. Most jobs open to women, however prestigious, do not pay enough to enable them to become economically self-sufficient. Unmarried women, even wealthy ones, rarely set up independent households. Jobs are seen as temporary measures on the way to marriage or as supplementary income afterwards. For young single women, they are primarily a venue for display, the ultimate aim of which is to secure a successful future in the private, rather than public, sphere.

Competitive display is thus often geared towards attaining desirable marriage partners. Marriages, like the wedding ceremonies commencing them, signify and engender social position. A daughter who obtains a prestigious mate raises, or at least reinforces, her family's lofty rank. Brides are chosen for a variety of assets, among which beauty and wealth are most significant. Damascenes value feminine beauty, and associate it with the city. A beautiful woman is said to have drunk the water of Damascus (*sharbaneh mayat al-sham*). While beauty is a key asset for women, wealth is what renders a groom desirable. For potential brides, complex distinctions are made among beauty, money and status. Such social measuring up often results in what a few decades ago would have been unimaginable – marriages between elite Damascene women, *banat ayal*, who often possess both beauty and status, and wealthy Alawi men.

A potential bride's desirability is not defined by the groom alone; choosing a partner is a family matter in which mothers and sisters are central. The marriage market in elite Damascus exists within a male-dominated economic system, but is not itself male controlled; powerful matrons direct the movement of people and statuses. Contemporary Damascus bears little or no resemblance to the drawing rooms of Jane Austen and Maria Edgeworth. Beauty and fortune are explicitly weighed and measured – usually by women themselves – to determine a woman's worth. In a few instances, however, and much like Lady Bertram of Austen's *Mansfield*

Park,[8] one Damascene informant repeatedly expressed surprise and indignation at an acquaintance who, although neither attractive nor rich, had married well. Not unlike nineteenth-century Britain, contemporary Syria is undergoing rapid social and economic transformations, with older kinship-based forms of distinction giving way to materially based ones, or at least a material idiom replacing that of kinship. Elites are redefining themselves, yet some things remain the same: the centrality of marriage and kin, and the basis of family honour. In this respect, the contrived gentility of Austen's England parallels the contrived chastity of contemporary Syria.

For all women in Damascus the ability to purchase, cultivate and embellish a look that highlights beauty, and suggests wealth, is crucial. For single women, appearance is central to obtaining a desirable spouse. Young women dress to impress not only men but, even more importantly, other women, given the central role mothers and sisters play in finding a young man a bride. But the pressure to present a stylish image does not disappear after marriage, as a wife's grooming and attire then signify her husband's and family's status. Competitive display is evident in elite in-spots: at the Sheraton Hotel pool, wealthy women may change bathing suits several times during an afternoon of sunbathing. A married woman, expensively coiffed and dressed, is one who has made an enviable match.

Acquisition practices among the elite are ranked, with those who can afford to shop in France or Lebanon at the top, those who buy at the better Damascene stores in the middle, and below them those who must resort to the cheaper synthetic local imitations of European catwalk fashions available in less expensive boutiques. Natural fabrics are rare and worn only by the uppermost stratum, or sometimes the Western educated.

Dress style, among both young and middle-aged women, tends to run to two extremes. On the one hand, there is a strong tendency towards highly marked sensuality or sexuality: tight, figure-hugging and sometimes cleavage-revealing clothing in vivid colours, heavy make-up, teased and moussed long hair, high heels, multiple gold or gilt accessories. One evening, as we sipped coffee in the Sheraton's al-Nawafeer Café, one of my two women companions glanced around at the parade of glitter and bemoaned the recent changes in taste. 'The aristocracy used to have class,' she remarked, 'now everything must be bigger, busier, heavier and shinier.' As a Syrian woman quoted in Lindsfarne-Tapper and Ingham's all-too brief description of Damascene wedding fashions put it: 'There is no place in Damascus now for classic simplicity'.[9] On the other hand, there is an increasing number of *muhajjibat,* who, with their white headscarves and simple blue or grey overcoats, eschew all local conventions of attractiveness. Here, to a considerable extent, Damascus contrasts with Cairo, where an industry in elaborate, ornate *hijab* clothing offers an alternative to the plainer styles worn in Syria. Women find it difficult to maintain a stylistic middle ground between the invisibility of the *hijab*, and the flamboyance of the coquette. As one Damascene woman put it (in English), 'we have cockteasers and *muhajjibat*, and nothing in between!'

More frequently, competitive display takes place beyond traditional domestic settings such as the *subhiyyah* (morning coffee) and *istiqbal* (afternoon reception). Major gathering spots, such as exclusive hotels, and numerous new restaurants provide venues for seeing and being seen. Young men and women gaze at each other in the safety of groups; they rarely converse one-to-one publicly. Young women are allowed, indeed encouraged, to attract men, but are forbidden to socialize with them. The aim is to attract a husband with her body, since young people of opposite sexes are rarely permitted enough time together for anything else to matter. This is why display, contained within certain spaces, is more acceptable than interaction.

In a context where image rather than achievement determines status, the presentation stakes are high. Every aspect of a woman's appearance is subject to close scrutiny and evaluation by other women. Losing or gaining a pound, drying one's hair differently, wearing a skirt instead of trousers or a slightly thicker line of eyeliner, all elicit comment; sometimes, but not always, in complimentary form.

In marked contrast to the social harmony among Middle Eastern women often depicted by feminist anthropologists, behind the appearance of intimacy often lurks bitterness and jealousy.[10] Syrian women have confided in me the difficulty they have making female friends amidst relentless rivalry. The constant competitiveness is wearing; nothing about the other goes unnoticed. Women compare themselves continually and mercilessly in an agonistic mode of sociability tinged with hostility. In her study of child-rearing in a Syrian village, Rugh finds that children have little time or opportunity to develop friendships outside the home, and that relationships with non-relatives were perceived as dangerous for the young and inexperienced.[11] This practice would more greatly affect females, whose restriction to the home continues well into adulthood. In her study of visiting practices in Yemen, Meneley describes a similarly agonistic form of sociability, an 'inclination for invidious distinction'[12] among the women of Zabid.

In elite Damascus, women alternate flattery with criticism, cruelty with kindness, and as one put it, 'build you up in order to knock you down again'. Cutting remarks are sandwiched between grand gestures of affection and generosity, so one seldom knows where one stands. One favourite form of female sparring is the back-handed compliment: 'You've gained weight, but it looks good on you', 'You look better in skirts than in trousers', 'You don't look short because you're fat.' Outright insults are also not uncommon. Once I was with a friend on holiday in the Latakia when she met an acquaintance she had not seen since the previous year. 'Are you pregnant?' asked the woman. 'No, just heavier', my friend replied. Instead of cowering in embarrassment, the woman continued, 'But this is really quite a change, isn't it? You really have gained weight!'

Foreign women living in Damascus often find themselves thrust into this ruthless competitive fray, as they are drawn – perhaps unwittingly – into local women's status contests. Local women often feel that foreign females get more male attention than they deserve, merely because of what they represent (sexual freedom, exoticness, novelty and, of course, the coveted prospect of a way out of Syria). Although relatively young and single, I fell far short, literally, of the local ideal. Damascenes hold that 'height is two thirds of beauty' (*al-tul tiltayn al-jamaal*); I stand four feet ten inches tall. Nevertheless, unwanted sexual attention occurred frequently, despite my care to dress modestly and interact carefully.

My fieldnotes bemoan the 'data' I may have lost as a result of the suspicion and resentment I evoked in other women. In one incident, a friend suggested taking me to a meeting of the Arab Club, then cancelled. 'My [male] cousin is busy, and I can't find another man to go with us. And I know the two women who told me of the meeting will be jealous if we go there on our own.' As Willy Jansen shows in the case of Algeria, adult women who lack male partners are socially ambiguous, falling between proper gender categories.[13] They are, in keeping with Mary Douglas's classic formulation, dangerously 'out of place'.[14]

When I did manage to sustain relationships with women, they often vied with each other for my affections, and chided me for perceived slights or preferences. I began to conceal my relationships with women from other women, but felt guilty for my disingenuousness. Later into my fieldwork I realized that I had adopted local women's strategies for social survival. What I discovered was that the intense competitiveness I sometimes encountered did not signify a failure to bond or gain access. Rather, these experiences of seeming rejection heralded my acceptance into circles of cultural intimacy where both hostility and affection characterize close relationships. Acceptance as a friend, or even fictive sister, means having to operate amid strong contradictory emotions.

I tried to take slights and insults in my stride, reminding myself of their ethnographic relevance, for I, like the women I studied, was often put in uncomfortable positions of competitive display. One particularly memorable instance occurred on New Year's Eve in my second year of fieldwork. My closest friend invited me to spend the evening with her family. She was organizing a party for about sixty people, hiring a hall, a caterer, a band and a dancer. Just before I left for the United States for Christmas, and again during the week after my return, she urged me repeatedly to try and find a date for the occasion, on the grounds that all the guests would be in couples. I continually refused, finally pointing out that her unmarried sister and brothers would be there without dates.

Knowing it was my birthday on the first of January, she ordered a cake as well. It was laid out in the middle of a semi-circle of tables early in the evening, a pink and white double heart with my name written on it. Shortly after midnight the band started to play 'Happy Birthday' and I was called over to blow out the lone candle and cut the cake. But it did not end there; I was obliged to dance a 'birthday dance' with the caterer/master of ceremonies, on the platform where the band was still playing 'Happy Birthday'. It went on for an endless five minutes. My friend's obvious delight made the embarrassment worthwhile. I sat down. I was just beginning to relax and enjoy the evening when the master of ceremonies called for beauty contest nominations. My first impulse was to run to the ladies' room, but young women were heading towards the stage with no coaxing, and I was afraid I would miss something interesting. I thought I would get away with hiding behind my friend's brother, where I could not be seen from the stage. I nearly succeeded; there were five girls lined up in front of the band, and the contest was about to begin when my friend and her two brothers, followed by the rest of her family, began to urge me to join in. I thanked them and declined. They persisted, and people from neighbouring tables joined in the coaxing. Finally my friend walked over and pulled me up. I continued to resist, but now realized that nothing short of a tantrum would relieve me from participating, I told my friend I would take part only if she did. Reading this as acquiescence she said that she could not join in because she was fat and pushed me onto the stage. So there I was, on the eve of my thirtieth birthday, in a conservatively flared black cocktail dress and pearl earrings, tacked onto a line of vibrant miniskirted, spike-heeled, moussed and painted nineteen year olds. We had to prance around the stage individually while the band played behind us. I tried to console myself with the thought that I was joining a long anthropological tradition of participating in unpleasant and humiliating rituals. When the judges made their decision, I was eliminated first, as numbers one, two, three, four and five were asked to come forward (I was number six). After a few more elimination rounds, the judges chose a winner, and the new blonde 'beauty queen' (*malikat al-jamal*) paraded in her crown and sash, as the defeated contestants left the stage in tears. As a group of us rode home in a hired minibus, my friend noted that the annual beauty contest had long been a sensitive issue. The next day she rang to apologize for any offence the incident caused, and confided that the outcome of the contest had been decided in advance, to rectify hurt caused by the previous year's result.

Attractiveness, the means to procure it and the access to spaces in which to display it are surpassing other measures of worth among the elites of Damascus. I am not suggesting here that Middle Eastern women are uniquely competitive. Indeed, the resonance with the eighteenth- and nineteenth-century Britain of Edgeworth and Austen precludes any impulse to particularize. Antagonistic relations among women are part of a system of oppression. Women are often their own harshest critics, and hold each other to a stringent set of moral values and aesthetic standards. As Georg Simmel notes, 'Women's position on the defensive does not allow the wall of custom to be lowered even at a single point'.[15] If patriarchal structures and the increasing commodification of social relations and physical appearances everywhere pit woman against woman, this is even truer of places with strong male dominance, like the Middle East.

As both judges and contestants, women direct the contests that shape the social world of Damascus. They create and are created by new consumptive patterns and leisure practices, and the social hierarchies these engender and maintain. The emergence of new classes and the intermingling of old and new money have heightened competition within the elite marriage market, which in turn pressurizes women into conspicuous display of bodies, and limits their involvement in public life in order to preserve chastity capital. As in all contests, some are more successful than others.

An examination of consumptive patterns, display modes and marriage practices among women in Damascus reveals an uneasy accommodation between old and new elites. Informants from various class, sectarian and regional groups often invoke an endogamous principle to describe Damascene, particularly elite Damascene, marriage practices: 'Damascenes never marry non-Damascenes'. Yet I observed numerous instances of elite Damascenes – often women – marrying wealthy non-Damascenes – often regime-connected Alawis. If young women serve as preservers of family honour and emblems of family prestige, it is unsurprising that their marriage to men from socially, if no longer economically and politically, inferior groups produces strong 'we' images. Marriage, with the alignment of families, the melding of cultural and economic capital it entails, is a primary locus of identity and sociability. I argue that it is the aspect of social life in which the accommodation of competing elites is most keenly felt and discursively resisted. It is also where the tension between old ideals and new realities becomes particularly apparent.

Bibliography

Armbrust, W., 'When the Lights go Down in Cairo: Cinema as Secular Ritual', in *Visual Anthropology*, vol. 10, nos. 2–4, 1998.

Austen, J., *Mansfield Park*, London: Penguin, 1966; original 1814.

Bourdieu, P., 'The Disenchantment of the World', in *Algeria 1960*, Cambridge: Cambridge University Press, 1979.

——*Distinction: A Social Critique of the Judgment of Taste*, London: Routledge & Kegan Paul, 1984.

Dialmy, A., 'Premarital Sexuality in Morocco', in *al-Raida*, vol. 20, no. 99, 2002/3.

Douglas, M., *Purity and Danger*, London: Routledge & Keegan Paul, 1966.

Early, E. A., *Baladi Women of Cairo: Playing with an Egg and a Stone*, Boulder, CO: Lynne Rienner, 1993.

Edgeworth, M., *Castle Rackrent and Ennui*, ed. Marilyn Butler, London: Penguin, 1992; original 1800.

Hoodfar, H., *Between Marriage and the Market: Intimate Politics and Survival in Cairo*, Berkeley: University of California Press, 1997.

Jansen, W., *Women without Men: Gender and Marginality in an Algerian Town*, Leiden: Brill, 1987.

Kabbani, R., 'Global Beauty: Damascus', in *Vogue*, vol. 164, no. 2394, January 1998.

Khair Badawi, M. T., *Le désir amputé; vécu sexuel des femmes libanaises*, Paris: L'Harmattan, 1986.

Lampedusa, Giuseppe di, *The Leopard*, New York: Pantheon Books, 1960.

Lindisfarne-Tapper, Nancy, and Ingham, Bruce, *Languages of Dress in the Middle East*, London: Curzon, 1997.

Makhlouf, C., *Changing Veils: Women and Modernisation in North Yemen*, London: Croom Helm, 1979.

Meneley, A., *Tournaments of Value: Sociability and Hierarchy in a Yemeni Town*, Toronto: University of Toronto Press, 1996.

Ossman, S., *Picturing Casablanca: Portraits of Power in Moroccan City*, Berkeley: University of California Press, 1994.

Rosenfeld, H., 'Non-Hierarchical, Hierarchical and Masked Reciprocity in an Arab Village', in *Anthropological Quarterly*, vol. 47, no. 1, 1974.

Rugh, A., *Within the Circle: Parents and Children in an Arab Village*, New York: Columbia University Press, 1997.

Simmel, G., 'Conflict', in *Conflict and the Web of Group Affiliations*, New York: Free Press of Glencoe, 1955; original 1908.

Thompson, E., 'Sex and Cinema in Damascus: The Gendered Politics of Public Space in a Colonial City', in Hans C. Korsholm Nielsen and Jakob Skovgaard-Petersen, eds, *Middle Eastern Cities 1900–1950: Public Spaces and Public Spheres in Transformation*, Aarhus: Aarhus University Press, 2001.

Watson, H., *Women in the City of the Dead*, London: Hurst & Co, 1992.

Notes

1. E. Thompson, 'Sex and Cinema in Damascus: The Gendered Politics of Public Space in a Colonial City', Aarhus, 2001.
2. P. Bourdieu, 'The Disenchantment of the World', in *Algeria 1960*, Cambridge, 1979.
3. Giuseppe di Lampedusa, *The Leopard*, New York, 1960, p. 40.
4. P. Bourdieu, 1979
5. See Khair Badawi, *Le désir amputé; vécu sexuel des femmes libanaises*, Paris, 1986, and A. Dialmy, 'Premarital Sexuality in Morocco', *al-Raida,* 2002/3, for evidence of this practice in the Middle East.
6. S. Ossman, *Picturing Casablanca: Portraits of Power in Moroccan City*, Berkeley, 1994, pp. 46–7.
7. W. Armbrust, 'When the Lights go Down in Cairo: Cinema as Secular Ritual', in *Visual Anthropology*, 1998, p. 418.
8. J. Austen, *Mansfield Park*, London, 1966, p. 65.
9. Nancy Lindisfarne-Tapper and Bruce Ingham, *Languages of Dress in the Middle East*, London, 1997, p. 32.
10. see H. Rosenfeld, 'Non-Hierarchical, Hierarchical and Masked Reciprocity in an Arab Village', in *Anthropological Quarterly*, vol. 47, no. 1, 1974; C. Makhlouf, *Changing Veils: Women and Modernisation in North Yemen*, London, 1979; H. Watson, *Women in the City of the Dead,* London, 1992; Early, E. A., *Baladi Women of Cairo: Playing with an Egg and a Stone*, Boulder, CO, 1993; H. Hoodfar, *Between Marriage and the Market: Intimate Politics and Survival in Cairo*, Berkeley, 1997.
11. A. Rugh, *Within the Circle: Parents and Children in an Arab Village*, New York, 1997, pp. 225–6.
12. A. Meneley, *Tournaments of Value: Sociability and Hierarchy in a Yemeni Town,* Toronto, 1996, p. 33.
13. W. Jansen, *Women without Men: Gender and Marginality in an Algerian Town*, Leiden, 1987, p. 10.
14. M. Douglas, *Purity and Danger*, London, 1966.
15. G. Simmel, 'Conflict', New York, 1955, p. 96.

In the Eye of Which Beholder? Beauty, Body Image and Sexuality in Contemporary Tunisia

Angel M. Foster

El-Hem's Story

El-Hem was twenty years old when she left her community near Gafsa to come to Tunis to pursue her studies at the university. Bright and dynamic, El-Hem intended to finish her university degree, start a career and begin a family, all by the age of twenty-six. The moment she arrived in Tunis she immediately felt out of place; she felt provincial, unsophisticated, and somewhat isolated. Physically she felt different. She had been raised in a community that she describes as 'traditional', both in dress and appearance. Women in her family and community were, or at least seemed to her, voluptuous, dark haired and dark eyed. El-Hem was thought of as the town beauty and she always felt that she fitted in. But when she arrived in Tunis she was struck by the thinness of those around her. She wasn't able to purchase the fashionable clothes of her peers; they simply didn't look right. And she believed that university men wouldn't be interested in her because of the way that she looked.

El-Hem eagerly decided to pursue weight loss with the same vigour that she pursued her studies. She began by denying herself food in the evenings. As the weight began to fall off her small frame she decided to eat only the afternoon meal, and then only in small portions. She dyed her hair blonde and began to wear fashionable clothes and make-up. Upon returning to Gafsa after the first year of her studies, her family was shocked. She had become so thin and looked so different. Her parents were concerned; how would she be able to marry a man from Gafsa if she looked so foreign? Over the summer El-Hem conceded to the parental pressure and put weight

> back on, all the while knowing that she would resume her dieting when she returned to university in the fall.
>
> And resume the dieting she did. For the next five years, El-Hem used dieting, laxatives and occasional purging to obtain the thin, svelte figure she believed to be ideal. She returned to Gafsa less frequently and instead spent holidays with relatives in Tunis; she simply found the pressure to gain weight from her family to be too intense. She also felt confused; in Tunis, she felt good about the way that she looked and the way that men responded to her. For the first time in her life she had boyfriends, and she knew she wouldn't have been able to date if she had continued to look like a rural woman from the centre of the country. But when she returned to her rural village, she no longer felt like she fitted in and she feared no one would want to marry her.
>
> El-Hem's pursuit of an ideal body began to take its toll on her energy and her health. She felt tired, distracted and unable to pursue her studies with the same dedication that she had previously. She explained that she spent so much time focusing on how she looked and what she ate that she wasn't able to concentrate on her studies. She twice failed her year-end examinations and at age twenty-six she remains in her final year at the university.[1]

As El-Hem's story demonstrates, young women in Tunisia face a number of competing pressures regarding physical appearance. 'Traditional' concepts of female beauty place value on voluptuousness, a body type associated with wealth, fertility and maternity. However, in part due to the recent infusion of Western media images, fashion and concepts of beauty appear to be changing among young urban women. Many young women report a desire for lighter hair, fairer skin and the svelte bodies of European models. For many women, these competing concepts of beauty have important implications for self-esteem, relationships and sexual expression.

This chapter investigates internalized and externalized concepts of beauty among unmarried women in Tunisia. Situated in the fields of medical anthropology and public health, an effort is made to draw on nearly two years of qualitative and quantitative fieldwork I have conducted in eleven of twenty-three Tunisian governorates over the last five years. After briefly providing an overview of historical and contemporary constructions of female beauty in Tunisia, I will then present the results of an orally administered open-ended survey conducted with 100 never-married female university students. The intention is to highlight both the competing images of beauty and the impact these pressures have on the behaviours of university students in Tunis. For comparative purposes, I will then turn to the results of a study conducted on a sample of 200 unmarried women who had never sought university education. The women here were all living in five regions of Tunisia.

The results reveal some striking regional differences in the perception of what constitutes female beauty and ideal body image. Since my informants were drawn from different settings, the women will most likely experience varying tensions in accommodating or reconciling the discrepant expectations while negotiating the images and identities they wish to subscribe to. I will, by way of concluding inferences, elucidate some of the probable implications these pressures have on women's health and sexuality, particularly among young urban women.

A brief note or caveat about the nature of my narratives and oral histories, which inform the bulk of my data, is in order here. A distinction needs to be made between the terms 'oral narrative' and 'oral history'. An oral narrative is just one step of the oral history process and refers specifically to the material recorded. In this case, oral narratives were collected through open-ended interviews. An oral history, it must be kept in mind, is a process and includes recording, transcribing and representing the oral narrative. These definitions are adapted from Gluck and Patai.[2] In an attempt to reconcile the realities of oral narratives with the requirements for academic writing, I have chosen to present oral histories in italicized script. The italicization indicates that this is a presentation/representation of the oral narrative, not the woman's words exactly as they were uttered. Direct quotes are indicated throughout the chapter in the conventional format.

Beauty and Body Image in Tunisian Popular Culture

Consistent with much of the Middle East and North Africa, traditional concepts of female beauty and attractiveness in Tunisia have been associated with voluptuousness.[3] Colloquial expressions, poetry and lyrics from popular songs emphasize the virtues of female plumpness. Long-standing cultural constructions of beauty associate a full figure with prosperity, fertility and maternity. These values are generally believed to be deeply entrenched. Indeed, recent studies dedicated to nutritional status in Tunisia have highlighted the connection between the growing prevalence of obesity and overweight and the cultural value placed on female voluptuousness. The rate of obesity among Tunisian women increased from of 8.7 percent in 1980 to nearly 23 percent in 2000.[4]

Tunisian women are over three times as likely to be obese as their male counterparts. Also the risk of becoming obese or overweight increases once a girl reaches adolescence. Urban women and lesser-educated women are more likely to be obese or overweight than their rural or educated counterparts. Efforts to address the public health consequences of obesity in Tunisia have been quietly launched. Although public health efforts surrounding obesity and overweight are in their infancy, the connection between this growing public health problem and cultural conceptions of female beauty has been widely acknowledged. As one Tunis-based physician noted, 'Beauty and fertility remain intertwined in Tunisia. Girls often get fattened up when they are eligible for marriage because in our society we associate fatness with fertility and fertility with beauty'.[5]

Yet not widely discussed in Tunisia are the emerging health implications of an increasingly popular and prominent construction of female beauty, one derived from Western societies. The infusion of Western images of female beauty constructed around thinness, through print media, satellite television, cinema and the fashion industry has grown significantly in Tunisia over the last two decades. Changing patterns of consumption have influenced the development of a growing marketing and commercial advertisement industry which place primacy on Western conceptualizations of beauty and body image. Images of thin, fairhaired, and lightskinned women abound. In the United States and Western Europe the commercialization and perpetuation of these types of images of thinness have been repeatedly linked to eating disorders, compulsive exercising and depression among women. But how influential is this Western conception of female beauty on Tunisian women? How do the competing concepts of beauty influence women's behaviours and self-esteem? And does this increasingly prominent conception of beauty have implications for women's health and sexuality?

Surveying University Students

To begin to address these questions I will now turn to the study that I conducted with never-married female university students. In 1998–2000

I completed a knowledge, attitudes and behaviours (KAP) study on young women's health and sexuality.[6] As a component of this study, I discussed body image and beauty with 100 women living and studying in Greater Tunis.[7] These women reflected both the socioeconomic and geographic diversity present in the university system.

Generally, the results from the survey indicate that Western images of female beauty shape the way that young women see themselves and their attractiveness. Sixty-nine percent of women stated that the most influential factor defining female beauty in Tunisia originates from Europe or the West. Approximately one quarter of women cited both Arab and Western constructions of beauty as being highly influential and only 9 percent of women sited Arab or Tunisian constructions of beauty as establishing the ideal for women. Many women noted that a shift has taken place recently. As a student from Tunis stated, 'For my mother, it was considered beautiful to be fat. But now it is different. French, Italian, American ... all of those models are what I see everyday. If I want to be considered beautiful, I need to look like them. The standards have changed'.[8]

When asked about the ideal body type for women, 75 percent of respondents described a thin or 'model-like' body. Fourteen percent of women articulated a body type ideal as being voluptuous, a body type associated with more traditional concepts of female beauty in Tunisia. However, nearly half of these women, almost all from rural areas of the country, went on to state that there were actually two ideal body types in Tunisia: one characterized by voluptuousness, one by thinness. As Samira, a student from Nabeul explained,

> In Tunisia there are actually two ideals. Men here want to date women who look like models, who are thin, and blonde, and fair. But men from my community want to marry women who are bigger, who are round and supple. I live in Tunis and I want to be able to go out and have fun. It is hard to do that if you are a fat girl.[9]

The remaining 15 percent of women, disproportionately originating from areas outside of Tunis, identified 'in the middle' as the body type ideal. I am fully aware that placing ideal body type responses into categories has the potential to be subjective, as being 'thin', 'medium' or 'voluptuous' means different things to different people. When the answer was unclear or could be interpreted in multiple ways, I asked follow-up questions for clarification. For example, I would ask the student to name a person who embodied the ideal (Claudia Schiffer was the most often named model) or ask for a description. When a student responded with 'a body like a European's', I would explain that European women have different body types and ask for a description or example. Women also often used their own bodies, stating for example 'like mine' or 'like yours'. In these cases I would always ask for clarification.

As was reflected in Samira's statement, beauty and body image are perceived as being intertwined with both relationships and sexual expression. This theme emerged prominently during the focus group discussions as well. By the mid-1990s the average age of first marriage for women in Tunisia was 26.4 years and consequently women are spending a longer period of their reproductive and sexual lives unmarried.[10] Patterns in dating and sexual behaviours have changed over the last two decades and recent studies have documented increasing premarital sexual activity by unmarried women in Tunis.[11] Many university students feel that dating and sexual activity have placed new pressures on women with respect to attractiveness. A woman from the central area of Kairouan commented:

> In the past women were desired for their maternity, their family, their intelligence. Being a big girl meant that your family was comfortable, that you could have children. It was considered beautiful. Now men are attracted to European women and the sexuality that this represents. For a woman to be attractive, or to have a boyfriend, she has to look like that.[12]

To be 'datable', many university students feel that they need to embody the Western ideals of beauty. When asked if it was problematic to be a heavy-set student, 78 percent of women responded with an emphatic yes. Student respondents repeatedly stated that being plump presented obstacles to dating, dancing and the ability to wear fashionable clothes. Women also stated that larger girls felt bad about themselves. As a student from Tunis explained:

> How could a girl feel good about herself if she was fat? Look around you. When girls are fat they are alone. Men won't want to go out with them and their [girl] friends pity them. If the [fat] girl is funny or smart maybe she can survive socially, but in general, it is very hard.[13]

The twenty-two women who stated that being voluptuous was not a problem were disproportionately from regions outside of Greater Tunis. Nearly half of these women went on to explain that, because their communities valued larger body types, voluptuous students would be able to find husbands and feel good about themselves. Rima, a student from the southern area of Tataouine, articulated this concept well:

> I am from the South. Women in the South want to be bigger than women in Tunis. It is natural for us, it is considered beautiful. European women are beautiful too and it is natural for European women to be thin, blonde, and made-up. But it is not natural for us. We look foreign. It is difficult to come to Tunis where girls want to look like European models. Why can we not look like ourselves? I don't think it is a problem for a woman to be fat. Okay, if she is obese then it is a problem. But if she has breasts and a larger rear and thick arms? Life would not be difficult for her in my town. She would be considered beautiful, she would have no problems getting married, and her parents would be very proud. But it would be difficult for her in Tunis. There is a lot of pressure to be thin here.[14]

The pressures on women to be thin appear to be multifaceted. Certainly, women's perceptions of men's preferences (which I did not independently examine) play an important role in shaping ideal female beauty. However, body image is also influenced by women's own perceptions of themselves and each other, independent of relationships, dating and marriage. A number of women, particularly those from Tunis, discussed how 'thinness' reflected success, intelligence and professionalism. Many women spoke openly of how their appearance affected their self-confidence and self-esteem and reflected a form of 'competition' between women. As a woman from Tunis remarked:

> You asked me what the ideal body-type is in Tunisia. It's like mine. I'm proud of the way I look. Some of my friends are jealous because it is easy for me. I look this way naturally. But, I feel good about myself and I like it that my friends want to look like me.[15]

In contrast to the above quote, many women, who do not see themselves as conforming to this body image ideal, reported feelings of low self-esteem, anxiety and depression. Of course, there is not a consistent definition of what it means to be 'fat' or voluptuous. And I was not in a position to clinically assess the BMI (Body Mass Index) or weight of the women who participated in this study. However, it was striking to me that the vast majority of women who expressed feelings of depression, defined themselves as fat and/or described their strategies for losing weight appeared to me to fall within a healthy weight range. A healthy appearing woman from the central region of El-Kef explained:

> I hate looking in the mirror. I look at my friends and they are all so thin. I wish I could be one of those girls who is comfortable with the way she looks, but I can't. I've tried to lose weight through dieting, but it doesn't work for me. It doesn't matter what I do. I hate going out with my girlfriends because I feel ashamed of the way that I look.[16]

Many women reported actively working to achieve the thinner body that reflects this changing image of ideal female beauty. It appears that the desire to obtain a model-like physique is impacting young women's health, as Nadia's story reveals.

Nadia's Story

> Nadia is a twenty-five-year-old university student studying in Tunis. After beginning her studies Nadia began to feel new pressures about her appearance. A tall woman, Nadia decided that she needed to lose weight in order to be more attractive and be able to wear more fashionable clothes. At first she dieted, eliminating pasta and couscous from her meals. When the results were not significant enough, she discussed strategies with her friends. One diet involved consuming only water three days a week, but Nadia felt tired and decided to try something else. Her friends advised her to take laxatives, but after a while they gave her stomach cramps and she ultimately decided to stop taking them. Finally, a friend advised her to start smoking as a way to curb her appetite. Nadia had never smoked before, but at the age of 23 decided to give it a try. Two years later, Nadia still smokes and is convinced that if she quits she will put the weight back on.[17]

Unfortunately, Nadia's experience is in no way unique. When asked about the strategies or methods by which young women actively work to achieve weight loss and thinness, respondents described a number of different options. Almost all of the survey participants offered dieting as a commonly used method of weight loss. However, when probed further on what constituted dieting, over a third of the students described behaviours which fall into the category of disordered eating, including routine fasting, 'fad' diets and the elimination of meals. Ten percent of students described dieting behaviours, such as routine purging, that would meet the clinical criteria of eating disorders. Ten percent of women discussed the use of laxatives and other medications in weight loss and 9 percent of women, who were twice as likely to be from Tunis, offered smoking as a weight-loss strategy. And my discussions with women about their personal experiences with dieting and weight loss confirmed disordered eating, eating disorders, laxative use and smoking were all being employed.

It is evident that university students in Tunis are being profoundly affected by exposure to the body image ideal characteristic of Western constructions of female beauty. The complex pressures on these women to achieve thinness have implications for women's perceptions of themselves, their sexual relationships, their relationships with their families and communities and their health.

Broader Perceptions of Ideal Beauty: Survey of Women without University Education

Thus far, I have focused exclusively on the conceptualization of beauty and body image within the female university student population. I shall now briefly turn to the larger study in order to draw some broader conclusions. In 2000, I completed the same study on young women's health and sexuality on a sample of 100 unmarried women without any university education. Respondents were all drawn from Greater Tunis. This was supplemented by a sample of 135 (also unmarried and without university education) from communities in the governorates of Sfax, Beja, Siliana and Sidi-Bouzid. Altogether the results revealed a few interesting and seemingly inconsistent findings. For example, educational background played no significant role in defining or shaping women's perceptions. Both those who have had the benefit of a university education and those without it evinced the same attitudes and preferences.

The majority of women in the Tunis study stated that Western images are the most influential in defining female beauty, identified the thin, model-like body type as being ideal and reported that it was problematic for a woman to be heavy-set. Again, consistent with the university-educated sample, these women often mentioned the dating/marriage dichotomy and identified active strategies for weight loss among themselves and their peers. However, fewer women in the sample of those without a university education described weight-loss strategies that would be broadly defined as unhealthy.

With respect to the other regions, the impact of Western images on women's conceptualization of beauty appears to be much less profound. The studies in Siliana, Sfax, and Sidi Bouzid found that the majority of women identified Arab constructions of beauty as being the most influential (57 percent, 71 percent and 93 percent, respectively). In Beja, and Sfax the majority of respondents identified 'medium build' as the ideal body type (77 percent and 94 percent), in Siliana the majority of women identified either 'medium' or voluptuous as the ideal body type (76 percent) and in Sidi Bouzid the ideal female body type was identified as 'voluptuous' by 80 percent of respondents. In Beja and Sfax some women reported that dieting was employed as a weight-loss strategy and no women described the unhealthy strategies of disordered eating, laxative use or smoking. In Siliana and Sidi Bouzid, the governorates in which voluptuousness was valued over thinness, the majority of women reported that it was, in fact, not problematic to be heavy-set and unmarried and virtually no women reported active weight-loss strategies. Indeed, several women discussed how they and their friends were actively trying to gain weight. Altogether one categorical and undisputed finding can be easily extracted from our results: unmarried women without a university education are more heavily influenced by Arab constructions of beauty. They are not engaging in the same behaviours as their Tunis-based counterparts. The beholder's eye, in other words, varies by region.

Despite the sampling and contextual limitations of the study a few striking findings and patterns stand out, both in their visible manifestations and consequences. Foremost, it is obvious that Western images of female beauty are becoming a powerful force in Tunisia. Furthermore, these nascent perceptions of beauty and body images appear to be intimately associated with perceptions that Western images of female beauty are becoming powerful markers of self-worth, eligibility for dating and marriage, familial and community identification and sexuality. The larger study reveals that young urban women, particularly those living in Tunis, feel considerable pressure to achieve the thin, svelte body type associated with Western images of beauty. Although these are more pronounced among university students, young urban women are beginning to actively employ a number of strategies to obtain this body image ideal. It appears evident from the study with university students that a number of these strategies, including disordered eating, laxative use and smoking, have profound implications for young women's social, psychological and physical health.

I contend that this is an emerging health issue in Tunis. However, recent attention on urban women has focused exclusively on obesity (albeit in a limited way). Adult nutritional status, overweight and obesity are issues of significant importance in contemporary Tunisia. However, the health needs of young women must also be considered. Only by assessing young women's perceptions of their bodies and their behaviours can we begin to understand the complex and nuanced relationship between body image and young women's social context and realities. And only after that assessment can we begin to address young women's health needs.

Bibliography

Foster, A., 'Young Women's Sexuality: The Health Consequences of Misinformation among University Students', in D. L. Bowen and E. Early, eds, *Everyday Life in the Muslim Middle East*, Bloomington: Indiana University Press, 2002.

Gluck, S., and Patai, D., eds, *Women's Words: The Feminist Practice of Oral History*, New York: Routledge, 1991.

Inhorn, M., *Quest for Conception: Gender, Infertility, and Egyptian Medical Traditions*, Philadelphia: University of Pennsylvania Press, 1994.

Mokhtar, N., Elati, J., Chabir, R., Bour,. A., Elkari, K., Scholossman, N., Caballero, B., and Aguenaou, H., 'Diet, Culture and Obesity in Northern Africa', *Journal of Nutrition*, vol. 131, no. 3, 2001.

ONFP, *La santé de la mère et de l'enfant*, Tunis: Ministère de la Santé Publique, 1996.

Sherif-Trask, B., 'Egypt', in B. Sherif-Trask, ed., *Women's Issues Worldwide: The Middle East and North Africa*, Westport, CT: Greenwood Press, 2003.

Notes

1. All names used throughout the paper are pseudonyms. Interview, Tunis, October, 1999.

2. S. Gluck and D. Patai, *Women's Words: The Feminist Practice of Oral History*, New York, 1991.
3. For a discussion of 'traditional' or 'historical' constructions of female beauty in the Middle East, see M. Inhorn, *Quest for Conception: Gender, Infertility, and Egyptian Medical Traditions*, Philadelphia, 1994, and B. Sherif-Trask, 'Egypt', in B. Sherif-Trask, ed., *Women's Issues Worldwide: The Middle East and North Africa*, Westport, CT, 2003.
4. N. Mokhtar et al., 'Diet, Culture and Obesity in Northern Africa', *Journal of Nutrition*, vol. 131, no. 3, 2001.
5. Interview, Tunis, June 2003.
6. In addition to the formal survey, I also conducted both informal and formal focus groups with over 250 university students. Throughout this chapter I will also draw on the perspectives, opinions and experiences that women related during those encounters.
7. Greater Tunis in this context refers to the governorates of Tunis, Ariana and Ben Arrous.
8. Interview, Tunis, 20 October 1999.
9. Interview, Tunis, 26 October 1999.
10. ONFP, *La santé de la mère et de l'enfant*, Tunis ,1996, p. 175.
11. A. Foster, 'Young Women's Sexuality: The Health Consequences of Misinformation among University Students', in D. L. Bowen and E. Early, eds, *Everyday Life in the Muslim Middle East*, Bloomington 2002.
12. Interview, Tunis, 25 February 1999.
13. Interview, Tunis, 19 October 1999.
14. Interview, Tunis, 1 May 1999.
15. Interview, Tunis, 8 October 1999.
16. Interview, Tunis, 27 October 1999.
17. Interview, Tunis: October 1999.

Breaking the Silence: What AUB Students Really Think about Sex

Roseanne Saad Khalaf

When I informed my creative writing classes that a number of our seminars would focus on the topic of sex, the initial reaction was silence followed by utter disbelief. 'Wow!' exclaimed one enthusiastic male student. 'Just what every guy dreams of but can't talk about openly.' Next a rather amusing incident occurred when two animated young women attempted to speak at the same time but managed only to produce strange, inaudible sounds. Unfortunately the laughter and commotion that ensued made it impossible for me to rescue them from this embarrassing situation. Later that afternoon, in the quiet calm of my office, Layla let drop the white veil that covered her mouth while Samar adjusted her tongue rings. As they engaged in articulate conversation I marvelled at how two female students, one traditional, the other postmodern, had eagerly attempted to express their views only to be hindered by contrasting differences in attire and adornment that ultimately rendered them silent.

Ironically, both have been 'deformed' and made speechless by the very values they adhere to. In a most visible sense, they also epitomize the dissonant normative expectations and lifestyles that continue to polarize certain segments of Lebanese society. That both are seeking an 'American' liberal education and happen to be in the same creative writing seminar makes the setting all the more compelling. The outwardly timid and reserved veiled student, along with her dauntless and liberated cohort, who flaunts the rings on her tongue and other parts of her sparsely dressed body as 'emblems of honour' and daring, represent extreme modes of adaptation which are manifest elsewhere in the Arab world.

Contrived as it may seem, a classroom setting devoted to creative writing offers a unique and discerning opportunity to explore sensitive issues related to sexuality, and allows a better understanding of how a group of intelligent students are groping to forge a meaningful and coherent sexual ideology. However, working critically with the writer's personal experience to relocate it to the classroom in a way that allows for a more meaningful engagement with experience can be immensely challenging.[1] In my study, the task became even more daunting because the topic of sex requires venturing into sensitive, often forbidden territory. To craft sexual narratives, students had to enter unmapped terrain as well as stretch language beyond neutral communication in order to express ideas and inhabit spaces not normally explored in the classroom. Delving into highly private realms of experience often required the use of sexually explicit language that ran the risk of exceeding the comfort zone of certain students and testing their threshold of tolerance. At times we even faced a 'linguistic void', ostensibly because students have not yet developed a comfortable or adequate way of expressing their views, nor have they found acceptable language to use in a classroom setting. Initially, it was somewhat difficult to generate natural rapport since language had to be carefully negotiated. Luckily students were quick to overcome the barriers and, to my delight, out of the closet tumbled amazing stories. Fortunately the rush of tales moved beyond the local and segmental allegiances to assume wider significance.

Not surprisingly, the questionnaire I administered in the early stages of this experimental study (see Appendix) revealed the majority of students to be multilingual, multicultural, highly mobile and diverse. Many are border crossers by virtue of having lived, together with their families, in a number of countries to escape the atrocities of the Lebanese civil war that ravaged the country for nearly two decades. Today, students struggle to reconcile the romantic and nostalgic Lebanese narratives told to them by their parents with the realities of a postwar society. What they are witnessing instead is a country in limbo populated with self-serving politicians and a dysfunctional government that remains, for various reasons, incapable of addressing any of the underlying issues and tensions that instigated the war in the first place. Predictably, whatever reserves of optimism and determination students possess are quickly depleted in the wake of countless daily obstacles they encounter. Unless they have the good fortune of joining a family business, decent jobs remain scarce, salaries low and the future highly uncertain thanks to regional political instability. Given this dire situation, it is little wonder that students are attracted to rampant consumer culture and quick fixes inevitably ushered in by the trappings of globalism. Postwar Lebanese society has instilled an insatiable desire to make up for lost time. This impetuous hankering for the 'good life', to enjoy the moment and not look back, is a desperate attempt to erase all traces of a violent past. As one perceptive student remarked, 'It seems that war and violence are never far away.' When peaceful times are perceived as nothing more than brief interludes, it is easy to comprehend why my students behave the way they do.

Creating a space where issues regarding sex can be openly debated, discussed and written about freely offered students an opportunity to give voice to their views on sexuality. By delving into such seemingly private zones of personal autonomy, they acquired an expansive sense of control and empowerment. As a result, students began to assume some of the enabling attributes of a diminutive 'public sphere' and/or 'third spaces'.[2]

This was only possible because our *contact zone* remained protected from the threatening outside gaze by the *safety net* of a classroom setting where critical exchanges that deal with difference served primarily to broaden awareness. The transformative power of discourse and personal writing was evident right from the beginning when repeatedly students expressed their desire to be change agents with regard to matters of sex. Yet they were acutely aware that the acceptance of diversity in our created 'third space' was a distant cry from their real and lived environment. Here there was no posturing for they were not being judged in any way. Whatever diverse practices and attitudes they revealed were welcome in our shared arena and, perhaps even more important, the information remained entirely within their control. The ability to engage in text creation under a safety net served to increase and heighten awareness, to unsettle and transform fixed, often rigid ways of seeing. In the end, the acceptance of difference gave new shape and meaning to their initial views on sexuality that developed into a sense, real or imagined, of empowerment and control. Despite the shifting uncertainties and complexities of postwar Lebanon, students now felt they exercised power in this particular sphere.

Six Thematic Categories

For the sake of clarity I have divided the recurring and salient ideas in the *sex narratives* and discourse of students into six thematic categories or rubrics, each of which is given an appropriate title: Breaking Away: Parent/Child Dualism, Writing in the Margins, Sexual Identity in Flux, The Exhibitionist: Indecent Exposure, Male/Female Sex Language, and The

Freedom to Choose and Imagine. It is essential to keep in mind that none of the themes are mutually exclusive: all inevitably contain overlapping material, presumably because notions regarding sex are more often than not interconnected, especially in discourse. The following pages contain a brief analysis of each thematic grouping along with excerpts taken from student narratives in an attempt to capture their voices and reveal their intimate thoughts and feelings regarding issues of sexuality.

Breaking Away: Parent/Child Dualism

Conflicts over sexuality between AUB students and their parents have to do with divergent views, a struggle between two opposing sexual ideologies. Students, on the one hand, view sex as a positive form of self-fulfillment and an opportunity for open experimentation. As such, sexual expression is given legitimacy in all consensual relations regardless of romantic or enduring bonds. Parents, on the other hand, emphasize the dangers involved in free sex outside the secure confines of love and marriage. Physical intimacies, they argue, must act as a prelude to enduring relationships. Consequently, it comes as no surprise that differences concerning sexuality between the two generations are hugely polarized, with each group attributing meaning and purpose to their particular views by drawing on an entirely different set of values. Such strong intractable positionings seem to account for the sharp divisions between the two generations.

Recurring themes of parent/child dualism depict an ongoing struggle over the role of sexuality in everyday life. Because the stories are told entirely from the moral perspectives of students, they offer a critique of their established positions as they act and react against the conservative values of their parents, with each strongly rejecting the sexual values of the other.

> My parents are limited. They just think like they have been programmed to think. They have experienced the 60s and 70s without the sexual revolution. So as far as they are concerned, being active sexually is bad. Taking drugs is bad. Bisexuality and gay people don't even exist. (Fadi)

An awareness of the attitudes assumed by parents is essential in order for students to negotiate and reinvent their sexual identity inside the parent/child dualism. Only when they have labelled and 'othered' the views of their parents can they be free to imagine and forge into existence entirely new visions and approaches. Careful examination and rejection of the ideas embraced by their parents allow for new alternatives that challenge the existing, taken-for-granted values, offering instead limitless possibilities.

> As for myself, I believe in sexual experimentation. Most of the older people I know, including my parents, are disgusted by gays, but I have nothing against them. Actually, I admire their honesty. I believe every individual should have the freedom to choose same sex partners if they so wish. (Maya)

Students are not only able to identify and account for these generational differences. They are also surprisingly quick to expose the problematic nature of their parents' traditional approaches to sexuality.

> My parents allow me to have a relationship as long as no sex is involved. No sex at all. No kisses, no hugs, and no nothing. Of course I know that what they are asking is impossible so I can never be open and honest with them on this issue. (Manal)

In assuming a more liberal stance as they react to the views of their parents, some students totally disregard or ridicule what their parents have to say about sex, while others attempt to come to terms with feelings of resentment and defiance as they search for a new voice capable of challenging what they perceive to be outdated ideas.

> At a young age I developed a morbid fascination with sex because it was a forbidden word in our household. (Hiam)

> My parents are convinced that by returning to Lebanon they will no longer need to worry about their children growing up in a promiscuous society. Now I will be able to catch a decent, rich guy from a good family who comes from a similar background and we will live happily ever after in total boredom. Naturally, I have no intention of living out their fantasies. My career will be the most important thing in my life. I certainly am not going to be bossed around by any guy. If I fall in love, I plan to live with my boyfriend so I can maintain my freedom. (Nour)

> A girl's virginity, my parents insist, guarantees the right and the ability to trap a worthy spouse (meaning rich and from a good family). I find the whole thing abhorrent. (Nadia)

Though the fortuitous and not-so-random nature of the sample under study does not allow generalization, the men appear to go beyond the disapproving stance of their women colleagues to decry and disavow the cultural predispositions that reinforce parental authority and allow parents to serve as arbiters and gatekeepers of social conduct. They are particularly concerned about those normative expectations associated with their exclusive and dogmatic role of safeguarding and upholding family honour and dignity. Others go even further by searching for strategies that will assist their efforts in forging more pliable images and patterns of conduct.

> Because I am the only boy in our family, my parents consider it my duty to be the guardian of my sister's virtue. If my sister is not allowed to have sex, why should I be any different, and above all, why should I or anyone else need to guard her virginity? (Adib)

Yet one of the major contributions of these narratives is the creation of images that focus on new ways of seeing and living outside the parent/child dualism. The forging of themes not only against but also outside and beyond the old attitudes offers fresh incentives and perspectives.

> I believe that sex is a personal choice that one makes and it plays an important role in self-discovery and maturity. Sexual experimentation is good experience and it does not always have to take place with a person of the opposite sex. Having a person of the same sex touch you or going to a gay bar will allow the discovery of something new. (Bahij)

Clearly an underlying moral divide exists between the two generations with respect to love, sex and intimacy. Seidman has attributed this dissonance to opposing schools of thought that he labels as sexual *romantics* versus *libertarians*.[3] The *romantics* view sex as a way of expressing intimate feelings that have to do with bonds of affection and love: feelings that should never be taken lightly because they involve reciprocal obligations. By contrast, a libertarian sexual ethic defines sex as a mode of bodily sensual pleasures. 'Libertarians intend to free individuals of the excessive social controls that inhibit sexual expression and stigmatize transgressive desires and acts'.[4] *Libertarians*, on the other hand, play a role in challenging sexual orthodoxies. They aim to free sex from excessive strictures, focusing more on its pleasures and expressive possibilities. Such views remain in sharp contrast to the dominant social groups that impose higher moral purposes such as procreation, love and family on sex.

It is interesting to note that the majority of students agree that their parents are definitely *romantics* when it comes to sex. Students themselves, however, do not all fit neatly into the *libertarian* category. Indeed, there are some who harbour serious ambivalence and uncertainty in this regard, for instead of assuming a liberal stance they are inclined to favour the views of their parents, seeing absolutely no reason to reject the values they grew up with.

> I was brought up by strict parents who do not believe in sex before marriage. However, by the time I entered university, I formed my own ideas that are not very different from those of my parents. I believe that when a girl loses her virginity before marriage, she loses the respect of her future husband as well as the people around her. (Maha)

To my surprise, a number of students touched on a highly sensitive and rather embarrassing issue, namely, the double standards, cynicism and social hypocrisy of their parents. Goffman's metaphors of *front stage* and *backstage* appropriately exemplify the contradictions students observed and criticized in the behaviour of their parents.[5] Backstage parents often relinquish their *nice scripts* by acting in ways that contradict the polite, moral front they maintain in public or in *front stage* situations. When parents uphold strict moral values that are not in step with their actual behaviour, their children are the first to notice.

The jarring dissonance between the overt righteousness and covert misconduct of their parents is to my students a microcosm of the deepening malaise they see elsewhere in Lebanese society. Such aberrant symptoms, particularly when their parents are presumably their own moral arbiters and role models, are not lightly dismissed.

> My parents lead separate lives. I know that they both have lovers. Well to be perfectly honest, my father fools around with many women. At first my mother was angry, but now she does her own thing. Of course, in front of their kids they act like a normal and happy couple. (Reem)

> How can my parents pretend to believe in traditional values regarding sex and marriage when their relationship has been dead for years. (Maher)

Clearly the insincerity of their parents compounds their sense of moral outrage. They are, after all, trapped in a socio-cultural setting that demands they pay deference to parents whose values and conduct are no longer relevant or meaningful to their own situations. Perhaps what is even more telling about these views of parental hypocrisy is that students embrace another set of romantic values, that relationships should be honest and not dead sexually.

Writing in the Margins

Although students are positioned in families and communities, the majority openly reject the sexual values upheld by mainstream groups. The very act of questioning and challenging the status quo moves them to the margins where they speak from silent places in an attempt to register their disapproval and eventually destabilize the centre. Here the self/other distinctions raise critical questions because by producing their own narrative subjectivities, student writers are excluding or 'othering' those who have 'othered' them. In this way, as DeVault reminds us, their personal accounts make excluded voices 'hearable'.[6] By writing their sex narratives they are able to articulate and give voice to their own stories. The ability to render the invisible visible is, in and of itself, an enabling act: a bold attempt to gain control of one important aspect of their lives.

> Unfortunately, my parents avoid the topic of sex. My generation is much more comfortable with our sexuality. We talk openly about it and experience it in ways that our parents would never approve of. I discuss sex only with my friends because I think it is entirely my business. (Kamil)

> On the surface our society is very conservative when it comes to sex. The reality is that older people have sex in secret with many partners while pretending to be virtuous. When young people talk openly about sexual relationships it makes older people uncomfortable because they feel threatened. I argue a lot with the older generation. I really hate it when they laugh or ignore my ideas. Mostly they shove my views aside as if they are of no importance. (Rami)

Such symptoms of recalcitrance notwithstanding, students' perspectives and views on sexuality remain worlds apart from the mainstream groups they are exposed to. As a result they feel their ideas are not taken seriously and there is a concerted attempt, at least in their view, to ignore and thus marginalize whatever they have to say about sex. Curiously, students were unable to imagine that their parents may have had other views when they were young.

Sexual Identity in Flux

Students' narratives not only define the essentialism and fixity of their parents' views on sex, they also prod them to examine and redraw the boundaries that categorize them as different. Positions and stories that create established parameters are rejected in much the same way that notions having to do with grounded or fixed ideas are quickly examined and dismissed. The formation of their positionings is not situated within some established public ideal but formed through the diversity derived from competing ideas. Their narrative voices are the outcome of shifting and conflicting tensions brought into play when sexual codes are viewed with apprehension and suspicion. Hence they are clearly inclined to favour more situational and constructed normative standards and actual modes of conduct.

By posing hard questions, new choices and endless possibilities start to take shape and provide more open-ended multiple models. There is an eagerness to move beyond invisible barriers, to resist the pressure to conform to rigid and absolute forms of sexual identity that translate into established and predetermined positions. By challenging the views of mainstream groups, students create a *fluid space*,[7] in which ongoing experimentation leaves room to construct new views and sets into motion a struggle against definition by others, against the fixity of what is considered normal sexuality as opposed to diversity in sexual patterns. Students consider sex to be shaped by difference, thus the labels given are seen as mere fictions serving primarily as a means of social control, since they inevitably block out the many subcultures and sexualities.

> Labels limit people in ways that they aren't even conscious of. Nothing is set in stone and I hate how the sexual complexities of our lives become diluted into one defining category: *the rape victim, the heterosexual, the homo, the lesbian, the pervert,* etc. Ironically, it was only when I stopped feeling the need to be labelled that I was able to be in a healthy relationship. (Hind)

Students reject simplistic, fixed labels because, in their eyes, sexual identities exist on uncertain ground and are constantly subjected to displacements. They challenge the idea of sexual normality substituting instead an ever-shifting terrain. In this sense, they are more inclined to veer in the direction of more situational than absolutist ethical yardsticks. Morality becomes, as it were, how one feels afterwards.

> Although I was also attracted to men my experiences with them were never fulfilling. At one point in my life, I decided to explore my attraction to women. After a year I became completely disillusioned with the lesbian community but I also knew that if I disclosed my feelings for men I would be shunned and called a traitor. Slowly I drifted away from the gay scene realizing that if there is no place for someone like me there I must create my own place. Now my friends are people like me who have rejected the term *normal* when it comes to sexual identity. (Fayrouz)

Like Fayrouz, students reshape and reinvent their sexual identity through experimentation with alternative frameworks, seeking to define themselves against a shifting landscape of possibilities. It is not surprising that, within such a fluid and negotiable setting, virtually everything becomes charged with sensual, erotic undertones and, hence, highly contested. Seemingly mundane and prosaic matters – i.e. dress codes, speech styles and the freedom to imagine alternate sexual attributes and practices – begin to assume primacy. Students are often in danger of viewing everyone as other and having their individual tastes become so 'selved' that they will never match up with the tastes of others. The question that arises here is how many of these individualized alternatives can be enacted in a world of others who are also equally individualized?

The Exhibitionist: Indecent Exposure

AUB campus is densely populated with women students wearing suggestive clothing that reveals tattooed and pierced bodies among other more lurid and sultry manifestations of eroticization. Why female students conform to a highly fashionable, exaggerated dress code that serves to exhibit the body in provocative ways initiated a lively and rather humorous class debate. To some (and Siham is a typical example), this investment in body image is not only seen as an intrinsic, natural desire to embellish their femininity and enhance feelings of self-worth, it is also readily recognized for its extrinsic, instrumental value: a means to seduce and attract men. Furthermore, as Rima candidly admits, the competition for this scarce commodity (men) is so intense that many women on campus are engaged in a competitive game of 'outdoing' each other.

> It is a natural and innate desire to wear sexy clothes in order to attract men. I know that my body is appealing and so it feels good to wear short skirts and low cut tops. It's a way of seducing men visually. (Siham)

Female students who wear suggestive attire use their sex appeal to tempt men but also to keep them at a safe distance. They exhibit their bodies to feel attractive and desirable while simultaneously sending a clear message that men can look but not touch. It became immediately evident that to many of my women students playing the role of a seductive temptress is fully exploited and thoroughly enjoyed.

> My friends and I try to out do each other when it comes to wearing sexy clothes. One of my friends comes from a very religious family that think she should dress in a modest and conservative way. Instead of fighting with them, she hides her clothes in my car and changes into tight jeans at my house before going to her classes at AUB. It's worth the inconvenience because we both enjoy looking cool in order to attract men. (Rima)

Though male students remain divided on this issue, they have been made readily aware of the games their women friends play. To Wael, the campus becomes an enchanting and great place to watch 'sexy females exhibiting themselves all day long'. Samir, however, decries the vulgarity and bland uniformity of this obsession with body image.

> AUB campus is a great place to watch sexy female students exhibiting themselves all day long. (Wael)

> Actually to me, most of the girls on campus look alike because they dress in the same vulgar way. (Samir)

> AUB is a place of extremes. Girls either reveal all or hide all. (Khatir)

The abandon with which the young are eroticizing their bodies should not be lightly dismissed as merely a trendy and fashionable craze. It is a reflection of a deeper and more nagging societal conflict; almost a textbook instance of anomie: i.e. a disjunction between normative expectations which condone, indeed cajole, young women to be *sexually attractive* but condemns them if they become *sexually active.* Many young women, even the most adept at reconciling these inconsistent societal expectations, are the ones, as therapists have urged, to bear the psychological toll. They are the surrogate victims of such cognitive dissonance but dissonance, after all, is the price of individuality as is anomie.[8] If students want to be 'different' or 'individual' the price is psychic dislocation and in scripting terms the intrapsychic is more important since it is the place where dissonance is negotiated.

This problem, incidentally, has been recently compounded by a disheartening demographic reality. Because of the disproportionate outmigration of young Lebanese men in pursuit of more promising career options, the sex ratio is visibly skewed. Demographers put the estimate at approximately four to one; i.e. one male for every four females in eligible age brackets. Once again, it is the growing pool of single women who must, in one way or another, deal with the scarcity of eligible men. The eroticization of the female body and other associated ploys to embellish their sex appeal seem like an appropriate strategy to gain a competitive edge over their cohorts when it comes to soliciting the attention of the scarce and coveted male. In the language of Bourdieu this eroticization becomes a judicious resource in the 'social capital' that single women need to cultivate and jealously guard.[9]

Male/Female Sex Language

Linguistic approaches are often used in discourse to provide evidence of gender differentiation. An analysis of men's and women's speech style reveal that they are mostly organized around a series of global oppositions, for example, men's talk is 'competitive', whereas women's is 'cooperative'; men talk to gain 'status', whereas women talk to achieve 'intimacy' and 'connection'.[10] These stereotypical notions or conventional language distinctions proved problematic among my students as the woman did not form a homogeneous group. Many positioned themselves alongside the men by assuming dominant discourses that conjured up a liberal sexual environment. Like their male counterparts, they adhere to the *opportunity-taking* narrative pattern in which they see themselves as the initiators, the 'doers' of sexual activity. In the context of my previous remarks this too becomes part of the 'social capital' women need to skilfully cultivate. Here, as well, women can no longer afford to remain passive and resigned victims. Instead, they depict themselves as active agents directly involved in resisting the circumstances that undermine their autonomy and well-being. As decision-makers, they assume complete control over their sexual activities. Moreover, sex is considered to be autonomous from love or intimacy. Subsequently as modern liberated individuals, they initiate, engage in and enjoy sex outside the confines of love and marriage. In their texts and discourse, they break with and undermine the stereotypical notions and conventions that resort to restrictive language and behaviour. Their sexual encounters are disclosed in language that is explicit and direct, with a surprising degree of distance and control.

Dalia is so unabashedly explicit in this regard that her sexual encounters are completely divorced from any ethical stance or intimate feelings. Indulging in sex becomes an unalloyed libidinal resource to be fully exploited. If her younger boyfriends fall short (because of their premature ejaculation) of fulfilling her expectations, she readily seeks older and more experienced men.

> Lately I have been having sex with older men because I got pissed off with guys my age who come quickly leaving me dissatisfied. Now that I have taken matters into my own hands, sex is pleasurable. I am beginning to enjoy multiple organisms with mature men who know how to fulfill my sexual needs. (Dalia)

This group of female students differs from their male peers only through the inclusion of resistant or emancipatory discourses that incorporate feminist rhetoric laced with fierce criticism of misogyny and prejudice. There is a strong determination among these women students to defend their rights.

> My father lectures me about the dangers of premarital sex because he wants me to be a chaste, ignorant virgin when I get married. My brother, on the other hand, is encouraged to indulge in sex, even with prostitutes. You might think that my father is an illiterate, old man but actually he is an AUB graduate. When I tell my father that I reject his double standards he threatens to cut off financial support. He considers me disobedient and says he is no longer proud of me. The truth is that I am not proud of him either. This is my life and I alone decide when, with whom, and how often to have sex. (Nayla)

In sharp contrast, a more conservative group of women students have developed strategies which enable them to approach the topic of sex alternately, from a more inhibited discourse rooted in polite, acceptable language. They are careful to avoid explicit terminology, adhering instead to expressions of a traditional and patriarchal kind. To be happy, they argue, a woman should seek a long-term heterosexual relationship. Not surprisingly, this group invoked the rhetoric of love, intimacy, chastity, romance, marriage and motherhood.

> Sex should be shared only with the person you marry. My virginity and faithfulness is a special gift I will offer to my husband because I

> want to be perfect and beautiful for him. (Suha)

Sexuality, as their texts demonstrated, is accompanied by a discourse of distaste and fear. Premarital sex is not only wrong and dangerous, but transgressive pleasure is closely linked to morality and social punishment.

> I believe it is immoral and unacceptable to have premarital sex. Our society is correct in punishing women who are promiscuous. In the past, Americans were moral and strict when it came to sex. Now it is as simple as eating or drinking. I do not mean to offend Americans, but their values are not acceptable in our culture. I, like most of my friends, cannot take sex lightly. (Manal)

> If I have sex before getting married I will live in fear that my family might find out and punish me severely. I really don't think it's worth the risk. (Youmna)

In general, this group of women seems comfortable acting in accordance with prescribed essentialist social rules: the sexually attractive woman is the beautiful one who, to please men, must guard her virtue. They favour the passive as opposed to the proactive narrative pattern but in restrictive and tentative ways, as their options remain closely tied to gaining acceptance through the *male gaze*. Because they long to be the objects of male desire, one overriding concern is the need to remain feminine, to be a *real* woman in the eyes of men. Once the centrality of men is established and confirmed in the narratives and discourse of this group of women students, they immediately focus on the need to achieve and maintain their femininity presumably to remain objects of desire. Yet ironically, the notion of femininity seems to create extreme feelings of anxiety and competition.

> It is very important for a woman to remain attractive especially if she wants to find a suitable husband. Some girls are lucky because they are naturally good looking. I have to work hard at it and I am sometimes afraid that men will go after the more beautiful girls. (Amina)

The sharp divide between the conservative female discourse of passivity that coexisted with one that assumed a far more liberal stance, constructing sex as autonomous from traditional relationships, assumed striking proportions and initiated lively and heated class debates. However, it remains the liberal stance and terminology towards sex-related issues, so boldly adopted by a considerable number of women students, that blurs the conventional distinctions between male/female sex texts. It is rather strange that none of my women students raised the possibility of being interesting to men or even happy with them in non-sexual ways.

The Freedom to Imagine and Choose

Given the ambivalence, fluidity and inconsistent expectations young students in Lebanon are subjected to, it is little wonder that a prosaic academic elective (a seminar in creative writing) should become an accessible and meaningful vector for the expression and mobilization of pent-up energy. Sheltered in the sanctuary of a classroom, students are released from the constraints of the outside world. The opportunity to write becomes both an outcome of, and direct agency for the articulation of this newfound freedom.

Of course writing itself can be viewed as a practice of freedom. Texts focus on the personal, and as such, they allow the *freedom to imagine* while blocking out the *freedom from interference*. The freedom to imagine is crucial if students are to develop a sexual identity that enables them to envision sexuality in ways that permit alternative possibilities because it identifies and innovatively addresses the gap between what is, as opposed to what is longed for. By creating diverse themes and navigating forbidden territory, students are able to articulate new ways of understanding crucial issues that have to do with their sexuality. Narratives provide the freedom to change existing norms through reinterpretation, thus offering fresh perspectives and new ways of seeing. The images that emerged in this study are those of diversity, daring experimentation and, ultimately, growth.

Narrative texts and discourse offered space away from and beyond the outside gaze, a space in which 'hidden transcripts' can be created and explored. Eventually these 'hidden transcripts' may hold the potential to counteract the cultural givens that might otherwise define the sexual identity of students. Weeks has, I believe, correctly argued that 'The radical oppositional identities which arise against hegemonic ones offer narratives of imagined alternatives which can provide the motivation for inspiration and change'.[11] Pushing beyond normalizing and imposing sexual strictures allows students to map out new sexual possibilities that widen their vision. They think and write boldly about unarticulated expectations, about what could or should be when it comes to sex-related issues and the control of their bodies. Imbedded in their narratives are themes that demand a collective awareness of the need to respect diversity, a call for the celebration of difference, including the right of each and every individual to choose. Most striking is an approach to sex that is at once rational, experimental and expansive, rather than moral and judgmental.

> I do not believe that one should be restricted to a single partner for life because it is possible and important to have sex with many people over time. (Serene)

> I like guys, but I'm not sure I don't like girls too. Sometimes I check them out and declare which is sexy, pretty, etc. I examine them like a guy would. Is this normal? If I lived abroad I might have sex with a girl just to see how it feels. Also because virginity is such a big deal here, I'm determined to lose it. (Ibtihaj)

> Who we love and have sex with is entirely our own business. No one has the right to decide for anyone else. There are enough rules to define our social lives, how can we allow people to control the sexual aspect of our lives too? (Nadim)

> My parents are divorced and I can't really remember a time when I saw them together in a loving relationship. This is probably why I hold my current view on the uselessness of marriage. I would like to experiment with different kinds of relationships and arrangements with the opposite sex before I decide how best to live my private life. (Joumana)

> To me, sex is art and art is freedom. To deny a person sex is the same as denying that person his/her freedom of expression. People say music is the universal language in the world, but I think sex is because its boundaries are limitless. (Hani)

> Religion, race, age and social class will never be a hindrance if I am attached to a person. Before I came to AUB I never thought this way. However, I have to admit that after watching a lot of love making on campus, I have changed my views and become much more liberal. (Dana)

> Sex is happening and girls are enjoying it too. I wish I could confront this hypocritical Lebanese society we live in and tell them that sex is a fantastic language between people. (Samir)

> Girls are told that the most precious gift they can offer their husbands is their virginity. But then why should a man not offer the same to his wife? No way! If he does, he'll be called weird names because a Lebanese man must prove his manhood. I think all this stuff is rubbish. (Ghassan)

Students do not regard heterosexual couples as the building block of social life, presumably because they do not envision any kind of 'proper' sexuality for all. The fixity of 'normal' sexuality is viewed with scepticism. Instead, they opt for the diversity of sexual patterns. Their scripts and discourse are impatient and defiant when it comes to set social constructions that demand the regulation of sexual behaviour. While to Suha fidelity and virginity are a 'special gift' she intends to offer her husband on their wedding night, Ibtihaj remains defiant.' 'Because it is such a big deal', she declares, 'I am determined to lose it.' She also need not confine herself to heterosexual sex. 'If I lived abroad I might have sex with a girl just to see how it feels.'

In other words, far from being unnatural or deviant, homosexuality is seen as a way of constructing or reconstructing sexual arrangements and relationships to suit real human needs. It is a personal choice one makes and, as such, deserves respect and acceptance.

> Although I am a heterosexual male I do not mind bisexuals or homosexuals since sex is about being comfortable with oneself and having the freedom to choose. (Ahmad)
>
> My sister is a lesbian but my parents don't know because she is afraid they will punish her. I don't see anything wrong with her sexual identity. I am still very close to my sister. In fact, I respect her courage and determination to be herself. (Rashid)
>
> I don't have anything against gays. In fact, I have many gay friends. My dad, however, insists they are abnormal and a threat to society. (Nina)
>
> Many people in Lebanon hate homosexuals. They think they are immoral. I think sexuality should be a matter of choice and I think it's fine to have a gay relationship. How else can one discover something new about themselves? (Zuheir)

Concluding Inferences

Initially, in undertaking this exploratory case study I was fully aware of the unusual nature of the sample and its rather contrived classroom setting; more so since it focused on textual material and discourse rather than actual sexual behaviour. Given, however, the resilient cultural taboos in Lebanon that continue to impose formidable constraints on free and candid discussion of sexuality, the classroom became an expedient and 'natural' sanctuary in which to explore such forbidden and censored issues. Judging by the positive reactions of students, the experience was more than just an expressive outlet of repressed desires and hidden fantasies. It proved also cathartic and didactic and, thereby, revealed the importance of providing such neutral settings and diminutive 'public spheres' where the young can freely communicate and share common concerns away from the public gaze.

Throughout the study, students persistently and repeatedly argued for a liberalized conception of sex. Collectively they voiced their determination to move sex into an arena where rational and experimental approaches rather than moral thinking and behaviour can and indeed should occur. If I am to invoke a common conceptual distinction, one can discern a shift from an essentialist to a constructionist perspective.

Students also recognized the urgent need for a new language. There seems to be no adequate vocabulary to articulate the expanding possibilities in the intimate sphere of their sexual experiences. Their healthy, open attitude towards sex allowed them to explore the vital role it plays in their lives with little or no inhibition, yet they all complained that language remained a constraining factor.

Finally, I would like to extract a few broad and unanticipated inferences from the study; particularly as they prefigure the need for a decentred and more public debate on such sensitive but contested issues. The fact that these voices represent no more than the cloistered views of students sheltered in the comfort zone of a classroom should not belittle or undermine the significance of the results, marginal or sketchy as they may seem. Pinar, among others, has urged that when marginal views are given voice they begin to circulate in the mainstream where they are invariably taken into account and recorded.[12] Although they remain in danger of being controlled or greatly modified by a regulatory regime, they still possess the power to disrupt and discredit those at the centre once they form a space capable of being analysed in articulation with others.[13] Judith Butler recognizes the need 'both to theorize essential spaces from which to speak and simultaneously to deconstruct these spaces to keep them from solidifying'.[14] Keeping sexual identities fluid leaves room for diversity, which will, in turn, open up yet more spaces from which to speak.

The students in my study, judging by subsequent conversations I have had with them outside the classroom, seem determined to continue exploring the changing shape of sexual differences. They also remain acutely aware that crossing boundaries only sets up new boundaries that must be continuously transgressed in order to avoid the strictures that accompany the static nature of rigid, inflexible views. Once again, in other words, the seemingly private emotional narrative engagement had the potential to expand further than the confines of our classroom setting. It provided students with the opportunity to move beyond situated literacy as well as the mere crafting of sex texts and discourse. In telling their stories they ventured out of the margins to negotiate public and private positionings. By externalizing their ideas they formed a realm capable of being analysed in articulation with others. The autonomous *comfort zone* was transformed into a participatory *contact zone* where diverse ideas could be openly debated against a shifting landscape of possibilities and alternative frameworks: where awareness could be refined and heightened through imaginative text creation, open and critical discourse. At the same time, all of this occurred under a safety net of confidentiality and trust. In our shared space, diverse perceptions concerning sexual identity served to increase and sharpen awareness among students in ways that ultimately unsettled and transformed rigid ways of seeing both in and beyond the classroom.

Appendix

Methodology

The study examines the personal texts and discourse of forty-three students enrolled in three creative writing sections over the course of one academic semester (fall 2003). Students were given a short questionnaire before being asked to craft personal narratives in which they explore their views, feelings and lived experiences with regard to sex. Emotional narrative engagement offered the opportunity to navigate the terrain of sexual identity by reflecting on the issues they themselves deemed to be of immediate significance to their lives.

From the very start, class discussions were informal, interactive and lively. Students proved highly adapt in critically engaging with and workshopping their texts. As our class discussions progressed, discourse took a more spontaneous turn when students eagerly and openly began exchanging opinions. Soon it became clear that I was not dealing with a passive group. They were as interested in my views as I was in theirs. Curiosity was quick to surface with questions ranging from why I had chosen to examine the issue of sexuality to what were the goals and scope of my research, and most importantly, what would I do with the findings? In many ways the queries of my students prompted me to face issues I had not, as yet, given much thought to. They knew all too well that the *sex texts* would provide a glimpse into the intimate details of their lives. Consequently, I found it necessary to reassure them that their real names would not be mentioned as a way of ensuring strict confidentiality when it came to publishing the data. Once this sensitive issue was settled, all were disarmingly eager to participate.

The Questionnaire

The structured questionnaire was self-administered during class sessions to forty-three creative writing students (three sections) during the fall semester of 2003. My intention was to better understand the sample that populated my classes before asking them to engage in personal narrative writing and discourse. The findings reveal that the majority of students are between nineteen and twenty-one years of age, nineteen of whom are male and twenty-four female. The sample consisted of four sophomores, twenty-one juniors, seventeen seniors and one graduate student. All came to creative writing, an elective course, from a wide range of disciplines. In fact, only six of the forty-three students are majoring in English. In terms of nationality, 62 percent of the sample is Lebanese, 11 percent hold dual citizenships, while the rest are from other countries around the world. High mobility and multilingualism seem to be distinguishing factors common to the majority of respondents.

Table 1: Age

Students	***Age***	***Percent***
3	18	7
18	19	41.9
12	20	27.9
5	21	11.6
3	22	7
2	23	4.6

Table 2: Sex

Students	***Sex***	***Percent***
19	M	44.1
24	F	55.8

Table 3: Academic Class

Students	***Academic Class***	***Percent***
4	Sophomore	9.3
21	Junior	48.8
17	Senior	39.5
1	Prospective Graduate	2.3

Table 4: Major

Students	***Major***	***Percent***
7	Graphic Design	16.3
5	Business	11.6
5	English Language	11.6
4	Computer Communication Eng.	9.3
3	Biology	7
3	Mechanical Engineering	7
2	Physics	4.7
2	Psychology	4.7
2	PSPA	4.7
2	Economics	4.7
2	Nutrition	4.7
1	Computer Engineering	2.3
1	English Literature	2.3
1	Mathematics	2.3
1	Civil Engineering	2.3
1	Computer Science	2.3
1	Education	2.3

Table 5: Place of Birth

Students	***Place of Birth***	***Percent***
22	Lebanon	62.7
6	Saudi Arabia	13.9
4	UAE	9.3
3	USA	6.9
2	Brazil	4.6
2	Kuwait	4.6
1	Germany	2.3
1	Jordan	2.3
1	Cyprus	2.3
1	Australia	2.3

Table 6: Countries Lived in

Students	***Countries Lived in***	***Percent***
16	1	37.2
8	2	18.6
15	3	34.8
3	4	6.9
1	5	2.3

Table 7: Nationality

Students	***Nationality***	***Percent***
27	Lebanese	62.8
4	Lebanese/American	9.3
3	Palestinian	7
2	American	4.7
2	Jordanian	4.7
1	Kuwaiti	2.3
1	Lebanese/Brazilian	2.3
1	Lebanese/German	2.3
1	Saudi Arabian	2.3
1	Palestinian/Jordanian	2.3

Table 8: Native Language

Students	*Native Language*	*Percent*
27	Arabic	62.7
5	English	11.6
4	Arabic/English	9.3
2	French	4.6
2	Portuguese	4.6
1	Armenian	2.3
1	Arabic/German	2.3
1	Arabic/French	2.3

Table 9: Languages Spoken

Students	*Languages Spoken*	*Percent*
13	2	30.2
21	3	48.8
9	4	20.9

Bibliography

Bauman, Z., *Liquid Life*, Cambridge, UK: Polity Press, 2005.

Bhabba, H. K., *Nation and Narration*, London: Routledge, 1990.

Bourdieu, P., *The Field of Cultural Production,* New York: Columbia University Press, 1993.

Butler, J., *Gender Trouble: Feminism and Subversion of Identity*, New York: Routledge, 1990.

Cameron, D., 'Beyond Alienation: An Integrated Approach to Women and Language', in M. Toolan, ed., *Critical Discourse Analysis: Critical Concepts in Linguistics*, London: Routledge, 2002.

Coates, J., 'Gossip Revisited: Language in All-Female Groups', in Jennifer Coates and Deborah Cameron, eds, *Women in Speech Communities*, London: Longman, 1989.

DeVault, M., 'Personal Writing in Social Sciences: Issues of Production and Interpretation', in R. Hertz (ed.), *Reflexivity and Voice*, London: SAGE, 1997.

Durkheim, E., *Suicide: A Study in Sociology*, New York: Free Press, 1951.

Foucault, M., *Power/Knowledge: Selected Interviews and Other Writings*, ed. C. Gordon, New York: Panthen, 1980.

Goffman, E., *The Presentation of Self in Everyday Life*, New York: Doubleday, 1971.
Habermas, J., 'Civil Society and the Political Public Sphere', in Calhoun, C., Joseph Gerteis, James Moody, Steven Pfaff, Intermohan Virk, eds, *Contemporary Sociological Theory*, London: Blackwell, 2002.
Hall, S., 'The Local and the Global: Globalization and Ethnicity', in A. D. King, ed., *Culture, Globalization and the World System*, Binghamton: SUNY, 1991.
Hannerz, U., *Transactional Connections*, London: Routledge, 1996.
Hertz, R., ed., *Reflexivity and Voice*, Newbury Park, CA: SAGE, 1997.
Kamler, B., *Relocating the Personal*, Albany: State University of New York Press, 2001.
Pinar, W., 'Regimes of Reason and the Male Narrative Voice', in W. Tierney and Y. Lincoln, eds, *Representation and the Text*, Albany: State University of New York Press, 1997.
Seidman, S., *Embattled Eros*, New York: Routledge, 1992.
Simon, R., *Teaching Against the Grain: Texts for a Pedagogy of Possibility*, New York: Bergin & Garvey, 1992.
Tannen, D., *You Just Don't Understand: Women and Men in Conversation*, London: Virago, 1991.
Weeks, J., *Invented Moralities*, New York: Columbia University Press, 1995.

Notes

1. B. Kamler, *Relocating the Persona*, Albany, 2001.
2. For an elaboration of these concepts, see J. Habermas, 'Civil Society and the Political Public Sphere', London, 2002; S. Hall, 'The Local and the Global: Globalization and Ethnicity', Binghamton: SUNY, 1991; H. K. Bhabba, *Nation and Narration*, London, 1990; U. Hannerz, *Transactional Connections*, London, 1996.
3. S. Seidman, *Embattled Eros*, New York, 1992.
4. Ibid., p. 188.
5. E. Goffman, *The Presentation of Self in Everyday Life*, New York, 1971.
6. M. DeVault, 'Personal Writing in Social Sciences: Issues of Production and Interpretation', London, 1997.
7. Z. Bauman, *Liquid Life*, Cambridge, 2005.
8. E. Durkheim, *Suicide: A Study in Sociology*, New York, 1951.
9. P. Bourdieu, *The Field of Cultural Production*, New York, 1993.
10. D. Cameron, 'Beyond Alienation: An Integrated Approach to Women and Language', London, 2002; J. Coates, 'Gossip Revisited: Language in All-Female Groups', London, 1989; D. Tannen, *You Just Don't Understand: Women and Men in Conversation*, London, 1991.
11. J. Weeks, *Invented Moralities*, New York, 1995, p. 99.
12. W. Pinar, 'Regimes of Reason and the Male Narrative Voice', Albany, 1997.
13. M. Foucault, *Power/Knowledge: Selected Interviews and Other Writings*, New York, 1980.
14. J. Butler, *Gender Trouble: Feminism and Subversion of Identity*, New York, 1990, p. 118.

Creating Queer Space in Beirut

Zones of Encounter within the Lebanese Male Homosexual Sphere

Sofian Merabet

How can one as an anthropologist write about 'queer space' and its socio-cultural creation in Lebanon in light of a perpetually changing global landscape at the beginning of the twenty-first century? Theoretically, one will have to look back on a long and complex intellectual tradition that is closely tied to twentieth-century philosophical thought. Similar to its analytical object – Lebanon's socio-cultural landscape – this intellectual tradition can neither be conceived of as one monolithic body with a coherent thread running through it nor as a chronological teleology proceeding from a clear-cut beginning to an explicit end. It is rather a fluid and at times contradictory tradition that has drawn from different and competing methodological angles. The knowledge of space, along with its social and cultural creation, indeed, constantly oscillates between cohesive description and circumstantial fragmentation. One describes objects within space or unrelated fragments of space while presenting either an anthropological field site or a geographical place. Yet one rarely reflects on the intricate ways in which space gets socially created and on the relations and consequences that a culturally conscious urban anthropology entertains with the geography of difference within whose realm it operates.

Lebanon's capital Beirut is one of these field sites where the anthropologist is constantly reminded of the historically rich and conflicting nature of the urban landscape, its shifting borderlines and entrenched interpretations of a variety of persistently contested spaces. In trying to illustrate my main point here, I shall focus on different places within the Lebanese capital that come close to the creation of what I wish to call 'queer space'. They are often places in which the socially assumed dichotomy between 'public' and 'private' becomes redundant and gives room to what I perceive as being 'zones of encounter', namely urban sites that foster attempts, not necessarily always with success, at transcending spatio-temporal fixities. These fixities, along with their socio-cultural correlates, sometimes come to be challenged by some individuals through symbolic representation. Both, i.e. fixities and correlates, display social relations that are subject to constant change. Thus they can be symbolically displaced on an endless basis as well as dissimulated by the homosexual individual.

Every so often, however, instead of being directly challenged, social boundaries become rather asserted and (sometimes) reinforced. The ensuing reproduction of fixities thus helps to maintain collective relations in a deceptive state of uncontested cohesion and coexistence. Within this contradictory reality of challenging and asserting the status quo, social space continually incorporates a panoply of social practices, those of commonly shared as well as individual content. They come into being and die, while their protagonists act out and sometimes undoubtedly suffer their consequences. Subsequently, practices of homosexuality have their altering impact, at moments contiguous and at others concealed, upon the creation of queer space in Beirut. Such a space denotes, of course, a foremost non-architectural term. It designates the geographical along with the socio-cultural fields in which various homosexual practices take place and are being integrated into the respective lives of different individuals. As a theoretical token, I prefer, therefore, to subscribe to the adjective 'queer', even if its equivalent 'gay' is more widely used in Lebanese vernaculars. It highlights the potential challenge and rupture that a corresponding space may pose to a number of social normativities along with their copious social conformities.

The integration of homosexual practices in Lebanon, however, forecloses the local existence of what could be termed a 'gay community', if one perceives a community as being a somehow coherent and comprehending group of individuals who share corresponding, although at times competing, convictions and aspirations, and where the sexual inclination becomes a fundamental concern regarding the many social convolutions of identity construction. Today, there is no such category that I can readily think of that implies that Lebanese homosexuals form anything but an externally – let alone internally – uncontested social entity. For that matter, there have been no effective spaces in post- civil war Lebanon that have unequivocally demarcated activities of an inclusive community which socially identifies itself with its homosexual orientation. I certainly do not want to overlook attempts, generally quite composite in their convictions, of self-appointed groups that have emerged over recent years, to reach out into what they call a 'community'. Unfortunately, as of late, many of these attempts have ended up as pipe dreams confined to the clear-cut boundaries of their contestants' overwhelmingly prosperous economic backgrounds.[1]

In contrast, the aftermath of the so-called "Cedar revolution," following the assassination of the former Prime minister Rafik Hariri on 14 February 2005, led not only to the withdrawal of Syrian troops, but also to an increased self-awareness and self-empowerment of large parts of Lebanese civil society. This development also included the partial re-imagination of local queer identities. In spite of the violence generated by the Syrian military retreat, the brief moment of perceived liberation was equated not only with a general shaking-off of fear, but also with a concerted "coming-out" by the local LGBT group HELEM whose nascent community activism has increasingly been reported on by the international media.[2] Moreover, the devastating war unleashed by the Israeli military against the whole of Lebanon in the summer of 2006, propelled many an advocate at the forefront of the humanitarian aid and transformed them into relief workers organized with other civic groups in an effort to help the scores of refugees who had been bombed out of their homes. Given the knowledge in public relations accumulated over the past couple of years, HELEM and its supporters will surely be able to capitalize on their commitment to humanitarian causes in the hour of general disaster in order to further their own agenda in a time after the end of the Israeli aggression.

Notwithstanding the various attempts to form and categorize an activist gay movement in Lebanon at the beginning of the 21st century, I am more interested in assessing the numerous spaces of intersecting and corresponding borderlines, and in stressing the individual lives of persons who are diverse in their individual experiences, larger socio-cultural affiliations, social status and economic interests. Moreover, local homosexuals, many of whom use the English word 'gay' as an individual qualifier, regardless of the language they actually speak, entertain distinct, albeit heavily charged, relations with each other as well as with society in general. More importantly, they have diverse and, at times, conflicting ways of approaching and coping with their particular lived realities.

The Homosexual Sphere

Given the difficulties and complications attached to the misleading implications of applying the social classification of 'community' to homosexuals in Lebanon, it becomes all the more pertinent for the anthropologist to look for an alternative and suitable category that comes close to assessing the complexity of daily-life experiences. Therefore, in order to grapple with the frame in which homosexual practices, along with their various representations, are presently taking place in and around Beirut, I choose to talk about a 'homosexual sphere', a space that is fluctuating and every so often ambiguous. This sphere is mostly a realm that consists primarily of gendered as well as sexual symbols in relation to which queer space is perpetually being created. Yet the fluidity of the homosexual sphere in Lebanon aside, the homosexual individual, almost as a rule, constantly falls back onto the insidious politics of fixities and categorization frequently associated with his social demeanour or her bodily posture.

Due to the notorious – and typically overwhelming – need in Lebanon to categorize people by putting them into a socially convenient set of drawers, it becomes increasingly pivotal to consider the less predictable dynamics regarding specific details and motivations in homosexual practice that go beyond any sort of fixities and that, particularly in this case, are often related to the individual minutiae of lived realities. These minutiae unfold precisely within what I have called 'zones of encounter'. Those (usually open) sites, which are part of the larger cityscape, do not just manage to transcend fixities of a spatio-temporal nature. Through symbolic representation by some concerned individuals, they also manage to defy an overwhelming normative orthodoxy and its socio-cultural correlates such as unquestioned compliance and mimicry. At first glance, this representation is a symbolization that dissimulates more than it shows. However, next to frontal, overt, that is to say declared and codified individual performances, this symbolization also encompasses relations that are hidden, clandestine and, therefore, linked to zones of encounter that are reminiscent of sites of transgressions, particularly those regarding sexual *jouissance*, together with their conditions and consequences. Thus an urban environment like Beirut contains zones of intersecting encounters and correspondences that the inhabitants of the city assign to specific places, which then in turn become appropriated and are varyingly interpreted by different people, including homosexual men.

In post-civil-war Lebanon, the representations of productive relations in spatial discourse do not only encompass relations of state and governmental power, but they also reflect a variety of alternative potencies that become crystallized within the larger context of their own dynamic representations. The spatial setting of such representations is related, for example, either to certain neighbourhoods or some street corners, or even to a variety of particular buildings scattered around the city. Thus while the formality of frontal relations is often brutal and based not only on the state but also on an assortment of less easily distinguishable social authorities, it does not completely prohibit individual clandestine and underground activities. In other words, there may not be power without accomplices and without police, but there cannot be power without those who resist it either.

Appropriating, Contesting and Representing Space

Today in Beirut, there is a spatial practice as it is officially perceived and sanctioned. It is a practice that comprises notably the production, reproduction as well as destruction of entire districts of the city. On the other hand, there are different representations – i.e. counter-appropriations – of space. For instance, the appropriations of the café or the nightclub whose clientele changes from day to night times, tuning itself into the continuous flow of spatial contestation. These representations are constantly shifting and they convert those frontal relations of production and reproduction into informal signs and codes that, in turn, are prone to being contested and struggled upon. Spaces of representation, for example, like the current social hubs along Monnot Street in the eastern neighbourhood of Ashrafieh or of the newly refurbished downtown area, are lived spaces for a more general (even if far from inclusive) public. Parts of them, however, also present complex symbolisms associated with the intricate social process of creating queer space in Lebanon. For instance, by encompassing a carefully selected list of social venues, the practice of 'bar hopping' may eventually become a kind of code shared by a particular group of people. It is not a mere appropriation of space, but rather of spaces of representation that include a reframing of these spaces in the form of a temporary displacement as well as some kind of collective, albeit contradictory, social identification.

Given the intricate interplay of social pressure and the potential individual resistance to it, how is it at all possible for the anthropologist to represent theoretically the appropriation of a space deemed queer in Beirut? First, the larger urban dynamics, along with their human crystallizations, must be grasped with a strong commitment to interdisciplinarity. In a time in which specializations become celebrated fixities in themselves, it is important to be reminded of the richness of scholarship born out of disciplinary transversality at the crossroads of philosophy, sociology, history, literature and linguistics. The idea of corresponding intersections becomes most relevant within the concept of the 'moment' purported by the French urbanist-philosopher Henri Lefebvre, an instant captured by philosophy, literature and politics that privileges the spatial over the temporal.[3] It is this concept that I endeavour to appropriate myself by talking about zones of encounter within which the homosexual sphere in Beirut is best captured in its complexity striving towards autonomy.

The encounter itself is an intimate moment, to be located first in time as well as in space. It is the very event in which people meet who would not necessarily do so had it not been for this particular time and place. Notwithstanding its discreet character, in Lebanon, the encounter is always linked to either one or more publicly accessible places, possibly a restaurant, a movie theatre or an internet café. For example, life on certain streets in Beirut unveils a kind of metaphysics of space, a poetic divinity, next to which thousands of people may pass without seeing anything, and which all of a sudden becomes sensitively tangible and terribly haunting for those who have a particular social stake in it. On some sort of canonical mental map, those concerned individuals will read the social topography of a neighbourhood not merely as a grid of real-life streets, but rather as a congregation of sites and cultural references that loom large in the imagination of the local homosexual.

I choose to capture Beirut's countless congregations of sites and cultural references by literally walking through the entire city. My choice translates into a challenging enterprise, for the social conformities of post-civil-war Lebanon coerce many Lebanese to approach their urban centre along the routes of a car driver's paradise. Beirut is not Los Angeles, however, and driving the latest American models of Sports Utilities Vehicles (SUVs) in the relatively small, and usually car-infested, streets of the Lebanese capital becomes an all-too-obvious exercise in indulgence. Thus the local politics of prestige and status symbolizations, privileging the unmistaken agenda of the big and brazen, often end up defining a man by his best phallic friend, the automobile. To wilfully walk through the streets and alleys of Beirut becomes, therefore, anything but a commonly shared activity. To confront with one's feet the notorious lack of sidewalks is, at best, something that only a nobody – i.e. a condemned pedestrian – may do. Yet, by moving against the grain of fumes and honks, it becomes also possible to experience an invigorating rupture within this particularly limiting scheme of things. As a person on foot in a city that almost makes natural locomotion impossible, the observing anthropologist starts distinguishing many of the urban spaces that bear the potential of creating alternative discourses.

As the young Walter Benjamin was smitten by Paris and what he perceived as being French culture, a central figure emerged from his eclectic work, namely that of what he understood the quintessential Parisian to be, the *flâneur*.[4] This idle stroller is continuously adrift in the city. While his passive senses are exquisitely attuned, his greatest luxury remains one of having no specific purpose. As an indulgent and solitary figure, he loves to contemplate the panoply of street life as an ambler whose own reflection is mirrored in the alleys and thoroughfares he decides to walk through. With the seemingly impartial gall of an infant, or sometime of a predator on the move, he gazes at passing strangers, one of whom may be himself, manifest in a fractured form that is reflected in some unexpected shopwindow. There is probably no more impersonal, and, for that matter, no more concentrated, distillation of intimacy than in the Benjaminian figure of the Parisian *flâneur*, who unremittingly strolls, loafs or idles.

I do not find it utterly improper to use the altogether male image of an early twentieth-century suit-wearing Berliner, most likely carrying some kind of mahogany walking stick, to convey my own methodological approach in making sense of the vicissitudes that rage in the Lebanese capital today. What some would see as unforgivable aimlessness is, after all, one of the city-dwellers' *arts de vivre*. However, the anthropologist who is walking through Beirut's urban maze, and this on an everyday basis for years, cannot be reduced to some elitist theoretical icon. Moreover, most anthropological fieldwork encompasses always individual struggles with a daily life that, by definition, lacks conventional glamour and is decidedly unacademic in outlook. Over the becoming, yet confining, figure of the *flâneur*, I favour, therefore, talk about the rather ordinary 'walker', 'stroller' or sometimes even the simple 'drifter'. I thus concentrate on his or her abilities to master the arts of impressions, circumnavigating the city as whim dictates, giving him or herself over to the spectacle of the moment, without the limitations of a particular agenda. But I also focus on the various attempts by the idle drifter at 'participant objectification' as well as on the importance of activating the senses in order to help the concerned person to succeed in understanding the complexity of various spaces and neighbourhoods in a city like Beirut, but also in coping with the hardships of daily life in Lebanon.

Hamra's Queer Topography

The Hamra district of Beirut, for instance, the 'Big Red' as it were, is a prime example of a busy neighbourhood that over the daily twenty-four hours goes through different stages of presumed collective perceptions and individual discoveries. During the day, store after store, snack stand after snack stand and a myriad of cars compete for the passer's attention. Regardless of whether it is in the daylight or during the wee hours, one has to ask him or herself if and how a large part of this human stream, which on an everyday basis transports innumerable waves of personal dreams on the city streets that cover the vast body of Beirut, is influenced by its environment and how an ostensibly mutual impact between city and people may possibly modify the entire current of thoughts of a neighbourhood, or perhaps of the entire world.

In the bustling and mundane streets of the Hamra district, a multiplicity of bars and 'amusement centres', including brothels carrying names like *Candle Bar* and *Rock Inn*, are barely noticeable in daytime. Although these establishments cater to a wide range of heterosexual patrons, historically, there has always been a number of social venues clearly drawing on homosexual customers. These have never been fixed places that remained stable in terms of their locations, names or design. On the contrary, we are dealing with bars, cafés and clubs that have emerged on a queer topography for various reasons at some point or another in the history of this pivotal neighbourhood. Some have vanished and been forgotten, others, while ceasing to exist, still continue to be remembered by those individuals who, for reasons of their own making, associate with them memorable times.

During the 1975–91 civil war, the most popular homosexual hangout in the area was to be found right at the start of Hamra Street, namely within the modernist premises of the so-called 'Horseshoe Building'. The café bearing the same name disappeared long ago, even though a fastfood restaurant opened in its stead in 2003. The current owners resuscitated the old alias, yet they made the Horseshoe into an entirely new place, in terms of design but also in terms of a new, family-oriented, clientele. In fact, the civil war, as well as its immediate aftermath, witnessed an active spatial contestation on the queer map in and around Beirut. Now vanished and almost completely forgotten nightclubs, like the indelible *King's* on the Corniche, harboured composite crowds of homosexuals in the days when the city was in physical shambles.

Still today, there remain in Hamra two run-down movie theatres, the *Edison* on Bliss Street and the *Khayyam* in an apartment building off Sidani Street, both of which host occasional homosexual encounters framed by European soft porn from the 1970s (often staged in German with Greek or Turkish subtitles) or East Asian Kung-Fu films. However, the main cinema that for a long time was the prime hub for ready man-to-man sexual interactions closed its doors in 2000. The *Pavillon*, named after the hotel on Ibrahim 'Abd El 'Aal Street in whose basement it was situated, is said to have attracted huge crowds of men during the civil war, some of whom took part in militia fighting. According to many stories that I have been told over the past decade, when West Beirut was under shelling and deprived of electricity, the power generators of the *Pavillon* movie theatre worked in splendid isolation from the terrors of the outside world in order to satisfy its faithful patrons. Not having been there at the time, I cannot vouch for the total accuracy of these stories. Nevertheless, echoes of years of overheard commentary, along with later personal visits to these very premises, made me realize the insinuated sharp dichotomy between an apparently licentious inside and a regulated spiteful outside. To know about these places means also that one knows about their socially illegitimate character. Thus, by becoming a form of release – or delusion, for that matter – inside the movie theatre, to be indulged in furtively, the strictly sexual encounter is often being recollected in shame on the streets outside.

This being said, the substance of homosexual desire, that of voyeurism and recollection, along with the issues of daydream, fantasy and delusion, cannot be eclipsed completely by the complex existence of a socially sanctioned homophobia in Lebanon. Through its spatially projected dimension, the local contestation of values, lived realities and collective performances has its continuous impact, notwithstanding any kind of spatial confinement, on social interactions at large. It is a contestation, moreover, that is not necessarily teleological in outlook. That is, the process, together with its impromptu results, can never be estimated in advance. In May 2002, for example, a bar/restaurant called *Café Sheikh Manoush* closed its premises in a basement on Bliss Street, a mere stone's throw away from the cornucopian campus of the American University of Beirut. A heedless observer may well have wondered why a restaurant would possibly shut down that, only a few months before its definite closure, was a packed place of seemingly undisturbed homoerotic consumption.

The 'Café Sheikh Manoush'

The answer as to why the café closed is located in the larger, and not seldom contradictory, ramifications of a socially widespread homophobia in Lebanon. Sheikh Manoush, without any doubt, managed over the two years of its successful existence to attract large numbers of local homosexuals. In fact, on Saturday nights during the summer of 2001, it became something of a pleasure-seeking hothouse of coy male glances and stares that found its legitimation as a springboard from which people later in the night proceeded to enjoy themselves in dance clubs, notably in the notorious and queer-identified *Acid* in Horsh Tabet, in the eastern parts of the capital. As success frequently comes coupled with a heightened public visibility, predictable problems were already looming on the horizon. But before embracing analysis, let me first render the idea of what the place, whose opening hours were limited to the night, was all about at the start of a weekend. Following is an uncensored excerpt of my notes that I took on a Saturday night upon embarking on fieldwork in 2001. As with all things uncensored, the ensuing paragraphs express a few of the methodological, but also simply human, flaws and weaknesses of the ethnographic novice. However, they further illustrate indirectly many of the theoretical questions that I, as an aspiring anthropologist, came to be haunted by during the entire period of my research.

> The primary colour in the locale is blue, as is the colour of the menu whose cover outlining an oversized compass suggestively reads in large English letters: 'Café Sheikh Manoush: Where West Meets East', as if intentionally designed for the Lebanese version of a collectively sanctioned *amour bleu*. One enters the premises from Bliss Street by going some steps down in order to reach an underground lounge decorated in Orientalist fashion *à l'arabe*. In the middle of the restaurant stand a bunch of low wooden tables around which one can sit on pseudo-traditional chairs that face each other. At the far left stands the bar where a group of men is sitting on high stools, two rather old fellows and two youngsters. One of the youngsters wears a muscle shirt that accentuates the developed lines of his gym-trained body. Despite the comparatively more mature couple at the bar, the rest of the customers seems to be quite young, mostly men in their twenties. The music is a concoction of 2001 Western summer remixes, but there are also moments when Arabic songs get played, thus enticing large parts of the audience into standing up and moving their trendy physiques to the tunes of local pop icons ...
>
> All of a sudden, a group of four male philanderers has dramatically entered the *Sheikh* before deciding to sit in the far right corner which, alas, is situated immediately behind me. I'm facing a dilemma now. On the one hand, I hate sitting in corners myself, or rather with my back to walls, reluctant to hide plainly from my surroundings. On the other, I hardly appreciate it when presumably interesting things

happen right in the rear of where I am.

Therefore, I have to weigh my own narcissism against my notorious curiosity. The other thing that bothers me is that I somehow recognize one of the two old men sitting at the bar. I must have encountered him in past years when the *Sheikh* was still in its old location above ground and somewhat less stylish, although still highly distinguishable by its intricate wood paneling that featured the names of famous, now defunct, singers, not just Arab, but also European and American. For some reason, I can't forget the Arabic letters denoting 'Edith Piaf'.

The old guy is looking at me with his squinty eyes. He actually looks freaky, I must admit. Perhaps he knows why his face looks familiar to me. I doubt it, though. To my right, there lingers a cute young couple. To tell the truth, there is just one who looks winsome to me, the other embodies something quite rigid and is endowed, I have to say, with anything but a pleasing face ... Why is this waiter coming and going in my direction? Judging from his eyes, it's definitely not because of me or because of my empty glass, but rather because of the enticing bachelors in full commotion behind me ...

Newcomers! And not only that. It's intriguing to note that another familiar face has just stepped into the *Sheikh*. And this time, I can even place the person. It's a fellow I literally met in the water. It was while swimming in the waves of Jbeil's 'Paradise Beach' some days earlier. Back then, he primarily struck me as being the only one on that stretch of littered sand who actually knew how to swim, indulging his athletic body in sound and studied movements that clearly distinguished him from his drifting peers. After floating inconspicuously next to each other under the burning sun for a while, we mutually broke the ice by talking about the sun's astounding reflection on the relatively smooth surface of the Mediterranean sea. He told me that he was originally from Beirut, however, had been working in Saudi Arabia over the past couple of years. Having left Jeddah only four days earlier, he already started missing the city. Whether he preferred the Red Sea over the Mediterranean, I thus sheepishly inquired. 'Not really,' he replied. It was rather the greater freedom that presently Lebanon was falling short to provide him with that he was longing for. (Later he told me that his family was awfully eager for him to get married as soon as possible.) 'In Saudi Arabia, anything goes and I don't feel looked after all the time like here,' he further explained. Soon later, our conversation started to lose in substance. He asked me where my towel was lying and, in stepping out of the water, offered me a ride back to Beirut, which I merrily accepted. But as the moment arrived to leave, I couldn't find him. Had he changed his mind or did something unforeseeable occur? I don't know. In any case, now he's at *Sheikh Manoush*, standing just about ten yards away from me and ignoring his former fellow bather as best he can.

The waiter finally took my empty glass in which I had been drinking, under compulsion, a rather nondescript cocktail called 'Tropicana'. Whatever the exact ingredients of this non-alcoholic mix may have been, I wonder ... The old guy, along with his younger companion, just stared intensely at me. I'm probably making this one up by way of projection because the eloquent swimmer from Jbeil continues blatantly to avoid paying the slightest heed to me. Nonetheless, I remain intrigued by the fact that next to the fifty-or-so- years-old bald and cross-eyed gentleman sits this attractive youngster with carefully fashioned sloppy hair. In the meantime, there are two further couples of the older generation making their eye-catching entry into the lounge which, by now, has become an exclusively male space. Notwithstanding all odds, I have to confess that, especially at this point, I'm anything but into the theatrics of these local sugar daddies. But look! One of them exchanges three kisses on the cheek with one of the *shabab*[5] sitting behind me ... Why is the bald man squinting in my direction again? Possibly just in order to get a glance of what is happening in my back where two of the chaps are leaving now, yet not before profusely saying 'bye' to the small crowd surrounding them. The attractive one brings them to the door, but comes back and proceeds with his distracted chat with the barman. In the meantime, the couple to my right is sharing some fruity cocktail. While bibulating the proclaimed exotic liquid out of their respective straw, they seem to be engaged in a balmy conversation. The cute one's affluent economic background is very much noticeable. He is most certainly some 'son of a family'. He sports a thin goatee around his secretive lips. His looks are quite intricate, some would later say that his demeanour has even a feminine touch to it. Whatever that is supposed to mean ...

To my left sit two other male representatives of the older generation. To me, they both appear like relatively square chubby hubbies. And, as usual, some Greek god makes his way into the *Sheikh* and greets them. Is this for real or am I just imagining those particular patterns of the plot unfolding in front of my eyes? In this case, anyway, we are talking about an I-shirted blond beauty with an aquiline nose, a tight butt, and significantly developed triceps, again ... It's getting too loud, and this annoys me because I have increasingly a hard time appreciating the blasting drums of the music in the background ... The 'son of a family' (or shall I say 'family son'?) to my right is at times pensive, nervously putting his straw in and out of his mouth ... It just occurs to me that I haven't mentioned yet the two TV sets behind the bar. Both are tuned to the very popular 'Fashion TV' and show the latest 'tendences' from Paris and Milan. At this point, it looks to me all the more like an unmistakable parade of vanities of some sort that is vigorously being mimicked by the very reality I find myself in tonight. Yet, at the end of the day, one may readily ask the question of 'what is fake and what is real?'

I call for the cheque, and here he comes, the waiter, that is. I guess now the stud from 'Paradise Beach' recognized me for sure (as if I have had tentatively doubts about it). Still, there is no explicit recognition on his part. Or maybe I'm just incapable of picking up the relevant signs. For that matter, it always strikes me how much can happen within the apparently mere exchange of a glance. Besides, there appears to be so much of an implicitly assumed acknowledgement that it doesn't need to be explicit or even cheaply overt anymore. No wonder that I'm in the midst of some thriving pick-up scene. This being said, at the end of the play, there are moments in which I fool myself in believing that I can take equal part in this exacting kind of a covert game. However, there are other moments in which I simply can't, let alone go – undisturbed – along with the thwarting rules.

The Queer Encounter in Beirut, a Probing Conundrum

As far as the lack of censorship of the above is concerned, I hope that the excerpt discloses the difficulty in approaching theoretical questions, often quite haunting in character, surrounding the tangled interactions among homosexuals in Lebanon. Yet before tackling the subject of homophobia by replying to the question as to why, in spite of all commercial and social success, the *Café Sheikh Manoush* ended up being shut down less than a year after I wrote my first observations, let me first indicate briefly some of the conjectures that partly delineate the probing conundrum of the queer encounter in Beirut. As becomes manifest in the excerpt, one of the striking aspects of that encounter is to be found in its intergenerational dimension. The seemingly undisturbed congregation of youngsters with their older cronies points to what I shall later examine within the larger context of paternalism. But for the moment, I will assess the complex politics of clothing and style as it is embodied by many a homosexual in Beirut. The wearing of muscle shirts – or so called I-shirts (i.e. tank tops) – is primarily intended to display the more or less muscular upper extremities of the concerned young man. Further, the willingness to exhibit a gym-trained body is presumed to reveal the sex appeal of the male protagonist, and, along with the appropriate accoutrements, underlines his wider aspirations to compete for a place within the local realm of a compound process of cultural globalization. Within this process, the politics of ideals is often limited to the basic setting of certain fixed types that are collectively reinforced by shared patterns of global consumption. However, such an individual bodily exhibition is usually also a collective attempt to indulge in a global culture whose major tenets revolve around the mundane consumption of fashion and style.

Similarly, music plays an important role in fostering the image of the smart and trendy. This being said, the cultural consumption of all things global can in no way be reduced to matters generally deemed 'Western' in form and content. The phrase 'Where West meets East' (and conspicuously not 'Where East meets West'), prominently featured on the cover of the menu of *Sheikh Manoush* may perhaps point in some cheap way to an essentializing cliché, but it is also a reference to the contradictory politics of self-definition that affects, among others, homosexuals in and around Beirut. Interestingly, within the past decade or so, along with the rest of the Arab world, Lebanon has witnessed an important revival and popularity of Arabic pop, making it almost impossible for local dance clubs not to play the relevant songs. For instance, within the homosexual sphere in and around the Lebanese capital, it would be difficult to find somebody oblivious to the salient fact that on weekends, at about 1.30 AM to be exact, the DJ at *Acid* puts on *arabi* (Arabic dance pop). Enframed by the beating remixes of a Said Mrad and the catchy vocals of a Nancy Ajram, the flashy dance club becomes packed with a plethora of belly-dancing aspirants trying their best to give the finest corporeal performances. It is precisely this wilful synchronization of fashionable bodies that rhythmically move to synthesized tunes under the attention-grabbing roof of an eclectic and stylish nightclub that best captures local interpretations of global habits of consumption.

However, the dominant aspiration for an individual place within the embattled local Lebanese realm of cultural globalization tends to translate into a politics of ideals that often limits itself to the basic assertion of fixed types drawn from the repertoire of a larger post-colonial predicament. As becomes apparent in the excerpt about *Sheikh Manoush*, the general appeal, as relating to bodily aesthetics and sexual attraction, is typically linked to the exoticism of a complex beauty ideal flourishing among the haunting ruins of a seemingly ageless colonial past. It is an ideal that, as an unfaltering social rule, has the tendency to privilege light complexions over dark ones. Corresponding to a paradigm, this ideal ends up being projected onto the blemished mirror of post-colonial haughtiness. Within the homosexual sphere of status-obsessed Beirut, the image of the 'blond (and preferably blue-eyed) hunk' transcends in desire, admiration and prestige the possibility of all other homoerotic categories, thus discounting practically any kind of counter-currents. This peculiar projection of exoticized images remains a pernicious one, however. To desire the fairness of the other – and not the other as such – by passing over any pigmentation regarded as being too conspicuous does not only put into perspective a rampant racism, it also uncovers the problematics of a continuously colonized society faced with the perpetual and deceptive processes of identifying itself according to contrived ideals that are primarily associated with some locally imagined and essentialized West.

Thus to assess these processes of identification by dwelling in one's own social space within the homosexual sphere in Beirut persists in being a delicate undertaking for the concerned individual. Further, the consequences that such a social challenge generates go well beyond any sort of latent narcissism on the part of the anthropologist. They also transcend any semiotic confusion, manifest through the possible exchange of misunderstood glares and gazes that may be an integral part of the researcher's interactions with his or her would-be informants. These interactions are always potentially predicated on the impending incapacity to pick up relevant signs which are themselves continuously displaced by all the involved protagonists.

Moreover, the displacement of the interactions between anthropologist and informant goes hand in glove with generalized mechanisms of projection and defence such as the exhibition of arrogance, indifference and aloofness that are an integral part of the broader social repertoire in Lebanon. Indeed, to recognize people – a happenstance hardly to be avoided in such a minuscule country – does not mean that person A has to acknowledge person B outright. Quite the opposite is *de rigueur*. As partly illustrated by the behaviour of the young Lebanese man working in Saudi Arabia, you can easily talk to a person at a particular time and in a particular place. However, once those temporal and spatial co-ordinates are shifted, the same person may refrain from looking at you altogether. Within the specificity of the moment and through a distinctive mobilization of covert gazes and gapes, familiar faces are always first screened, that is to say, evaluated by the respective party according to their particular relevance to him. If somebody happens to lack, for one reason or another, the attributes of a timely social significance, he is generally met with indifference or some equivalent attitude suggesting that he barely exists.

Nonetheless, if someone manages, for better or worse, to entice the attention of his target audience, he will find himself most probably at the centre of some propitious interest. As an unrelenting consequence, the question ends up boiling down to how the homosexual individual is to provoke the undisputed acknowledgment of his peers. The answer partly lies in the strategic ability to display successfully one's own aloofness in the presence of others. It is an ability that amounts to a collective power play of sorts where the presumably desired individual, in a stroke of conscious glamour, indulges himself in taking up the part of the unreachable icon. Such an individual is endowed with a number of social dexterities ranging from a deliberate short attention span to the capacity of forging false promises – or straightforward lies, for that matter. These skills help him to get rid of his respective interlocutors in order to move on to somebody, hopefully, more becoming in appearance and benefit.

In addition, such an effective protagonist rapidly assesses his own potential interest – or lack thereof – in his counterparts and acts accordingly. The question is how to prepare a face for such a cursory world and how such world shows itself in the resulting face. To play at being hard to get reflects the ideal of anonymity in encounters within the Lebanese homosexual sphere that discount the very idea of sustained relationships, let alone the identifiable commitment this would generate. Yet it also points to local ideals of anonymity in a very small country that is notoriously anything but anonymous. At the same time, to play the role of the aloof chap highlights the deceitful determination to protect oneself. It is a determination that comes in the shape of a latent – sometime quite manifest – denial of one's own ultimately anti-normative sexuality. In turn, the production of desire becomes a skill in itself that highlights personal characteristics which are made to be well received by one's entourage. It is a production that includes, for instance, the particular looks of a fellow as well as the various ways he is capable of mobilizing to exhibit actual – or oftentimes made-up – material wealth.

Here the aforementioned complex issue of paternalism comes into play. Generally, the purported prestige associated with an older man is linked, whether directly or through the tangled ramifications of a psychoanalytical projection, to that person's socially perceived status. In an arrestingly patriarchal society like the Lebanese one, that is so much predicated on the fallacies of categorizing people, the phallic figure of the seemingly affluent and mature male, generally in the shape of a local heavyweight, remains central. This centrality is anything but a simple one, however. From it, and beyond the local obsession of relentlessly putting individuals into preset drawers, originate large webs of complex individual and collective desires and dependencies as well as conformist acquiescences which equate male maturity with the opportunities of a prevalent power that every so often wants to be defied yet ends up being reinforced all the same. It is a paradoxical equation, for it makes evident the pitfalls of a mainly ordinary situation where structures of oppression are adamantly reproduced precisely by those who are understood to suffer most from their repercussions but who, nonetheless, indulge in the deceitful comfort of normative conformity as well as in the volition of looking and acting alike generated from it.

This presumption – albeit incomplete – and coupled with the paradox alluded to above point together directly to the subject of homophobia. Despite all commercial and social success, the reasons why the *Café Sheikh Manoush* closed its doors are to be found in the conflicting ways in which a collective *raison d'être*, discounted as 'conspicuous behaviour' by Lebanese society at large, becomes gradually visible only before ending up as a subject of suppression. On a trivial level, it would be possible to limit my analysis to pure facticity, for example, in simply stating that the café's owner suddenly stopped wanting to have a queer-identified crowd as his primary clientele before closing the place. In part, it would even be pertinent to hint at the post-civil-war alacrity of the Lebanese in catering to a home-grown culture of excessive consumption that tends to be predicated on a social craving for immediate gratification, one that in the long term can hardly be satisfied by just one venue, whether queer-identified or not. Hence the ubiquitous practice over the past decade of opening and closing innumerable restaurants all over Beirut. Yet, in the case of the closure of *Sheikh Manoush*, all of the above cannot do justice to the totality of the different shapes that the knotty process of homophobia takes up in Lebanon. In fact, this process is all about bumps and hitches.

Visibility and the Politics of Homophobia

By the early summer of 2001, the *Café Sheikh Manoush* had not only become one of the hot spots of Beirut's homosexual sphere, it also started to attract a male crowd that was in a vigorous process of asserting its social visibility.

As illustrated by my excerpt of field notes, the place had quickly converted into a stage of alternative contestations where the intricate interplay of social pressure and individual resistance materialized into a succession of competing skirmishes. In the end, they remained nonetheless cautious and rather feeble as well as close to an ultimately overpowering conformist normativity. Part of these contestations was the display of what would later be denounced by the detractors as 'conspicuous demeanour', i.e. an inappropriate behaviour 'where men act like women', for instance. Not that such a conveyed 'femininity' had ever been foreign to male homosexuals, or even to society at large, in Lebanon. Quite the opposite is true. Despite its limited and officially unacknowledged nature, an understated yet effective local permissiveness had always allowed for socially marginalized identities in Beirut to prosper to a certain point. However, when the corresponding intersections of visibility were perceived as becoming all too excessive, i.e. potentially threatening the order of all things social, suppression made itself manifest as the almost inevitable answer.

Suppression, in fact, can be spelled out differently. What interests me here is less state suppression *per se*, even though it continues to be potent and pivotal by way of official persecution, legitimized by Article 534 of the Lebanese Penal Code that outlaws all 'sexual activity that is contrary to nature'. I am rather concerned by the complex dynamics of what I call an internal as well as perpetually internalized homophobia that is operative and very much present within – and not merely without – the homosexual sphere in Lebanon. Odd and trivial as it may seem, the closure of the *Café Sheikh Manoush* must be explained by the notorious droplet of excess that caused the glass of microsocial contingencies to spill over with its presumed transgressive content. An increasingly asserted 'feminine behaviour' on the part of some young customers started not only to antagonize the normative mental comfort of the café's owner, but also that of many a male homosexual customer eager to demarcate himself from any kind of potentially incriminating conspicuousness. This eagerness to be different from – i.e. better than – the effeminate *tanteht*[6] leads to a peculiar kind of homophobia that, I argue, is internal to the homosexual sphere in Lebanon as well as successively internalized by a great number of its protagonists. It is a demarcation that bears at its core a complicated apparatus of disavowal. However, the widespread and emphatic proclamation *ana mesh heyk*, 'I'm not like that', coupled with particular interpellations denouncing the effeminate other, by extension, also include the general rejection of any alternate idiosyncratic differences that may characterize the other, regardless of whether external or internal.

The result is a neurotic and awfully frustrated performance that clearly privileges a mimicry of the normative over a common recognition of difference, thus implying xenophobia in its most literal sense. This, first somewhat hesitating, then violent performance, so strange to the observing eye, bears a frightening potency and removes horror to the realm of social tragedy: if you are not like me, looking up to similar ideals and sharing compatible desires, you cannot possibly be part of the world I inhabit. Therefore, I shall look – if at all – through you and ignore your very existence. The underlying neurosis of such a performance may, paradoxically, be based on a profound individual urge to express oneself. Yet this urge tends to mutate into a conformist mimicry that coerces the concerned person into acting out a projected ideal image that he wants to partake in. Often enough, the material affluence in personal backgrounds is all but pretended. The lack of money, together with the opprobrious compulsion to look physically like the normative rest, is another instance where relations of paternalism come into play. It is an instance that turns more than just a few youngsters into various relations of patronage where special (e.g. sexual) favours are exchanged for material means.

To stage this unbridled mimicry in front of television screens featuring a Fashion TV that is committed to the latest trends from Europe establishes a parade of vanities where the observer, in his relentless attempts at participant objectification,[7] struggles in vain to distinguish between what is fake and what is real. It is precisely this interplay between phantasm and actuality that best characterizes the lived reality within the homosexual sphere in Beirut. Thus the conceivable comedy of the ensuing encounters, reckoned as public and where challenge along with compliance rapidly mellow into melodramatic cliché, overlays certain tragic realities of contemporary Lebanese society. The structural poverty of individual opportunity forces young people to surrender before the potent and fortified walls erected to protect and preserve social normativity. Tensions between the personal quest for perpetual attention and the contradictory display of arrogance toward others, the burning issues of repression and disavowal, as well as the conceptual divide in the propagation of ideals that exoticize the fair and flaxen-haired by proclaiming its occasional representative as the epitome of beauty – itself predicated on a post-colonial sense of inferiority – often result in an individual suffering that is founded on the collective effort by many a homosexual in Beirut to accommodate impotence.

I argue that it is the particular conjectures, ranging from the larger context of paternalism to the notorious politics of aloofness and the rampant internalization of homophobia, which partly delineate the probing conundrum of the homosexual encounter in Lebanon. Ultimately, they are, to a great extent, responsible for the closure of the *Café Sheikh Manoush*. Nevertheless, to display a demeanour generally understood as 'feminine', or 'effeminate' for that matter, does not have to be interpreted as a detrimental transgression *per se*. At times and in certain situations, it may even be welcome. Yet, the event of a favourable circumstance notwithstanding, such behaviour, if perceived as increasing in visibility, will most surely turn into the declared target of a notoriously violent internalized homophobia. That is to say that intensifying visibility invites the tendency of getting conflated with the possibility of a consequential threat to the patriarchal order of things and, therefore, the protected ideal of male – i.e. masculine – supremacy. It must thus, by all means, be chastized.

As mentioned earlier, the more the *Café Sheikh Manoush* evolved into a prominent hangout for homosexuals in Beirut, the more economically successful a business enterprise it became. As indicated, however, this success, however, also meant the increased visibility of individuals who were regarded as behaving 'conspicuously'. A double backlash followed. On the one hand, the initial stages of an internal permissiveness gradually mutated into hostility, not only on the part of the owner of the establishment, but also among those homosexual customers who saw their normative social comfort challenged. In many ways, both opted for the deceitful safety of auto-censorship instead of confronting a challenge they sensed would potentially compromise their presumed undisturbable status – or a social reputation, for that matter – commonly referred to in all local vernaculars as 'prestige'. Ultimately, such an option was predicated on affliction and the fear of being oneself socially disparaged. Yet to censor oneself only became possible after the concerned individuals managed to separate themselves conceptually from the people whose 'conspicuous' behaviour they exalted in denouncing. On the other hand, the resulting ramifications of an internalized and perpetuated homophobia, which takes up various forms of latent as well as manifest aggression and bellicosity, ironically prompted the majority of the clientele to a progressive withdrawal from the café. Thus, after staying empty for a couple of months, the *Café Sheikh Manoush* ended its formerly lucrative business and was forced to close its doors in May 2002.

Even during the summer of 2001, *Sheikh Manoush* had, of course, never been the sole social venue welcoming homosexual encounters in and around the Lebanese capital. I rather draw on the example to illustrate the many complications that creating queer space in Beirut forcefully entails. After the closure of the café, the general visibility of a queer-identified crowd, as well as the enduring presence of the potentially 'conspicuous' detractor, on the image-wary surface of Lebanese society did anything but decrease. Instead, what happened was that the local homosexual sphere started to appropriate a multiplicity of alternative – closed as well as open – spaces, thus putting forth a tangled process that remains not only one of inherently mocking the easily scandalized but also one of violent contestation, antagonism and suffering.

The Corniche

One of these alternative – and open – spaces is, for instance, the city's eventful seashore promenade, known to everybody as the Corniche. Situated not far from the Hamra district in the western part of Beirut, the Corniche has managed to retain into the post-civil war era a sort of timeless social substance. In a lot of ways, the promenade embodies a perpetually enacted microcosm within the clashing context of the macrocosmical social theatre of one of Beirut's main stages. During its rich and conflicting urban history, it has by and large remained a twenty-four-hour experience. On its various sections, stretching from 'Ain al-Mraisseh in the east to Ramlet al-Bayda in the southwest of the city, all of which are altogether different in their respective character, the bustle of urban life is always present, day or night. In spite of the manifest enactment of a larger social macrocosm within the spatial confines of a parading ground, today's the Corniche is also the socio-historical product of a postwar society widely obsessed by the importance of hierarchies and the sore politics of segregation. Therefore, only to the to the idealistic observer does it seem as if the Corniche were one of the few places in Beirut in which almost everybody congregates. The truth about Lebanese patterns of congregation is also that, in spite of all limitations, there are always individuals who manage to contest and appropriate certain spaces that go way beyond the social confines of normative conformity.

Similarly, the impediment of spatio-temporal coordinates does not stop at an active creation and appropriation of what I have been calling queer space. According to the time of the day or the night and the particular part of the Corniche, even the most fleeting partaker encounters *shabab*,[8] who generally are mostly in groups but who are also sometimes alone, leaning on the railing and selectively gazing at those who pass by. Although there are always people on the Corniche, the seashore promenade gets crowded in the evening, good weather permitting that is. After the last glimpse of the setting sun finally disappears in the composed summer waves of the eastern Mediterranean, the Corniche is packed with people and there is no apparent change ahead. All of a sudden though, the blackness of the night makes itself unmistakable. Because of enduring electricity problems pertaining to the larger and long-lasting crisis of the local energy sector, some of the city's streetlights remain often turned off. Oddly enough, it is precisely this lack of immanent visibility on the Corniche that allows for a heightened social activity related to the sociable undertakings in this blackened place of bustling urbanity.

Considering that during the day Beirut is a haven for flings and flirtations of multiple kinds, it is easy to fantasize that in the dark anything may go. But this remains a fantasy, even if some lived realities sometimes appear to come close to it. What a bitter irony, therefore, to recognize how even a lack in the industrial energy sector may be converted into a social happening or even a personal adventure where the appropriation of space challenges the contestation of personal dispositions and identities. But this, of course, is always liminal and limited to specific sites and areas that are capable of defying order, authority and convention, albeit they may ultimately be prone to reconfirm them.

If one abandons after midnight the immediate area closest to the reconstructed downtown district and diverts one's stroll towards the sea, ones leaves behind the newly furbished but still empty marina to the right at the eastern end of Beirut's historical hotel district district, namely the very site on which a bomb hit the convoy of the former Prime minister Rafik Hariri in the spring of 2005, killing him and everybody in his entourage. The haunting place gives way to a promontory where over the next couple of yards, the entire acoustic ambiance seems suddenly to change. The babel of supposed socially permissible activity that stirs men's and women's voices against the Corniche's background transforms into an altogether different universe across the street from the mosque of 'Ain al-Mraisseh. Within the labyrinth of shadows stretching westwards in the direction of the recently inaugurated lighthouse some canonical magic is taking forceful effect. By the very nature of its architectural imposition and casually intimidating character, the 'new Manara', as the concrete structure is commonly called, not only takes up the material shape of an omnipresent watchtower but also of the unmistakable significance of the urban phallus *par excellence*. In its igniting shadow, the strolling pedestrian becomes himself the observer of multiple forms and physiognomies in the almost all-encompassing night. Faces of all shapes and colours gaze with feverish intensity at each other. The only continual assertiveness is the cacophony of car noises but also of different intonations and dialects that resound at that late hour from every possible back corner.

Passing the military baths at the very tip of Ras Beirut promontory, one distinguishes, particularly during the summer months from June to August, the privileged acolytes of Lebanese army officers as they enter the heavily protected premises. It is easy to imagine them sunbathing on their martial *chaises longues* while at the same time being watched by overendowed soldiers whose most coveted equipment, apart from their ubiquitous machine guns, is their professionally developed triceps. The less fortunate, however, are denied access and thus proceed by foot towards Beirut's effervescent Luna Park where folks, mostly from the capital's southern suburbs, indulge on weekends in the humble but popular joys of riding a slightly decrepit Ferris wheel while simultaneously listening to the blasting sounds of overly recycled tunes sung by one or more of the countless Lebanese pop divas, such as the barely tolerable Najwa Karam. Moving slowly away from these acoustic discharges and making one's way up the only real hill that characterizes the Corniche's otherwise relatively horizontal topography, one reaches the area of Raouche, originally famous for its two pigeon rocks that define its coastline. Even from the outside, the chichi atmosphere of such restorative places as the so-called *Petit Café* and its *Grand* counterpart imposes itself on anybody who happens to walk by. Between the indistinguishable aesthetics of small and big, the Orient, and whatever its current global incarnations may yield in terms of postmodern consumerism, is near its best in blatantly orientalizing itself.

Step after step on this particular stretch of Beirut's seashore promenade, the restless spirit of hollowness gets successively reinforced. While the so-called Palm Springs complex with its ever-packed Starbucks Café could not look more false in its painful imitation of Floridian hacienda-style architecture (itself a brazen fake), it does not need much to rival the unusually large, yet equally bursting, Burger King division next door. This being said, the recently inaugurated Arabian phantasmagoria of a Movenpick Hotel on the other side of the street, flying the flags of Lebanon, Saudi Arabia and Switzerland tellingly in the Mediterranean sun, beats them all in providing a mirror, even if a largely unnoticed one, for many a fair of local vanities that pose in breathing the air of the world while in fact choking on the self-imposed rules of conformist mimicry. However, it would be ultimately misleading for the anthropologist, in his relentless Bourdieusian attempt at a 'participant objectification', one that is intended to gain a reflexive distance from a despair-provoking subject matter whose sheer proliferation of self-indulgence can easily make him weep, to limit his observations to the overtly phallic manifestations of normative power, whether in the form of architecture or within the intransigent frame of social hierarchies. Everywhere on these sections of the Corniche, next to those suffocating from the ramifications of their inimically performed privilege, there are always others to whom, for a multiplicity of reasons, access to the illusory heights of this earthly paradise is denied, or at least made difficult.

Even if the margins are generally adamant in asserting their potential for resisting any sort of dominant current, within the nervous context of post-civil-war Lebanon, the quietest transgressions often tend to be engulfed by the powerful whirlwinds of social conformity where the actual lack of belonging to certain ideals not only results in gawky mimicry but also in a widespread suppression of difference. In a variety of ways, the Corniche provides the stage for this upsetting paradox. At the southern edge of the pompous Movenpick Hotel, for instance, one passes the now closed but still famous Carlton, itself a tourist resort whose past glory is incidentally not only associated with the seemingly undisturbed hedonism of the 1960s and early 1970s but also with the highly entertained homoerotic joys of its mayoral owner from the Lebanese mountain district of Kesserwan. While awaiting demolition, the Carlton, in its state of dilapidation which, thanks to varying strategic alliances, is due only in part to the war, bears hauntingly witness to a scarred and painful past. But the now empty building also looks down upon the deterring animations of a present that does anything it can to repress its troublesome pedigree.

Ramlet al-Bayda

Leaving the Carlton behind, the Corniche makes a slight descent and, at its southern end, turns into a boulevard that, on the left, borders a row of luxury apartment highrises and, on the right, a sandy beach called Ramlet al-Bayda. From a distance, one could almost mistake this part of the city for some sort of local Ipanema, however, as with many things in Lebanon, seeing them close up reveals actual vistas that are quite different from the initial fantasy. In spite of sands that are anything but white these days, but rather widely littered and washed by a sea whose smell and colour frequently tend toward a questionable green, the beach still retains a popularity among those crowds who cannot afford the high entrance fees to the trendy resorts outside of Beirut. The contradiction could not be more graphic. On one side of the street there are the rich and beautiful sitting high up on their 250 square feet balconies while sipping the most exotic cocktails under the Mediterranean sun, and on the other, there is, down there, the noise of the populace who try hard to have their share of a summer diversion. The blatancy of spatially fixed and fixing social hierarchies is evidently not limited to this particular site, nor are its human representations reduced to manifestation in daylight. On the contrary, Ramlet al-Bayda is one of the foremost zones that facilitate the initiation into male homosexual encounters in Beirut – at night transforming into a parading ground for anticipated sexual gratifications, but occasionally also for yearning romantic desires.

One can stride at any time during the night on the sidewalk of Ramlet al-Bayda and encounter a variety of men, young and old, walking or sitting in their cars, who all seem to be waiting for something to happen. The confrontation with suggestive gazes, and sometimes evocative bodily postures, makes it clear to the observer that the apparently nonchalant dude leaning on the railing *khasso*, 'is concerned' according to the elaborate local vernacular. In fact, this inherent state of suspended intentionality very well summarizes what kind of activity homosexual cruising is all about within the parameters of an open space in and around Beirut. Before any kind of direct interaction involving speaking, let alone physical contact, takes place, it is up to the ubiquitous exchange of gapes and stares to respectively assess and categorize the potential object of desire. Nonetheless, there is a certain shared familiarity to this demeanour, and everybody who is part of it seems to abide by some set of informal codes and criteria that regulate what takes place on this particular stretch of the promenade. As persuasively portrayed by the first pages of Nabil Kaakoush's photomontage entitled 'Hey Handsome' (*Ya helo* in Arabic), to visually register the presence of somebody who is concerned (*khasso*), is usually followed by a supposedly credulous, yet highly calculated, verbal interaction intended to confirm the respective protagonists' motives.[9] Following the never-failing inquiries about the exact time or about borrowing a cigarette ensues a rehearsed, yet only seemingly disinterested, dialogue about the contrived coincidence of being in the same place at the same time.

Ali, a teenage boy from the southern suburb of Chouifat, said to me after we finally engaged in a conversation that took place weeks after I first saw him strolling around and paying attention to some of the cars parked conspicuously next to the sidewalk, 'when I initially came here, I used to feel like a child who lost his parents on an extended walk in a strange city, in a foreign land'. 'Have you ever been afraid venturing out here and hooking up with the wrong people, getting in their cars and so on?' I somewhat obliquely inquired. 'Not really', asserted Ali sharply. According to him, he had successively become more than a regular cruising customer at Ramlet al-Bayda, solicited by a few car-owning sugar daddies who sat silent but definitely alert in their motored vehicles. 'On the contrary,' Ali later replied to my question, 'even if I have been at times abused by those guys, deep in my soul I detect a profound sentiment of affinity that draws me to this multiplicity of individual faces who are not that bad after all. They may be foreign [i.e. from different confessionally defined neighbourhoods in and around Beirut] but certainly not strange.'

It did not take me more than a couple of nocturnal field trips to figure out that the 'affinity' that Ali was talking about had a little, albeit crucial, material twist to it.

There are times, especially after midnight on weekends, when I felt I was standing in some laboratory of pleasures, a kind of voluptuous labyrinth, and at the same time being the witness of an upsetting of local practices of strolling prostitution. The straight-running beach boulevard, recently named after the late Prime Minister Rafik Hariri (in material terms, the formerly most potent man in the country) more or less stretches from the Movenpick compound in the north to the Summerland Hotel and the Algerian embassy in the south. At night, Ramlet al-Bayda converts into an informal strip where the commodification of homosexual love has become *de rigueur* in spite of the regular patrols of local gendarmes, some of whom have their own dubious stakes in apprehending the individuals they decide to watch closely. This overt commodification of homosexual love often but not always involves, on the receiving end (depending on one's perspective, that is), boys who are materially and, therefore, socially marginalized. Ali is a case in point. As a Palestinian from one of the many southern suburban neighbourhoods of Beirut, he hardly sees his family. As he informed me, after a number of the relatively brief interactions we had, his mother repudiated him some years ago, nominally because he is a *tobji*.[10] He told me that as a result of a situation involving economic and physical hardship, he became a *sharmût*, a male prostitute. 'And after all,' he continued as if he had to justify himself before me, 'the entire world feeds on cocks! *Ma heyk?!* [No?!]'

The inherent state of suspension that tends to characterize homosexual cruising within the risky, even if sometime thrilling, parameters of an open space in Beirut begs the question as to who exactly is gazing at whom, and why? Is Charbel glancing at the marvel of Ali's bodily contours, or is Ramzi staring at Paul's feigned stripped anatomy? On an urban site like Ramlet al-Bayda, the archetype of the gaze is of pivotal relevance. It always assumes its powerfulness because it projects the common terror, as well as the ostensible fantasy, represented when we dream about being naked in a public place. It reminds us that what we normally experience as the solidity and comfort of ordinary life, coupled with the whole insidious set of social expectations, ranging from heterosexual normativity to the maintenance of hierarchies and parochial principles, is actually a deadly abyss. To that generalized dread of places where passages are open to nostalgias opposing public morale, one can always add a corridor that gives way to impromptu bedrooms whose doors are set ajar. Yet it is usually in a concocted bathrobe of conformist mimicry in which a long-rehearsed song unwraps a weary happiness. In the eagerness of incipient transgressions, fingers unlace themselves and an overcoat comes instinctively down, leading the way to the semi-anonymous physical journey, however, never before eventually going up again, restoring the never totally jeopardized land of supposed social respectability.

Spatial Alienation and the Myth of Queer Subjectivity

But let's turn back to some of the crucial theoretical issues pertaining to the spatial creation of certain experiences and their constant interpretation and appropriations of space by groups of individuals who are in the need of perpetually finding, if not imagining, sites where what I call the 'encounter' takes place. The space in and around Beirut, as an open or closed frame for the homosexual encounter, where material, psychological and spatio-temporal foci converge, often turns into 'alienation'. This is a notion that Karl Marx had first introduced as *Entfremdung* in the original German of his early *Grundrisse* (Outlines).[11] In this general theory of capitalism, he accounted for the transformation of human relations into things through the action of money, commodity and capital. I want to extend this notion of alienation to aspects of individual as well as social identity creation and locate it spatially. In so doing, I shall be able to further point to the ways in which, within the homosexual sphere in Beirut, this particular understanding of alienation not only renders commodity fetishism possible, but also how it eventually gives way to psychoanalytic associations concerning spatial identification that range from outright repression to more complicated practices of disavowal. In the meantime, these transformed human relations exert their coercive and lasting power over individuals, and lead to an understanding of the creation of space as being a culturally as well as socio-politically overdetermined product where the individual identity is perpetually shaped by the spatial production and reproduction of social relations.

As mentioned at the beginning of this essay, one of the most striking aspects of a spatially conceived creation of 'queerness' in Beirut is that it actually draws its practitioners to look for places that could become signs, 'spatial signs' of sorts, that are convenient references capable of displaying their difference as identity. Therefore, what ends up becoming a place of identification, like, for instance, the *Café Sheikh Manoush* or the Corniche, is neither the actual material 'thing' (i.e. the premises of the café or the particular stretch of the promenade) nor its sign (i.e. closed or open space for the homosexual encounter), but the idea of the relation between the two. Although I do not intend to overemphasize the distancing notion of an 'idea' that may overly separate the individual from a given place, I underscore, nevertheless, the importance of the relational aspect regarding the creation and reproduction of space and thus dismiss an absolute (i.e. unyielding) understanding of it. In fact, the site of the absolute does not exist, or, if at all, only as an emptiness, one that evokes an esoteric mystery. With this relational aspect of space in mind, the spatial creation of what may be termed 'queer' in Beirut then transforms into a para-referential discourse that ultimately becomes associated with the lived idea of a social 'lack'. It is an idea that, eventually, turns out to be inseparable from Lacanian psychoanalysis and its definition of human desire, namely a desire that is based on the inevitability of having to contend with lack and that, as a consequence, in the context of this essay points to the myth of queer subjectivity in Lebanon.

The Hammam an-Nuzha al-Jadid

Before endeavouring to conquer the Lacanian maze of bodies and mirrors, I want to go back to another set of field notes of mine and draw attention to an ethnographic zone of encounter that further exemplifies my theoretical assumptions. Let me pay a brief but intense visit to the oldest of the few local bathhouses functioning in Beirut, the *hammam an-nuzha al-jadid*, the 'new amusement bathhouse' as it were. If one approaches it from the Corniche, that is, from the west, the strolling observer has to pass first through the labyrinth of 'Ain al-Mraisseh's shadowy streets where the bulk of the *harat ash-sharamît*, the local whores' quarter, is to be found. Behind the quarter lies the pre-civil-war red-light district, the legendary *zeytuna*, whose still recently battle-inflicted lunar landscape, by now turned into a surreal real-estate utopia, has to be crossed when going eastwards towards the historic, and now lost, Jewish neighbourhood of Wadi Abu-Jamil. From afar, it is possible to make out Beirut's synagogue, one more 'preserved' ruin within this downtown pantheon of ruins where, as Jad Tabet tellingly remarks, 'the wartorn city [clashes with] the memory of the future'.[12]

In the middle of the site of an almost totally annihilated urban centre, stands the ugliness of a revived modern concrete building called Starco that shelters, among other things, the Ministry of Culture and a quite defunct Planet Hollywood. In Beirut, the memory of a violent past tends to get obliterated altogether and, in its stead, a repressed version emerges, but never without betraying a future whose potential for bearing disaster haunts for all time the present. This version is captured in a projected future that holds Beirutis once more as hostages, this time, caught between the disrobing mirror of the past and the idolatry of an imagined present that is shaky at best.[13] But reality, regardless of how deeply repressed, always resurfaces somehow. Behind Planet Hollywood, the walking drifter quickly reaches the neighbourhood of *Zokak al-Blat* whose ruined palaces once housed European and American consulates under the Ottomans. Today, on the top of these palaces, converted into makeshift shelters for refugees from the south, Union Jacks and Stars and Stripes are anything but visible, instead the green of *Amal* and, increasingly more so, the yellow of *Hizbollah*, both symbolizing the current Shi'i protagonists within the highly contested Lebanese political arena, have since become the favourite colours.

However, *Zokak al Blat* ('the cobblestone alley' in Ottoman Arabic) is not only known as a borough of vanished official splendour where old bourgeois family residences like the Hneine and Ziyade Palaces now await destruction in order to provide room for the new, increasingly ubiquitous and car-infested highways that have been madly promoted by the government. On a queer mental map, *Zokak al Blat* is synonymous with the local bathhouse. *Hammam an-nuzha al-jadid: Bains turcs*, that's all the French-language notice outside says. Next to it, on the left, are green-framed posters of the 'vanished' Moussa Sadr. Nuredine, the muscular Iraqi refugee from Kurdistan, who grew up in a Damascene shanty town, gives every customer a towel at the entrance to this voluptuous purgatory. There is a strong link in the minds of many between bathhouses and sensual pleasures. In spite of its Orientalist resonance, it is an old idea that contributes to the mystery of these public establishments, a mystery that has always been half brothel half magic. But, who knows? In the caldarium the 'concerned' person may, after all, only find the promised purifying waters, clear and chanting. Not quite. In the steam room, there is Elie, his towel loosely covering his best parts. A golden cross cruises around his neck to formally demonstrate that he is from the 'other side', that is to say, from the east and beyond the former green line. Personal interaction:

> After making me reveal the formality of my own residence within the city that has consistently been a western one, Elie asks me how I could have possibly lived next to Sabra and Chatila in Beirut's southwest. 'Isn't it dangerous down there?' 'Well danger, you know ...' I mumble, '... it's kind of relative.' Raising his right eyebrow, he leaves the steam room and climbs up the ladder to the dry sauna. During this brief interaction, Hussein, a hairy hubby, was quietly sitting on the marble in the left corner of the room. We start chatting about the weather outside and the steam inside. Having found out after the sixth sentence that my intonation revealed my western Mediterranean origins, he asks me, referring to the intricacies of the 'amusement' haven we are in, whether in our cities 'something like this – you know what I mean' existed. I guess, my answer is once again a sheepish one. 'You know,' I say to him, 'I left the islandless country of the islands when I was barely sixteen, so I was too young to get introduced to the delights of high rising temperatures.' I discern another brow wanting to rival its sister, and I wonder whether the reason for that is Hussein's disbelief in my story or whether he was mocking my rather late maturity. Luckily, it's getting too hot in the caldarium, I crave for the cold shower.

For the moment, it remains contrary to its apparent character to imagine that this locale may only be in the service of bodily hygiene. There is always a great temptation in the unknown, and in the possibility of danger an even greater one. The 'new amusement bathhouse' gives way to those dangerous dreams: a double mythical sentiment that close to nothing may articulate. First, the intimacy at heart of an assumed public, yet intimate, if not altogether secret, place; a forceful contrast, effective only for the person who has already experienced these kinds of hydrotherapeutic follies. To undress, under any pretext, can be a symptomatic act. Or a simple imprudence. The ostensible references to Orientalist *rêveries* that sometime may very well be attached to the experience of the *hammam* notwithstanding, within its undoubtedly limited frame, this experience remains an integral part in more than one homosexual life in and around

Beirut. By allowing the homosexual encounter to happen as such, regardless of whether in the form of one or more timely diversions, in Lebanon, the *hammam* perseveres – and this, despite all setbacks – in playing a pivotal role in the creation of local queer space.

> Back in the steam room, I meet both Elie and Hussein again. This time they are joined by Pierre who, after all, prefers to be called 'Peter'. 'We are "open-minded"[14], *ma heyk*? [aren't we?].' How ephemeral the art of naming is! I say to myself. It is a mere deterministic categorization that the society at large bestows upon you. And it goes both, if not more, ways: 'Boutros' turns easily into 'Pierre' and 'Pierre' melts lightly down into 'Peter'. What comes next? At any rate, for the moment, I avoid the migraine that results from trying to digest what Lebanon appears to be all about. Sitting on the marble bench, I adopt the appreciativeness of a child. Wandering through this steaming labyrinth of voluptuous pleasures seems now like the mixing of colours on an artist's palette. I start imagining the task of anthropology as mixing with a fragmentary fantasy the different locales and their people before applying them on a huge theoretical canvas, one that leaves no room for superfluous justifications. The game with the other does not express life, through the gaze it precisely makes it – even if in limited forms. And yet, life withstands gazes: the spectacle will always go on. Moreover, in this infernal place, gazing at each other becomes also a play before the play, where the sexual intercourse with the bearers of orifices represents a challenge to all the participants. It is a mating meeting in which each one throws his performative weight into the scales of mutual competition – seldom mild but often without pity.

While discovering the maze on the stage of 'amusement', where the scale model of the bathhouse meets the greater universe of Beirut, the initially merely gazing individual experiences a sexually inspired complex that translates into an unusual congregation of bodies in which the protagonists may at times, in almost formal a fashion, represent different sides of Lebanon's spatially segregated sectarian communities. For brief moments, the fixed spatialization of mental maps appears to crumble here and there by opening up – albeit, ultimately, in just an ephemeral vein – to what I have called the 'encounter'. The interlacing polyphony of bodies meets the polyphony of communitarian loyalties, and sometimes is even able to undo them in time and space – never mind the brevity of the moment. Subsequent to the experience of individual gratification, many are the ones who return from their arousing journey, not only reasserting the 'right' links to a solidified chain of invented traditions, but also often as the incarnate guarantors for any form of social normativity, ranging from innocent repression to unruly self-denial. It is a guarantee that potentially harbours consequences that are even more berserk, especially when unachieved immediate sexual gratification gives way to frustration.

In all the hazy politics of steam and virility taking place in a Beiruti *hammam*, the involved anthropologist cannot but be absorbed by profound and defying thoughts, or, at least, so I felt at the time. Like food, drinking, sleeping and bathing, the effects of a vapory intercourse can be intense. They do not last, however. The search for gratification becomes a pattern and is repeated. Nonetheless, it cannot be but a finite one. Life reveals itself as some near-death experience, and our latent, sometime manifest, surreptitious minds will do anything to make it intriguing, and, if possible, repeatedly so. In the meantime, moreover, excrescences and orifices, places where borderlines between two bodies and between the body and the world as such are overcome, regularly manage to converge fleetingly with locations where exchanges and reciprocal orientations are – in spite of everything – carried out.

Bodies, Space and Mirrors

The relation between the body and the space it inhabits is necessarily a social one. Within such a thoroughly contested setting like Beirut, this association sustains an inherent immediacy by altering itself perpetually. The urban space in and around the Lebanese capital, as well as the various ways its appropriating inhabitants try to conceive of it socially, presents the homosexual individual with a living image and, therefore, with a mirror in which his body can be seen, or gazed at. In anthropology, the classical fieldwork situation is a 'stage in point'. When the anthropologist arrives in a foreign city or a distant country, he or she experiences the originally unknown space with the entire sensory apparatus of the body. Smells and tastes, legs and feet – for walking is essential to make sense of the environment one lives in – orient, or oftentimes disorient, the adapting anthropologist. With the sense of hearing, *he* perceives the contradictory qualities of voices, sounds, and noises as they may be felt, for example, on certain stretches of Beirut's Corniche. What happens spatially around *her*, regardless of whether in- or outside, becomes apparent through the intricacies of the relentlessly gazing eye. But, ultimately speaking, in a city like Beirut, what kind of bodies is the eye gazing at?

As Friedrich Nietzsche forcefully avows in his collection of aphorisms, misleadingly titled *The Will to Power*, 'every form belongs to the subject'. Within this tangled association between a ceaselessly moulding form and an ultimately diachronic content, what is being foreseen are bodily interactions where 'the seizure of the surface [happens] *through* the mirror'.[15] By perceiving surface, and by extension space, in a transcendent way – that is to say, 'through' and not 'in' the mirror – reflection and, therefore, self-awareness transform the body into a contextualized and spatial entity. The body – or, for that matter, the subject – is the one who, through the mirror, sees, and thus becomes aware of, him- or herself. However, as discussed within the context of the probing creation of what I call 'queer space' in Beirut, instead of breaking the moulds of society, these moulds often end up breaking many a concerned homosexual individual. Subsequently, to apply space to the body or, for instance, to coerce the subject into calibrated social moulds, shows that numerous are the subjects who, as a consequence, 'belong' to their respective forms, and not the other way around.

Notwithstanding this comparatively effective relationship of force, the body can never be conceived of as a unified entity. It is rather always, and necessarily so, a fragmented one. Thus it is only among the countless mirror reflections, involving bits and pieces of a bursting body which are slipping away from the claws of the dominant structure, that one can localize the emergence of alternative discourses which, in turn, may, or may not, defy the rigidity of social constraints.

In Jacques Lacan's seminal seven-page rendering of what he famously coined as 'the mirror stage',[16] the revealing reflection permits the subject who sees to elude the fragmentations of the body through language, in a way making sense of it by using words. However, instead of only 'forming the function of the I' and condemning the Ego to synchronic rigidity, the mirror stage also indicates a surpassing towards and within a space which is at once practical and at the same time symbolic, that is to say, imaginary. But if we conceive of Lacan's mirror as the very place where identities get created, one has to differ from the French psychoanalyst's interpretation and argue that the function of the mirror is not limited to sending back to the I (i.e. the subject or the Ego) its own image. The mirror, as an evanescent and fascinating object, also points to the immanent spatial repetition of the body. The I (i.e. Ego or the subject) and its other (i.e. the image seen and gazed at) face each other, they are seemingly similar, and even identical, yet differ utterly from each other; the image having no depth and no weight.

For instance, right and left are there, but they are reversed.

Significantly, the Ego perceives not only its double, but also the very context within which its identity gets created, and this mirror-context is, by definition and before all, a spatial one. Therefore, to analyse the spatial creation of a culture in Beirut reckoned as 'queer' translates not only into the necessity of emphasizing the importance of Lebanese group dynamics along with their individual crystallizations, but also that of the spatial context of the capital city itself in which identities get perpetually created. Beirut, as a buzzing, unsettling and ever-thrilling playland of hyperanimated people and streaming automobiles is the very context in which any number of cultures or 'spheres' get created, appropriated and unremittingly contested. As a consequence, my space is, in a way, the context of which I would be the text. Both my body and my body's other follow their space like its very reflections and its shadows. The moving intersections in Beirut between what touches, reaches, threatens or favours my body, and all the other bodies, form a zone that ultimately favours the encounter between myself and the other. This duplication, based on the inherent fragmented nature of the body, allows for gaps and tensions, contacts and cuts, it repeats and yet creates a difference that, down the road, may constitute an alternative space where encounters between different individuals become possible. Through this opening up, space comes to be lived in its profundities that themselves are composed of duplications, of echoes and repercussions. Socially speaking, space ends up having a double nature, a general double existence, proceeding from what is ostensibly invisible to the ordinarily visible.

Making the Invisible Visible and Vice Versa

To think about the double nature of space does not stop with the image of a Beiruti homosexual looking into the social mirror of Lebanese serendipities – or the lack thereof. Theoretically, the principles surrounding the very concept of the double are concomitant with Merleau-Pontyan phenomenology where the study of essences, including the essence of perception and consciousness, forms the core of the French philosopher's concerns.[17] This philosophical approach, however, is intended to provide an immediate description of human experience, namely as a direct mode of access to reality, whose very background is perception. Yet the peculiar urban amalgamations of Beirut, a self-declared – albeit crushingly provincial – metropolis that according to all appearances invites the invisible to become visible, but which nevertheless actively suppresses visibilities that are judged as being too conspicuous by rendering them invisible again, urge the participant observer to push his or her understanding of phenomenology a little further, thus surpassing the philosophical considerations of Maurice Merleau-Ponty.

As mentioned earlier, the inherent fragmentation of the body, as manifest in Lacan's 'Mirror Stage', not only contradicts the existence of essences, it also provides the site for difference to emerge. In recovering some of the bits and pieces of a fragmented body, the homosexual individual in Beirut is able in part to appropriate spaces in and around the city that pose a challenging alternative to the otherwise very overbearing social normativities of Lebanon. After having been coerced into social invisibility, for example through the closure of a particular social venue (e.g. the *Café Sheikh Manoush*), the concerned individual becomes visible once more, and this time in a different place within the larger urban geography. Contrary to the direct understanding of experience in Merleau-Pontyan phenomenology, in Beirut, the actual spaces of regained (queer) visibility are necessarily circuitous ones. While sharing a double nature, these spaces are completely indirect, and yet they remain pivotal. Generally, they amount to double spaces that allow for individual performances. Such performative spaces, however, do not just display real doubles that facilitate alternative and challenging openings. Often enough, these spaces make the regaining visibility almost obsolete, for they reveal fictive doubles where the individual becomes the prisoner of a false self, revolting against the artifice of conventional discourse. These fictive doubles provide, moreover, the stage for a widespread neurosis that defines (not only) the homosexual sphere in Beirut. It is a neurosis that is itself motivated by an overwhelming frustration, ranging from the vicissitudes of the sexual encounter to the larger ramifications of social life.

A common self-denial, in spite of occasional claims to the contrary (i.e. 'We are 'open-minded', *ma heyk*?'), is often coupled with a generalized rejection of difference, idiosyncratic or not, that may characterize the other. As the unfaltering consequence of a neurotic and exceedingly frustrated performance, many a homosexual individual in Beirut ends up opting to re-make himself, along with others, invisible. To indulge in the deceptive politics of normative mimicry instead of recognizing, let alone accepting, difference, becomes the undisputed and definitive outcome. In Lebanon, such a mimicry always takes place together with the overall social pressure to conform to certain fixed ideals and behaviours. Discouragingly enough, this anxiety often pushes the most genuine characters into the deceitful trap of social normativity whose pitfalls tend to materialize in projected arrogance and – sometimes – aggression. Within such an impasse, people are repeatedly made unhappy (and sometimes miserable) by those who have been coerced into unhappiness in some irrevocable ways. As a poignant paradox, moreover, such condescending pretence is itself, generally at least, based on a profound individual – albeit hopelessly aborted – urge to express oneself. The secret desire for difference notwithstanding, one that is akin to a desperate cry that bears no recognizable acoustic discharge, the results of this urge tend to mutate into a social coercion where the concerned person is made to believe that once he is no longer protected by the imperial garments of social conformity, his life is bound to collapse. Thus he is compelled to act out ad infinitum a projected and fictive ideal image that, fearing exclusion, he feels obliged to uphold and partake in.

Nevertheless, by providing the stage for an interference of gazes and stares, where different actors, the public, and the text along with its author, meet, the double spaces of individual and collective performances are, in spite of all kinds of social prohibition, appropriated in various ways by the homosexual sphere in Beirut. In further twisting Merleau-Pontyan phenomenology with its altercations between what is made visible and what not, the capacity of these double spaces can also be located in transposing the individual body from the constraints of a supposed 'real' everyday space, with all its hitherto limitations of an immediately and directly lived experience, to a 'perceived' space which may be real in its own terms, yet which is constantly shifting in meaning and by which frontal relations of identity construction are converted into signs and codes that, in turn, are prone to perpetual contestation. By giving way to an opening, this perceived space can potentially develop into a sort of 'third' or 'alternative' space which is neither real nor fictive, but an authentic zone of encounter that may become, in the long run, a socially transforming site that unquestionably sanctions the assertion of a lasting visibility and difference.

The Importance of Disciplinary Transversality in Socio-spatial Analysis

In furthermore capturing theoretically this zone of a possible homosexual encounter in and around Beirut as it relates, for instance, to specific places like the *Café Sheikh Manoush*, the city's Corniche or the *hammam*, it remains crucial to keep highlighting the importance of different methodological angles in making sense of the intricate social politics of appropriating and contesting urban space. A disciplinary transversality that manages to integrate philosophical, sociological, historical, literary, as well as linguistic concepts into corresponding theoretical intersections becomes increasingly central in delineating the venturesome interplay between socio-cultural normativities and the various tendencies that, within a spatial context, may potentially defy them. Historically, there has been a number of attempts, not all of which have accomplished their objective in accounting for this interplay. During the second decade of the twentieth century, the surrealists, for example, proceeded in deciphering what they called 'espace intérieur' and made an effort in expounding the passages from this particular kind of (intimate) experience to social life as a whole.[18] Yet in rejecting the very notion of the 'everyday' (i.e. actually lived experience) as a 'bourgeois excrement of the mind', as André Breton disparagingly put it, the identification of the correspondences between an intimate subjectivity and the larger world, as well as the ways in which the latter was supposed to be challenged by the former, became increasingly a task bordering on the impossible. Rather, what the surrealists claimed was to subscribe to what Walter Benjamin, within his own conjectural cogitations, had termed 'profane illumination'.[19] In so doing, they opted for a mellow evasion into what they called the 'marvellous' (*merveilleux*).[20]

In an altogether different – yet, to a certain degree, related – vein, the French eclectic thinker Georges Bataille wanted to link the surrealists' space of 'interior experience' not only to the space of physical nature, let alone to the evasive shores of a hypothetical 'marvellous', but also to what he, in the most compelling fashion, understood as being 'social space'. For him, social space featured a much higher complexity than the concept later advanced by Henri Lefebvre in his own writings on urbanism. Bataille's social space disclosed, as an ultimate foundation, the 'forbidden' or 'prohibited' (*l'interdit*), a category that he associated in his later magisterial work *Eroticism* with the *non-dit* (the 'un-said'), itself a key notion that demanded what he called 'transgression'.[21] Having as their focal point the multifarious production and reproduction of social relations, Bataille's theoretical writings are highly illuminative in tackling the sensitive subject of socially marginalized identities in a place like Beirut. To navigate on a daily basis through the normative waters of Lebanese prohibitions and taboos, a large number of which are socially condemned in an almost Althusserian fashion, by interpellating exclamations ranging from *'ayb!* and *haram!*, to the disavowing *ana mesh heyk!* ('shame on you!', 'this is forbidden!' and 'I'm not like that!')[22] is a strenuous enterprise for almost anybody careful enough not to fall prey to the many drowning undercurrents. Yet, within the composite context of a social space where, according to the most marvellous paradox, the kernel of what is forbidden is made clear to everybody, while, at the same time, prohibitions are asserted by avoiding to talk about their very inceptions, transgressions of any sort become difficult to articulate. Instead, what tends to prevail, and this not just within the homosexual sphere in and around Beirut, is a reproduction of social relations where the multitudes of half-baked individual compromises, or sometime straightforward acquiescence, triumph over transgression and, for that matter, possible change.

Individual arrangements and adaptations are, of course, themselves reflections of the fragmented body mentioned above, some of whose bits and pieces may potentially bear the social ingredients for a timely opening. The tenuous process of creating, as well as asserting, a queer space in Beirut is, moreover, intertwined with a complex category of time, along with a spatial appropriation of sex that itself goes beyond a seemingly ready distinction separating homosexual from heterosexual tendencies. The differentiation and close analysis of the normative reproductive function and the greater spaces of *jouissance* is pivotal. Marking the core of a perpetually contested social space in Lebanon, the various individual and collective attempts at spatializing and asserting *jouissance* in the capital city consume and devour the living being through all sorts of social sacrifices and, sometimes, even suffering.

This being said, if the libido forms the organizing forces of all activities leading to *jouissance*, all these activities have to be considered as the productive images of the ever-copious death drives that make a spatial appropriation of sex in Lebanon possible in the first place. Within a socially overdetermined homosexual sphere like the one in Beirut, the casual and disengaged pursuit of homosexual gratification as well as the continuous – albeit challenging – search for times and spaces of constructive creations are two sides of the same medal. It is a working example, in some ways contradictory, where the bodily drive to return to the state of quiescence that preceded our socio-cultural birth explains why a lot of individuals are drawn to embrace casualty and disengagement and thus end up repeating painful or sometimes traumatic events (even though such repetition appears at first glance to contradict the drive to seek pleasure). Moreover, through such a compulsion to repeat and indulge in supposed comfort, many a homosexual in Beirut attempts to 'bind' the experienced trauma, thus allowing himself to return to a state of undisturbed quiescence, never mind its illusory character.

In discerning the continuous – albeit difficult – search for times and spaces of constructive creations, it is helpful to paraphrase Henri Lefebvre, for whom time, with all its socio-cultural constraints and limitations, inscribes itself continually onto space whose very own relation with the lived reality of nature is but the 'lyrical and tragic writing' of the relation that links time to nature.[23] Contestation is, therefore, not a mere prerequisite for appropriation. In order to create a particular social space in and around the Lebanese capital, the concerned individual has always to confront the phallic dimensions, not necessarily immediately visible, of local spaces already in place. Like many other cities that placidly experience the constancy of proclaimed transitions, Beirut translates into an urban realm that overtly privileges the treacherous assurances of built verticality. Within such a context of architectural phallocracy, violence, in its multiple manifestations, is not just latent and hidden but very much on display in physical form as well as in the shape of numerous 'prohibitions' that come into play perpetually. Such violence becomes also manifest in suppressing individual contestations to which gets opposed, or rather added, in an almost necessary social overtaking, the failure of their own potential transgressions.

Spatialized Phallocracies

The spatial existence of phallic – if not phallocratic – verticality, expressed in architecture and urban design in all but the exposed parts of Beirut, parts that are always prone to imminent physical destruction at any given time, originates within the various, and hierarchically highly self-conscious, local socio-cultural pedigrees. The social as well as architectural manifestations of these pedigrees, ones that take up the form of arrogance and authoritarianism, point to the inherently compulsive and segregated nature of social space in Lebanon. Such compulsion demands, of course, a detailed social interpretation, especially since its manifestations are not always to be distinguished by merely looking at them from afar. In general, social space is, after all, primarily a lived space and an architecture of concepts, forms and laws whose abstract reality always imposes itself upon the individually experienced reality of meanings, bodies, intentions and desires. As the Lebanese historian Samir Kassir, assassinated in the aftermath of the "Cedar revolution," argued in his stately *Histoire de Beyrouth*, the tension that has been characterizing the compulsions of social space in Lebanon since the local inception of modernity in the later part of the nineteenth century is played out unmistakably between what he called 'individual affirmation', on the one hand, and self-imposing 'collective dynamics', on the other.[24] However, both currents and their various strained points of intersection cannot be understood without their respective and mutual spatial references.

Kassir used the revealing notion of 'mimetic space' in order to delineate the practised mimicry of a society that obstinately indulges in advertising an illusory diversity but, nevertheless, chokes on the compulsive prescriptions of social conformity. To pressure anyone to adhere to fixed types of ideals and categories is the most potent compulsion that collective dynamics carry in coercing individual affirmation. It is a compulsion that may be strictly abstract or, with reference to the important repertoire of its perpetually interpellating exclamations of which *'ayb!* and *haram!* are but trivial examples, very much manifest within the social fabric at large. Moreover, beyond the boundaries of such a fabric, social compulsion always has a concrete and shaping impact on the spatial – and, more particularly, architectural – configuration of the society it is a product of. It is an impact that, in turn, constrains directly any sort of alternative affirmations that may be perceived as bearing some potential in defying society. For Kassir, throughout the modern history of Beirut, the 'phenomenon of mimicry ... went hand in glove with the [spatial] development of the city'.[25] Whether one looks at the so-called Palm Springs complex in its painful replication of an imagined Floridian hacienda, or at the unabashed Disneyesque make-up of a decidedly commodified urban enclave that proclaims itself the 'downtown' of a city whose very own general character could not be further removed from the celebrated glitzy arcades on the centrally located Maarad street, imitation wins over adaptation.

The compulsive presence of the seemingly most ordinary places in a city like Beirut, such as a particular building complex or even an entire neighbourhood, conveys an urban 'scene' that, along with its stage and actors, is (visually) 'seen' by everybody who feels pressured enough to be a part of it. However, while a multiplicity of bodies nonchalantly parade on the exhibition grounds of a city where something perpetually happens on the various catwalks of local vanities, there is certainly always an 'obscene' component, one that, according to the inherent logics of Lebanese society, cannot and should not materialize in this space, but which is, nonetheless, perpetually in relation to it. The fragmentation of the body is precisely the material that feeds obscenity, for it is, once again, in the bits and pieces of an alternative individual affirmation that collective dynamics and their resourceful compulsions can be challenged. However, the homosexual subject, one that is by definition marginalized in a variety of ways by the local politics of ideals and commendabilities, has a difficult time in manipulating the risky, even if enabling, techniques of obscenity. Therefore, to confront either the intricacies of Beiruti social space or its distinctive exhibition of signs and symbols tends to result in a large-scale sublimation that involves a compromising social mimicry rather than overt revolt. Moreover, having partly to recognize, on the one hand, the natural, sensual and sexual differences imbued in homosexual *jouissance*, but experiencing at the same time a sustained social adversity, on the other, literally freezes the homosexual sphere in Beirut and, in so doing, makes it particularly vulnerable to various kinds of internal aggressions as well as to a rampant politics of internalized homophobia.

To a great extent, skilful spatial practice, with its numerous techniques of contestation and appropriation, as well as the resulting representations of space, expressed through particular signs and symbols, help in creating spaces that come closest in providing the homosexual sphere in Beirut with the possibility to find suitable niches and avenues. Social space in general reflects the morphology of a society whose multifold nature includes zones of intersecting encounters and correspondences which, in turn – through individual or collective forms of representation – are assigned to specific places. As Lefebvre advances, 'space is social morphology; it is to any "lived" experience what the form is to any living organism, i.e. intimately linked to its functions and structures'.[26] Yet it is even more than that. To fully comprehend the social process of creating a space deemed as queer in Beirut, one cannot but emphasize enough the centrality of the body and its 'morphological' capabilities of fragmentation. Any given subject's relation to urban space implies also the basic relation to his or her own (fragmented) body. To be sure, social spaces are anything but inert things. As sites of lived experiences, they interpenetrate and overlap each other constantly. In Beirut, the fractious conflation of a triplicity regarding what is being perceived, conceived and lived, is never a simple – or stable – one. It is not an abstract model. Rather, in their coexisting (albeit immanent) contingency, the moments of perception, conception and lived experience must be linked together in order for the subject, as an intricate and dramatic member of any sort of social group, to pass from one to the other without getting lost – and thus marginalized – in the process.

Struggling for Difference

That the right to being different makes only sense through actual struggles to differ is an obvious statement. Similarly indubitable is the assertion that the differences created during these practical and, necessarily, theoretical struggles differ themselves from the socio-cultural particularities and distinctions that are induced within an existing and unremittingly lived everyday space like, for instance, the one experienced in Beirut. The differences that merit to be kept within the field of the critical anthropologist's attention, upon whose reinforcement theory and practice can count on, can only be disclosed through a conscientious analysis of social space and the numerous ways and techniques which enable many an individual and groups to continuously contest and appropriate it. As an integral condition of sorts, such an analysis must draw from disparate, and sometime competing, methodological angles, putting together anew dissociated – yet very much related – elements, in order to cover the whole panoply of the metonymies that define the complexities of inhabiting social space.

In other words, it is impossible to understand the creation of a particular space, like the one contested by the homosexual sphere in Beirut, along with its conditions and ongoing intricate processes, without putting it in a critical perspective that highlights the importance of its specific socio-historical location. All particularities notwithstanding, a distinctive location like the ever-enterprising, yet greatly supercilious, Lebanese capital is far from forming some sort of cultural bubble, removed from its general environs and enjoying the fruits of some splendid isolation. In spite of all self-declarations advertising the contrary, Beirut is rather an integral part of a larger world, regional and global, with which the city entertains continuous and stern relations of appropriation and contestation. For that matter, any cogent anthropological approach trying to assess such an urban space will have to deal with the countless ways and techniques in which any number of different individuals inhabit space while, at the same time, dynamically transforming it into the highest complexity of human dimensions. In so doing, this kind of urban anthropology will ultimately have to deal with specific socially appropriated places and their larger context. More concretely, it will need to examine the socio-cultural distribution of bodies within these places. Apart from being perpetually in relation to one another, these bodies also hold in their hands the capacity of fragmentation and, therefore, the latent ability to engender difference and (potentially) change.

The difficult and inveterate process of creating queer space in Beirut has to be understood along these sensible lines. It is a process that operates by generating practices, sometime astute and sometime contradictory, which it is incapable of separating itself from due to the fact that it is, simultaneously, one of its delicate products. At the end, and after having expounded the intricacies of its own formation, the spatial creation of just any sphere or, for that matter, culture (where the theoretical concepts are intrinsically linked to practical reality) will necessarily disclose itself as a challenging social process, one which underscores the crucial elements of an everyday life subjected to perpetual metamorphosis. It is, moreover, a process which must go *beyond* any assumed normative discourses that uphold the treacherous politics of dichotomies and naturalized hierarchies, as well as one which embraces the multiplicity of human possibilities.

Bibliography

Bataille, G., *L'érotisme,* Paris: Les Editions de Minuit, 1957.

Benjamin, W., *Illuminationen: Ausgewählte Schriften*, vol. 1, Frankfurt a. M.: Suhrkamp Taschenbuch, 1977.

Benjamin, W., 'M [der Flâneur]', in *Das Passagen-Werk*, vol. 1, Frankfurt a. M.: Edition Suhrkamp, 1983.

Bourdieu, Pierre, *In Algerien: Zeugnisse der Entwurzelung*, ed. Franz Schultheis and Christine Frisinghelli, Graz: Camera Austria, 2003.

Breton, A., *Manifestes du surréalisme*, Paris: Gallimard, 1999.

Kaakoush, N., 'Hey Handsome', in Roseanne Saad Khalaf and Malu Halasa, eds, *Transit Beirut: New Writing and Images*, Beirut and London: Saqi Books, 2004.

Kassir, S., *Histoire de Beyrouth*, Paris: Librairie Arthème Fayard, 2003.

Lacan, J., 'Le stade du miroir comme formateur de la fonction du Je', in *Écrits*, vol. 1, Paris: Éditions du Seuil, 1999.

Lefebvre, H., *La production de l'espace*, 4th edn, Paris: Anthropos, 2000.

Marx, K., *Grundrisse der Kritik der Politischen Ökonomie*, Berlin: Dietz, 1953.

Merleau-Ponty, M., *Phénoménologie de la perception*, Paris: Gallimard, 1963.

Nietzsche, F., *The Will to Power*, New York: Random House, 1967.

Tabet, J., *al-ia'mar wal-maslaha al-aama fi al-turath wal-hadatha: Madinat al-harb wa dhakirat al-mustaqbal*, Beirut: Dar al-Jadid, 1996.

Whitaker, B., *Unspeakable Love: Gay and Lesbian Life in the Middle East*, London: Saqi Books, 2006.

Notes

1. In 2002, a group was formed and christened HELEM (Arabic for 'dream'). It is also

the acronym for *himaya lubnaniyya lil mithliyeen wal muzdawijieen wal mughayireen* (Lebanese Protection for Lesbians, Gays, Bisexuals, and Transgenders).

2. Brian Whitaker, *Unspeakable Love: Gay and Lesbian Life in the Middle East*, London, 2006, p. 41.
3. H. Lefebvre, *La production de l'espace*, 4th edn, Paris, 2000.
4. W. Benjamin, *der Flâneur*, Frankfurt, 1983.
5. Arabic plural of *shab* that translates as 'male youngster' in English.
6. Lebanese plural of the French work *tante* (English 'auntie'), defining any male homosexual who is declared to be effeminate.
7. P. Bourdieu, *In Algerien: Zeugnisse der Entwurzelung* (Graz, 2003), p. 16.
8. See n. 5.
9. N. Kaakoush, 'Hey Handsome', London, 2004.
10. Local derogatory term for describing a male homosexual. The closest English equivalent would probably be 'faggot'.
11. K. Marx, *Grundrisse der Kritik der Politischen ökonomie*, Berlin, 1953.
12. J. Tabet, *al-ia'mar wal-maslaha al-aama fi al-turath wal-hadatha: Madinat al-harb wa dhakirat al-mustaqbal*, Beirut, 1996.
13. As part of a constructed self-confidence that feeds on a latent inferiority complex towards an imagined 'West' and converts it into one of superiority towards what is considered the 'East,' the English term 'open-minded' has been widely used in recent years as a local self-description in Lebanese Arabic.
14. J. Tabet, beirut, 1996. p. 225.
15. F. Nietzsche, *The Will to Power*, New York, 1967, p. 211.
16. J. Lacan, 'Le stade du miroir comme formateur de la fonction du Je', Paris, 1999, pp. 92–9.
17. M. Merleau-Ponty, *Phénoménologie de la perception*, Paris, 1963.
18. A. Breton, *Manifestes du surréalisme*, Paris, 1999.
19. W. Benjamin, *Illuminationen: Ausgewählte Schriften*, Frankfurt, 1977.
20. A. Breton, 1999, p. 25.
21. G. Bataille, *L'érotisme*, Paris, 1957.
22. The English translations are only approximate ones, for they do not render the complex moralizing connotations of these exclamations.
23. H. Lefebvre, 2000, p. 114.
24. S. Kassir, *Histoire de Beyrouth*, Paris, 2003, p. 246.
25. Ibid., p. 247.
26. H. Lefebvre, 2000, p.112.

Transition Beirut: Gay Identities, Lived Realties

The Balancing Act in the Middle East

Jared McCormick

> *Is there a universal gay identity linked to modernity? ... [we need] to question the extent to which the forces of globalization can be said to produce a common consciousness and identity based on homosexuality.*[1]

The new global economy and the flow of goods that inevitably succeed it have transformed local markets. These trades, sparked by liberal capitalism, are applauded for shoring up development and economic integration, though they are often berated for their increasing homogenizing effects. Note how the widespread prevalence and growth of technologies, of the new world order, such as satellite television channels and the internet are threatening the very fabric of local social hierarchies by altering not only how we access information, but more importantly, what we choose to access. Moreover, particular ways of living, ideas and values are becoming linked to an internationalized standard through global integration. Therefore, it is no surprise that with the increasing inroads of globalization, 'sexuality becomes the terrain on which are fought out bitter disputes'.[2]

Sexuality, and its effects, remains, notwithstanding a few recent exceptions, a relatively unexplored phenomenon in the context of Arab societies. Given the emotionally charged and contested nature of sexuality, any open treatment or recognition of this highly sensitive issue is tabooed and stigmatized. This is more so of homosexuality; an even greater proscribed topic. Other than a few journalistic, sensational accounts and feature stories, empirical and grounded studies are very scant, if not non-existent. In contrast, Lebanon, particularly since the millennium, has experienced a growing gay social scene. Discussions of homosexuality have become part of the public discourse. More compelling and certainly unprecedented elsewhere in the Arab world, Lebanon can now boast of establishing the first gay rights voluntary association – *Helem*, the Arabic word for 'dream'. Interestingly, this is the acronym for *Himaya Lubnaniyya lil-Mithliyien* (Lebanese Protections for Homosexuals). Statistically, there has been a perceptible increase in gay men who are not only openly gay but defend their 'lifestyle' with more audible voice.

Fieldwork for this essay was carried out in the fall of 2005 and conducted using multiple interviews with twenty Lebanese men who all self-identified as gay. The term 'gay' is employed to mean the existence of a 'social life: not only same-sex desires but gay selves, gay neighbours, and gay social practices'.[3] The intention was to examine the processes by which they graft this way of living and the beliefs it connotes with their lived reality. This process of grafting was of particular relevance to those who had discovered and acted upon their inclinations while outside of Lebanon.

Six subjects were Lebanese who, in some capacity, had been in the West for at least eight years working/studying or were born/raised in Europe or America, most having dual citizenship. Their gay identity was characterized by more openness, clarity and general acceptance in comparison to those born and raised exclusively in Lebanon. Still they had to face the painful task of renegotiating an identity in a comparatively unreceptive socio-cultural setting. It became evident from the remaining fourteen that their gay identity was not entirely locally produced but rather was greatly inspired by the imported paradigm of the 'global gay' character.

Today, self association with the term gay does not translate to a *precise* tailor-made set of behaviours or a common ethos, yet both groups of men have ongoing challenges with the cultural import of the gay identity that undoubtedly requires a juggling act with the subject's lived reality in Lebanon. Incidentally, the informants were religiously mixed, representing virtually all the major sectarian groups: Shi'i, Sunni, Maronite, Catholic, Greek Orthodox and Druze. This juggling act is most clearly seen by the balance of being 'out' of the closet while still being 'in'. Family members – especially fathers – were almost always not privy to the subject's sexual history, whereas many of the subject's friends and perhaps a sister might know.

The social context of sexuality in Beirut is rapidly changing and the precursors and outward manifestations of a gay identity are increasing. The gay community is gaining momentum, aided by technology and the growth of *Helem*. Given such, it is worthwhile to pause for a moment and consider not only the importance and consequence of coming out, but also what local and international forces are influencing this phenomenon. With the transfer of the modern gay identity, which has never existed as a way of life in the Middle East, so begins the complex negotiation and appropriation of the individual's identity between their local identity and the values of their imported identities.

It is hoped that this exploratory study will provide an instructive case study observing a portion of the transition that 'out' Lebanese men are facing as they negotiate their masculinities and validate their gay identities among friends and family. Hence, it could well provide some grounded and instructive instances of how they are forging and validating their own identities with the increasing interconnectivity of modernity.

Local Negotiation of Identity

> *I don't see an[y] hope or signs of change in the Arab world regarding the GLBT (Gay, Lesbian, Bisexual, Transgender) rights unless they start becoming more pro-West.*
>
> (Comment from *Helem* discussion board, posted 4 December 2005)

In order to explore the changing character of sexual identity being caught, as it were, in the process of reformulating itself, it is necessary to view the process within three historical contexts: the post-independence interlude; the massive number of worldwide Lebanese emigrants who return, in some form, with a hybrid set of cultural, economic and social pressures; and the religious and ethnic diversity which characterizes Lebanon. These factors are offered to illustrate, albeit very briefly, how Lebanon's landscape, in comparison to neighbouring Arab countries, helped lay the groundwork for the ostensibly liberalizing social situation witnessed today.

Additionally, in 1989, the Taif Agreement effectively ended the Lebanese Civil War which ravaged the country. The abating wartime mentality created fertile grounds to redefine some of the social boundaries repressed during combat, including a tacit exploration of sexual definitions. Around the millennium, with the prevalence of the internet, coupled with the foundation of *Helem*, the scene became more conducive to the development of a gay identity; or at least access to identified places where a small community of men could assemble.

Today, Beirut has an international reputation as a decadent and outlandish postwar hotspot. To some extent, this characterization also applies to the gay scene. A recent feature article in *Out Traveler* focusing on Lebanon declares Beirut 'the Arab World's most gay-friendly city'.[4] The article normalizes the homosexual scene in Beirut and in essence only mentions venues which are accessible to the economically predisposed. This may be misconstrued to mean that socioeconomic status could be a major consideration in accounting for one's gay identity. Yet the overall profile of informants selected for this research does not support such deterministic impressions or monocausal interpretations. If anything, they reflect a plurality of characteristics and predisposing circumstances. It is possible, however, to single out a few common experiences which my informants converge upon or share in, of course, to varying degrees. First, access to capital may indeed be a factor as nearly all the men interviewed *self*-perceived their families as upper to middle class compared to the average Lebanese family. Moreover, all those interviewed were working towards their bachelors degree, at the minimum, while most were starting or had finished higher degrees of learning. Their access to education clearly precipitated more exposure to contemporary ideologies and surely it offered greater access to foreign languages, as all spoke English. The third palpable theme was how well-travelled the men were. All, save two individuals, had travelled outside the Arab world, with most having visited Europe at least once. This is not to imply that wealth led directly to their open formation of a gay identity, yet it might be inferred that their economic status allowed them access to many spheres of life unviable to one without economic resources.

Interestingly, the group of six who spent at least eight years outside Lebanon clearly showed less dissonance between their lived identity and their gay identity. The disjunction between sex life and private life was less manifest and more of their friends, associates and family knew they were gay. These men who returned to Lebanon also had fewer difficulties translating their desires into action in comparison to their counterparts who remained. Though the evidence might be limited, one could nonetheless infer that the significant amount of time they have spent in the West influenced their ability to bridge their biculturalism in favour of the 'global gay' model.

In contrast, a number of the men born and raised in Lebanon whom I attempted to interview were ambivalent, hesitant and often uncertain while talking about their sexual identity. Many, in fact, did not unequivocally identify themselves as 'gay', despite their vast and varied connections in numerous pockets of the homosexual scene. Many would say 'yes' in the beginning, only to later recant their responses. Rather than believe they were trying to dissemble their gay identity, it illustrates the struggle of navigating between various identities inwardly and externally. The schism of this negotiation was most often observed in their responses to preferred/assumed sexual role as the active or passive partner. The informants expressed frustration in finding an equalitarian homosexual relationship, in terms of sexual and emotional reciprocity and support, because of the strict adherence to a sexual dichotomy which stresses a role based on the subject's function as 'active' (masculine) or 'passive' (feminine). One quite effete informant seemed insulted by my research, believing my goal was to make everyone with homosexual inclinations come out. Rather, I alerted him to the fact that nearly three-quarters of my informants said that coming out was less than totally liberating because of the other drawbacks it created, especially as Tahir noted, '[having people know] is a liability, you can't control it ... and Lebanon is small'.

Effects of Gay Identity in Lebanon

> *Beirut has a gay scene, Lebanon doesn't.*
> (Kamal, twenty-six years old)

Inevitably a major point of departure for those who adhere to the term 'gay' begins with migration to Beirut. The informants in this study originally came from all over Lebanon but currently live in greater Beirut for studies or work. However, because of Lebanon's size, it is conceivable that one could 'migrate' to the city, not to reside, but for the city's social networks and for an outlet to the gay scene.

Among my informants the very idea of a gay community remains amorphous. While some felt part of a tightly knit group, others questioned the existence of a few clubs, bars and chat rooms as a viable or meaningful definition of a community. There seems to be little, if any, semblance of a full community outside of *Helem*. By and large, the homosexual community consists of small groups of men of varying identities in a secretive web. The different conceptions of community became visible as some subjects compared Beirut's gay community to Europe, while others equated community to mean the 'gay scene'. There does indeed exist a community in the sense of a group of men sharing a characteristic. It lacks though a cohesive meaning and contains little depth in comparison to the Western model which emphasizes it as a shared struggle. As one informant put it:

> [There is] no community in [the] sense of the European communities, it's very fragmented and underground. [It's] repressed because it's such a small country and people only do this kind of stuff in Beirut. (Marwan, twenty-three years old)

The estrangement between a homosexual lifestyle and the full gay identity accounts for the lack of community. Hani, a nineteen-year-old Shi'i noted, 'people see gays as just a way to have sex. Not a lifestyle. If it is a lifestyle then it clashes with our Lebanese lifestyle.' Forging a gay identity seemed a complex process for most informants. Though the incorporation of some element has had an impact in informing the advocacy character of the movement, it has had its problems; as it is ultimately incompatible with parts of their lived experience in Lebanon. When asked, for example, if they looked to the West to define their meaning of being gay one responded it was 'automatic'. Another quipped 'of course, what else would it be?' Others 'took it as [a] guide to start discovering [their identity]', while an insightful returnee to Lebanon, who studied in an American high school and state university, perhaps shed light on what people find in the foreign gay identity by replying, 'America allowed me to be who I am. [It] said who I am was OK.'

Such reflections might appear like a natural progression to adopting the global gay identity since Lebanon lacks any rubric or local framework to support the meaning that a modern gay lifestyle has taken. However, this prompts one to question the underlying beliefs which might have pushed them to this foreign paradigm and pulled them away from their local identity formation. Likewise, in reference to gay men acting 'Americanized', one informant from the American University of Beirut suggested that 'people need to take risks, but remember to be Lebanese'. This only supports, by his own admission, that the gay identity is not of Lebanon and conceivably unable to meld with the local ideals.

Modernity and globalization appear to have advanced the prospects of overall worldwide sexual acceptance. In spite of that, Lebanon's values in general are not advancing at the same rate. One difficulty each member of the gay population in Lebanon negotiates is the role they play in the public sphere as gay men. The matter ultimately rests on the degree of their openness with their homosexuality. Hence the basic question: 'should more men come out in Lebanon?' generated many unexpected responses. The opinions of the informants varied and did not converge on a set of common expectations.

While there were a variety of replies, many seemed to overlap on the realistic necessity of being in Beirut for exposure of the 'community'. There were divergences of opinions, however, as some expressed coming out as less than they had 'bargained for'. Nader, an eloquent twenty-seven-year-old, expressed his apprehension of coming out because it is practically irreversible and comes with such high stakes that 'affect the rest of your life'. It was most bluntly put by Loay, a twenty-five-year-old Lebanese, born and raised in America: 'only [come out] if you can make it without your family'. All of the informants actively supported others to come out, but having done so themselves they understood the costs associated with it and implicitly seemed to understand any apprehension.

Hesitation exists, as there is obviously a high cost to coming out. It looks as if a number of consequences are an expression of the primacy and centrality of the family as an agency of socialization for enforcing societal norms. To fully understand how these men are grappling with their identity transformation, one must appreciate what is to be lost by positively identifying as gay. The rights and responsibilities of being a man are threatened by straying from Connell's idea of a 'hegemonic' masculinity.[5] Most Lebanese still do not consider a gay 'way of life' as an acceptable or viable identity. From my interviews, it seems that the continuation of such a view might well account for the predispositions of many informants to lead sections of their lives in secret, especially in relation to their family.

As a result, the psychological cost of living such diametrically opposed realities cannot be demeaned. Many felt they did not have a balancing act of being 'out/in' the closet, but through accounts of their actions around older/immediate family members gave the impression that sometimes their behaviour reverted to something more socially acceptable, whether they were conscience of it or not. Hussein said his conduct did not change when he spent time in his village in the south, but he continued to act 'normal'. This indicated his belief that gay behaviour is unorthodox yet his own is not; thereby expressing the conflict between his gay identity and his family life. One could easily infer from this that in cultures where family loyalty is not as intense, the conflict might not assume such forms. Donham noted in a study of the South African gay community that the 'gay identity is different to the degree that it does not rely upon the family for its anchoring, indeed if anything, it has continually liberated itself from the effects of family socialization'.[6] It seems that the gay identity did not draw the subjects away from their families but did alienate them in some regards because of the covert lifestyle they have been inclined to assume outside the home. The anxiety and fear that the family might somehow discover their true identity remains one of their most menacing concerns. Therefore their homosexual life is kept tightly private.

Given such realities one can begin to understand and appreciate the circumstances which sustain the apprehensions against coming out. They are largely a byproduct of economic considerations and the security the family continues to provide in this regard. Considering all emotional involvement aside, their support comes through financial means and family connections which are subject to change should such a status-changing event, such as coming out, disrupt the balance of their own gender/sex paradigm in their family. Imagine funding one's own education without family support or finding a job with no *wasta* (favours). There are too many compelling pressures for men not to reveal any non-heteroseuxal proclivities until they can be more financially independent of their families. It is within this context that the prospects of coming out remain inextricably associated with the survival of the family as a venue for economic security.

Unyielding as these circumstances may seem, it is not difficult to discern that there are additional trends/phenomena that have become apparent in Lebanon that are changing the lived and perceived realities of homosexual men. Three such realities stand out: the establishment of *Helem*, the role of the internet and the changing character of growing global consumerism/marketing. An explanation of these will help us understand the predicament that homosexuals are facing in forging and validating their sexual identities.

Helem

'Fight to Exist' because 'Silence is Death'
(*Helem* slogans, from printed material)

Helem, founded in 2001, is effectively the first non-governmental organization (NGO) fighting for LGBT rights in the Arab world. There is indisputably no other place in the Middle East from which *Helem* could operate besides Beirut. *Helem* is jointly registered in Quebec, Canada and

Lebanon. Nonetheless, it has not, as of yet, received an official registration number from the Lebanese Ministry of Interior. George Azzi, the coordinator of *Helem*, said, 'according to the current jurisprudence, the fact that we have paid and received an acknowledgment of registration will be accepted in courts as proof of state recognition'.[7] This does not mean *Helem* has *carte blanche* to push and propagate its agenda and all its alleged objectives. It is significant that they have followed the proper protocol with the Lebanese government, which has granted, in a way, tacit approval through the absence of any restrictions.

Currently, there exists an internal debate regarding the strategies the group should pursue; i.e. should they subscribe to a more politically expedient mission or work on grassroots development and public opinion. They have set up a lobbying subcommittee to work not only on the removal of law 534 from the Penal Code but also to seek positive modifications that would actively protect homosexuals. There are two lawyers who advise *Helem* on legal issues, and they seem to be on the brink of making a slight dent into the political realm for gay rights. Some members acknowledge that even if – by some stroke of luck – the law was changed, it would do little to transform the overall mentality against homosexuality. Certainly some members believe a legal framework to safeguard homosexuals is necessary before it will be feasible for more people to come out. A minority, on the other hand, prefer to stress the social acceptance and understanding needed to change public opinion.

Another goal of *Helem* is to raise the general discourse surrounding homosexuality. Advocating such a sensitive issue in public within the Arab world is seen by Massad as an 'incitement to discourse'.[8] The Lebanese are generally tolerant, yet increasing dialogue on homosexuality might have unfavourable consequences. A member of *Helem*, Ahmed, expressed his view that *Helem* walks a fine line between increasing awareness and pushing the limits too quickly. The latter is unavoidably, in his view, to spark a backlash against the NGO or gay frequented establishments. One might indicate in this regard that the last police raids of two gay-frequented nightclubs happened at Acid on 12 November 2005, when seven were arrested, and roughly a week later at X-OM with no arrests. One could cite this as evidence of a backlash; however, it does not provide a convincing case of 'cracking down', as both clubs are flourishing more than ever. There was admittance of underage individuals and suspected drug use at both.

Ahmed's apprehensions are legitimate as *Helem* and the gay community must strive to support men as they struggle to reconcile the desired elements inherent in a global gay identity model in light of the morals and ways of life in Lebanese society. Put another way, can the local society and culture sustain and absorb *Helem*'s professed goals and objectives?

Interestingly, *Helem*'s incitement to public discourse has been recently aided by their development of a gay press (another first in the Arab world) with the publication of the magazine *Barra*, meaning 'out' in Lebanese colloquial Arabic. Launched in 2005, *Barra*'s content is mixed between French, English and Arabic and provides analysis and commentary on current issues that assail the gay community. It is distributed in limited locations around Beirut and also online. The publication has grown so much that they are hiring a freelance sales representative to handle advertising and the subsequent issue (March 2006) will include nearly eighty pages, of which most is Arabic with some English and French additions. The previous two issues, which were roughly thirty pages, are available on the *Helem* website and 5,000 have been downloaded thus far.[9] *Barra*, along with *Helem*, may eventually help to solidify the 'internationalized' gay identity, as was observed in Bolivia when an outreach clinic opened to support HIV education to the homosexual community.[10]

Moreover, *Helem* must overcome the financial and socioeconomic divides that split the homosexual community to attract a diverse following and membership in addition to the sectarian rifts already omnipresent in Lebanese society. One informant, for instance, remarked that because out gay men were already on the fringes of Lebanese society, he believed the close association with 'gays and the West' allows one to de-emphasize his confessional identity, thereby entertaining the prospects of supplanting one for the other. However, I do not have sufficient data to substantiate this interesting inference.

Helem is struggling to solidify a gay identity within the fabric of local content – which is predominately a homosexual community of men having sex with men (MSM) with little or no association with the gay identity. They aspire to increase public awareness, move the community to a more solid common ground regarding sexual openness, and address issues that beset the gay community such as HIV and hate crimes.

Recently, the Dutch embassy provided funding that will sponsor production of a booklet on positive sexual health for the LGBT community. 'This booklet will be the first of its kind in the Arabic language and will serve as a comprehensive resource on sexual health.'[11] While I do not question the necessity of the information on sexual health, it raises issues of how the gay community and their individual values are being shaped to conform to the global gay identity as 'a product of foreign imaginations, being invented, as it were, in the service of obscure international agendas'.[12] The emergent outlines or emancipatory efforts to formulate a gay identity appears to ride on the coat tails of globalization as Western countries continue to advocate rights for this way of life, their policies and by granting aid money to NGOs. One informant, as Westernized as he was, considered the encroaching 'global gay identity' as another form of imperialism. Even though the Lebanese are eager to invoke conspiracy theories, his perceptions might carry some weight. At the least, it deserves further verification and validation to examine how the manifestations of this global gay identity are being reflected in beliefs and lifestyle throughout the world. Incidentally, other studies have shown the delicate balance between such global identities and their local counterparts.[13]

Role of Internet in Gay Identity Formation

> *I'm straight but I make exceptions for foreigners.*
> (Man outside Acid nightclub)

The 'internet revolution', by allowing access to material otherwise deemed inappropriate, has shaped many modern trends in terms of sexual identity. The dilemma of how agents, living in a culture that is ostensibly repressive towards their identity, can adapt to find ways to express themselves is partially solved by the internet serving as an accessible and expedient outlet.

The expansion of the internet has created a new avenue to explore one's sexuality, and at present, there are roughly 600,000 (or 13.4 percent of the population of Lebanese) online with 100 percent growth rate from 2000 to 2005.[14] The role of the internet is of utmost importance in the Middle East as it allows a negotiation and flexibility of the inner and outer identities of an individual. It also allows the subject to 'role play' and briefly experience something outside of himself in a clandestine manner. 'It may allow a subject to explore various possibilities, while maintaining a safe distance from those possibilities and their consequences'.[13] Because of this safety it is likely that authentic feelings come out online and the 'true gender is performed'.[14]

This elicits questions of whether Lebanese who have experience online become more predisposed to come out. From the twenty informants for this research, the fourteen raised within Lebanon all seem to recognize the internet as a major factor in their gay identity. So much so, in fact, that I would consider internet access as a possible prerequisite on the path of entering the homosexual subculture in Lebanon. Many said it started with curiosity, but as chat-rooms served as a viable and socially less intimidating way to meet men, they found an easy gateway to the homosexual community, all the while circumventing the associated social disgraces.

A large majority of informants, more exclusively the youngest ranging from seventeen to twenty-three years old, are regular chat-line users. Almost all admitted to meeting men 'offline', some declaring that they had recently stopped. Bassam, a very thoughtful twenty-four-year-old, cast doubts on the internet when he said it is 'not healthy, not social. This does not form a community. It should be a phase as it's helpful to discovery. But it has to move to something real off the computer.' His thoughts add to the argument of the missing gay community. People are not willing to accept coming off the 'anonymous' internet to bear the social costs of association with the identity or are unwilling to place themselves in this archetype.

The importance of the internet for *Helem* is also noteworthy. By far the majority of the information on homosexuality and gay issues available on the web is written in languages other than Arabic. While the Lebanese are known for their polyglot predisposition, which would allow them to access material in French or English, it is a watershed that the *Helem* website is in both English and Arabic. The English site hosts full content while the Arabic, currently under construction, covers the majority of the subject matter. It is also curious that the message boards and discussions are almost exclusively in English, save a few transliterated words from Arabic. It is feasibly one of the first sources of gay material in Arabic and surely one of the first from an NGO on Arab soil. One can imagine many Arab nationals viewing the growing collection of coming out stories, news updates or message boards, bearing in mind that the traffic reaches over 50,000 hits per month.[15] Roughly 6 percent of those visitors are from Saudi Arabia and only an estimated 5 percent are from within Lebanon.[16] This illustrates the importance and function of *Helem* in the changing sexual context of the Arab world. Therefore, it is no surprise that during religious holidays hundreds of 'Gulfies' (citizens from the Arab Gulf countries) are visible in the clubs/bars as Beirut is a growing destination for tourism. The expanding sexual flexibility affords 'breathing space' and brings neighbouring Arabs flocking to Beirut because it is familiar and physically closer than Europe, while curious non-Arabs enjoy it as an exotic new playground.

The final ground-breaking facet of the *Helem* website, and perhaps the most explicit, is how openly they disclose gay venues. Under the 'Queer Lebanon Guide', *Helem* has an exhaustive list of gay friendly clubs, bars and 'theatres' in Beirut. There are maps to clubs/bars including descriptions of the crowd, music, time and costs. Furthermore, the guide lists public cruising areas like Ramlet El Baida and 'theatres' where it is possible to pick up men and how to connect to gay chat lines on IRC (Internet Relay Chat) – all the while warning the would-be participant to 'beware of thieves and undercover police'. It is only that much more significant considering the geospatial location of Beirut in the Middle East. By publishing this information *Helem* appears to be trying to bridge the dissonance and stigma between the gay and straight realities in Lebanon, but in presenting information from the same perspective as a Western gay rights NGO it may cross the line of social tolerance in Lebanon.

Consumerism and Marketing

> *There is a growth in identity-based movements, and there is an impact of the global gay identity where people throughout the world are seeing themselves as part of a larger global movement.*
>
> (Cary Johnson, 2005)

The global gay identity in Lebanon is also being reinforced by imminent consumerism and marketing. Take for example the possibility of downloading the latest issue of *Barra* online for just $5 in addition to purchasing items from affiliates' ads on *Helem*'s webpage. Raynbow, an online store selling gay pride merchandise printed and manufactured in the USA but shipped worldwide, is Lebanese-owned and donates a portion of their proceeds from each sale to *Helem* (www.raynbow.org). One of their recent additions, the 'Lebanese Hunks Calendar for just $17.99', offers semi-clothed men in a graphic facsimile of similar such global marketing ventures. Not to undermine the mission or question the sincerity of their fundraising, it is, however, interesting to cite the experiences of the American gay community. Research has noted many websites strive to gain from constructing an image of community.[17] Raynbow, along with others, are embracing and purposely marketing to the homosexual Lebanese community. It is forming a small, albeit growing, industry by outwardly playing off of gay pride and Lebanese pride with men becoming the sexualized object, as is quite visible in the 'Lebanese Hunks Calendar'.

Another example is the travel company LebTour, which arranges and runs tours throughout Lebanon (www.lebtour.com). They advertise on the *Helem* website and apparently seem to specialize in serving a gay clientele as rainbow flags adorn every side of their website. In addition to the religious and eco-tourism tours there is a section offering 'gay tours' throughout Lebanon. It could indeed serve as an easy access point for foreigners into the Lebanese gay scene.

Yet, the larger question remains: how tolerated will the gay identity become in Lebanon even in view of such symptoms of commercialization? Apparently, from a service standpoint, it is bound to become more accepted. Take for instance the billboards of the chic department store Aïshti. In 2005 they produced a full ad campaign around Lebanon titled 'Vote for Tolerance', which showed models re-enacting the colors of the gay pride flag and included two male models in a near embrace. Furthermore, the number of 'gay nights' at various bars/clubs/cafes in Beirut currently accounts for five nights of the week. All subjects for this study responded positively to frequenting some of these establishments that either market or cater to the homosexual community.

Another case in point is a club, UV, near the infamous Monot Street. In 2005 it offered an 'Oriental Night', 'Halloween Party', or an extra drink ticket for guests who arrived before a certain time. The means of communication was via SMS from cellular phone numbers they collected at the door. I offer this instance to illustrate a new balance of tolerance in some parts of Beirut as managers and owners use subtle marketing ventures and embrace technology to promote their businesses. Perhaps gay marketing will increase in Beirut as the homosexual community is viewed as an economic entity to serve. Interestingly, the importance of homosexuals' betrayal of the hegemonic masculinity in Lebanon may well become obscured by the size of their wallets.

Conclusion

> *The development of a homosexual identity is dependent on the meanings that the actor attaches to the concepts of homosexual and homosexuality, and that these meanings are directly related to the meanings that are*

> *available in his immediate environment; and the meanings that are available in his immediate environment are related to the meanings that are allowed to circulate in the wider society. The commitment to a homosexual identity cannot occur in an environment where the cognitive category of homosexual does not exist.*[18]

I offer this example of the Lebanese community as further proof of Dank's argument while at the same time revealing transformations he had not anticipated. Even though *Helem* has started to provide the context and support needed in the 'immediate environment' for a gay identity to develop, I suggest the role of the internet is crucial and has added an unforeseen component to homosexual identity negotiation in Lebanon. The 'immediate environment' of the subject is altered by the cyber world, which allows one to stretch the limits and borders of local reality. Accessing the global gay identity, something historically unavailable, allows them to transcend the values of their immediate environment. One significance of the internet becomes more pronounced when we recognize that to virtually all the younger subjects the internet was singularly instrumental in their exposure to aspects of the global gay identity.

Another important theme, which was not considered, is the role of the Lebanese government. In nearly any Arab state an open gay rights group advocating a public agenda of acceptance would have only existed for a few days at best. While the Lebanese authorities are not particularly friendly to *Helem* they have done little by way of constraining them. Should this be taken to signify an implicit or tacit approval from the leadership – or a more pragmatic speculation, is the state too strained by other weighty concerns to really care? It is interesting to note that the intense political situation in 2005 coincided with *Helem*'s largest growth; however, linking the two is pure conjecture. Yet the magnitude of the political crisis might have distracted the concerns or public gaze of certain governmental agencies. Likewise, declining tourism might also account for this seemingly lax and permissive attitude of public officials who are anxious not to disrupt the crucial flow of revenue from tourism.

Regardless of the internal situation in Lebanon it is important to question on a larger scale how this global gay identity spreads across the world with Lebanon as another 'convert'. It provides little or no room to express a same-sex identity without the rubrics of the Western gay model, therefore it is no marvel that a foreign term denotes something not-of-Lebanon. I argue that the imported global gay identity has been embraced by a small number in the homosexual community and will continue to grow along with *Helem*'s support. Most 'out' men have taken the Western gay archetype as a guide. Hence, the 're'-localization of their identity cannot occur until a more liberal socio-sexual setting begins to contain some of the elements associated with a homosexual identity.

It is interesting to note in this regard that a few informants, particularly those who had not been abroad, admitted that, in the absence of such local venues, those in the midst of forging meaningful and coherent sexual and gender identities have little choice but to revert to the borrowed and mediated role models, transmitted through the global media.

The experience of Beirut, though still in a formative period, is quite useful. Throughout Beirut's checkered socio-cultural history, it has managed by virtue of its mixed and hybrid composition to evince a greater readiness to experiment with novel and cosmopolitan lifestyles. The relatively accommodating, at time felicitous experience of homosexuals in grafting a coherent identity, is a case in point. At a time when their counterparts elsewhere in surrounding countries are being demonized, repressed and incarcerated (and at times sent to their deaths, as in Iran), the gay community in Lebanon has succeeded in creating a voluntary association, a media (print and virtual) and numerous public venues.

It is hoped this brief study has touched upon the greater significance of a gay identity in Lebanon. The outward development of this identity involves many 'firsts' in the Arab world. *Helem* is inciting discourse, engaging in civil society and hopes to gain more active members. There are also expanding resources in Arabic regarding sexuality and a diversifying scene in Beirut.

In closing, this chapter does not suggest that the development of a gay identity in Lebanon is strictly limited to the influences and experiences of the West through the 'global gay' identity. Altman notes: 'It seems clear that *some form* of gay and lesbian identity is becoming more common across the world'.[19] The global gay identity has arrived and those who have adopted it have grafted this to their other identities due to their education, experience online and more extensive travel experience. Indisputably this quest for a local gay identity is ground-breaking and will play a large role in the advancement of sexuality in Lebanon, while Beirut is the apposite location for the entry of gay rights into the Arab world.

Bibliography

Altman, Dennis, 'Rapture or Continuity? The Internationalization of Gay Identities.' *Social Text,* No. 48, Duke University Press, 1996.

—— *Global Sex,* Chicago: University of Chicago Press, 2001.

Binnie, Jon, *The Globalization of Sexuality,* London: Sage, 2004.

Campbell, John Edward, *Virtually Out: Internet Affinity Portals and the Marketing of Gay Identity,* Association of Internet Researchers Conference, Chicago, IL, 2005.

—— *Getting it On Online: Cyberspace, Gay Male Sexuality and the Embodied Identity,* Harrington Park Press, 2004.

Connell, R.W., *Gender and Power,* Oxford: Polity Press, 1987.

—— *Masculinities,* Cambridge: Polity Press, 1996.

D'Augelli, Anthony, 'Identity Development and Sexual Orientation: Toward a model of Lesbian, Gay and Bisexual Development', in E.J. Trickett, R.J. Watts and D. Birman, eds, *Human Diversity: Perspectives on People in Context,* San Francisco: Jossey-Bass, 1994.

D'Emilio, John, 'Capitalism and Gay Identity,' in Snitow, Stansell, and Thompson, eds., *Powers of Desire: The Politics of Sexuality,* New York: Monthly Review Press, 1984.

Dank, Barry, 'Coming Out in the Gay World,' *Journal for the Study of Interpersonal Processes,* vol. 34, 1971.

Dickel, Michel, 'Gender: Virtual Disruptions of Gender and Sexual Identity', in *Electronic Journal of Communication,* vol. 5, no. 4, 1995.

Donham, Donald L., 'Freeing South Africa: The 'Modernization' of the Male-Male Sexuality in Soweto', in Robertson, Jennifer, ed., *Same-Sex Cultures and Sexualities,* Oxford: Blackwell, 2005.

Fraser, Nancy, *Justice Interruptus: Critical Reflections on the 'Postsocialist' Condition,* New York: Routledge, 1996.

Gilmore, David, *Manhood in the Making: Cultural Concepts of Masculinity,* New Haven: Yale University Press, 1990.

Goffman, Erving, *Presentation of the Self in Everyday Life,* New York: Anchor, 1959.

—— *Stigma: Notes on the Management of Spoiled Identity,* New York: Touchstone Books, 1986.

HELEM, *Helem Pride Monthly Newsletter,* vol. 1, issue 2, January 2006.

Henderson, Christian, *Lebanese Group Tackles Biggest Taboo.* Al Jazeera, 5 January 2006.

Herdt, G. and Boxer, A., 'Introduction: Culture, History, and Life Course of Gay Men', in G. Herdt, ed., *Gay Culture in America,* Boston: Beacon Press, 1992.

Herdt, ed., *Gay Culture in America: Essays from the Field,* Boston: Beacon Press, 1992.

Internet World Stats, Internet Usage in the Middle East, 31 December 2005.

IRIN, *Lebanon: Homosexuals still Facing Discrimination,* 8 December 2005.

Massad, Joseph, 'Re-Orienting Desire: The Gay International and the Arab World', in *Public Culture Journal,* vol. 14, no. 2, 2002.

Murray, David, 'Between a Rock and a Hard Place: The Power and Powerlessness of Transnational Narratives among Gay Martinican Men', in *American Anthropologist,* vol 102, no 2, June 2000.

Phillips, Oliver, 'Constituting the Global Gay: Issues of Individual Subjectivity and Sexuality in Southern Africa,' Herman and Stychin ,eds, *Sexuality in the Legal Arena*, London: Athlone, 2000.

Smith, Lee, *Beirut Unexpected*, Out Traveler, January/February 2006.

Stychin, Carl, 'Being Gay' in *Government and Opposition* 40 (1), 2005.

Torbey, Carine, *Lebanon's Gays Struggle with Law*, BBC News, 29 August 2005.

Wikan, Unni, 'Man Becomes Woman: Transsexualism in Oman as a Key to Gender Roles,' in *Man*, New Series, vol. 12, no. 2, August 1977.

Wright, Timothy, 'Gay Organizations, NGO's and the Globalization of Sexual Identity: The Case of Bolivia,' in Robertson, Jennifer, ed., *Same-Sex Cultures and Sexualities*, Oxford: Blackwell, 2005.

Notes

1. Dennis Altman, 'Rapture or Continuity? The Internationalization of Gay Identities,' *Social Text*, 1996, p. 79.
2. Dennis Altman, *Global Sex*, Chicago, 2001, p. 1.
3. G. Herdt and A. Boxer, 'Introduction: Culture, History, and Life Course of Gay Men,' in G. Herdt, ed., *Gay Culture in America*, Boston, 1992, p. 4.
4. Lee Smith, *Beirut Unexpected, Out Traveller*, 2006, p. 1.
5. R. W. Connell, *Gender and Power*, Oxford, 1987, and R. W. Connell, *Masculinities*, Cambridge, 1996.
6. Donald L. Donham, 'Freeing South Africa: The 'Modernization' of the Male-Male Sexuality in Soweto,' in Robertson, Jennifer, ed., *Same-Sex Cultures and Sexualities*, Oxford, 2005, p. 273.
7. IRIN, *Lebanon: Homosexuals still Facing Discrimination*, 8 December 2005.
8. Joseph Massad, *Re-Orienting Desire: The Gay International and the Arab World*, Durham, 2002.
9. *Helem Pride Monthly Newsletter*, 2006.
10. Timothy Wright, 'Gay Organizations, NGO's and the Globalization of Sexual Identity: The Case of Bolivia,' London, 2005.
11. *Helem* website, 2006.
12. Donald D. Donham, 2005, p. 289.
13. David Murray, 'Between a Rock and a Hard Place: The Power and Powerlessness of Transnational Narratives among Gay Martinican Men,' *American Anthropologist*, 2000.
14. Internet World Stats, Internet Usage in the Middle East, 31 December 2005.
15. Michel Dickel, 'Gender: Virtual Disruptions of Gender and Sexual Identity,' in *Electronic Journal of Communication*, 1995, p. 2.
16. Ibid.
17. *Helem Pride Monthly Newsletter*, 2006, p. 1.
18. Christian Henderson, Lebanese Group Tackles Biggest Taboo, *al-Jazeera*, 2006.
19. John Edward Campbell, *Virtually Out: Internet Affinity Portals and the Marketing of Gay Identity*, Association of Internet Researchers, 2005.
20. Barry Dank, 'Coming Out in the Gay World,' in *Journal for the Study of Interpersonal Processes*, 1971, p. 288.
21. Dennis Altman, 1996, p. 85.

Sacred Prey and Fatal Mirror: The Female Body Written by Amjad Nasir and ʿAbduh Wazin

Asʿad E. Khairallah

Dealing with sex in modern Arabic poetry spans the full spectrum, from Gibran's ideal of chastity to the open sexual language and idiom meant to express rebellion and dissidence. But rebellion is a relative matter. In most conservative societies, for example, just mentioning the sex organs by name or clear hints may sound quite revolutionary. Here we find much poetry having sex as its main subject, yet presenting no novelty whatsoever when seen from a classical Arabic or a modern Western perspective. Yet, besides the majority of such writings, one can find some really daring poetry wherein sex is manipulated as a powerful subversive weapon.

The most intentionally shocking or outrageous in this respect is the early work of a major poet, Unsi al-Hajj (b. 1937), who already in the late 1950s had launched his frontal attack on religious, social and moral taboos against sex. He also employed graphic, raw, blasphemous language. Al-Hajj was followed during the 1970s by a group of Surrealists in exile, led by ʿAbdalqadir al-Janabi (b. 1944), in Paris, who went to an even greater extent in their blasphemous extravagance. This attitude is still found, but in a much more attenuated and subtle form, in recent poetry; such as Hashim Shafiq's collection called *Ghazal ʿArabi*,[1] where we have a kind of exhibitionism, probably meant to show one's sexual liberalism and emancipation, as well as to call for such emancipation. This is quite typical of repressive societies that still suffer under the burden of sexual inhibition, but does not add much either in vision or in structure. It generally expresses a type of teenage erotic longing and experience, yet with the clear intention of showing off one's 'philosophy' of carnal pleasure. This often finds expression in rather prosaic, crude reference to love making and sexual organs.

In the mean time, some of the most beautiful love poetry was written by Adunis (b. 1930), singing not only of the spiritual side of union with the beloved, but especially the physical one, and the sheer ecstasy in experiencing the erotic world in its plenitude.[2] We also encounter this, though endowed with a strong mystical dimension, in the poetry of Edwar al-Kharrat (b. 1926), and in some poetic passages of his novels.[3] But this was exceptional during the period of the Pioneers in the 1950s and 1960s, who wanted to change society, and for most of whom erotic poetry was not suitable for a revolutionary poet. For some, women were even 'the ruin of the revolutionary'.[4]

Yet the more we advance in the last century the more explicit focus we observe on the sexual act itself, stripped from its possible social and moral dimensions. This chapter will not deal with the sociological aspect of sex, but with the poetic attempt to isolate sex and explore it in itself. It is my hope that such an effort will shed some light on a particularly salient phenomenon in much of modern Arabic poetry in the last two decades; namely the gradual withdrawal of any discussion of sex from social concerns, if not from society altogether. Such obsession with the eroticization of the individual body, and especially the sexual act, can be seen, naturally, in two contexts: as a way of satisfying one's personal desires, and as a rejection of the dominant discourse in all social, political, religious and moral realms.

Indeed this phenomenon has been becoming more salient since the early 1970s, especially among emigrant poets and intellectuals, whose attacks on sexual taboos became all the more vehement with the rise and entrenchment of religious fundamentalism at home. Much of this poetry, however, is still too aware of its rebellious stand to be able to talk about love in a really free manner and as an existential experience in itself apart from social restrictions, ideologies and taboos.

A good example of such poetry may be a poem by the Iraqi exile poet, Sargun Bulus (b. 1944), who is a leading figure among the Surrealist poets. His poem, 'The Kings of Christmas Eve',[5] starts by talking about the same old star inclining since eternity over a certain crib, and the Magian Kings hurrying to Bethlehem. Then the lyrical persona goes on to talk about the star:

> It itself bends also
> Over us in this bed: I and a woman
> Warm from the land of snow (a queen

who visits me at night
From her rainy kingdom)
Asleep she is now, asleep
(I? I dream. I watch the star)
And 'it' [meaning his penis] is asleep, at last
Asleep between her fleshy thighs
a lizard
inert
sun-bathing in the Valley of the Kings.

Bulus may not necessarily have meant to be provocative here. Still, the demystifying effect of his words is quite obvious. They present a striking contrast between the traditional piety when talking about such an event as the birth of a God (or of God Himself for the believers) and the lightness with which this birth is treated by the poet's persona. The mention of the Valley of the Kings between the thighs of the woman is another desacralization of what used to be a sacred place for the ancient Egyptians. One would have expected him to say 'The Valley of the Queens', since he is sleeping with a queen, but I think the displacement is meant to be another sarcastic hint at the Magian Kings. Yet, even if the poem were not intentionally blasphemous, it remains clear that the persona's only dream on Christmas Eve is not to pray or meditate about the birth of the Christian God, but to have sex with a Nordic woman, with a clear satisfaction about his enjoyment of life without being chained by old beliefs or superstitions of innocence or sin. It may be interesting to note that Bulus is Christian; otherwise he would probably have been more restrained in his sarcasm.

This consciousness of sin does not exist in the two texts I intend to analyse, namely, Amjad Nasir's *Surra man Ra'aki*[6] (Joy to Your Beholder, 1994) and 'Abduh Wazin's *Hadiqat al-Hawass* (The Garden of the Senses), which has been banned since its appearance in 1993. Both are beyond the stage of dealing with sin, or good and evil. They express, instead, a new attitude to love in a period when old ideologies, mythologies and ideals seem to have died. Hence, nothing is left behind other than the individual and his body as a final source of redemption. In this respect, instead of dying for a remote or abstract cause, the only thing which seems worth living and dying for is love. Physical love for a specific body, in other words, and not love for humanity, nature or God is the source of well-being and ultimate redemption.

This new erotic poetry is also basically different from the love poetry of the celebrated Nizar Qabbani (1923–98), who used to boast having a reading public of 50 million Arabs. For Qabbani, often dubbed as a Narcissistic Don Juan, poetry of the body and all its paraphernalia are omnipresent, but not the act of love itself. Thus, even when Qabbani claims to be defending and gives the impression of worshipping women, he remains essentially macho. His women remain no more than profane tools.

In contrast, a fundamental change in both the general outlook and in the specific attitude to love and sex is achieved by our two poets. The first is the Jordanian Amjad Nasir (b. 1955) who started his poetic and journalistic activities in Amman, then moved to Beirut where he worked as a journalist in the early 1970s. But the disruptions of the civil war forced him to emigrate, first to Cyprus, and then to London in 1987, where he helped found the newspaper *al-Quds al-'Arabi* (1989), of which he has been the literary editor. Since then he has published seven collections of poetry and two travel memoirs. The second is the Lebanese poet 'Abduh Wazin (b. 1957), who is also a journalist and critic, and has been the editor of the literary supplement of *al-Hayat* newspaper. He has published six collections of poetry, some translations and many articles.

Not only are these two poets among the most daring in addressing the sexual experience, they also share an attitude that takes love so seriously it often borders on the sacred. Yet, despite this basic similarity between them, they are quite distinct in vision, character, style, imagery, diction and mood.

Nasir's Sacred Prey

The metaphor of hunter and prey informs much of Nasir's discourse. But it is a ritual hunt. While unfolding through the whole collection, it expresses patriarchal values without much apology for them. It is thus understandable how, more often than not, this relationship is violent: it is a conquest, with an illicit or explicit sense of triumph mixed with pride and gratefulness. The prey is generally linked to a treasure, a prize, a trophy, but mostly to a symbol of fertility in the shape of a fruit or a plant. Thus the female organ appears as a flower, a truffle or a pear. But the male, the primitive male, is far from being a gatherer. He is a hunter who is mostly likened to a ferocious animal, a lion, a tiger, a panther, a male viper (referring to the male organ, while, in this case, the female sex is the bird, as I imagine). The male organ is also an arrow, a spear, a sword, a blade and the like, while the act consists of stabbing, splitting, etc. Resembling a goddess of fertility the beloved is a field, and the male would plough her with a bull's horn. Her coveted organ is soft and white, although it may in fact be blonde ('White is the blonde one guarded by ever wakeful grass'.[7] It is proud of its ornaments and lacework. It is a legendary treasure, well-guarded (privately and publicly), a little master sleeping in its cottons, a cone of sugar melting with desire.[8] It has a dark burgeon, and is also the opium flower spreading its fragrance in the fissure.[9]

But the most striking characteristic of this poetry is the mixture between a docile and nearly worshiping attitude in front of the female sex, on the one hand, and the burst of violent emotions and intentions, on the other. So, we often read incantations full of submissive admiration, such as the following:

> The white, the powerful
> Which drove us out stripped of all inheritance
>
> O white, victorious
> Carrier of odours and shakings
>
> Sleeping in its cottons
> My little master does not wake up
> To the flutes of the hand
> A cone of sugar melting with desire
> Greenhorn
> Proud of its ornaments and lacework.[10]

On the other hand the female sex could be a real prey, taking an animal form, especially as a bird fixed by the male organ, 'the viper squirming with impulsive force / the big eye staring',[11] or as 'the bird of the hill'[12] split by the male arrow. And we are often struck by the basic shift in language, when the relation becomes one of explicit violence as if transposing the hunter spirit to the farmer within the fertility context. Thus, in another part of the poem, the softly sleeping, white and powerful little master becomes the centre of a field addressed with the following mixture of metaphors:

> I will plough you with the force of primitive people
> And extract your treasures with hands that lead the horn
> To a scream for help that bloodies the skin of the white one,

> The graciously self-satisfied.[13]

The violence of this language is obvious, but one has to be familiar with the poet's metaphors in order to grasp the full sexual meaning of his imagery here. At the same time the poet could reject the accusation of 'unethical' writing, since he never calls things by their real names. Nor does he do that in his other expressions, such as his image of 'the plough that splits the truffle (*kama*)', or the abovementioned 'arrow that splits the bird of the hill'.[14] It may be difficult to see here a clear reference to defloration, as it is difficult for a censor or a judge to prove conclusively the existence of anything pornographic in these words.

This is true of Nasir's whole collection, for the strength of his language resides in that it is fully metaphoric. His imagery often relies on the interplay of the sacred and profane. The best example is his explicit exploitation of the Quranic metaphor of ploughing for love making. He practically never mentions sexual organs. He resorts, instead, to agricultural and animal metaphors. He also relies a lot on colours and odours, the odour of the woman functioning almost like that of a female animal in heat.

The dialectic of sacred and profane is much enhanced by Nasir's usage of intertextual effects. This technique allows him a very daring yet ambiguous interplay between a more or less innocent profanity of the religious tradition and the employment of a device that places the beloved's body and sex on a sacred pedestal. In his poem, 'The Passionate Lover's Ascension' (*Mi'rag al-'ashiq*, the term being traditionally used for the Ascension of the Prophet Muhammad), the various possibilities of the root *sarara* are used, thus coming up with the following verses:

> Joy to your beholder (*surra man ra'aki*)
> To the one who puts a hand on the knee
> Who dips a finger in the navel (*as-surra*)
> And smells a secret (*sirran*)
> Joy to him, who lets an arm hang down
> On the slender waist
> Who approaches the source and sees (*sharafa n-nab'a wa-shaf*).[15]

One cannot fail to recognize in this kind of litany and in the whole poem, where this term *surra* is repeated, a reminder of the religious and especially Christian term *Tuba* ('Blessed are' at the beginning of the Sermon on the Mount). On the other hand, the final verse is a clear play on the mystical terminology, since he reaches a kind of blessed vision through approaching the source and 'seeing', whereby the source (or the fountain of life?) is nothing but the female sexual organ.

In another context he refers to penetration by saying: 'For it is not easy to enter the kingdom from the roundness of the ring',[16] in a clear allusion to the saying of Christ: 'It is easier for a camel to go through the eye of a needle than for a rich man to enter the kingdom of God' (Matthew 19: 23–5). The same image is reiterated in the Quran (7: 40) which says of the unbelievers: 'nor will they enter the Garden until the camel goeth through the needle's eye'.[17]

In the same spirit, but in a more complex intertexual ploy, he blends hypotexts from the Gospel and the Quran and comes out with his own melange of sexual metaphors. So, the pious Quranic *Adkhilni mudkhala sidqin* (Let my entry be by the Gate of Truth and Honour: 80) is blended with the Gospel image of the narrow gate ('Try to enter through the narrow gate', Luke 13: 23) thus begetting his persona's way of addressing the beloved: *Adkhilini mudkhala diqin / li-nas'ada bil-alam* (Make me enter a narrow entry, so we rise in pain).[18]

Some maybe inclined to consider this subversion of religious tradition as merely playful. Others, especially the self-appointed guardians of the faith, may consider it blasphemous. What prompts us, however, to plead again and again for a more 'positive' interpretation is Nasir's insistence on deifying the beloved rather than belittling the deity. For example the following usage is a hypotext from the Quran:

> We get you and we lose you
> We surround you from all sides
> With branches and spears
> But you are cunning (*fa-tamkurin*)
> Your hand is above our hands.[19]

Here is a clear reference to the Quranic mention of God as the Cunning, the best plotter, if you wish, against those who try to deceive Him or plot against the Prophet. 'They plot, but Allah (also) plotteth, and Allah is the best of plotters' (8: 30). At the same time it is coupled with another clear Quranic reference to God's power: 'The hand of Allah is above their hands' (48: 10).

But in spite of the female's cunning and power, the persona, like Moses on the Mount, insists on seeing 'the source', imploring: *Arinih ... Uridu an arah* (p. 41: Let me see it ... I want to see it), as if to reach the mystical vision which makes him 'rave in love trance'.[20]

This is a very special mysticism though. It is the total fascination with the presence here and now of a particular body, exciting the instinctive, libidinal sexual desire of a seemingly primitive male, whose perfect union with the beloved's body is sometimes described in mystical terms.

One of the best poems which includes most of the aforementioned motifs and imagery is *wardat ad-dantil as-sawda'* (The Black Lacework Rose, meaning vagina), which is about a fleeting and casual sexual act between a male and a female who meet in a fortuitous way while travelling on a train. The act has no real location and the relation cannot strike roots since it takes place in a vehicle symbolizing mobility and change. Yet, one feels as if this occasional encounter had been predestined since eternity, and that the two dissonant parts of the same soul and body have finally come together.

The poet presents this act without any predetermined plot or narration in mind and, thereby, stripping it of all past and future, describing nothing but the bare, wild sexual desire, with no consideration whatsoever of anything intellectual, spiritual, or the like. The two persons have neither names nor clear colour or nationality, unless we suppose that she is British, because of her whiteness and freckles, and that he is an Arab or Asian, since he is referred to as 'the stranger'.[21] They do not talk; they exchange looks and feel each other's burning desire, or may even smell it. We are not told of any preliminary caresses or any love words. All we hear are the words of the male, probably uttered in his heart, wishing that the woman would part her legs more, so he can have a fuller and more sensual of view of his object of desire. Perhaps his being from the conservative Arab world makes him hungrier for sex and simultaneously more attractive on that level, to the point that a European girl could be enticed by his seething desire. Although the poem reveals little about the girl's feelings, we must infer that both are strongly attracted to each other, otherwise the love act would not have been consummated. In describing the emotions, fantasies and imaginative flights of the man, the whole poem revolves practically around one centre, the woman's sexual organ, and the psychic and physical negotiation of the love act. This act finally occurs on the train, between two strangers who would most probably remain so.

The idea of love at first sight is not mentioned but implied. Yet, the encounter has neither consequence nor future and seems far from resulting in any fruits. This sounds paradoxical when we remember all the agricultural and animal imagery and the incantations reminiscent of old Babylonian fertility rites. Still, the poem makes no clear allusion to any permanence in the new relationship that remains between two itinerant strangers, two train passengers, reflecting the poet's life as a foreigner in England, and maybe a certain vision he holds of life in general and of the erotic relationship in particular. The spirit moving this particular poem is that of the hunter, not the farmer. Thus, extracting the relation from all past and future allows the poet to focus exclusively on the sexual act itself and on its immediate physical and biological consequences, such as the liquid traces that the orgasm leaves on the man, and the deflowering on the young woman.[22]

Do we have here two particular male and female meeting by sheer chance on a train, the perfect symbol of relentless and unanchored movement and change of localities and passengers? Or is it rather the train of life? Does the love act, in its primal nudity, foreground the intense fixation of *this* male on the female sex and his craving to possess it, or does it highlight the overwhelming power of sexual desire as such?

In this respect, one cannot totally separate the persona from the poet. The Bedouin, nomadic spirit seems to be the driving force in the whole poem. The woman too is called 'the Bedouin of the cold'.[23] All through the book, the male appears as the stranger or passerby, while the female bestows not only a momentary ecstasy, but also a kind of transitional belonging and identity. The original identity of the male is lost; he is uprooted, away from his tribe and land; and he feels cold. Only the charms of the female would give him warmth and make him feel like a master, in a cold country that treats him as a foreign non-entity. This is why, perhaps, he is triumphant after the act, mixing his sense of triumph with some delight in the failure of his competitors, at least, or of all the others who aspire for the prominence of social prestige and elevated standing. They all covet the female goddess, but he alone reaches her and possesses her, usually like a real hunter and sometimes like a cunning thief.[24]

Yet, a legitimate question remains: is this love or only sex? Is the body in Nasir's poetry sacred or profane? Here I should like to suggest that the ritual atmosphere makes the relationship more than sheer sex, more sacred than profane. For despite the ephemeral contact between these two lovers, and I insist on calling them lovers, they seem to me to be more real and more involved in their mutual attraction than the kind of blasé and disenchanted bourgeois relationships we find in Qabbani. Indeed, Qabbani's lovesick and romanticized rendering of amatory encounters, with their prosaic inventory of lipsticks, socks and perfumes, seem banal and passionless in comparison. To a large extent this is also true of Hashim Shafiq's poetry. Without telling us much about the woman's body, Nasir's poem masterfully embodies the overwhelming desire of a male hypnotized by his own craving to possess the female, and once at the climax, 'raving in love trance / gulping whatever air is left'.[25]

Nasir's remarkable achievement lies in his inventive use of language and imagery and in his nuanced, often cunning, ambiguity in creating his persona and evocative narrations. This is even more lyrical in the way he treats the woman's 'sacred fruit', as he calls it, with a type of hymn that could well be inspired by mythology of Mesopotamian, Canaanite or biblical injunctions. No wonder his lyricism seems at times as though he is addressing a divine being, praying for rain, or enchanting a wild animal rather than face the treacherous prospect of hunting the beast down. The moment the reader thrusts himself into his unabashedly graphic portrayal of sexuality, one is overwhelmed by how the love act is seen as a wild and brute force resembling an aggressive fight with a sacred bull, having the final kill as its climax. The urge is so strong the lovers cannot help but yield to their devouring desire. Thus the act is not a simple sexual exercise nor does it resemble an encounter at a whorehouse. The ritual hymns and litanies which inform and sustain its basic tone bestow a sacred atmosphere on the whole scene.

In short, if one should infer any worldview from the scene, one may say that life is a short journey, whose highest purpose is to reunite the two split parts of the same human being, thus bringing them back to their paradise-like state, if only for some moments. In this reunion the male is the driving force. For him, one's ultimate ends justify any mean; fair or foul. Hence, ferocious instincts, violent weapons, as well as enchanting prayers, become legitimate. Possessing the sacred prey ends in a kind of total union, not a spiritual one between the human and the divine, but a concrete one between two human beings, in body for sure and maybe in spirit too.

Wazin and the Fatal Mirror

A quite different vision of love and sex is presented by 'Abduh Wazin, who takes the obsession with the erotic to its extreme. His lovers are not chancy, erratic passengers in a train, but a man and a woman in love, who for some undeclared reason decide to put an end to their life. Wazin's text is much less concerned with love making in itself or the longing to act on one's wildest instincts than in the body-in-love as the door to a hidden world that fascinates the poet's persona. This is why the text is rather contemplative and sometimes genuinely meditative, with the body of the beloved as its focus. And although the love match is described very fervently and explicitly, the effect is not primitively animalistic, nor is it all that exciting, notwithstanding the sexual description of the details of flirting, kissing, excitement, penetration, orgasm, swooning and the like. The reason for this is the atmosphere in which the whole text bathes, namely, that of two lovers facing death by choice. Furthermore, a meditation on love, life and death cannot make for a really exciting sexual game. It is true that this cerebral persona practises sex with total engagement. Yet sex is far from being his means for self-realization. In this realm, he has nothing to compare with the violent libidinal urgency of Nasir's persona. Thus, in a passage that well represents the vision, mood and style of the whole text, we read:

> Death had ripened within us, and we had ripened in its darkness, and we had prepared our two bodies as a last banquet. We chose to die together as we finished together and we were bored our deep boredom. *We chose to die like one who dies in front of a mirror*. Like one who dies with his shadow. We had come together in order to end all that had brought us together, all that had separated us. We did not meet in order to begin; it is in order to end that we met, to wipe (out) our wounds and eliminate our boredom ... We did not die, maybe because we so much prepared our death and so much waited for it that it became our own waiting and we became our own death.[26] italics mine

Two lovers meet in a kind of a small apartment, of which only a bed, a window, and a shower come into play, in order to prepare their death. We are not told how they were supposed to die: through pleasure, hunger or suicide. They fail to reach the end they had set for themselves; they seem to have become so used to the idea that it lost its interest. The woman ultimately gives up and leaves, not being ready to realize the project. She leaves the door opened behind her as if inviting the man to follow suit.

This is a summary of the 'narrative' which is no narrative in fact. And one may rightly ask, what makes the book of 134 pages and how come it is called *The Garden of the Senses*? The answer is that the book is a long meditation on the nature of love between a man and a woman, told by a male persona, in an attempt to recreate or rewrite the female's body, once it became absent. It is almost an attempt to pierce the secrets of life and death through the body, the living and dying, shining and dimming, calm and throbbing body of both beloved and narrator. Narrating their indulgence in preparing their death, the author focuses on the contemplation of the female body and on the act of love in its most intense moments. Although the book has been censored in Lebanon, there are no real pornographic scenes, since the author is not really interested in the love act as much as he is intent on seeing the backside of the mirror. This means that the female body, the other half that is supposed to make him whole, is at the same time his own Narcissistic waters, in which he is constantly contemplating himself, his own life and death. He is as enamoured of himself as he seems to be of this woman. Indeed, if their project to die together ultimately fails, it is probably because they have lost their unity in love and gone back, each to his and her shell of solitude and total isolation. This goes to the point where love making becomes another kind of masturbation. In fact, they do masturbate in front of each other.[27]

And this is the paradox, since, instead of reuniting with each other, each one becomes a kind of hermaphrodite, self-sufficient without being really whole. Neither of them needs the other, nor are they fully content with themselves.

> We were together in order to enter our isolation, our utmost isolation from the world, from our two bodies, from our burning and simultaneously empty desires; a male and a female we were, a male and a female I was, a female and a male she was.[28]

This is the crux of the frequently repeated notion of the lovers becoming identical, i.e. practically sexless as far as their mutual attraction is concerned. Failing to be the real mirror or missing half, the woman disappears, leaving enough space for the man's intensive brooding and Narcissistic self-contemplation. The Narcissistic mirror here could of course be poetry. Indeed, the other major theme in the book is the act of writing. This is driven to an extent where one often thinks that it is the fundamental aim behind the book, whereas love and the body are merely the pretext for writing. There is a dialectical relation between physical love and writing, each one negating the other in the register of desire. In this respect we have another passage that is central to the vision and style of the text:

> Writing is the desire of writing. It is the sudden pleasure which overtakes you while you surrender to it in complete calm. Yet, I did not lose the desire to write until I entered the desire of the body. I did not miss the habit of writing until I embraced the habit of the body. I did not get out of the hell of writing until I drowned in the hell of the body. Suddenly her body rose up in front of me ... At that moment, desire which was vague and bright like lightning became a faint thread that separated between the body and writing, between the body and its past, writing and its death.[29]

Such is the type of writing with which we have to do here. In order to be aware of the full meaning of this passage, one should perhaps remember what the body means to the two lovers. This comes out in the narrator's saying: 'I had really failed to understand the world, not because it was sufficiently vague, but because I was myself vague, vaguer than the world itself. I could not justify or explain my existence in it.' Then, a little later, he adds:

> When I decided to change the world, I secluded myself with my body, her body. I made my body, her body, a substitute for the world. I closed on myself; we closed on our two bodies. I started facing myself; we started rolling over in the darkness of fiery thoughts. And it happened that I was cut off from the world, the hateful, despondent, stuffy world, the dead, monotonous, boring, cold world, which was not the world itself ... When I was in seclusion with my body, her body, I became fully aware that I could change the world.[30]

This is, in sum, the new way of changing the world. It has evolved from (1) the prophetic vision aiming at changing the spirit, as with Gibran, to (2) the ideological commitments intent on changing society, as with the Pioneers, and finally to (3) this new avoidance of all grand projects, thus falling back on the possibilities of the individual body, either yielding to its desires or exploring its mystery.

But could one call this exploration real love?

When one loves one would like to stay alive, to perpetuate the moment. But, here, love is purely physical. The relationship is focused on the two bodies, but as mirrors to each other. Nor is it realistic to have a woman who never opens her mouth. This is also another element which makes the scene very special in its zeroing in on the sexual activity as observed by a persona who is a writer. Emotions are not involved in this activity. So, one wonders, if it is love at all, beyond a burning sexual desire. The persona is intensely interested in piercing the secret of the body, not the psyche. It is as if the whole psyche were incarnated in the body. The presence of death puts the relationship under a specific light with magnifying lenses. The soul is mentioned, but in a rather abstract way. It is the *ghayb* (the beyond), the principle of life probably, the secret beyond the body. But the psyche remains strangely absent, as if totally closed. The lovers are not only silent with words; they are also silent with emotions, so to speak. The only phenomena that exist are those of their bodily desires that are infinite.[31] He loves her for her nakedness.[32] There is no talk, neither between them, nor by the narrator, about society, art, thoughts or anything outside the immediate body and its states. The narrator is simply fascinated by her body, and now that she is gone, the exceptional details of her absent body, in all its aspects and positions, at rest and in motion, are a concrete expression of the narrator's intention to recreate that beloved body through language.

Within such a setting, one may begin to understand Wazin's obsession with the minute descriptions of her various parts, her face, her back, breasts, thighs, navel, sex, etc. under their various colours, shades and movements, in bed, under the shower, by the window, awake as in sleep. While all of this often seems like a precise phenomenological description, the text suddenly slips back into the consciousness of death and of what is beyond appearance. For instance, when he talks about her navel, he first describes its shape and the few fine hairs surrounding it as a source of excitement, and then continues in a rather metaphysical leap: 'it is the point of the body, its vanished memory, its death and rebirth'.[33]

When, like Nasir, he compares her sex to a flower, he does not do that in a flimsy metaphor. He dwells on the subject, endowing it with mysterious dimensions.

> The sight of her sex [her shame, 'pudendum', as he calls it] had certain vagueness about it. Like a flower it was, like a flower that does not articulate itself, a flower of vague desires, desires that happen and do not happen. Her sex was the nightly part of her body. Her sex was the night of her body. It was her night.[34]

Here again, the phenomenological description leaps into the metaphysical.

The vagina becomes the night of the body, its well of secrets:

> Her sex excited in me more than one desire, a feeling full of what makes death and life a single light, a single darkness. That fissure opens up on an abyss, the abyss of our two bodies, as they penetrate each other and become one. It is the abyss of pleasure surrounded by a deep void, the void of what is before and after the body. That open wound was our trace that we did not leave behind, our trace that did not leave us so as to witness for us, for our deep desires, and for our nostalgia that is deeper than death.[35]

The author does not tell us anything about the object of this nostalgia. It certainly cannot be the hateful world. As for the void of what is before and after the body, let us remember that it is the space of writing; writing as substitute and sublimation, possible only before and after this Eve's concrete bodily presence. And here one may wonder: was she ever really present, or is the whole thing a figment of the persona's mind? Or is it a deeper nostalgia to an imaginative Garden of Eden where the pleasures of the senses are not forbidden fruits and do not necessarily end in exile and death, and where the 'white, powerful one', as Nasir calls it, does not drive us out 'stripped of all inheritance'? Or is it simply a means for creation through recreating the woman's body and focusing on that fissure, wound or abyss of pleasure that opens up on 'the void of what is before and after the body'?

The importance of Nasir and Wazin is that each of them takes to the extreme a certain tendency that is becoming increasingly current. Wazin represents the rather meditative attitude that takes sex as the meeting point of life and death and yearns to discover its secret, whereas Nasir stands for the much more widespread carpe-diem spirit, or unavoidable yielding to an overwhelming, blind instinct that does not want so much to understand as to pass to immediate action and be satisfied. Nasir's poetics is that of overwhelming presence. He mixes muscular violence with tender incantations. Wazin's is that of the dialectics of presence and absence, of contemplation with erotic fascination. For his persona the vagina represents the strong presence of pleasure, yet it is always surrounded by 'the void which is before and after the body'.[36]

Both texts are highly ambiguous: Nasir's because of its pretty wild imagery and Wazin's because of the whole situation plunged in mystery with no explanation, or rather with too many possible interpretations.

Yet both are very clear about the 'sacredness' of this source of life that is the female's sexual organ, though with a major difference, namely that Wazin insists on highlighting it as the dialectic centre of both Eros and Thanatos, the enigmatic source of both life and death, while Nasir speaks of the joy and the quasi mystical bliss of approaching that source and seeing it, as if in a vision of union with the totality of Being. Between these two extremes, the last decades have known the full spectrum of shades and nuances, the sum total of which make for a dynamic and fascinating picture of the erotic imagination in modern Arabic poetry.

Bibliography

Adunis, *Mazamir al-ilah ad-da'I* (The Lost God's Psalms), in *Awraq fi r-rih*, Beirut: Dar Majallat Shi'r, 1957.

——*Tahawwulat al-ashiq*, in *Kitab at-tahawwulat wal-hijra fi aqalim an-nahar wal-layl* (The Book of Metamorphoses and Migration in the Regions of Day and Night), Beirut: al-Maktaba l-'asriyya, 1965.

——'Jasad' (Body), in *Mufrad bi-sighat al-jam'*, Beirut: Dar al-'Awda, 1977.

——*Amwaj al-layali*, Beirut, Dar al Adab, 1992.

Khairallah, A., 'Love and the Body in Modern Arabic Poetry', in R. Allen, H. Kilpatrick and E. de Moor, eds, *Love and Sexuality in Modern Arabic Literature*, London: Saqi Books, 1995.

Nasir, A., *Surra man ra'aki* (Joy to your Beholder), Cairo: Dar Sharqiyyat lin-Nashr wat-tawzi, 1994.

——*Al-A'mal al-Kamila*, Beirut: el-Mu'assasa l-'Arabiyya Lid-Dirasat wan-Nashr, 2001.

Pickthall, M., *The Meaning of the Glorious Koran: An Explanatory Translation*, New York: New American Library, 1956.

Sa'id, H., *Al-Kashf al Asrar al-Qasida*, Baghdad: Manshurat Matabat al Tahir, 1988.

Shafik, H., *Ghasal 'Arabi*, Beirut: Riyad ar-Rayyis, 2001.

Wazin, A., *Hadiqat al-Hawass*, Beirut: Dar al-Jadid, 1993.

Notes

1. Hashim Shafiq is an Iraqi poet born in 1950 and now living in London. See his *Ghazal 'arabi* (2001).
2. Adunis, *Tahawwulat al-ashiq*, in *Kitab at-tahawwulat wal-hijra fi aqalim an-nahar wal-layl* (The Book of Metamorphoses and Migration in the Regions of Day and Night), Beirut, 1965, and 'Jasad' (Body), in *Mufrad bi-sighat al-jam'*, Beirut, 1977.

3. Adunis, *Amwaj al-layali*, Beirut, Dar al Adab, 1992; A. Khairallah, 'Love and the Body in Modern Arabic Poetry', in R. Allen, H. Kilpatrick and E. de Moor, eds, *Love and Sexuality in Modern Arabic Literature*, London, 1995.
4. H. Sa'id, *Al-Kashf al Asrar al-Qasida*, Baghdad, 1988, p. 160.
5. The poem was written in Germany, where the poet was invited on a grant, in Villa Waldberta, Feldafing. Since the late 1960s Sargon Boulus – as he spells his name – has lived in San Francisco and, since the mid-1990s, has often been on long visits to Europe, especially to Germany. See his 'Muluk Laylat al Milad', *'Uyun*, 2/4, 1997, pp. 71–2.
6. The collection was first published in 1994, then in a shorter form within a selection of his poetry called *Athar la-'abir*, 1995, then in a little larger edition, 1996. The collection I am using here. His *Collected Works, al-A'mal al-Kamila*, 2001 includes four additional poems under the single collection *Surra man ra'aki*, which, in my opinion, do not add much to the main spirit of the work, and sometimes even lessen its strong impact.
7. A. Nasir, *Al-A'mal al-Kamila*, Beirut, 2001, p. 22.
8. Ibid., p. 27.
9. Ibid., p. 63.
10. Ibid., pp. 25–7.
11. Ibid., p. 29.
12. Ibid., p. 30.
13. Ibid., p. 88.
14. Ibid., p. 30.
15. Ibid., p. 55.
16. Ibid., p. 86.
17. See M. Pickthall, *The Meaning of the Glorious Koran: An Explanatory Translation*, New York, 1956.
18. A. Nasir, *Surra man ra'aki*, Cairo, 1994, p. 85.
19. Ibid., p. 59.
20. Ibid., p. 40.
21. Ibid., p. 22.
22. Ibid., p. 33.
23. Ibid., p. 18.
24. A. Nasir, 1994, pp. 93–95 and *Liss as-Sayf* (The Summer Thief), pp. 97–111.
25. A. Nasir, 1994, p. 40.
26. A. Wazin, *Hadiqat al-Hawass*, Beirut, 1993, p. 130.
27. Ibid., pp. 128–9.
28. Ibid., p. 116.
29. Ibid., p. 25.
30. Ibid., pp. 15–6.
31. Ibid., p. 93.
32. Ibid., p. 95.
33. Ibid., p. 100.
34. Ibid.
35. Ibid., p. 98.
36. Ibid.

Sexuality, Fantasy and Violence in Lebanon's Postwar Novel

Maher Jarrar

Sexuality and the Arabic Novel

In her introduction to a volume on *Love and Sexuality in Modern Arabic Literature,* an outcome of a seminar organized in 1995, Hilary Kilpatrick advances the following argument:

> [T]he search for love is intimately connected with the individual's desire for freedom and fulfilment, while the frank affirmation of sexuality, of whatever kind, represents a challenge to a rigid and hypocritical social order. In both cases the act itself cannot be separated from its expression, and innovative attitudes to love and sexuality are bound up with literary renewal. Above all, the writer who takes up these issues knows that his or her handling of them is a social act, implicating the whole community. Much more than in most West European literatures, discussions of love and sexuality in modern Arabic literature are intricately connected with ideas about society and the individual's place in it. They are central to contemporary Arabic culture.[1]

The study of sexuality in literature is embroiled with many difficulties. At least three such problematics are self-evident. First, some of the ambiguities are inherent in the striking fluidity of sexuality in virtually all its manifestations, biological, cultural, as well as personal. Second, they are also an expression of the symbolic meanings of sexual communication and negotiation. Finally, they could well be a reflection of the complex and highly charged nature of the literary text itself. Conceptually, much of my discussion is informed by the constructionist perspective of Jeffrey Weeks, Anthony Giddens and others who argue that sexuality can be more realistically understood if it is seen as an outcome of the social forces and diverse cultural settings it is embedded in. Weeks, thus, argues that

> sexuality is something which society produces in complex ways. It is a result of diverse social practices that give meaning to human activities, of social definitions and self-definitions, of struggle between those who have power to define and regulate, and those who resist. Sexuality is not given, it is a product of negotiation, struggle and human agency.[2]

Anthony Giddens stresses, as well, that sexuality 'is a social construct, operating within fields of power, not merely a set of biological promptings which either do or do not find direct release'.[3]

How does the Lebanese postwar novel give sexuality a language to articulate its social construct? To address this question, I have studied three recent Lebanese postwar novels published between 2001 and 2002, these are: Rashid al-Da'if's *Tustufil Myrel Streep*, Ilyas Khuri's *Yalo* and 'Alawiyya Subh's *Maryam al-hakaya*. The narrative time of two of these novels (by Khuri and Subh) covers a rather long interlude, starting at some point at the beginning of the twentieth century and extending to postwar reality. The narrative time of the third, al-Da'if's *Myrel Streep*, is confined to nearly a decade, from 1991 to 2000. All three novels are samples of Arabic 'nouveau roman', experimenting with modern narrative techniques and with a rich and novel mixture of vernacular dialects and classical Arabic language, creating polyphonic discourses.

The novel, more than any other genre, is capable of artistically articulating the complexity of the realities in which it is anchored. This relation of *referentiality* is actualized in the novel through different techniques. Nevertheless, as Peter Zima puts it, '[T]he very idea of an objective description of reality is an illusion based on the untenable assumption that a particular discourse can be identified with the real'.[4]

The Lebanese Novel and the Civil War

Let us turn our attention first to Lebanese society, the originator and the victim of a dramatic civil strife that lasted for seventeen years (1975 to 1992). Samir Khalaf, in one of his most recent books, writes that:

> Since Lebanon was, for nearly two decades, besieged by every conceivable form of collective terror, it is pertinent to assess the impact of these beleaguering encounters on those entrapped in them ... [T]he magnitude of damage to human life and property and the psychological and moral consequences of relentless violence have been, by any measure, immense – especially since they involved a comparatively small and fractured society with a bewildering plurality and shifting targets of hostility ...
>
> The scares and scars of war have left a heavy psychic toll which displays itself in pervasive post-stress symptoms of nagging feelings of despair and hopelessness. In a culture generally averse to psychoanalytic counselling and therapy, these and other psychic disorders are more debilitating. They are bound to remain masked and unrecognized and hence, unattended to.[5]

The connection between sexuality and the Lebanese civil war, as portrayed in the novel, has been the subject of a number of studies written, interestingly, by mostly female authors. Evelyne Accad, defends this hypothesis by claiming

> that although both female and male novelists make the connection between sexuality and war, their ways of expressing it and most of all the solutions implied are quite different. Women writers paint the war and the relationships of women, men, and their families in the darkest terms: sexuality is tied to women's oppression and the restrictions put on their lives; the war brings destruction, death, and despair ... [M]en writers also paint the war relationships among the men and women in the bleakest terms, and they emphasize the connection between the two. But their depression does not lead them to the search for alternatives different from the historically accepted ones: heroism, revenge, and violence as catharsis.[6]
>
> In both women's and men's writing, the war is used to break down the patriarchal system and the traditional order. The female protagonists do it through masochism, while the male ones use cruelty and sadism. But such actions and reactions lead nowhere because the use of war to free oneself from domination and oppression only reinforces the authoritarian order by reproducing the power structure with different colours.[7]

Regarding the question of poverty and class consciousness, Accad claims that this question

> emphasizes women writers' awareness of these issues. This awareness leads them to search for positive alternatives, while men writers use their recognition of the problems to justify violence. Both male and female authors show the links in the fate of the dispossessed, their struggle to overcome it, women's oppression and war.[8]

These and other such inferences, though partly convincing, emerge from Accad's own analysis of novels she is presenting. Indeed, they originate from her misconstruing of the texts. She even misreads the titles of the Arabic originals.

Miriam Cooke, on the other hand, perceives Lebanese women's war literature as providing

> examples of women's construction of new gender norms. Some heroines escape from a male controller and train to become combat-ready; others deliberately enter into zones forbidden to all, but especially to women, by the well-advertised presence of a sniper. Lebanese war literature creates a hyperspace in which women can transform themselves from passive observers to military discursive participants.[9]

Sex and Ideology: Rashid al-Da'if's Tustufil Myrel Streep[10]

Narrator, storyline and time

Al-Da'if's novella covers 141 pages in the form of a long monologue that is not divided into chapters. The voice which opens the narrative is that of a first person recounting his own experience. In the course of the first few pages, the reader comes to know that he is called 'Rashshud', a diminutive form of the proper masculine name Rashid (the first name of the real author, al-Da'if). Such diminutives are meant as nicknames and are used by the addresser as a sign of familiarity and intimacy towards the addressee. They are usually saved for children or for a beloved one. Diminutives as the names might be, they are often used to belittle the addressee and to emphasize that he is not being taken seriously. Adding insult to injury, is actually the mother-in-law who calls him 'Rashshud'.[11] As the narrative goes on we understand that the use of this form by his mother-in-law refers to a kind of disrespect or belittling. She demeans him as an immature person, a nuisance or a dummy. A character with an emblematic name, argues M. Riffaterre, 'usually acts as if the name, instead of being bequeathed to him, had been chosen as a tag for his way of life or his temperament. The text thus proceeds by verifying the kind of action expected of the type through a convincing, that is to say, tautological, story'.[12]

As is clear from his other narratives, al-Da'if has a cherished familiarity, and an affinity, with the name Rashid. It is, after all, his own name. It is the name he chooses for the first person narrator both in his quasi-autobiographical "Azizi al-sayyid Kawabata' (*Dear Mr Kawabata*, 1987) and in his latest narrative 'Insi 'l-sayyara' (*Forget about the Car!*, 2002). By giving the narrator a name familiar to the reader that s/he, consciously or unconsciously, relates with the author al-Da'if intends to generate more authority for the narrator's voice, enhancing therefore the nature of the narrative.

The narrating 'I' in al-Da'if's story represents an intrusive narrator who provides a nuanced and decidedly subjective angle to the events: from the first pages, the reader encounters a baffled man in dilemma. Al-Da'if is, of course, far from unique in employing this 'I-narrative form'.[13]

Now, let us move to the story line which can be easily extracted from the episodic plot. With breaks in the temporal continuity we learn that Rashshud is thirty-five and lives alone in Beirut. His maternal aunt arranged his marriage to a neighbour of hers. His widowed mother resides in their native village, whereas his brothers and sisters, like one-third of the Lebanese, are immigrants in the Gulf States and Australia. Rashshud is obsessed by two things: owning a TV set and sex. For him getting married is eventually like buying a TV set and having free sex.

The main narrative space is dominated by closed rooms: living rooms, bedrooms and toilets. Nevertheless, many encounters take place in cafés. These encounter-spaces are used in order to portray Rashshud's conservative, macho attitude towards women. The only two open spaces are those of fantasy: one is unreal, signified by the electronic TV media; whereas the other involves the fantasy of the body. Hence, the narrative could be read as an apartment narrative. An apartment is a captive space closed to the outside and it sets constrictive and confining limits on what an individual can make of himself.[14] The apartment is not simply an expression of the individual's identity; it is also constitutive of that identity; or as Bachelard puts it, 'Our house is our corner of the world'.[15] Henry Lefebvre suggests that 'the relationship between home and ego borders on identity because both are a "secret and a directly experienced space"'.[16] The first thing Rashshud did when he moved to 'his' new apartment was to buy curtains to protect him from the piercing gaze of the neighbours, the others. Nevertheless, he created for himself a voyeuristic space, where he can watch pornography channels and where he can cast his gaze at the body of his bride.

From the outset of the *story* the reader gets to know that Rashshud's bride – whose name, curiously, remains unknown all through the novella – did not want to move with him to 'his' new apartment. She avoids him and tries to get away from any sexual contacts with him; she despises him and compares the new apartment to a tomb. She prefers to stay at her mother's or with his maternal aunt. The strategy Rashshud uses in order to persuade her to join him in the apartment is to convince her that the TV set he has bought is much better than the one they watch at her mother's. She rarely joins him in the apartment and whenever she does she avoids any sexual contact with him. Rashshud on the other hand waits till she sleeps (or pretends that she is sleeping) in order to rub his organ on her body, penetrate her quickly, for his ejaculation is abrupt and uncontrolled, or he masturbates on her. Rashshud is a very jealous and self-absorbed person, who throughout the narrative is trying to convince himself (and accordingly the reader) through long distorted soliloquies that his wife is betraying him with another man.

As is clear from the above, the story line is simple and it ends with divorce after his wife gets pregnant and he accuses her of a relationship with a French student. This is a melodramatic theme typical of al-Daʿif's last three novels, where melodrama functions as a means of revising notions of value and behaviour.[17] What make the skeleton of the narrative proceed in space and time are themes that represent an obsessive repetition of the same dilemma. There is no escape from the grip of the narrator's fixated point of view, from his misunderstanding, bad faith and assiduous jealousy.

The story time, as implied by the narrator, started in 1992, when he was watching George Bush on TV announcing the beginning of a 'new world order' after the Gulf War. It ends with divorce some months later while his wife was in her second month of pregnancy. The narrative time, on the other hand, is anachronous, filled with lacunas and is moreover contradictory: it includes events that occurred in 1995, 1998 and 2000 (alluding to Hizbullah's victory). This anachronous sequence is filled with faults, lapses, slips, chance delays and false analogies, leading to the discursive and spotty character of the narrative. Such techniques have been long established in modern narratives by James Joyce, Henry Miller and Alain Robbe-Grillet who seem to form part of al-Daʿif's referential frame. These techniques have been a common 'sensibility' among Arab novelists since the 1960s.[18]

Main character

Oddly, but perhaps consistent with al-Daʿif's intention, no hint is given as to his occupation or regular mode of employment. He seems to have time at his disposal to indulge his whims. And he does so with considerable abandon. He whiles away his time watching TV programmes, particularly erotic and hard-core pornography. He is an avid reader of local and foreign newspapers. Likewise, he is devoted to his favourite radio and TV stations, particularly the BBC. Religiously, every Thursday, he hangs out with his friends in Blue Note, a bistro-like restaurant/bar for the liberal, left-of-centre set. He belongs, most probably, to the white-collar stratum. He is a kind of a pseudo-intellectual, who exhibits naïveté on both domestic and public concerns. His ethos, in conformity to his middle-class background and learning, is to cling to the vision of a more or less small world, sustained by equal economic units and linked organically to a community, a common culture and a way of life belonging to the reality of a Lebanese middle class, made vulnerable under the oppressive weight of destructive social forces, yet lacking the consciousness of its situation.

Two themes occupy the novella: first, the effect of the electronic media and globalization on the life of individuals and families; second, the degrading norms and demoralization of the Lebanese postwar society. The axis around which these themes move is that of *sexuality*. This axis is woven with a multilayered language: first, there is the level of a modern-classical Arabic; second, the level of colloquial Lebanese with its French and English derivatives; and third, the language of classical Islamic law and juridical sex manuals.

The electronic media

As a result of electronically mediated interactions, the definition of situations and behaviours is no longer determined by physical location. By altering the informational characteristics of place, as Meyrowitz argues, electronic media reshape social situations and social identities. 'The electronic media destroys the specialness of place and time. Aspects of group identity, socialization, and hierarchy, that were once dependent on particular physical locations and the special experiences available in them have been altered by electronic media.'[19]

So pervasive is the electronic media that much of the social fabric in cities today moves toward hyper-reality. This is most visible in the replacement of geographical space with the screen interface, the transformation of distance and depth into pure surface, the reduction of space to time, of the face-to-face encounter to the terminal screen.[20] From 1995, the novel gadgetry of the electronic media, i.e. the internet, the cable channels and the cellular phone, were starting to become available for the population at large in Lebanon. Hard pornographic films invaded the privacy of homes in Beirut and they became a common subject in everyday discussions. Some neighbourhoods, as well as religious authorities, organized campaigns against this unwelcome intrusion. People were talking about 'The New World Order' and globalization in the same breath they talk about a porn film or the Lebanese economy or indulge in a heated sectarian discussion.

Rashshud, as well as his wife and her parents, are all avid TV fans. Their lives rotate around the screen. Through television, strangers are experienced as intimates. Heidi Nast maintains that

> as an arena of news and entertainment shared by both sexes, television alters women's perspective. The power of television to reshape the traditional relations between men and women – which were supported by the literacy gap and industrialization – is suggested clearly by the romantic notion of the 'home' as a separate domain apart from the 'hostile society of the outer world'.[21]

Television and other electronic media bring this world into the home and, in doing so, change both the public and domestic spheres.

Rashshud seeks to find a parallelism between his relation with his wife and that of Meryl Streep and Dustin Hoffman in *Kramer Versus Kramer*. Al-Da'if intends, of course, to build one of his main narrative kernels on this film. His attempt remains, nevertheless, very loose and not persuasive, since any other film from this genre would have served equally well. Most of Rashshud's energy and fantasy are, instead, fixated on sex. Rashshud is a conservative, a true son of his patriarchal society, a hypocrite with double standards. While he condones, for example, honour crimes against women, he condemns premarital sex. He is also vehemently opposed to abortion. With such a stern, moralistic mindset one would expect Rashshud to display a modicum of virtuous conduct consistent with stringent precepts he demands from others. Far from it, he is often unabashedly indulgent and unrestrained when it comes to his own conduct. For example, he evinces no misgivings whatsoever when he tries to rape the neighbourhood veiled seamstress who came to fix their curtains at home! Likewise, he watches porn films with much abandon. Hard-core episodes and porn stars become his role models and sources of fantasies. His wife is given no chance to resist or demure his acts. He forcibly attempts to try all kinds of sexual techniques with her: fellatio, anus licking, anal penetration, etc. Rashshud, as well, is an underwear fetishist. When he was young , his mother used to find sperm traces on his underwear, both frontal and from behind so that she accused him of being a passive homosexual. Most of all Rashshud enjoys masturbation.

Language

This brings us to the language employed by al-Da'if. His narrative reveals modernist characteristics common to other contemporary Arab novels. He does though display a few peculiar, if not anomalous, linguistic proclivities which have invited a scurry of recent interest.[22] On the level of modern Arabic language, he employs a prose that deliberately ranges between a classical vocabulary, indulging heavily in mixed metaphors, and a vernacular language, coloured with the colloquial and free from casual connectives, that focuses on the small, mundane aspects of existence.[23] At times it descends to a fatuous language of ribaldry. In this way he incorporates the tension and contradictions created by the use of language in a single narrative voice. A third level brings the narration to a still higher tension when al-Da'if resorts to the language of Islamic juristic treatise on sexuality. Instances of such expressions are legion throughout his narration.

His excessive playfulness and virtuosity in taking linguistic liberties become at times too burdensome, artificial and, hence, unconvincing. They also tax the sensibilities of the ordinary reader. Such excesses seem more pronounced since al-Da'if is a professor of linguistics at the Lebanese University, a national institution which normally attracts a mainstream and conservative constituency. This is particularly visible in his explicit, laborious and relentless graphic rendering of sexual encounters and fantasies. By employing such linguistic collages and hyperboles, he clearly exceeds the limits of tolerance. It is then that al-Da'if's narrations slip away from eroticism into pornography.

Pornography

Can one differentiate between eroticism and pornography in literature? Do experimentation and a pathological sexual *idée fixe* give licence to a vulgar language describing aberrant sexual preferences? Or is art, as some are inclined to suggest, a mere experimental masturbation for art's sake? The debate about obscenity in literature has a long history both in medieval and modern Arabic as well as in Western literatures.[24] It has been approached from two points of view: aesthetics and realism. It involves breaking taboos by speaking about subjects that are not supposed to be disclosed openly. Its purpose is to awaken, to usher in a sense of reality. Hence, what reality shares with erotic literature is not inherent in content but in form.

D. H. Lawrence argues that

> the plain and simple excitement, quite open and wholesome, which you find in some Boccaccio stories is not for a minute to be confused with the furtive excitement aroused by rubbing the dirty little secret in all secrecy in modern best-sellers. This furtive, sneaking, cunning rubbing of an inflamed spot in the imagination is the very quick of modern pornography, and it is a beastly and very dangerous thing.[25]

Much of the strategy of al-Da'if's novella is built around voyeurism, the manly gaze, secrecy and hypocrisy. Other than their evocative sensuality and eroticism, it is my view that these are all aspects that reveal acts of male power and surveillance against the women's body. Bodies and spaces in his narrative are made up through the production of relations of power. As such it is not enough to argue that pornography should be accepted in postwar novels because eroticism has a long tradition in Arabic literature and because pornography has become a part of modern consumer culture and has invaded the very privacy of our homes. It must be borne in mind that without secrecy and manifestation of power there would be no pornography. But if pornography is nurtured and embellished in a socio-cultural setting of secrecy, what is the result of pornography? The effect on the individual is manifold, and always insidious. But one effect is perhaps inevitable: 'the pornography of today, whether it be the pornography of the rubber-goods shop or the pornography of the popular novel, film and play, is an invariable stimulant to the vice of the abuse of the other and the self', as D. H. Lawrence argues. Does Rashshud resemble us, 'i.e. we, the Lebanese', asks Mary al-Qusayfi, one of the critics who reviewed al-Da'if's *Meryl Streep*.[26] Her answer is that of affirmative doubt.

By way of conclusion I wish to extrapolate, tentative as they may seem, a few inferences about the form and outcome of sexuality as a literary genre in a postwar setting like Beirut. The most striking, perhaps, is that al-Da'if's strategy must not be seen merely as a radical experimentation with narrative themes and playful prose, inventive and appealing as these may seem. Such virtuosity can be easily seen, as has hopefully been demonstrated in this chapter, in al-Da'if's inventiveness and skill (at times excessive) in readily manipulating both these literary elements. The narrative, I am suggesting, entails a *disguised phobia*; both at the level of gender and the reassertion of social and religious affiliation. This indifference to, or phobia of the other is an expression of what Samir Khalaf labels 'Geography of Fear'[27] and has become much more pronounced in postwar Lebanon.

The structure of desire in al-Da'if's discourse is triadic, there is always another male hidden: whether sexually or on the level of language. This antagonist allows Rashshud to establish himself as a subject, yet at the same time he gives him a dose of his own inferiority. Rashshud meditates on the desire to command his wife, a desire provoked by his wish to control her activities. The narrative confirms the very patriarchal norm whose violation it supposedly applauds. It manifests, on the first level, a loss of confidence in the status and meaning of masculinity in a postwar era and fear of emancipated femininity. On the second level, the social spaces of the narrative are concentrated either in a neighbourhood of veiled women or in the Shi'i and Kurdish quarter of Burj al-Murr, where his friend, the porter at Beirut Airport, lives. The porter functions as an object of desire and as a sexual antagonist and rival. These sectarian spaces culminate in an episode that takes place in South Lebanon. It is in this representational space that a cousin of Rashshud's wife had penetrated her when she was still nine years old as she was sitting on his lap in a car. Oddly, this incident happened while Arab visitors and local crowds were celebrating the victory of Hizbullah and the liberation of South Lebanon from the Israeli invaders.

The liberty of experimentation in the use of language which mounts up in a satirical parody of many voices and languages, and particularly, his parody of the language of Islamic law and of Arabic love manuals regarding sexual relations and techniques, reveals an anxiety of the symbolic phallus of the other.[28] This fear of 'the other', which creates for Rashshud a sense of inferiority, is conveyed through more than one Freudian *lapsus* that make the fabric of the narration. Eros becomes here a disguised expression of aggression and a prelude to war. This kind of disguised phobic discourse is unprecedented in the Lebanese novel. Are we here confronting a new type of writing provoked by the degradation of the social and political system which is becoming manifestly sectarian, excluding a major portion of the society and reinforcing lack of democracy and constant violations of civil rights? Whatever the causes, the consequences of such a literary trend might be drastic.

Levantine History, Civil Violence and the Schizo: Ilyas Khuri's Yalo

Despite its classification as a postwar novel, *Yalo*, Khuri's latest novel, explicitly depicts the atrocities of war and its repercussions on a society, which scandalously fails to accommodate its wounded sons or cater for their pressing needs. In a sense then, the novel lingers in the Lebanese civil war's deepest enclaves – engulfed by its manifold carnage, while at the same time dwelling on the latter through the lens of a fragmented persona. The novel often seems to feed solely on the image of its main protagonist –Yalo – whose prominent/singular male voice takes the lead and starts digging deep into his memory, in order to weave a meaningful narrative – one that finally comes out puzzling and closer to hallucination.

Daniel (nicknamed Yalo) the main character is an anti-hero. Of Syriac ethnic origin (*suryani*), he was born in Lebanon in 1961. His grandfather Ephram had fled the massacre of 1915 carried out by the Turks and the Kurds against the Syriac and Armenian citizens of his native village Ain Ward, near Mardin in Anatolia.

Yalo's father leaves the family after Yalo's birth and migrates to Sweden. Yalo knows of no aunts, uncles or relatives. The grandfather takes care of his daughter and her son. He perceives his small family as a counterpart of the Holy Family – father, son and Holy Spirit – the mother being the Holy Spirit. At the age of twelve or thirteen, the 'holy family' flees the atrocities of the Lebanese Civil War and becomes displaced from its quarter. They move to the eastern part of Beirut, the so-called Christian area. At the age of fourteen he joins the paramilitary friends of the Lebanese Christian, powerful and fearful militia, *al-Quwwat al-Lubnaniyya* 'Les Forces Libanaises'. At the age of seventeen, he becomes a fighter.

Yalo is a victim. He is an innocent boy, son of Syriac immigrants who fled the massacres of 1915–17 in Anatolia, becomes a fighter, actively involved in the making of a horrible civil war. He is a 'victim' of a divided, deeply religious family, existentially aware of its uprootedness, and of its ancient and rich heritage. A typical example of many of the fighters in the Lebanese civil war: an innocent boy, pampered with machoism, a fervid ideology, drugs, sex and the game of war. At the end of the war, the last months of 1989, he flees to Paris. There, he wanders penniless as a vagabond for three months until he is picked up by a Lebanese millionaire, nouveau riche, Michel Sallum. Mr Sallum, weapons dealer, brings him back to Lebanon to serve as a guard – 'my wife is frightened of dogs, or else I would have bought a dog to guard the villa', Mr Sallum tells him.

The novel's story line highlights Yalo's prewar life. Principally, it is an attempt to demonstrate how the war did not help in restructuring his survival in postwar Lebanon. Rather, it is the juxtaposition of war and the predisposition of his society to become more dysfunctional, which turned Yalo/Daniel/Berro into a character with many uncertain identities.

None of these identities, however, were coherent or meaningful. They all reveal, in varying degrees, a sense of betrayal coupled with an underlying tone of unappeased hostility that one can detect from Yalo's biographical account(s). This pent-up hostility stems at first from the dislocation permeating his relationship with his domineering grandfather, with his mother and overall entourage. He feels entrapped but alone. Like any other form of bondage, he is *in* but not *of* the group which envelops his life. This disaffection develops further in both war and postwar settings, where Yalo never fits or manages to understand the mechanisms of his detested surroundings. Thus, the constant impression is that Yalo is hallucinating while attempting to recollect his tenuous and ambivalent memory.

Yalo is arrested for a crime he did not commit. Shirin, his alleged victim, claims that he had raped her, whereas he insists on her consent and on the smell of incense that filled his being. He is forced to admit, under torture, a crime he did not commit. He was made to be part of an underground 'terrorist' group that work for Israel. Yalo writes/narrates and rewrites his story four times, a story which begins with the massacre of Ain Ward and ends with crucifixion.

Ioan Davis explains that the dominant space of a prison-like setting may degrade the graphology of the prisoner, 'by compelling him to write in order then to mock him by destroying or distorting what he has been compelled to write'.[29]

In the stormy wave of hallucination however, only sympathy can be developed for this problematic protagonist. Having been acted upon rather than an actor, even during sexual performances (e.g. with Mme Randa who drew him into the world of porn), Yalo retaliates by practising hard-core voyeurism: flashing secret lovers down the hill. Yet it was after he joined the war that Yalo learnt to become an ardent voyeur. By sniping and flashlighting, he used to punish 'lusty' wanderers in the valley. Bullied throughout his entire life, he suddenly decided to bully people in turn and earn some power out of forcibly disempowering his 'preys'. Obviously, Yalo carried his war like mentality forward and turned it into a defensive lifestyle. In a disintegrated society, each individual possesses his/her own ramified sexual stories outside the fixed boundaries of understandable relations (e.g. Mme Randa who cheats on her husband Michel Sallum, Shirin who engages in numerous random sexual encounters, Gabi, Yalo's mother, and her older lover Ilyas Shami). There are no institutions that could absorb the children of an ugly war. These children suffer nevertheless from a host of crippling dysfunctions that render them sexual objects and push them beyond the edge of reason.

If sexuality is as problematic on all levels, could Yalo have really raped Shirin, who accuses him of sexual assault, followed by a sequence of blackmailing operations? Since the act of raping itself does not constitute part of his patched-up memory, Yalo provides the reader (and more importantly, himself) with a detailed yet sporadic account of how he fell in love with her – an unexpected infringement on his embittered night world. What he fails to do is to provide a coherent account of how the overall incident was triggered. Instead, Yalo puts forward a story that diverges from Shirin's own; one with many altered beginnings and a monolithic end. That is, Yalo's selectivity in concentrating on the post-rape nature of his involvement with the girl often makes him question the possibility of his guilt as a rapist, but never confirm it. For, in his relationship to Shirin, Yalo gradually adopted an engaged/engaging attitude. He tried, it seems, to understand his own past in light of her presence in his life. Sex did not remain a commodity with her; instead, it was transformed into a meaningful interaction associated with his becoming a man. Through the smell in her arms, he embarked on a new but short-lived life, marked with his reacquisition of the power of speech. From then on, things seemed endowed with the kind of meaning that even the aftermath of war failed to procure.

Nevertheless, Shirin did not understand anything beyond her 'victimization': not the words, not the songs, not the metaphors, not his confused past, not the lies he made up to look 'manly' in her eyes. At times, Yalo is depicted as her sexual prey rather than her own aggressor. In a sense then, Yalo can be deemed innocent, albeit from a misplaced commitment – one of many others he was rather passively drawn into. Even where love was allegedly found, sexuality remained problematic. Yalo seems to be eternally trapped in war, despite its presumed extinction. Unfortunately, if the overt physical violence had disappeared, its crashing impact never did. Instead, it translated into social havoc, tormenting in the first place the fighters who possessed no means of reintegration at home. Thus, Yalo became an outcast, living on the margin of Shirin's life; let alone everybody else's.

It is noteworthy here that each of the voices in this novel speak from the outskirts of life. That is, all the characters are marginalized by the mere fact that they speak the language of war: a language of lies and treachery. 'Truth has become a disease', reiterates Yalo when he briskly discovers the vice of unmasking his inner self, of 'stripping naked' (as George Bataille would label it) before the other's gazing eye. For, there is no 'other' in Yalo's context that wishes to caringly stare at a distorted self, at a product of war that may well replicate who they deeply are and, hence, splinter their fabricated/defensive social shields.

Mothers, Sisters, Wives and Male Violence: Alawiyya Sobh's Maryam al-hakaya

While Khuri's *Yalo* depends on a narrative provided by a single male protagonist, 'Alawiyya Subh's *Maryam al-hakaya* draws instead on a thread of narratives, conveyed sequentially from one female voice to the other across three different generations. *Maryam al-hakaya* takes the form of stories embedded within a frame-story that is narrated by a certain 'Alawiyya (which, as in al-Da'if's novels, is also the real name of the author). Nevertheless, the implied narrator, 'Alawiyya, dedicates for each one of the characters, who are personalities either related to her by kin or are her close friends, a whole chapter that is narrated by the character itself. The polyphonous nature of the novel lays before the reader an array of distorted human samples.

The main framework of *Maryam al-hakaya* captures a migration movement within Lebanese society (from sometime during the 1930s until postwar society). Maryam's family abandons the countryside (South Lebanon) to relocate in Beirut. Much like other displaced groups, she carries over her own distinct cultural baggage, dreams and aspirations for a brighter world. Women, in particular, are bound to suffer because their dislocation is not alleviated by the geographic shift. Actually running away from their besiegement is merely like the act of escaping their proper shadows: a 'hope-filled' but unrealistic journey. Stories of virility – or lack thereof – keep sprouting throughout the novel, in view of elucidating how the manifold female protagonists all share a similar fate especially where sexuality was at stake. From rape and the impact of bestiality in the depraved countryside to betrayal in the heart of a warning city, fairytale-like accounts of suffering and anguish are intimately laced together. Without succumbing to dogma or futile preaching, the power of speech is virtually lost.

Across generational lines, women in *Maryam al-hakaya* all seem like victims of unfulfilled sexual dreams and expectations. While the majority of older characters (Maryam's mother or Umm Yusuf who perceive sex as an unclean act, *najis*) remain confined to disparaging matrimonial bonds, younger females (Ibtisam, Maryam and 'Alawiyya) venture into the realm of sexuality from an allegedly wider doorway, allowing for a multiplicity of unrequited love affairs and sexual encounters to unfold. However, in their failure to transcend the inherited sexual codes of virginity, honour, virtue and virility, daughters like mothers end up facing further victimization.

Indeed, war brutally engulfs the protagonists' memories, eats them up from within and imposes a sense of unprecedented loss. For instance, Umm Ahmad loses bedsheets and garments as proof of her daughters' honourable initiation into marriage. Hence, she becomes unjustifiably paranoid about society's potential allegations against the family's protected honour. By the same token, Ibtisam – the educated activist – relinquishes her faith in revolution as well as her belief in relationships due to her break-up with her Christian lover, Karim, who marries a woman from his own religion. She, as a consequence, embarks on a traditional marriage, which compounded her vulnerability and despair.

Such episodes are emblematic of the war's inherently deceitful nature and the vivid attempts by women to adapt in rather than stay 'out' – for fear of becoming outcasts. Umm Ahmad, who has not experienced any injustice attributed to her sexuality, wishes nonetheless to protect her daughters' reputation – even years past their marriage. The blood-stained towels she dearly preserved in her closet before the bloodier hand of war snatched them away probably represented her sole recelebration of sexuality. What Maryam's mother, Umm Ahmad and Ibtisam have in common is not only deception but the perfidy of being raped. Yet Ibtisam, who willingly offers a body animated with love to Karim, has her dreams and ardent beliefs violated by a weak partner. At a very crucial moment in his sexual encounters with Ibtisam, Karim becomes painfully aware about the link between revolution and sexual debauchery. Soon after this incident, Karim surrenders to society's pressing urges, which allegedly address him from within. Seemingly, a primordial 'nerve' keeps flicking and it is this powerful 'nerve' that brings him back to the comfort of his proper clan/religion/region; in sum, to his people rather than to the feared 'other' that Ibtisam now represents, after love and sexuality have faltered.

Maryam somehow undergoes an identically distorted sexual experience with 'Abbas, a married man who practises with her, in secret, the unspoken language of open desires. The pleasure Maryam derives with 'Abbas is only ephemeral and its progeny bound to disappear. Hence, an impregnated Maryam drags her feet to the doctor – like many of war's desperate females – to abort both the foetus and her tickling yet temporary sensation of ruling the world through motherhood.

One of the novel's most intriguing features lies in the abundance of spaces within which characters happen to move furtively. Nevertheless, mobility and their aptitude to transcend geographic barriers (even to other countries like Syria, Iraq or Palestine) do not diminish the confinement that strangulates all protagonists – namely females. In fact, the plethora of reported spaces are endowed with an inherent sense of restriction that forces characters to run away in vain. The entire novel is actually structured around incapacitated individuals on the run. If the act of running is instigated by excessive misery, its outcome culminates in further destruction on both the physically and emotionally damaged. Faced with an impeding lack of alternatives – even where they have attempted to adopt an active stance – women in *Maryam al-hakaya* are gradually drawn into a hysterical mode. A symptomatic absence of identity and the availability of a social audience that fuels such unfortunate absence by forcing females outside the vicinity of the so-called 'conscious subject position' explicitly reassert the pathological nature of war and the society that hosts it. A pertinent illustrative example would be Maryam's aunt, Naziha, who becomes a prostitute in al-Mutanabbi Street, Beirut's 'red light district',[30] named, oddly enough, after the most famous Arab poet of the tenth century. The infamous street is a location frequently portrayed by Lebanese male novelists, primarily in their accounts of initiation into manhood.[31] The particularity of this novel culminates, however, in the fact that it meticulously depicts the 'making' of a prostitute and the flagrant schism permeating her personal life. If Maryam's aunt stretches her role to the fullest – even after she is compelled to give up her job – it is because she was stripped throughout the years of any identity other than being labelled as a sex object. To her parents, she was dead. To the host of men who discovered their virility in the warmth of her body, she was yet another prostitute – whose desirable flame was meant to fade away with age. Hence, the enunciated fullness with which she assumes her role stems from the inherent absurdity of her situation. Oscillating like a shadow between a farfetched world she aspires for and another that monstrously devours her energy, the disadvantaged country girl spends her days flirting with a wrecked dream: reacquiring proof of existence as a human being in a community that harshly rejected her. Even when she came back with repentance, Maryam's aunt did not constitute the crux of her family's attention; her wealth did, until it was squandered.

As stated earlier, I am arguing with Anthony Giddens that, sexuality 'is a social construct, operating within fields of power, not merely a set of biological promptings which either do or do not find direct release'. The three Lebanese novels that were discussed were chosen to answer the following question: how does the Lebanese postwar novel give sexuality a language to articulate its social construct? The novels under scrutiny reveal different forms of sexual behaviour. Al-Da'if's novel exposes a hypocrite, middle-class, pseudo-intellectual who lives in Beirut in an era of rapid changes on all levels in postwar Lebanon and in a society unable to handle its political and social dilemmas. The main character swivels around the electronic media. Passive consumption, voyeurism and pornography draw all his attention, leaving him unable to start a love relation with women, whom he perceives as sex objects. As argued earlier, al-Da'if's novel entails a *disguised phobia*; both at the level of gender and the reassertion of social and religious affiliation.

Khuri's novel on the other hand portrays Yalo, the main character, as a victim, a stranger and an *idiot*. Yalo is indeed one of war's crippled creatures. Even so, the problematic nature of his life stretches beyond the occurrence of war itself. From the onset, Yalo had grown in a broken family, distinctly marked with the absence of a viable 'orienting' fatherly figure. Dominated by his grandfather's strict and overbearing personality, Yalo developed a major imbalance that jeopardized every venue of his life, including sexuality. The great sense of disempowerment which haunted him in his disintegrated home was also primarily reinforced by the fact that the multi-communal Lebanese society treated him as an undermined minority, in constant need of assimilation. Hence, nursed and nurtured in a chauvinistic society where sex is defined as mere commodity, Yalo underwent manifold but forced 'initiation rites' that made him link sexuality with machismo.

The third novel, *Maryam al-hakaya*, depicts the life of female characters. They proliferate images of more marginalized individuals as they suffer the repercussions of war on a society that has never been less than predisposed for further sectarianism, corruption and striking 'machoism'.

Note

I would like to thank Professor Samir Khalaf for his unlimited support, valuable advice and generous comments. Many thanks are also due to Ms Nisrine Jaafar (Oxford) for the valuable discussions on theoretical matters that inspired parts of this chapter.

Bibliography

Accad, Evelyne, *Sexuality and War: Literary Masks of the Middle East,* New York: New York University Press, 1990.

Aghacy, Samira, 'Rachid al Da'if's *An Exposed Space between Drowsiness and Sleep*: Abortive Representation', Journal of Arab Literature, vol. 27, 1996.

—— 'The Use of Autobiography in Rashid al Da'if's *Dear Mr. Kawabata*', in R. Ostle, E. de Moor and S. Wild, eds, *Writing the Self: Autobiographical Writing in Modern Arabic Literature,* London: Saqi Books, 1998.

Allen, R., Kilpatrick, H., and Moor, E. de, eds, *Love and Sexuality in Modern Arabic Literature,* London: Saqi Books, 1995.

Bachelard, Gaston., *The Poetics of Space*, Boston: Beacon Press, 1969.

Badawi, Muhammad, *al-Riwaya al-Jadida fi Misr: dirasa fi 'l-tashkil wal-idiyulujiya,* Beirut: al-Mu'assasa al-Jami'yya lil-Dirasat wal-nashr, 1993.

Bal, M., *Narratology: Introduction to the Theory of Narrative*, Toronto: University of Toronto Press, 1997.

Barton, James L., *Turkish Atrocities: Statements of American Missionaries on the Destruction of Christian Communities in Ottoman Turkey, 1915–1917*, Ann Arbor, MI: Gomidas Institute, 1998.

Bouhdiba, A., *Sexuality in Islam*, London: Routledge & Kegan Paul, 1985.

Cooke, Miriam, 'Death and Desire in Iraqi War Literature', in R. Allen, H. Kilpatrick and E. de Moor, eds, *Love and Sexuality in Modern Arabic Literature*, London: Saqi Books, 1995.

al-Da'if, Rashid, *'Azizi al-sayyid Kawabata*, Beirut: Mukhtarat, 1995.

Dalrymple, William, *From the Holy Mountain*, London: Flamingo, 1998.

Davis, Ioan, *Writers in Prison*, Oxford and Cambridge, MA: Basil Blackwell, 1990.

Giddens, Anthony, *The Transformation of Intimacy*, Cambridge: Polity Press, 1992.

Harlow, Barbara, *Resistance Literature*, New York: Methuen, 1987.

Hays, M. and Nikolopoulou, A., eds, *Melodrama: The Cultural Emergence of a Genre*, London: Macmillan Press, 1999.

Jaafar, N., 'The Blue Flame and the Red Flame: Love and Eroticism', unpublished MA thesis with Professor Anthony Synnott, McGill, 2002.

Kellner, D., *Media Culture*, London: Routledge, 1995.

Khalaf, Samir, *Prostitution in a Changing Society: A Sociological Survey of Legal Prostitution in Beirut*, Beirut: Khayyats, 1964.

—— *Civil and Uncivil Violence in Lebanon: A History of the Internationalization of Communal Conflict*, New York: Columbia University Press, 2002.

al-Kharrat, E., *al-Qissa al-qasida*, Cairo: Dar Sharqiyyat, 1995.

—— *al-Hasasiyya al-Jadida*, Beirut: Dar al-Adab, 1997.

Khuri, Ilyas, *al-Mubtada' wa'l-khabar*, Beirut: Mu'assasat al-Abhath al-'Arabiyya, 1984.

Lefebvre, Henry, *The Production of Space*, Oxford and Cambridge, MA: Blackwell, 1997.

Marcus, Sharon, *Apartment Stories*, Berkeley: University of California Press, 1999.

Meyer, Stefan G., *The Experimental Arabic Novel: Postcolonial Literary Modernism in the Levant*, New York: State University of New York Press, 2001.

Meyrowitz, Joshua, *No Sense of Place: The Impact of Electronic Media on Social Behaviour*, Oxford: Oxford University Press, 1985.

Miller, Henry, 'Obscenity and the Law of Reflection', in *Pornography and Obscenity: Handbook for Censors. Two Essays by D. H. Lawrence and Henry Miller*, IN: Fridtjof-Karla Publications, 1958.

Nast, H. and Pile, S., eds, *Places through the Body*, London: Routledge, 1998.

Prince, Gerald, *Dictionary of Narratology*, Lincoln: University of Nebraska Press, 1987.

al-Qusaifi, Mary, *An-Nahar*, Beirut, 1 December 2001.

Riffaterre, Michael, *Fictional Truth*, Baltimore: Johns Hopkins University Press, 1995.

Scarry, Elaine, *The Body in Pain: The Making and Unmaking of the World*, Oxford: Oxford University Press, 1987.

Sidawi, Rafif R., *al-Nadhra al-riwa'iyya 'ila al-harb al-lubnaniyya, 1975–1995*, Beirut: Dar al-Farabi, 2003.

Stanzel, Franz, *Theorie des Erzählens*, Göttingen: Vandenhoeck & Ruprecht, 1991.

Takieddine Amyuni, Mona, 'Style and Politics in the Novels and Poems of Rashid al-Da'if', *International Journal of Middle East Studies*, vol. 28, 1996.

Ternon, Yves, *Mardin 1915: Anatomie pathologique d'une destruction*, Revue d'histoire Arménienne contemporaine (special issue), vol. 4, 2000-2.

Thomson, David, ed., *A Biographical Dictionary of Film*, New York: Knopf, 1995.

Weeks, Jeffrey, *Sexuality*, London: Routledge, 1986.

Zima, Peter, 'The Sociology of Texts: Position and Object', in Bart Keunen and Bart Eeckhout, eds, *Literature and Society: The Function of Literary Sociology in Comparative Literature*, Brussels: Peter Lang, 2001.

Notes

1. R. Allen et al., *Love and Sexuality in Modern Arabic Literature*, London, 1995, p. 15.
2. Jeffrey Weeks, *Sexuality*, London, 1986, p. 24.
3. Anthony Giddens, *The Transformation of Intimacy*, Cambridge, 1992, p. 23.
4. Peter Zima, 'The Sociology of Texts: Position and Object', in Bart Keunen and Bart Eeckhout, eds, *Literature and Society: The Function of Literary Sociology in Comparative Literature*, Brussels, 2001, p. 29.
5. Samir Khalaf, *Civil and Uncivil Violence in Lebanon: A History of the Internationalization of Communal Conflict*, New York, 2002, pp. 3–4.
6. Evelyne Accad, *Sexuality and War: Literary Masks of the Middle East*, New York, 1990, pp. 167–8.
7. Ibid., p. 170.
8. Ibid., p.170.
9. Miriam Cooke, 'Death and Desire in Iraqi War Literature', in R. Allen, H. Kilpatrick and E. de Moor, eds, *Love and Sexuality in Modern Arabic Literature*, London, 1995, p. 189.
10. Beirut: Riyad El-Rayees Books, January 2001. *Tustufil* or *tistifil*, is a word used in Lebanese dialect meaning something like 'I care less with what so-and-so thinks or does' (its etymology is still unknown to me). The English title on the back of the Arabic titlepage reads: 'To Hell with Meryl Streep'. For Meryl Streep, see David Thomson, 1995,

pp. 722–3.

11. Rashid al-Da'if, *'Azizi al-sayyid Kawabata*, Beirut, 1995, p. 8.
12. Michael Riffaterre, *Fictional Truth*, Baltimore, 1995, pp. 722–3.
13. For its salient use and varied forms, see Gerald Prince, *Dictionary of Narratology*, Lincoln, 1987; Franz Stanzel, *Theorie des Erzählens*, Göttingen, 1991, pp. 109–48, 285–94; M. Bal, *Narratology: Introduction to the Theory of Narrative*, Toronto, 1997, pp. 120–6.
14. Sharon Marcus, *Apartment Stories*, Berkeley, 1999.
15. Gaston Bachelard, *The Poetics of Space*, Boston, 1969, p. 4.
16. Henry Lefebvre, *The Production of Space*, London, 1997, p. 121.
17. On the role of melodramatic plays as cultural genres, see M. Hays and A. Nikolopoulou, eds, *Melodrama: The Cultural Emergence of a Genre*, London, 1999.
18. For this and related considerations, see E. al-Kharrat, *al-Qissa al-qasida*, Cairo, 1995 and *al-Hasasiyya al-Jadida*, Beirut, 1997; Muhammad Badawi, *al-Riwaya al-Jadida fi Misr: dirasa fi 'l-tashkil wal-idiyulujiya*, Beirut, 1993, pp. 79–168; Stefan G. Meyer, *The Experimental Arabic Novel: Postcolonial Literary Modernism in the Levant*, New York, 2001, pp. 1–97.
19. Joshua Meyrowitz, *No Sense of Place: The Impact of Electronic Media on Social Behaviour*, Oxford, 1985, p. 117.
20. D. Kellner, *Media Culture*, London, 1995, pp. 2–8.
21. H. Nast and S. Pile, *Places through the Body*, London, 1998, p. 210.
22. See Samira Aghacy, 'Rachid al Da'if's *An Exposed Space between Drowsiness and Sleep*: Abortive Representation', Journal of Arab Literature, vol. 27, 1996, and 'The Use of Autobiography in Rashid al Da'if's *Dear Mr. Kawabata*', in R. Ostle et al., *Writing the Self: Autobiographical Writing in Modern Arabic Literature,* London, 1998; Mona Takieddine Amyuni, 'Style and Politics in the Novels and Poems of Rashid al-Da'if', *International Journal of Middle East Studies*, vol. 28, 1996; Stefan G. Meyer, *The Experimental Arabic Novel: Postcolonial Literary Modernism in the Levant*, 2001; Rafif R. Sidawi, *al-Nadhra al-riwa'iyya 'ila al-harb al-lubnaniyya, 1975–1995*, Beirut, 2003.
23. Meyer, 2001, p. 222.
24. See, among others, A. Bouhdiba, *Sexuality in Islam*, London, 1985; N. Jaafar, 'The Blue Flame and the Red Flame: Love and Eroticism', unpublished MA thesis with Professor Anthony Synnott, McGill, 2002.
25. Henry Miller, 'Obscenity and the Law of Reflection', in *Pornography and Obscenity: Handbook for Censors. Two Essays by D. H. Lawrence and Henry Miller*, Michigan, IN, 1958, p. 14.
26. al-Qusayfi, *an*-Nahar, Beirut, 2001, p. 18.
27. Khalaf, 2002.
28. See Sabbah, 1984; Bouhdiba, 1985.
29. Ioan Davis, *Writers in Prison*, Oxford and Cambridge, MA 1990, pp. 63–4; on confession of prisoners, Elaine Scarry, *The Body in Pain: The Making and Unmaking of the World*, Oxford, 1987, pp. 29–35; on the power of writing, Barbara Harlow, *Resistance Literature*, New York, 1987, pp. 125–32.
30. Khalaf, 2002.
31. Ilyas Khuri, *al-Mubtada' wa'l-khabar*, Beirut, 1984, pp. 16–17; al-Da'if, 1995, pp. 122–5.

Postscript and Acknowledgments

Samir Khalaf

Despite the massive and relentless volume of research and writing on sexuality, both scholarly and sensational, issues pertaining to sexuality, desire and eroticism continue to arouse uncertainty, confusion and moral anxiety. Attempts to demystify this most primal of human resources remain suffused with considerable ambiguity. Precisely because of its strong emotive powers and sensibilities sexuality, in the words of Jeffery Weeks, one of the most authoritative commentators on the subject in recent years, is tantamount to a 'transmission belt' for some of the most passionate sentiments and abiding commitments: 'love and anger, tenderness and aggression, intimacy and adventure, romance and predatoriness, pleasure and pain, empathy and power.' (Weeks, 1986:11).

Difficulties in exploring such intimate and contested human phenomena are also inherent in the chameleon-like predisposition of sexuality to appear in many guises and forms. Hence it is not surprising that it should become the terrain for some of the highly charged and fierce ethical and political debates and polemics which continue to polarize various groups and constituencies within society. Indeed in recent years, even in the presumably liberal and permissive cultural contexts of North American and Western Europe, many of the so-called 'social issues' provoked by the resurgent conservatism of the 'New Right' are essentially a byproduct of concerns associated with the changing character of sexuality.

The range of such concerns touch an extensive and overlapping numbers of vital issues and basic human values: the sanctity of family life and the contested association of sexuality with the virtues of intimacy and reproduction, the nature and place of sexual education, changing perceptions of homosexuality, the stigma associated with forms of 'sexual deviance', intimate violence and muffled sexual abuse, matters of gender, the reassertion of sexual identities between the sexes, the role of feminist and radical sexual movements in challenging trenchant patriarchal sentiments. These and related issues have become defining elements in shaping the political agendas of conservative constituencies in both developed and developing societies.

The advent of globalism and post-modernity have exacerbated the sense of uncertainty and moral confusion. In addition to the conventional forms of socio-economic discrimination associated with income, class and ethnicity, there are added risks and uncertainties emanating from a new 'cosmetics of affluence', mass leisure, consumerism and sexual tourism. With the erosion of state loyalties, sexual outlets have been released from some of their traditional constraints. Access to such outlets is being increasingly marketed via the global venues of the Internet, videos and chat rooms, where digital and virtual worlds are accessible at the click of a mouse. Access is also being extended to other aberrant areas such as pornography, pedophilia and trafficking in child prostitution.

The pursuit of such novel opportunities demands the cultivation of new lifestyles where notions of beauty, body image and sexual appeal are coveted forms of 'social capital'. Hence any symptoms of ugliness, obesity, lack of decorum or disinterest in sexuality are held with disdain and become sources of public embarrassment. Within such a salient and irresistible context, reinforced by the global appeals of the mass media, the sources of ambiguity and uncertainty are bound to become more compelling and unsettling. This is most visible in the growing dissonance between, on the one hand, the aroused passions of global consumerism, commodified sexuality and eroticization of public life and, on the other, the preponderance of fundamentalist reactions seeking refuge in the imagined authenticity and security of traditional norms of familiar realities. Hence, obsession with youthfulness, sensuality, the eroticization of one's body through cosmetic surgery, suggestive mannerisms and risqué and evocative fashions coexist with those that compel women to preserve their modesty and sexual purity.

Indeed the prevalence of such jarring manifestations is symptomatic of the unresolved character of sexuality. Most evident in this regard are the disparities between sexual abandon in the private sphere of seeming timidity, and temperance in the public sphere, the persistence of double standards which condone, often celebrate, the sexual powers of masculine libido but abnegate the unbridled female sexuality as *fitnah*, a source of seduction and chaos in society. The most poignant, perhaps, is the persistence of 'honour crimes' and the preponderance of female circumcision and 'hymnoplasty'. The former is intended to preserve a woman's purity while the latter is an effort to restore it. Both, often dismissed as benign 'cultural gestures', are forms of social reconstruction to safeguard a woman's virtue (i.e. virginity) as her most cherished 'social capital'. These, like the polarized juxtapositions of bared midriffs, head scarves and veils one encounters in public spaces, are emblematic of the dialectical interplay between the appeals of trendy fashions and the weight of traditional norms. Young women in particular have to bear much of the burden of negotiating a sexual identity that reconciles both expectations.

Despite the grievous implications of such inconsistent and unsettling realities and the growing public awareness of the importance of sexuality in Arab society for emotional well-being and in forging a coherent and meaningful sexual identity, there hasn't been any open or informed public debate about such issues, let alone empirical or grounded exploration of some of their problematic dimensions. Recently the popular media, feminist groups, human rights advocates, medical and public health practitioners, NGO's and policy-makers have been making repeated appeals to address the dire consequences of some of these problems. Little has been done, however, by way of heeding such calls. Sexuality remains a mystified, taboo and unexplored dimension of Arab culture.

This is, at least, anomalous given the historic curiosity the topic inspired and the persistence of the distorted and denigrated images propagated by orientalists, nineteenth-century travellers and current sensationalist accounts. Indeed some of the contemporary images of the dualistic nature of women and Arab sexuality continue to perpetuate the same misconceptions propagated by European romantics and colonialists; namely that the Muslim women are either voracious and over-eroticised or submissive repressed and silenced.

Naturally such misconceptions have not remained unchallenged. By reformulating the classical work of Imam al-Ghazali, a handful of contemporary scholars sought to identify the defining elements of sexuality in Islam and to elucidate their impact on the social construction of marriage, gender, sexual desire, romantic love, even misogyny and mysticism. Abdel Wahab Bouhdiba, Fatima Mernissi, Nawal al-Sadawi,

Salah-eddin Mounajed, Malek Alloula, among others, have offered insightful analyses of the interplay between sexuality, colonization and imperialism. And of course, the seminal work of Edward Said regarding the orientalist representation of sexuality stands out in this regard.

Such groundbreaking work notwithstanding, the tenacious taboos surrounding research or open and candid debate on sexuality continue to be politically charged and culturally constructed. The thought of hosting a conference bringing together scholars, activists and practitioners became all the more urgent and legitimate. If only to 'break the ice', as it were, and to open up areas of research thus far unexplored, obscured or muffled to objective and critical inquiry. It was also felt, given the sensitivity of the topic, that convening the conference outside the Arab World would be a more conducive setting for the objective presentations we wished to solicit from participants. A Ford Foundation grant made possible the collaborative efforts of St. Antony's College, Oxford and the Centre for Behavioral Research at the American University of Beirut (AUB). A steering committee, composed of Eugene Rogan (Oxford), Samir Khalaf (AUB), Huda Zurayk (AUB), Basim Musallam (Cambridge University) and Jocelyn DeJong (University of Manchester), formulated the overall objectives and scope of the conference, set out specific topics and panels and invited participants.

The nine panels addressed the following issues: marriage and sexuality; sexual knowledge in childhood, adolescence and among university students; health and sexual knowledge; the body; honour killing; men and masculinity and AIDS. About thirty participants were drawn from multi-disciplines (history, anthropology, sociology, demography, public health, psychiatry, medicine, therapy, social work) and cross-cultural (Tunis, Morocco, Egypt, Jordan, Lebanon, Turkey, Palestine). The conference was held on 23–25 June 2000, at the Middle East Centre of St. Antony's College, Oxford. Angel Foster must be complemented for writing a succinct but very informative report of the conference proceedings. She introduced the themes and contexts of each panel and provided a summary of the contributions by highlighting their significant empirical findings and broader theoretical inferences.

Encouraged by the success of St. Antony's conference we started to consider prospects for holding a sequel in Beirut. We also concurred to extend the scope of our concerns to explore, within a more academic context, some of the broader conceptual socio-historical dimensions of sexuality, to elucidate the ways sexual identity, sexual desire, fantasy and the body are perceived and lived in a variety of cultural settings. Consideration of how sexuality is narrated and expressed in Arabic literature and poetry could be, we felt, instructive in this regard. Equally important, given the recent surge in the public manifestations of homosexuality, is to provide empirical substantiation of the forms it is assuming and the issues it is provoking.

The three-day Beirut conference (5–7 December 2003) was organized around a set of six interrelated panels: socio-historical perspectives, sexuality in literature, issues of sexual identity, sexuality in the family, sexual health in Lebanon, and the eroticisation of the human body. We were keen to call on scholars currently engaged in works which had direct relevance to the themes and issues of the conference. The presentations and discussions displayed a 'freshness' of work-in-progress.

We were fortunate to attract John Gagnon, Professor Emeritus of Sociology at New York State University at Stonybrook as keynote speaker. As a prominent and prolific scholar he has, during much of his resourceful career, been engrossed in research and writing on various aspects of human sexuality. His opening address on the local/global tensions in comparative sex research provided an apt and meaningful context for our deliberations. Unlike the fairly closed sessions at St. Antony's, the Beirut conference was open to the public. The event received considerable media coverage mixed with bemused attention and curiosity.

An editorial committee (John Gagnon, Eugene Rogan and Samir Khalaf) reviewed all twenty-eight contributions and recommended ten for publication. Unfortunately, because of other pending commitments Eugene could not continue to serve as part of the editorial team. The task of editing papers and preparing the volume for publication fell to John Gagnon and myself. I must nonetheless acknowledge and laud the time and resources Eugene and his spirited colleagues at the Middle East Centre invested in this project. Both notable ventures, at St Antony's and AUB, could not have materialized without their sustained interest and support. Their collaboration did much to upgrade and safeguard the desired quality of the contributions. The participation of John Gagnon was remarkable in more than just his invaluable scholarly contributions and informed input. He was beset, as we were engaged in the process of editing, with an apprehensive and unsettling medical problem. He audaciously went on, not yet fully recovered from his bypass operation, to pursue his share of the work. All of us – and I speak on behalf of other colleagues – are enormously grateful.

Like other such joint projects the ultimate outcome is always much more than the sum of its individual parts. Also, in most such instances, the final product could not have been possible without the support, insight and feedback of colleagues and friends who were not directly involved in the conferences. Perhaps because of the engaging nature of the topic and the probing and intimate debate the papers provoked, we were always prodded to speed up the process of publication to give the prospective volume the wider exposure and readership it deserves.

By a fitting coincidence, while editing this volume I was presenting a new seminar on sexuality and society. The transparent and animated discussions, often disarmingly candid and explicit, were very instructive and revealing. They were a tangible and vivid proof of some of the overriding themes which inform the essays, particularly the dissonance between the expected and lived sexual realities of young people in Arab society.

André Gaspard and Mai Ghoussoub of Saqi Books deserve special recognition for their sustained encouragement and willingness to put up with the unavoidable delays we faced in delivering the final manuscript. Their professional team must be acknowledged for their accomplished skills and collegiality in attending to their respective tasks. As copyeditor, Jane Robson, was adroit in two invaluable senses: she had a quick eye but a light hand. For better or worse, she was very sparing with the original text. Lara Frankena was efficient and genial as commissioning editor. Ourida Mneimne displayed all the desired aesthetic skills in designing the layout of the book. I also wish to acknowledge the contribution of Christine Shuttleworth in preparing the index. Finally Mrs Leila Jbara worked laboriously in preparing the various versions of the manuscript.

Biographical Notes

Angel Foster has a D. Phil. from Oxford in Middle Eastern Studies. She is an Associate at Ibis Reproductive Health and in the fourth year of the MD program at Harvard Medical School. Her current research involves medical abortion, reproductive health education, and emergency contraception in the Middle East and North Africa. Her research and dissertation focused on women's comprehensive health care in Tunisia.

John Gagnon is Distinguished Professor of Sociology Emeritus at the State University of New York at Stony Brook. He received his degrees from the University of Chicago. Gagnon is the author or co-author of such books as *Sex Offenders, Sexual Conduct, Human Sexualities, The Social Organization of Sexuality, Sex in America* and *An Interpretation of Desire.* In addition he is editor of many books as well as the author of many scientific articles. These days he lives mostly in Nice, France.

Ghassan Hage is an Associate Professor of Anthropology at the University of Sydney. He is currently Visiting Professor in the Department of Social and Behavioral Sciences at the American University of Beirut (AUB). His works include *Arab Australians, White Nation* and *Against Paranoid Nationalism.* He is currently writing an ethnographically based work on the Lebanese diaspora.

Jens Hanssen has a D. Phil. from Oxford and teaches modern Middle Eastern and Mediterranean History at the University of Toronto. He has published Fin de Siècle *Beirut: The Making of an Ottoman Provincial Capital* with Oxford University Press, co-authored *History, Space and Social Conflict in Beirut*, and co-edited *Empire in the City; Arab Provincial Capitals in the Late Ottoman Empire.* He has held junior research fellowships at the AUB and the Deutsche Morgenlundische Gesellschaft in Beirut form1997 to 1999. In 2000, he was Socrates Fellow at the University of Aix-en-Provence, Marseille, and in 2001 he received a Thyssen postdoctoral fellowship to study the Arab renaissance in 19th-century Syria.

Maher Jarrar is a Professor at AUB and Director of the *Anis Makdisi Program in Literature*. He has a PhD in Arabic and Islamic Studies from the University of Tubingen. He has served as Visiting Professor at Harvard and Fellow at the Wissenschaftskolleg Zu Berlin. His publications include *Die Prophetenbiographei in islamischen Spanien, Ein Beitrag zur Uberlieferungs – und Redaktionsgeschichte*. He is the co-editor of *Myths, Historical Archetypes and Symbolic Figures in Arabic Literature* and has written many articles in refereed journals.

Ray Jureidini has a PhD from Flinders University of South Australia and is Associate Professor of Sociology in the Department of Social and Behavioral Sciences at the AUB. He has taught Sociology at LaTrobe, Deakin and Monash universities in Melbourne, Australia. He is principle editor of an introductory sociology text-book *Sociology: Australian Connections*, and has authored numerous book chapters and journal articles. He has been executive editor of two scholarly journals *Labour & Industry* and the *Journal of Arabic, Islamic and Middle Eastern Studies*, foundation vice chairman of the *Australian Arabic Council* and national secretary of the *Australian Sociological Association*. His current research focuses upon human rights and international labour migration, in particular, the dynamics of female guestworkers in the Middle East.

As'ad Khairallah has a PhD in Middle Eastern Studies and Comparative Literature from Princeton University and is Professor of Arabic at AUB. He held a Professorial Appointment at Freiburg University in Germany before he returned to his position at AUB in 1998. Professor Khairallah is widely published. Of relevance to the present conference are the following: *Love, Madness, and Poetry: An Interpretation of Majnun Legend* and 'Love and the Body in Modern Arabic Poetry' in *Love and Sexuality in Modern Arabic Literature,* ed. R. Allen et al.

Roseanne Saad Khalaf is Assistant Professor of English and Creative Writing at AUB. She received her Ed.D in Creative Writing and Linguistics from the University of Leicester. She has held the position of research specialist at the Princeton University Development Office and worked as a consultant for the

Educational Testing Service. Her publications include *Once Upon a Time in Lebanon* and *Lebanon: Four Journeys to the Past.* She is co-editor of *Themes*, a twelfth-grade English textbook written for the National Center of Educational Research and Development and *Transit Beirut: New Writing and Images,* an anthology of complex urban experience that brings together personal writing, journalism, short stories, photography and animation. Most recently, she has edited, *Hikayat,* an anthology of short stories by Lebanese women. *Cleo, The Hotel Cat* and *Cleo Visits Downtown Beirut* are the first two stories in a series of children's books. She is currently working on the topic of relocating lived experience to the creative writing classroom.

Samir Khalaf is professor of Sociology and Director of the Center for Behavioral Research at AUB. Educated at Princeton University (PhD), he has also held academic appointments at Princeton, Harvard, MIT and New York University. He is the author of numerous journal articles and book chapters on comparative modernization, socio-cultural history, urbanization, and post-war reconstruction. Among his books are *Persistence and Change in Nineteenth-Century Lebanon*, *Hamra of Beirut*, *Lebanon's Predicament*, *Recovering Beirut* (with Philip Khoury), *Beirut Reclaimed*, *Cultural Resistance: Global and Local Encounters in the Middle East*, *Civil and Uncivil Violence in Lebanon: A History of the Internationalization of Communal Conflict.* He has been a recipient of several international fellowships and research awards and appointed on the international jury to review master plans for the post-war reconstruction of Beirut. He is trustee of several foundations and serves on the editorial boards of a score of international journals and publications.

Akram Khater is Associate Professor of History at North Carolina State University, and Director of the Middle East Studies Program. He holds a PhD in History from the University of California, Berkeley. Before coming to Raleigh, he taught at Ball State University in Indiana. His books include *Inventing Home: Emigration, Gender and the Making of a Lebanese Middle Class, 1861-1921*, and *A History of the Middle East: A Sourcebook for the History of the Middle East*. Professor Khater has also contributed to the Middle East and North Africa section of *The World and Its People*, a high school textbook. He has published a substantial number of articles and reviews and was awarded a number of teaching accolades and grants during his tenure at N.C. State. His professional affiliations include the Middle East Studies Association, American Historical Association, Triangle Islamic Studies Group, and Mediterranean

Studies Group, and the Chair of the Committee on Middle East Studies at NC State. He also sits on the editorial boards of several journals and book series.

Jared McCormick is a MA candidate in Middle Eastern Studies at the AUB. He is currently finishing his thesis which examines 'gay' identity in Lebanon and changing masculinities.

Sofian Merabet is an associate researcher at the Center for Behavioral Research at the AUB and a doctoral candidate in the Department of Anthropology at Columbia University. His doctoral dissertation focuses on the constructions of socially marginalized identities in Beirut with an emphasis on queer space. From February 2002 until June 2003 he taught sociology and anthropology in the Department of Social and Behavioral Sciences at AUB.

Christa Salamandra is a Visiting Fulbright Professor at LAU. She received her PhD from Oxford. She has held appointments at Oxford, the School of Oriental and African Studies and the University of London. She has published a score of professional papers on the construction of social identity in global and migrant settings and has been the recipient of several scholarly awards and prizes. A revised edition of her PhD dissertation *A New Old Damascus: Authenticity and Distinction in Urban Syria* was published in 2004.

Index